The
DAUGHTERS
of
GEORGE III

DOROTHY MARGARET STUART

Publishers' Note

This text by Dorothy Margaret Stuart was first published in 1939. This revised edition has minor updates, but in large is as Miss Stuart wrote it. The few original illustrations from the 1939 edition have not been included in this revised edition and instead a new colour section with 50 images is added to the text.

The extracts in this book from the Royal Archives at Windsor are indicated this—(w).

Fonthill Media Limited
Fonthill Media LLC
www.fonthillmedia.com
office@fonthillmedia.com

First published 1939
This revised edition first published in the United Kingdom
and the United States of America 2016

British Library Cataloguing in Publication Data:
A catalogue record for this book is available from the British Library

ISBN 978-1-78155-485-2

Typeset in 10pt on 13pt Sabon
Printed and bound in England by CPI Group (UK) Ltd, Croydon, CR0 4YY

Contents

1

Charlotte Augusta Matilda, Princess Royal-Queen of Würtemberg, 1766–1828

I

On 29 September 1766, within the unassuming brick walls of Buckingham House, was born the eldest daughter of George III and Charlotte of Mecklenburg-Strelitz. The anxiety felt by a large part of the nation for the continuance of 'the glorious House of Hanover and Protestant succession' had already been allayed by the birth of three lusty, pink-cheeked princes, but no man could have foretold how swiftly and steadily the royal nurseries would be filled.

It is, as Lord Melbourne hinted to Queen Victoria, a little curious that so many good-looking children should have been born of the union between George III and Queen Charlotte. His florid youthful comeliness soon passed, leaving him with protuberant eyes and pendulous lips, and even the Queen's best friends could not describe her as anything but plain. Yet these two found themselves in course of time surrounded by a family of seven sons and six daughters all of whom were, at least in their earlier years, more than passably handsome. Before the combined influences of dissipation and heredity played havoc with their contours the sons were a personable septet; and of the daughters Fanny Burney exclaimed, with characteristic fervour, 'Never in tale or fable were six sister princesses more lovely!' A visitor from America wrote in 1788, 'The four eldest princesses are thought surprising beauties. They are certainly handsome'; and Peter Pindar called the whole six 'the beauteous boast of Britain's Isle'. When Gainsborough was painting for Queen Charlotte the series of family portraits which now hang in the Queen's Audience Room at Windsor, he spoke with rapture to Angelo the Elder of the royal children. 'He used', records Angelo the Younger, 'to tell my father he was all but raving mad with ecstasy in beholding such a constellation of youthful beauty.' Elsewhere he remarks, 'The sweetest, the most lovely female countenance of the youthful group always appeared to me to be that of the Princess Royal'.

The six Princesses were so spaced in order of time that they tended to fall into two equal groups: the elder Charlotte Augusta Matilda, Princess Royal, born in 1766; Augusta Sophia, born in 1768; Elizabeth, born in 1770: and the younger—Mary, born in 1776; Sophia, born in 1777; and Amelia, born in 1783, the interval between Princess Elizabeth and Princess Mary being marked by the successive arrival of their brothers, the Princes Ernest, Augustus, and Adolphus, and that between Sophia and Amelia by the brief lives of Prince Octavius and Prince Alfred. The senior group had this advantage over the junior, that their childhood was not chequered by the shadow of their father's madness. His earlier lapses into oddity were probably not conspicuous enough to come to the knowledge of such of his children as were then in existence, and when the first serious attack occurred in October 1788, it was Mary, Sophia, and Amelia who were more likely to be badly frightened by their visits to a parent whom they had seen far off, watching them with bloodshot eyes as they walked on the lawn at Windsor, and who now welcomed their entry into his secluded apartments with wild and shrill serenades on the flute. That the poor King himself was conscious of the time-space between his two clusters of daughters is shown by the inscription he wrote in a book which he gave, in January 1789, to the eldest, whom he calls his 'Ever Dearest Daughter, Matilda, Governess to her Three Younger Sisters'.

The official governess to the royal children had been appointed on the birth of George, Prince of Wales, in 1762, and did not retire till thirty years later. She was Lady Charlotte Finch, *née* Fermor, second daughter of Thomas, first Earl of Pomfret, and wife of the Honble. William Finch, second son of the seventh Earl of Winchilsea. Though perhaps less charming than her kinswoman, for whom Pope wrote *The Rape of the Lock*, she had brains, breeding, and culture. Horace Walpole met her, with her sister Lady Arabella, at Florence in 1740, and called her 'the cleverest girl in the world'; he also added that she spoke 'the purest Tuscan, like any Florentine'.

Melbourne may have been right when he said that George III did not like clever women, but his Majesty certainly did not choose a stupid one for his daughters' governess. All the family were devoted to 'Lady Cha', whose name crops up in royal letters long after her death in 1813. The Queen of Würtemberg wrote to Lady Harcourt that 'Lady Cha's' picture always hung in her closet, and that she never moved from Louisbourg to Stuttgart without taking it with her— and when those words were written her Majesty had been an exile in Germany for nearly twenty years.

Under the vigilant eye of this lady, Miss Planta taught the Princesses English; Mademoiselle Moula and Mademoiselle Krohme, assisted later by M. de la Guiffardière, taught them French; and Mademoiselle Montmollin instructed them in fancy needlework, beadwork, and the netting of silk purses. For drawing in its various branches there was an unexpectedly large number of instructors. Biachio Rebecca taught some of the Princesses 'to draw the human figure'; Mr Cooper taught them landscape-drawing in chalks; Miss Black was engaged as a teacher of 'painting in crayons', *i.e.* pastels; M. Rustan, a Fleming, initiated them into the art of drawing heads, hands, and feet on a large scale, in black chalk— and in the process made himself so grimy that his royal pupils nicknamed him

Count Smudge. Dancing was the province of M. Desnoyer, geography of Sir George Bolton, and music, among others, of Mr Webb of Windsor.

No efforts would have made an accomplished musician of the Princess Royal, who, according to Fanny Burney, had no taste for music and 'heard it almost with pain'; but she wrote a beautiful copper-plate hand, her grammar and spelling reflect no discredit on Miss Planta, and she could express herself both in French and German with perfect ease. Her religious training, like that of her sisters, was mainly in her mother's hands, and when she took charge of the education of her stepdaughter 'Trinette' (Catherine of Würtemberg), she wrote to her father that she would try to make her 'go through the same course of religion that Mama made us read with Schräder'[(w)]—the German chaplain at St James's.[1]

Windsor Castle having fallen into a ruinous condition, George III decided, pending its restoration, to house his family in two existing buildings enlarged and adapted for the purpose, to the south-east of the Castle; Upper Lodge, demolished in 1823, and Lower Lodge, formerly Burford Lodge. The young Princes and Princesses were distributed at Kew between the now-vanished White House, the Dutch House (later called the Palace), and the little houses round the Green; at Windsor the elder Princesses lived with their parents in the Upper Lodge, the younger Princesses with their governesses in the Lower.

When Mary Hamilton, Sir William's attractive niece, joined the royal household in 1777, she thus described Upper Lodge:

> . . . the Queen has 7 or 8 rooms furnished in a style of elegant simplicity, beautiful paper hangings, light carved gilt frames for looking glasses, worked chairs and painted frames, every room different. Curtains of fine white dimity with white cotton fringe—one set of chairs are knotted floss silk of different shades sewn on to imitate natural flowers. . . .
>
> N.B. Her Majesty has done a great deal of the knotting herself.

Ten years later the furniture of the Princess Royal's apartments at Upper Lodge included a sofa, twelve chairs, two pier card-tables, a pembroke table, and two pairs of curtains 'of a warm, dark-red damask lined with white'.

It is hardly surprising that Miss Hamilton should have won the affection of the young Princesses, or even that she should have evoked rather crude and uncouth demonstrations of regard from their already-susceptible eldest brother. The Princess Royal in particular seems to have been attracted by this lively Scotswoman, who played Dumb Crambo and other strenuous games with so much abandon, and whom after only a year's acquaintance she addressed as 'Dear Hamy' or 'my dearest Hammy'. In one of the letters she sent to her the twelve-year old Princess wrote, 'Pray love me, for I love you very much, so it is fair; the Publicans and Sinners loved those that loved them'; and in another she says contritely, 'I am very sorry to have tormented and hurt you in not learning my lesson for M. de la Guiffardière'—the same whimsical French Protestant pastor who figures in the journal of Fanny Burney as 'Mr Turbulent'.

Another personage destined to loom large both in the lives of the daughters of George III and in the pages of Miss Burney was the sub-governess Miss Martha Carolina Goldsworthy, otherwise 'Gooly' or 'Goully'. She was a daughter of Burrington Goldsworthy and his wife Philippia, *née* Vanbrugh, and a sister of Colonel (afterwards Lieutenant-General) Philip Goldsworthy, Equerry and Clerk Marshal of the Mews to George III, and 'the wag of the Court'. In the possession of Mr Hubert Carr-Gomm are two admirable pastels by Russell of this brother and sister, who strongly resemble each other in their dark-blue eyes, long noses, and rather humorously puckered lips. 'Goully' wears a voluminous fichu, revealing a thin gold neck-chain with a small pendant key—probably the key of the Queen's jewel-casket.

From 1786 onward Miss Goldsworthy had an able and vigilant coadjutor in the person of Miss Jane Gomm, daughter of Mr William Gomm, who is described on his mural tablet in Bath Abbey as being 'formerly of the British factory in Petersburg and late secretary of his Majesty's Embassy at the Hague'. An early portrait of Miss Gomm, also in the possession of Mr Hubert Carr-Gomm, shows her with dark, heavy eyebrows and sharp features surmounted by a wreath of pink rosebuds. Miss Burney, who did not like Miss Gomm, wrote of her, 'she is very sensible and well-informed, but her manner is not pleasing to strangers'. After their retirement the two ladies lived together in a house in Hill Street, Berkeley Square, and upon Miss Goldsworthy's death in 1816 she bequeathed to Miss Gomm the manor of Rotherhithe which she had inherited from her brother, the General. Princess Mary wrote to the Regent apropos of 'Goully's' demise, 'She has been breaking all this year, but was particularly well on Sunday last—was out in her carriage—saw many of her friends and made a good dinner'; but in the evening 'complained of spasm in her chest', and died between 12 and 1, 'quite easy at the last'.[w]

In spite of the alleged remark of the Princess Royal in 1789 that the lives of herself and her sisters had hitherto been spent 'in a cloister rather than in a kingdom', it is a mistake to suppose that Queen Charlotte brought up her daughters in an atmosphere of unrelieved seclusion and gloom. When they were young children they were allowed to romp freely with their brothers at Kew, and in July 1770 Lady Mary Coke noted admiringly in her journal that the Princess Royal was 'the best humour'd Child that ever was', after seeing her 'a good deal try'd by her brothers, who pull'd her about most unreasonably'. Later, the Princesses were encouraged to make friends with girls of their own age, and some of these friendships, such as that between the Princess Royal and Lady Louisa Stuart, ended only with their lives. Balls and theatres in London, bathing and yachting at Weymouth, visits to Bulstrode or to Nuneham, during which their mother described them as *la Bande Joyeuse*, can hardly be described as cloistral occupations, and just before the King's illness we find the elder Princesses watching him review the Blues, accompanying him and their mother to inspect 'Miss Morgan, the celebrated Welsh Fairy', and going with either parent on what were apparently cheerful and informal expeditions in the neighbourhood of Windsor. When the Princess Royal was only eleven years old she was present at a dramatic reading of *Lethe* by David Garrick, but this occasion may have been the reverse of gay, as Horace Walpole reports that 'all went off perfectly ill, with no exclamations of applause'. A year later Miss Ann Murry, dedicating to the Princess her book *Mentoria, or the Young Lady's Instructor*, urges her to model herself upon the Queen, so that 'two such animating pictures may influence the manners of posterity and enhance the merit of Female Virtue'; but all Queen Charlotte's children regarded her with awe rather than with affection, and it was no baseless raving on the part of the poor King when he said during his dementia that they were afraid of her.

In the journals of the artlessly sycophantic Fanny Burney we are so constantly called upon to admire the 'sweet condescencion', the 'elegant civility', of the 'second female in the land', and the Princess is so consistently held up as a figure of almost inhuman excellence, that it is quite refreshing to find her asking Fanny in a confidential whisper, 'Pray, is it really true that in your illness last year you coughed so violently that you broke the whalebone of your stays in two?' She was certainly full of kind attentions, holding the Queen's snuffbox while Fanny filled it, sharing her *orgeat* with her when they both had colds, and sitting alone in the firelight rather than disturb her in the middle of dinner. There was good-nature, too, in the way in which she regularly conveyed news of Mrs Delany to her ecstatic friend. More life-like is the portrait traced of the Princess by Mrs Harcourt, sister-in-law of Queen Charlotte's Master of the Horse, who saw her from a different angle, and was not dazzled by her rank:

> Princess Royal has excessive sensibility, a great sense of injury, a great sense of her own situation, much timidity: without wanting resolution, she wants presence of mind, from the extreme quickness of her feelings, which show themselves in her perpetual blushes. She has excellent judgment, wonderful memory, and great application. . . . She is unjustly considered proud, and a peculiarity in her temper is mistaken for less sweetness than it deserves.

Mrs Papendiek's verdict was:

> She was always shy, and under restraint with the Queen . . . never elegant in exhibition, though her figure was good and imposing. Timidity, with a want of affectionate confidence in the Queen's commands and wishes, always brought her Royal Highness forward as ill at ease, while out of the Queen's presence she was a different being.

Another shrewd observer, Lady Louisa Stuart, said of her 'she had sense, though not brilliancy, a thoroughly right mind, and real dignity', and that 'she dearly loved her poor father, whom she resembled in many points of character, and she was his comfort and darling'.

On 29 September 1788, Miss Burney noted in her journal:

> The birthday of our lovely eldest Princess. It happens to be also the birthday of Miss Goldsworthy: and her Majesty in a sportive humour bid me, as soon as she was dressed, go and bring down the 'two Michaelmas geese'.

Poor Queen Charlotte! her 'sportive humour', one of the most attractive things about her, was soon to be in eclipse. In the following month those about the King began to observe an increase in his natural garrulity and irascibility. Among the most anxious of the watchers must have been his eldest daughter, who, as Fanny Burney had observed, was the most affected by the attempt made on his life by the crazy Margaret Nicholson two years before. 'All the Princesses', Miss Burney then wrote, 'looked very ill, the Princess Royal particularly.' She was with her father when the crisis came on 5 November 1788.

> At noon the King went out in his chaise, with the Princess Royal, for an airing. I looked from my window to see him; he was all smiling benignity, but gave so many orders to the postillions and got in and out of the carriage twice, with such agitation, that again my fear of a great fever hanging over him grew more and more powerful.

It must have cost the Princess an effort to come in cheerfully and give 'in German a history of the outing and one that seemed comforting'. At dinner the same night the King 'broke forth into positive delirium'.

When it was decided that the patient should be moved from Windsor to Kew some three weeks later, he was anxious that the Princess Royal should go in the carriage with him; but this the doctors would not permit. Not till 16 January was she allowed to see him, when she, Princess Elizabeth, and Princess Augusta accompanied their mother on a visit to the rooms set apart for him. They saw him play a game of picquet with the Queen, and though both she and Dr Willis declared that the patient had behaved with perfect propriety, he afterwards told his pages that the Queen had consented that Lady Pembroke, for whom he had suddenly developed a fantastic passion, should come to him; and his bemused mind was at that time so full of that lady, whom he had admired in his young days, that it seems improbable that he was able to keep her name out of the conversation.

During the months which followed not one of the King's young daughters was spared the pain of seeing him. The Princesses, says Robert Fulke Greville, 'took their regular turns' in accompanying the Queen, and when at last the cloud lifted the designers of popular mementos, 'transparencies', pottery, silken ribbons, woodcuts, etc., were not slow to react to the sentimental appeal of their youthful sorrow turned into joy. In many of these pieces of loyal propaganda two or three of the Princesses figure, usually in attitudes of pious ecstasy.

Many years later, as Queen Dowager of Würtemberg, the eldest Princess, when in company with Mrs Williams Wynn (mother of the famous 'Lady of Quality'), reverted to those unforgettable days. According to Miss Frances Williams Wynn, the Queen

> spoke much of her father, of his recovery from his first illness; mentioned the story one has often heard of his wishing to read *King Lear*, which the doctors refused him, and which he got in spite of them by asking for Colman's works, in which he knew he should find the play as altered by Colman for the stage. . . . When the three elder princesses went into the King he told them what he had been reading. He said, 'It is very beautiful, very affecting, and very awful'; adding, 'I am like poor Lear, but thank God I have no Regan, no Goneril, only three Cordelias'. The Queen wept in relating this.

When the recovery of the King had been recognized by his physicians, his ministers, and his subjects, life resumed its wonted train. The dispersal of his sons was ready beginning—Prince William had gone to sea; the Princes Edward, Ernest, Augustus, and Adolphus were in Hanover; but the daughters were still tied closely to the maternal apron-strings. It was characteristic of Fanny Burney that she should have imagined that because in her presence Queen Charlotte and the Princesses observed a certain restraint, there was among them 'an annihilation of all nature and all pleasantry'. The Queen's letters to her children abound in little jokes, and allusions to family sayings and incidents, and one hazards a guess that neither Lady Harcourt nor Mrs Delany would have endorsed Miss Burney's views. None the less, it is possible to detect an excess of formality in the existence of the 'five amiable Graces', as their mother once called them.

'Grace' was, perhaps, hardly the chief merit of the eldest. Though a personable young woman, in the slightly exuberant style which the age considered 'fine', she was negligent in her dress and awkward in her deportment. An instance of this not unlikable *gaucherie* has been recorded by the anonymous author of *George III, his Court and Family*, in connection with a Birthday Ball, where the Princess appeared in 'white and gold with a green spot, the beautiful manufacture of England', but where she was unlucky enough, when 'going down the first country dance', to get the fringe of her petticoat entangled in the buckle of her shoe.

On recovering from this accident her Royal Highness appeared rather embarrassed; but the involuntary blush which this circumstance called forth added to her native beauty. This incident, however, gave rise to the following piece of ingenious levity:

> 'Twas at the birthnight ball, sir,
> God bless our gracious Queen,
> Where people great and small, sir,
> Are on a footing seen;
> As down the dance
> With heels from France
> A royal couple flew,
> Tho' well she tripped,
> The lady slipped,
> The Princess lost her shoe;
> Her highness hopp'd;
> The fiddlers stopped,
> Not knowing what to do.
>
> Amazed at such a pause, sir,
> The dancers, to a man,
> Eager to hear the cause, sir,
> Around the Princess ran;
> Lord Hertford, too,
> Like lightning flew,
> And tho' unused to knuckle,
> Laid down his wand,
> And lent a hand
> Her royal shoe to buckle.

What a missed opportunity for the 'group of the most fashionable dancing-masters in London', who, according to Henry Angelo, 'were constant attendants at the birthday ball'!

In 1790, when the King's health was thought to be re-established, the Princess Royal so far overcame her timidity as to 'set herself against the Queen', whose habit of 'constantly inviting to Windsor the daughters of such families as were attached to the Government' seemed to her own eldest daughter highly reprehensible. Mrs Papendiek declares that her Royal Highness 'now averred that she never liked the Queen . . . and went so far as to say that she was a silly woman'; but it is difficult to imagine the Princess uttering such blasphemy, whatever may have been her personal opinion.

The insurmountable reluctance of George III to arrange marriages for any of his daughters has puzzled historians. There was probably some truth in the statement of his brother, the Duke of Gloucester, that the King 'had not looked for Continental alliances from a notion that they would be unwilling to leave England'; and it is certain that he sometimes had what Macbeth called 'compunctious visitings', as when he spoke vaguely of taking the Princesses to Hanover and giving balls to all the eligible German princes. In any event he took no steps towards acquiring sons-in-law, and obstructed every move made by others. When, in 1805, Queen Charlotte's brother, the Duke of Mecklenburg-Strelitz, desired to send his eldest son to England with a view to his paying court to one of the younger Princesses, the Queen, who obviously desired the match, wrote to her husband: 'I have never named the subject to any of the princesses, for I have made it a rule to avoid a subject in which I know their opinions differ with [*sic*] your Majesty's, for every one of them have at different times assured me that happy as they are they should like to settle, if they could, and I feel I cannot blame them'.[w]

That one of his daughters should mingle royal with ducal blood seemed unseemly to King George III, who, however much he may have 'gloried in the name of Briton', in this matter broke away from the tradition established in Scotland by the Stuarts, and in England by the Plantagenets.

The nation was now beginning to take an interest in the King's daughters, and not only that part of the nation which was able to throng the Terrace at Windsor when the Royal Family, complacent or reluctant according to their several dispositions, took their ceremonial promenade. In 1782, when the Princess Royal was sixteen, Horace Walpole wrote to the Rev. William Mason:

> A man, I forget his name, has made a drawing which he says is for a companion to Copley's 'Death of Lord Chatham'. As the latter exhibits all the great men of Britain, this is to record the beauties: but what do you think is the subject he has pitched upon? The daughter of Pharaoh, saving Moses. The Princess Royal is the Egyptian Infanta. . . .

Two years later a rumour that the King was seeking German husbands for his daughters reached Robert Burns and inspired the following stanza in 'A Dream':

> Ye, lastly, bonnie blossoms a',
> Ye royal lassies dainty,
> Heav'n mak ye guid as weel as braw,
> And gie you lads a-plenty:
> But sneer na British boys awa',
> For Kings are unco scant ay;
> An 'German gentles are but sma',
> They're better just than want ay,
> On onie day.

As early as 1781 the Duchess of Chandos had attempted to arrange an alliance between the Emperor of Austria and the Princess Royal of England, and as the century entered its last decade possible suitors multiplied both for that Princess and her next sister, Princess Augusta. The Prince of Wales, his uncle, Prince Ernest of Mecklenburg-Strelitz, Countess Harcourt, Queen Charlotte's charming and poetical Lady of the Bedchamber, Mrs 'General' Harcourt, and Madame Schwellenburg (Fanny Burney's 'Cerbera') all took a hand in the match-making game, and the candidates included the Crown Prince of Denmark, Prince Ferdinand of Würtemberg, Prince Frederick of Orange, the Duke of Ostrogothland, brother of the King of Sweden, and George III's nephew, the eldest son of his sister, Augusta, Duchess of Brunswick.

As the years passed the life of the Princesses did not grow easier. Even after the King's health was re-established he remained excitable, incalculable, and odd; their mother's temper showed no signs of becoming more accommodating; and three at least of their much-loved brothers, 'G. P.', Augustus, and Edward, were causing distress to their parents by their conduct. 'I do not believe', wrote Mr (afterwards Sir James) Bland Burges in 1794, 'that there is a more unhappy family in England than that of our good King.' Of the Princess Royal he wrote:

> She is naturally nervous, and susceptible of strong impression. Convinced that she now has no chance of ever altering her condition; afraid of receiving any impressions of tenderness or affection; reserved and studious; tenderly loving her brothers and feeling strongly every unpleasant circumstance attending them, she is fallen into a kind of quiet, desperate state, without hope and open to every fear; or in other words what is commonly called broken-hearted. This has operated strongly upon her health, and Sir Lucas Pepys, under whose care she is, expresses considerable apprehensions for her, and even privately hints that he thinks she is in very great danger, as from her particular situation there is no chance of her being able to marry, which he pretty plainly says is the only probability he can foresee of saving her life or her understanding.

Neither the King, whose darling she was, nor the mother whose first-born daughter she had been, seems to have thought of doing anything to release the Princess from this bondage to despair. It was her rakish eldest brother who came to her aid. Towards the end of 1795 the Prince of Wales was enlisting his mother's brother, Prince Ernest Gottlob of Mecklenburg-Strelitz, in an endeavour to bring about a marriage between the Princess Royal and Peter Friedrich Ludwig of Oldenburg. '*Comme vous êtes fort lié avec lui*', wrote the younger Prince, whose intentions were better than his French, '*ne pouviez vous pas lui faire sentir que s'il s'arrivait de demander la Princess Roiale en marriage que sa recherche ne serait que bien recue?*' And he adds that his sister '*en enferme tout son bonheur depuis qu'elle a appris de la bouche de tout le monde l'excellent caractère et les aimables qualités de ce Prince'.*[w]

A few months earlier Mrs Harcourt had encountered Peter (Holstein) of Oldenburg, Prince Bishop of Lübeck, at Osnabrück. His wife, Frederika of Würtemberg, had died ten years before, leaving him with several children, and he was at that time acting as *Landesadministrator* for his feeble-minded cousin, whom he did not succeed as Duke till 1823. The lady was enchanted with him, and it is hardly surprising that her word-picture should have inclined the Princess Royal towards the suggested alliance. He was, wrote Mrs Harcourt, 'indeed a delightful man', tall and upright, with a long, deeply-lined face, looking older than his years; his manners were charming, and at the same time perfectly simple. When he told her that he was thinking of sending his children to be educated in England, she at once improved the shining hour.

> He praised England; said he was once there; and what he particularly admired was the domestic happiness he observed there; and spoke of his having once enjoyed it himself. I was going to seize this opportunity of leading his thoughts towards what we wish when four ladies came to be introduced to me. I could have seen them beaten with pleasure, but I did say a good deal, and seemed so well-informed about him that he was surprised, and asked how I came to know so many particulars.
>
> I answered that I had the honour of living a great deal with our Royal Family, and that virtues like his must naturally be the object of their attention, but I was sure they would be glad to see him, and that I wished he would visit them when there was a Peace. He said he was afraid his friends in England had forgotten him. I replied I did not want him to see any friends but the Royal Family.
>
> Surely this, with what Madame de Walmoden said to the *Grand Maréchal*, must suggest to him the idea that an alliance might take place?

Two undated letters from the Princess Royal to her brother belong to this period. She writes concerning the Duke of Oldenburg that she was perfectly convinced his character was such that, 'could it be brought about, it would be the properest Situation',[w] and she is anxious that the Prince of Wales should send a letter to 'Prince E.'—that is, to their Uncle Ernest of Mecklenburg-Strelitz—under cover to Madame Schwellenburg, expressing his 'approbation'. The Prince did better than this; he wrote urging his uncle to come to England with the Duke of Oldenburg, when he was '*sur que dans bien peu de semaines tout serait conclu*'.[w] So nearly was 'everything concluded' that in August 1795 Princess Elizabeth, writing to the Prince of Wales, referred to their eldest sister as the 'Dutchess of Oldenburg', and remarked that 'her maiden-blush cheek is turned into a Damask Rose whenever the Duke's name is mentioned'.[w] Nothing came of this plot—but when the Princess did find a husband a year later he was the brother of Peter of Oldenburg's dead wife, and, like him, a widower with young children.

Frederick of Würtemberg found, as his brother-in-law had found, powerful allies in the Harcourt family. Another mediator was John Coxe Hippisley, a Somerset barrister who, after an honourable career in the service of the East India Company, had acted as agent between the British Government and the Vatican, and had been instrumental in making the financial difficulties of Cardinal York known to George III, with results equally creditable to the King and agreeable to the Cardinal.

Hippisley laboured to smooth away the difficulties which several times threatened to bring his scheme—and Lady Harcourt's—to naught; and when at last it bore fruit, he well deserved the baronetcy which he received, together with the Order of Würtemberg and the privilege of bearing the arms of the Duchy, with the motto *Amicitiae virtutisque fidus*. He was also commissioner and trustee of the marriage settlement.

In 1771 England had been, to all intents and purposes, the guaranteeing Power of the constitution then conceded to the Würtembergers by their Duke. Five years later the Duke had been in England, negotiating the hire of his troops by George III; and it was his nephew, Frederick William Charles, forty-year-old Hereditary Prince, in whom Lady Harcourt and Mr Hippisley descried, in spite of his extreme corpulence and his previous ill-starred venture into matrimony, an eligible suitor for the hand of the Princess Royal.

Other obstacles besides the intractable temper of George III held up the negotiators. The most formidable of these was the mystery and scandal surrounding the death of the Hereditary Prince's first wife, George III's own niece, Augusta of Brunswick, sister of Caroline, later Princess of Wales. After their marriage in 1780 the Hereditary Prince entered the Russian service. His sister, Sophie (Maria Federowna), had four years earlier become the wife of Paul I, and their daughter, the Grand Duchess Catherine, was to become the wife successively of the younger son of Peter of Oldenburg and of the elder son of Frederick of Würtemberg. Till 1786 the Prince lived in St Petersburg with his flighty, foolish wife, and there three children had been born to them.

In the Windsor Archives are several letters written in 1781–82 by Augusta to her mother, the Duchess of Brunswick. The handwriting is unformed, the French is erratic, and there is on every page a suggestion of high spirits and irresponsibility reminiscent of her sister Caroline. She is eager to revisit Brunswick, and bring with her the baby which every day grows plus *gros et gras, comme sa maman*, but it would be *une tristesse affreuse* to leave her *cher mari* behind. A year later she shows less anxiety to get away from St Petersburg. *Je vole*, she exclaims, *de fête en fête, de bal en bal*. She is trying to learn Russian and has succeeded in mastering a few words of Polish, which makes a confusion terrible in her head. She thinks it a joke that people should call her *Altesse Royale*, under the impression that she is the daughter, not the niece, of the King of England, and she is amused when the Russians show some surprise at her total ignorance of English.[w]

Nothing in these letters suggests any disagreement between the Princess and her *cher mari*. 'For some time', said her sister Caroline, Princess of Wales, more than twenty years later, 'she behaved well . . . though her husband was very jealous of her from the beginning and beat her cruelly. 'We may accept this last statement with reserve, but it was certainly indiscreet of Augusta first to 'become enamoured of a man who had been the Empress's lover', and then to give birth to a baby some time after she had ceased to live with her husband. Frederick appealed to his father-in-law, who agreed that the Princess should be 'removed out of Russia', but Catherine the Great, from motives which may have been either magnanimous or malicious, refused to let her accompany her husband and children when they left the country in 1786. A fortnight later the Empress dispatched the unhappy woman to the fortress of Lhode (her sister Caroline says, of Reval) on the Baltic, and there she remained until the news was formally conveyed to the Hereditary Prince that she had died of 'a putrid fever', or, according to another account, of haemorrhage, in such a manner that immediate burial was necessary. Persistent rumours, in which the Princess of Wales firmly believed, spread all over Europe to the effect that Augusta had escaped from her prison and joined one of her Russian lovers. Did not a wandering Jew arrive at Brunswick and vow he had seen her at the Opera House at Leghorn? Not unnaturally George III hesitated to consent to a marriage between his 'comfort and darling' and the husband of his embarrassingly resurgent niece!

In December 1795 the Hereditary Prince wrote to *Sa Majesté le Roi d Angleterre*:

> *Les éminentes qualités autant que les vertus universellement reconnues de Madame la Princesse Royale son auguste fille ont fait nâitre en moi le plus vif désir de voir mon sort uni au sien, pénétré comme je le suis des avantages qu'une aussi illustre alliance aura pour mon bonheur particulier autant que pour la gloire de ma maison.*[w]

The ground had been prepared a month earlier by Baron de Wimpfen, his Grand Master of the Household, in a letter to Lord Grenville, Secretary of State for Foreign Affairs, in which it was stated that a negotiation had already been opened by the Duke of Brunswick relative to an alliance between the Hereditary Prince of Würtemberg and the Princess Royal—'or one of the other Princesses'.

Four months later, however, so little progress had been made that the suitor's father, growing impatient, proposed to withdraw his representative, Count Zeppeline, from London, and break off the negotiations. Rather plaintively, but not without dignity, the Prince wrote to Zeppeline:

De tout tems ma réputation a été intacte, et je crois avoir atteint l'âge de quarante avec la réputation d'un homme d'honneur et de bon sens. Si j'ai été mal jugé sur mon premier malheureux mariage, certainement je ne le dois qu'a la délicatesse de ma facon de penser et d'agir. . . .

The harassed envoy appealed to the Prince of Wales and to Lord Grenville protesting that the Emperor of Russia, the Empress Catherine, and the House of Brunswick united in approving the proposed alliance. The Empress even wrote wishing the Hereditary Prince success. Then John Coxe Hippisley flung himself into the fray. 'Can it be supposed', he wrote to Lady Harcourt, 'that the Duke and Duchess of Brunswick, the Emperor and Empress Queen, would *all* enter into a conspiracy against his Majesty, and sacrifice the Princess Royal to a Prince so undeserving of Her Royal Highness?'

Apparently it could. And the situation was still further complicated by the *délicatesse* which had made the Hereditary Prince conceal from his mother-in-law, the Duchess of Brunswick, the real nature of his dissatisfaction with her daughter's conduct in Russia. 'To this moment', writes Hippisley, 'it is supposed that Her Royal Highness is unacquainted with much of the dark History of former days.' Enough was now revealed to her to show that she had no just grounds of complaint against her son-in-law, nor any reason to demur at his marriage with the niece whom she had wished to see united to her own eldest son. Documentary support for Zeppeline's assertions was soon forthcoming both from Brunswick and from St Petersburg, but George III did not emerge into the open till July 1796, when he asserted his desire to give his daughter complete liberty of choice, adding, as a slight encouragement to the suitor, '*Elle se flatte de trouver dans l'union proposée cette douce tranquillité que sa disposition l'a toujours inclinée à souhaiter*'.[w] Fanny Burney's remarks after *l'union proposée* had taken place afford a curious commentary on the King's words, and suggest a doubt as to whether he had read his daughter's disposition aright:

> She is born to preside, and that with equal softness and dignity; but she was here in utter subjection, for which she had neither spirits nor inclination. She adored the King, honoured the Queen, and loved her sisters and had much kindness for her brothers; but her style of life was not adapted to the royalty of her nature, any more than of her birth; and though she only wished for power to do good and to confer favours, she thought herself out of place in not possessing it.

The Hereditary Prince was a man of pertinacity. Not until March 1797 did he receive from his future father-in-law a portrait of his future wife. But on the Queen's birthday in January the Princess Royal was observed to be wearing 'a medallion of the Prince of Würtemberg suspended to a diamond necklace', and it may be that if the design of her gown was reported to him he read into it a cheering significance. It was embroidered by herself with artificial flowers, 'and on one side an anchor, tastefully wrought in gold, had a very novel and beautiful effect'. She had been ill with jaundice in the previous November, but fortunately by the end of the year her yellowness was 'beginning to go off'. This tendency to liver trouble was probably responsible for that 'yellow mark' which Lady Mary Coke had noticed upon the cheeks of the two-year-old Princess Royal in 1768.

Even when George III's reluctant consent had been given, procrastination was not at an end. The Prince wrote to Lord Grenville in August 1796 that he would be ready to embark at Hamburg early in December; but he was recommended to defer his journey on account of the inclemency of the weather. Finally, in March 1797 the King instructed the Duke of Portland, as Home Secretary, to draw up the treaty of marriage, following as closely as possible the tenour of the treaty concluded between the Duke of Brunswick and Princess Augusta of Great Britain in 1766, when an annuity of £5,000 was settled out of his Majesty's Irish revenues. The Duke of Portland was directed to 'concert' with the Lord-Lieutenant of Ireland the proper method of obtaining the sanction of the Parliament of that kingdom to a similar grant on this occasion.

The weather was as inclement in April as the anxious prophets had feared it might be in December, and the Hereditary Prince was the worse for a very bad crossing when he disembarked at Harwich on 10 April. Even then he was not allowed to come straight to London and claim his prize. Either to give him a chance to recover from his indisposition, or to obtain a further respite for financial negotiations, he was informed that the King thought it would be well if he were to remain incognito for a time, 'in order to obviate the inconveniences which would otherwise be felt by both parties by a prolonged ceremonial'. It was suggested that in the interval the Prince might take a tour through the country.

On 28 April the Prince intimated that he would come to London in strict incognito on 4 May, 'on private business', and would set out on the tour through the country five days later. It cannot have been a very extensive tour, as it was on 13 May that Lord Malmesbury and Sir Stephen Cottrell went, in 'one of his Majesty's coaches, drawn by six horses', to fetch him from Isleworth where he had been the guest of Sir Joseph Banks. His host, a valued friend of the Family, was sworn of the Privy Council very shortly before the arrival of the Hereditary Prince.

In the meantime, on 3 May, the King had sent a Message to the House of Commons announcing the marriage, and reminding them that the bridegroom, like the royal dynasty of Hanover, was descended from the Electress Sophia. The King went on:

> . . . the many Proofs he has received of the attachment of this House to his
> Person and Family leave him no room to doubt of the concurrence and

assistance of this House in enabling Him to give such a portion to His Eldest Daughter as may be suitable to the Honour and Dignity of the Crown.

The House voted a dutiful Address in response, and the Committee of Supply passed a resolution *nem. con.* that the sum of £80,000 be granted to his Majesty as a marriage portion for the Princess Royal.

On the same day the Marriage Treaty was signed. Among its clauses were the following:

> The children of the marriage were to be brought up in Würtemberg, but might not marry without the consent of the King of England or his successors.
>
> The whole of the marriage portion was to be placed in British Funds, and paid to the Princess half-yearly.
>
> If her husband should predecease her, she should be at liberty to return to England, bringing with her 'the whole of her paraphernalia, rings, jewels, etc.', including those 'obtained during her marriage'.
>
> The Irish annuity, to be received by the Commissioners for the marriage, would be paid to the Princess for her sole use.
>
> Her English attendants were to leave her, and her German attendants to join her, at Hanover, but she was to be free to celebrate [*sic*] divine service according to the rites of the English Church.
>
> The Princess was to take with her to Würtemberg three English female servants, a German footman, and a hairdresser, 'from hence'.

The possibility of children was contemplated with a hopefulness almost amounting to certitude. According to Miss Disbrowe, who was at Stuttgart soon after the Queen-Dowager of Würtemberg died, 'with her trousseau she had received two sets of children's clothes, supposed to last for the first three years— one for a boy, one for a girl.

They were never needed, and were sold at her death.' Gillray published about this time a cartoon entitled 'Le Baiser a la Würtemberg'. In this the suitor, in a gorgeous uniform, with orders dangling from every button-hole, is saluting a fiancée only a little less portly than he; and on the eve of the wedding another cartoon, in even more questionable taste, appeared from the same hand. It was called 'The Bridal Night'. Once more the Duke is seen bedizened with orders (there is even one depending from the ribbon of his tie-wig) and his proportions explain the nickname bestowed upon him by the wits of the time 'the Great Belly-gerent'. (Napoleon was to observe not long after that he believed God had created this Prince to demonstrate the utmost extent to which the human skin could be stretched without bursting.) A further delicate allusion is the figure of Cupid perched on the back of an elephant, which he enchants with the music of his flute. Pitt, then Prime Minister, carries a bag labelled '£80,000'; George III bears the candlestick; and the walls are hung with a tapestry representing the Triumph of Love.

Among the characteristics of the Princess Royal observed in her youth by Lady Louisa Stuart was her indifference to externals in the matter of dress. 'She did not', says Lady Louisa, 'take notice whether your gown was a new or an old one', though the Queen and her sisters 'took an exact account of everybody's wardrobe and trinket-box'. It is true that she insisted on embroidering her wedding robe with her own hands to the very last stitch, 'knowing well that three stitches done by any other hand would make it immediately said it was none of it done by herself', but her trousseau was arranged by the Queen, who, writing many years later to the Prince Regent, remarked, 'For your sister, where I managed everything, I had only made up what was absolutely necessary to wear here, and she took most pieces of silk, and muslin, and lace over to make up in the fashion they dress abroad'.[w]

The Prince of Würtemberg, having quitted the hospitable and scientific company of Sir Joseph Banks, arrived in London; but the resourceful Hippisley had one more hurdle to negotiate on his behalf. This was the question of a *cadeau de noce* from the bride. Anything, the Prince declared, however trivial, would answer the purpose, perhaps a hair-ring set with brilliants; but he should 'really find himself mortified if on his return home he were compelled to admit that he had received nothing'. Lady Harcourt, to whom Hippisley had applied, rejoined that every country had its own customs, and that it was as reasonable he should then be satisfied with those established here, as it soon would be for the Princess to adopt those of the place she was going to. Hippisley persisted, however. 'The subject', he declared in a second memorandum, 'is very near the Prince of Wgs feelings. He says it is impossible for us, unaccustomed to the Etiquette of Germany, to imagine the ill impression resulting from the omission.' Lady Harcourt, equally obstinate, declined to speak to the Princess, for the following excellent reasons:

> . . . it would be impossible for her to suppose that *from myself* I should suggest to her any thing that is not usual in England; and if she thought I had receiv'd a hint from others it would be very painful to her to find that there was any dissatisfaction, after all the pains that have been taken to show every attention.

Small wonder that Princess Elizabeth reported to the Prince of Wales about this time that 'Royal' was 'very fussy and agitated' after news came that her fiancé was in England.[w]

Any soreness occasioned by this refusal must have worn off before the Prince was presented to his bride, for there is no suggestion in Fanny Burney's second-hand description of the scene that it was marred by stiffness on his side. To Mrs Locke Miss Burney wrote:

A private letter from Windsor tells me the Prince of Würtemberg has much pleased in the Royal House by his manners and address upon his interview, but that the poor Princess Royal was almost dead with terror and agitation and affright at the first meeting. She could not utter a word. The Queen was obliged to speak her answers. The Prince said he hoped this first would be the last disturbance his presence would ever occasion her. She then tried to recover, and so far conquered her tumult as to attempt joining in a general discourse from time to time. He paid his court successfully I am told to the sisters, who all determine to like him: and the Princess Royal is quite revived in her spirits again, now this tremendous opening sight is over.

It is to Fanny Burney that we owe the preservation of Princess Augusta's impressions:

... when I told her that I had heard her Royal Highness the bride had never looked so lovely, she confirmed the praise warmly, but laughingly added, ''Twas the Queen dressed her! You know what a figure she used to make of herself, with her odd manner of dressing herself; but Mamma said, "Now really, Princess Royal, this one time is the last, and I cannot suffer you to make such a quiz of yourself: so I will really have you dressed properly". And indeed the Queen was quite in the right for everybody said she had never looked so well in her life.' The word 'quiz' you may depend was never the Queen's.

'Her Royal Highness the bride' wore, according to the *Lady's Magazine*, 'a nuptial habit of white satin, with a train or pellice of rich crimson velvet with fur trimmings'. Under the coronet her hair was arranged in long ringlets. She seems to have been eclipsed, however, by the bridegroom, who wore a suit of 'silk, shot with gold and silver richly embroidered; gold and silver flaps and cuffs; under his coat the order of St Catherine; over his shoulder the blue watered ribbon insignia of the German Order of the Golden Fleece'.

After the ceremony they left in the King's travelling post-chaise; but not before his daughter had, in obedience to a promise given to her husband the day before, written to beg that his Majesty would be so gracious as to join his influence to that of the two Imperial Courts to support the interest of the Würtemberg family. Evidently the Prince was still quite as much preoccupied with the glory of his house as with his *bonheur particulier*. To his only daughter, Catherine, he wrote: *Depuis jeudi 18 vous avez une nouvelle mère, qui fait, et qui fera le bonheur de votre père et qui par conséquent vous aimerez et respecterez comme lui.*

A letter from Princess Augusta in the unpublished Harcourt MSS. shows that the bridegroom had very thoughtfully 'sent on express' a charming portrait of George III after Gainsborough, so that his bride should find that familiar and well-loved countenance waiting to greet her in a little closet beyond her own suite of apartments.

After a sea-passage so bad that it left the Princess Royal miserably giddy and faint they reached Cuxhaven, where they were met by Prince Adolphus, 'all kindness, much improved in his understanding and conversation', but his appearance much altered by his 'having let his Hair grow as long as Ernest's was'.[w] They spent the night at Admiralty House, and set off next day, travelling by way of the ancestral domain of Hanover. 'In all the places we came through', wrote the Princess to her father, 'the Peasants enquired which was their King's daughter, and then came up and spoke to me, entreating that I would persuade your Majesty to come among them.' Meanwhile the Hereditary Prince had written to his father-in-law, '*Le bonheur de mes jours, sire, sera dorénavant un bienfait reçu des mains de votre Majesté*'; [w] and once more he repeats his plea for English support of his House.

On 28 June they reached Stuttgart, with its baroque palace adorned with painted ceilings, columns of blue marble, and sculpture 'in the manner of Canova'. Two days later they arrived at the even more pretentious palace of Louisbourg (Ludwigsburg), surrounded by long avenues of chestnuts and limes. When, twenty-one years later, Princess Elizabeth visited her eldest sister she was equally impressed by the number and splendour of the lustres at Louisbourg, and the huge size of the place. She gravely records that her husband, the Landgrave of Hesse-Homburg, had to take 'four hundred long steps' when passing from the Dowager Queen's apartments to their own on the same floor, and to reach his dressing-room 'one hundred more'.[w] Her comparison of the building with the Castle of Otranto was hardly happy; anything less 'Gothick' than this synthetic Versailles it would be difficult to conceive.

It was here that the Hereditary Prince and his bride were received by the young Princess Catherine—'a very handsome girl, the very image of her father'. At a dinner party the same night 'God Save the King' was performed with both vocal and instrumental music—the Princess Royal's imperfect ear did not prevent her from recognizing the familiar strain. 'I own', she wrote to her father, 'that I required all the Strength in my power not to burst into Tears. However, I fought with my feelings and behaved pretty well.'[w] Queen Charlotte was not exaggerating when she wrote to the Prince of Wales a few weeks later, 'Every word of her letters bespeaks inexpressible bliss'.[w] The Princess was charmed with her new home, the height of the corn, the size of the cattle, the Spanish sheep grazing on clover-speckled lawns. The Hereditary Prince took her on a short tour of the more mountainous districts of the duchy, because, as he explained to his daughter, there are no mountains in England—a very natural conclusion if we remember that his impressions of this country were chiefly derived from the flat cabbage-fields round Isleworth.

In conversation with Dr O'Meara at St Helena some twenty years later Napoleon remarked of the Princess Royal of England, whom he had first met when he marched upon Ulm in 1805, 'I had the pleasure of interfering to

Charlotte Augusta Matilda, Princess Royal her advantage when her husband, who was a brute, though a man of talent, had ill-treated her, for which she was very grateful to me'. Even in the Family opinions were divided as to the success of the marriage, and diplomatic dispatches seldom show Frederick in an amiable light. The enthusiasm of the Princess certainly cooled a little as the years passed, but she seems to have remained pleased with her husband, and after his death in the autumn of 1816 she wrote to the Prince Regent:

> Now, my dearest Brother, I must slightly touch on a part of your letter which has given me great pain and at the same time astonishes me, as certainly the idea of my ever opposing a wish of my adored Husband's was as far from my Heart [sic] as from my Heart. Believe me, dearest Brother, never could I have been as happy with him as I was had not our minds been congenial. You will from this imagine how deeply you have wounded my feelings by attending to the idle Reports of those whose only object must have been to do mischief and who ever wish to blame the Conduct of all Sovereigns.[w]

It is difficult to imagine how a 'brute' could have acted as the Princess describes her husband acting in a letter to her father dated 'Scharnhausen, 10 August 1797':

> ... On Saturday at four o'clock the Prince was so good as to bring me some Letters, and told me he was going out of shooting [sic]. I followed him to the Door, and saw him mount his Horse. When I returned to my Room I was seized with such an unaccountable uneasiness that I could not go on with my Book, and taking my work went up to set with Madame de Spieghel in her Room. I had been there about a quarter of an hour when a servant came in and called her out, telling her that Prince Frederick had something to say to her. This alarmed me very much. In about three minutes she returned, and saying that I looked ill with fright begged I would go into the Garden. This confirmed my fears, and the moment that I had reached a Bench I burst into Tears, entreating that she would acquaint me with what had happened to my Husband. She then by degrees told me that he had fallen from his Horse. In a short time Prince Frederick came from his Father to fetch me back to the House, where I found the Prince in bed, and he then told me himself that his Arm was broke. It is a great mercy that he was not killed. ... His eye was much bruised, but providentially not hurt essentially. He never lost his presence of mind for before they could lift him off the ground [he] gave Directions that I should be taken into the Garden that I might be spared the pain of seeing him lifted out of the coach. When I came to him he forced himself to appear chearfull, and though in dread-full pain (as from the distance the surgeon could not arrive for six hours after the Fracture) he kept laughing and talking

with me for above three hours, when he insisted on my going to supper, and the moment I left him he fainted away.[w]

There was, however, a special reason why at that time the Prince should be solicitous about his wife. As a result of his accident he was still unable three weeks later to do more than sign his name with his left hand, 'and', wrote the Princess, 'does not think it respectfull to acquaint your Majesty in that manner that he has reason to hope I am with child'.[w] When congratulating his father-in-law on the victory of Camperdown in October 1797, the Hereditary Prince thus expressed himself on the event impending in his family:

Vous allez jouir des doux plaisirs de l'affection paternelle, auxquels votre cœur est si sensible—une fille chèrie qui fait le bonheur de ma vie va bientôt me donner un titulaire, et m'attacher par de nouveaux liens à la Haute Personne de Votre Majesté.[w]

By the death of his father in December 1797 Frederick became Duke, and his wife Duchess of Würtemberg. They moved from Scharnhausen to Louisbourg, and when the old Duchess died early in 1798, her successor took charge of 'Trinette'. 'One thing', she wrote to her father, 'gives me great pleasure in this undertaking—that from the very beginning she took to me very much, and her age being the same as my dearest Amelia's makes her doubly interesting to me.'[w] To the Prince of Wales, after some affectionate remarks about his 'dear little Charlotte', she confessed, 'I look forward with great anxiety to the moment when I shall be equally blessed'.[w]

Already the Princess seems to have won the hearts of her subjects, for the Court Chamberlain, Baron de Wimpfen, reported to Hippisley that when her hour came the churches were continuously full of people with tears in their eyes, and the *bourgeoisie* were making ready to celebrate the occasion on a scale unknown in the annals of the duchy.

Characteristically, the Princess was eager to spare her good father unnecessary suspense. Monsieur de Reder was waiting to carry the news to England, and she had desired to send a few lines by his hand, 'but the Duke dreads so much that I might hurt myself that I have been obliged to give up the thoughts of writing for some time afterwards, and as a Compromise write now'. They intend to move into the country whenever she is well again, and she entreats his Majesty to send a 'pair of cangaroos' for the menagerie which they hope to have. On 5 April she observed, upon her and the Duke taking the Sacrament together, that it was the first time since 1732 that the Duke and Duchess had not been of different religions.[w]

When at last Monsieur de Reder set out for England he was the bearer of bad news. '*Nos ésperances les plus chères ont été anéanties*', wrote the Duke on 27 April.[w] The Princess, after a long and difficult labour, had given birth to a stillborn daughter.' *Une grande et belle fille*', de Wimpfen told Hippisley. To the Prince of Wales Charles Arbuthnot, English Minister at Stuttgart, revealed, 'Her Royal Highness's situation was, it must be confessed, at first extremely critical, for having been delivered of a dead child, and having suffered very greatly in her lying-in, so much fever ensued that for a short time the physicians were apprehensive of her safety'.[w] They were afraid at first to tell her that the baby was not alive.

On 4 May, in a small and shaky hand, the Princess wrote to her father, 'I trust that I feel this as a Christian, and submit with resignation to the will of the Almighty, but Nature must ever make me regret the loss of the little thing I had built such happiness on'. She pays a tribute to the Duke, 'who really is the best of Husbands, and who, God knows, has suffered cruelly from his anxiety on my subject', and to the delicacy of Mr Arbuthnot, who had planned to give a great ball to the Duke in honour of the birth of her 'dear Infant'; when he heard of her misfortune, 'the preparations being made', he wished to give the ball in honour of her recovery; but when he heard how deeply she was afflicted, he 'had the goodness to give it up'.[w]

When early in June she was established at Louisbourg, she was not strong enough to walk, but spent most of the day in the little flower garden the Duke had made for her. Later he planned a small farm 'quite in the English style', and a cottage 'covered with moss, which adds much to its comfort', but her efforts to introduce 'the true Gothic taste' into Germany do not appear to have met with much success. During a visit to the Black Forest she is charmed by a medieval ruin, and her first thought is that if her father could see it it would lead him to build a tower in the Great Park on the same plan. She is constantly mindful of his interest in farming and in building, and gives him practical information, with comments added by her husband, on German methods of agriculture. She walks in the fields and mentally compares the crops with her recollections of those at Windsor. 'Had the Ears of corn appeared fuller or longer than those in the Great Park, I should not have failed sending some to your Majesty but . . . I examined them closely, and found no difference.' She tells Farmer George that in some parts of the country they have driven the hogs into the fields, which have devoured the mice, but many people are against this, 'as they think it will give the Hogs an epidemical illness'.[w]

The Princess follows with the keenest interest the King's building enterprises at Windsor and at Kew, and allusions to Wyatt and 'Capability' Browne constantly recur. In November 1802 she writes that she thinks his Majesty's alterations at Windsor Castle 'must quite restore it to its ancient Gothic beauty, and the new building at Kew be Lulworth Castle improved'. She draws chair-covers 'with a Pen on Velvet' for the chairs intended for the new Palace, and sends her father a broth-cup made of Louisbourg china after her own design. Her husband, Elector of the Empire since 1803, is also building, not only a house for the still-desired kangaroos, but 'a long picture gallery of artificial marble', to which she hopes to add portraits of her parents, when 'the delight of looking at them will be easier felt than described'.[w]

In the grounds of the château was a pleasant house, the Mathildenhof, with a garden of its, own, and it was there that she did most of her painting on porcelain, signing each piece on the bottom with her initials, C. A. M. When the Disbrowes were at Stuttgart shortly after her death, 'an oven for baking china' was still to be seen. Some examples of her handiwork are preserved at Frogmore House, large vases, loaded with gold paint, and adorned with landscapes and garlands in monochrome. One particularly 'Wertherish' design shows a mossy tombstone, inscribed *Erinnerung*, on the verge of a gloomy stream.

The letters written by Charlotte Augusta Matilda to her father between 1797 and 1805 give many sidelights upon her character, revealing her as a singularly pleasant person, with cheerful and intelligent tastes. She enjoyed sledging, theatre-going, and the company of young people. Her piety, though perhaps its utterances may sound strange in modern ears, was dyed in grain and stood wind and weather. Doubtless her father read with pleasure her occasional excursions into philosophy; as when, for example, she wrote to him on 6 July 1798:

> Ever since twelve o'clock we have had a dreadful Storm, Thunder, Lightning and Rain. Whilst we were drinking coffee I heard a sad crash and could not help saying that I wished all those who chose to pretend being unbelievers might frequently meet with such Storms, as I thought it must impress them not only with great awe but also with the conviction of there being a Supreme Being.[w]

Her own views on philosophers were such that she would have repudiated any suggestion that she herself was a dabbler in divine philosophy. After 'Admiral Nelson's noble victory' at the battle of the Nile, when she thought she discerned a rift in the clouds that had been darkening over Europe ever since 1789, she wrote:

> I am thoroughly convinced that it is owing to the sad loss of principles that we have all suffered so cruelly, and shall ever look on the odious Philosophers as the Beings through whom these misfortunes originated.[w]

Indeed, her usual code was so austere that she disapproved of Kotzebue, who 'tries to render vice plausible and virtue insignificant, in addition to which he weakens every principle'. This was not the opinion of Thackeray, who held that 'in the midst of the balderdash there runs that reality of love, children, and forgiveness of wrong which will be listened to wherever it is preached, and sets all the world sympathising'.

Through all her letters there flows like a recurrent refrain her affection for her father. 'I am like an Infant on those occasions', she wrote, after a visit from Lord

Minto had given her an opportunity to hear first-hand news from Windsor; and when Mr Villiers followed a year later she exclaimed, 'One must have been as long parted from one's family as I have to feel the delight of conversing comfortably about them!' On one occasion a letter from the King 'had suffused on her countenance such a look of happiness' that the first question her stepchildren asked was what had given her so much pleasure. The aching separation from her family was destined to last till within a year of her death; and after 1805, when the shadow of Napoleon crept across Würtemberg, all direct communication between her and her father was broken off. According to Miss Williams Wynn, Napoleon gave the Princess 'facilities for correspondence with her own family at the time that the state of Europe would have made it nearly impossible', but in the Windsor Archives are preserved the first letters she wrote after communication was re-established at the end of 1813, and in one of these she says categorically that she had been for nine years cut off from 'all confidential correspondence with the best and dearest of relations', and in the other that she had been 'unhappily deprived of all direct communications with the Royal Family of England'.[w] A few letters percolated through from the Continent perhaps with the connivance of Napoleon—but her friends in England had to rely for news of her mainly on Continental newspapers and the reports of neutral diplomats.

These were sad years for a daughter of George III, married to a puppet-king who was Napoleon's assiduous liegeman as long as the sun of Austerlitz shone, step-mother-in-law to Jerome Bonaparte, and in constant friendly contact with the enemies of her native land. Through it all she seems to have borne herself with a simple dignity that did honour to what she described as 'the pains that were bestowed on me at home'.

Emma Sophia, Countess Brownlow, relates in *Reminiscences of a Septuagenarian* how she was taken by her parents to Louisbourg during that short interval after the Peace of Amiens when the Continent was considered safe for English family parties. The Duke, playing whist at a table curved in order to admit his immense figure, did not impress the young visitor favourably. 'His face was handsome', she says, 'but there was something suspicious and not agreeable in his countenance. He seemed to be watching the Duchess, and trying to hear what passed between her and my father and mother.' The Duchess, on the other hand, 'had a pleasant, good-humoured face, without any pretensions to beauty'. With a turban of some soft material on her head, and her hair frizzed and powdered, she sounds charming; but Emma Sophia's comment, 'HRH was also very large, but not in the same way, being shapeless and like a figure of snow', suggests an analogy with Mr Mantalini's two admiring friends, one of whom 'had no outline', while the other's was 'a demd outline'.

II

When the Princess Royal of England went to Würtemberg as a bride in 1797 one of the first things she noticed was the heavy furrows made in the roads by the Austrian cannon.[w] The country was overrun with Austrian troops, which the Court of Vienna was supposed to maintain, but which were actually a burden, and a grievous one, on the finances of the Duchy, already suffering from the marching and counter-marching of the French armies commanded by Moreau. The distant thunder of French artillery makes itself heard in the Princess's letters in March 1799, when her husband wants to send her off hastily to Anspach, and allows her to remain with him only on condition that she will go 'at a moment's warning' if he has reason to think that she would be 'exposed to anything unpleasant'.

Confusion and uncertainty now prevailed, and nervous persons saw a French spy behind every bush. Though the Würtembergers had urged their Duke to remain in their midst, they were placing every imaginable obstacle in the way of his raising troops. Meanwhile his sister, the Empress of Russia, was exhorting him to 'take an open and active part in the war', which he not unreasonably hesitated to do without the assistance of the Great Powers. The Princess wrote, evidently at his instigation, to beg her father, the minute they should be 'free of those monsters', to take the Duchy under his protection and to take into British pay the troops which her husband was willing to raise, to fight as part of the Austrian army against the French. In April 1800 this wish was realized, but in the interval there had been alarums and excursions, and the Princess noted with concern that revolutionary principles were infecting the local nobility, 'and the system of equality is constantly attempted, which', she adds, 'will make it difficult for me to find Ladies'.[w]

On 28 August the Duke hurried his wife off to Göppingen at midnight, but, thanks to what she regarded as divine intervention, the expected French advance on Louisbourg did not take place. By the beginning of October she was back in Stuttgart, dreading a winter marked by further French invasions, unless the Austrians would leave two or three regiments of infantry near the Rhine, 'as the Heavy Dragoons make it a rule to fly the moment they are attacked.

Indeed', adds the Princess, 'it is cruel to place them there, as the whole country is not made for them to act in. The receiving orders on every occasion to retire is enough to make these fine Regiments totally lose their courage.'[w]

There is a gap in the correspondence until the beginning of 1800. The Duke, in March of that year, dissolved his State Assembly, which, unabashed by an Imperial Rescript, refused to submit until 'threatened by the military'.

The French armies, having crossed the Rhine, thrust deeper into the Duchy, and on 12 May Frederick sent his wife to Weitlingen, where he joined her. Hence they were shortly afterwards compelled to flee to Erlangen, in the Franconian territories of the King of Prussia. The Princess's letters to her father are full of the perfidy of the Austrians, who abandoned the Duke without warning, and the rapacity of the French, who, having been content in 1796 with a 'contribution' equivalent to '£4 millions sterling', paid one-third in specie and two-thirds in horses, corn, etc., now demand an indemnity of '£6 millions and will accept nothing but specie or plate'. The Princess is anxious to sell her jewels, and she entreats her father to 'encourage' the loan which her husband, having stripped himself of all his ready money, proposes to raise in London.[w]

In the midst of all this pother the kangaroos arrived. How it chanced that they followed the fugitives to Erlangen is not clear, but the 'very pretty spot' prepared for their reception at Louisbourg was now in the hands of an uncomprehending enemy, and it is pleasant to know that they found quarters to their liking in Franconia. 'This house', writes the Duchess to her father, 'being partly built round a Court, the Duke has found means to place them in it, and they appear to enjoy themselves very much. Several painters have attempted to take their pictures, and I believe intend to engrave them.' A little less than a year later she is able to report that the kangaroos 'are in very good health, and two young ones have been born, which are great Beauties'.[w]

It was a melancholy year for the Princess, who, having pined at Louisbourg for English verdure, now, in a land of conifers and sand, longs for the clover lawns of her Swabian home. Her two younger stepchildren, Catherine and Paul, were with her, but between August and December 1800 the Duke was away at Vienna, trying without much success to further the interests of his hard-pressed Duchy. In December, after Moreau's victory over the Austrians at Hohenlinden, the streets of Erlangen were full of French soldiers, so that the Duchess was practically a prisoner; and during the engagement which resulted in the capture of Nürnburg by Augereau she could hear the shots 'as distinctly as if we were at a Review'.[w]

Early in 1801, when the First Consul was busy welding Russia, Denmark, and Sweden into a weapon with which to castigate England, the Duchess ventured to offer her father 'some hints concerning Russia'.

Painful though Frederick's experiences in St Petersburg had been, he seems to have felt no reluctance in discussing Russian personalities with his wife, who, from what she has heard him say of 'those he lived with in Russia', has been able to form some judgment of the Emperor's character. She is anxious that, in order to improve the relations between the two Powers by passing 'a spunge on all sides over the unpleasant transactions that have taken place', George III should 'try to employ a person who, being fortunately equally attached and related to both Courts, might more easily succeed in softening things without opposing the dignity of either monarch—I mean the Duke'. She begs that the King will repose her whole confidence in his breast, as it is the only time in her life she has ever hidden anything from her husband.[w]

The suggestion came to nothing, and the Northern Powers entered into the Bond of Armed Neutrality, which suited Napoleon's game to perfection, and might have had uncomfortable consequences for England had Nelson not won the Battle of Copenhagen on 2 April 1801.

The Duchy of Würtemberg, tossed like a cork on the waves of Central European politics, enjoyed a brief interval of ease after the Peace of Amiens. The Duke and his wife returned to Louisbourg, where she took up her interrupted china-painting again, and sent her father some flower-pots of her own design. But if Frederick was, as Napoleon said, 'a man of talent', he can have had no illusions about a Peace so disingenuous, sworn by parties of whom neither trusted the other, and of whom both had pledged themselves to conditions impossible of fulfilment. It was a truce rather than a peace, and nobody can have been less surprised than the First Consul when England declared war on France in May 1803—a little more than a year after its conclusion.

Frederick, during the interval between his return to Louisbourg and the French triumphs at Ulm and Austerlitz, comported himself with an assiduous adaptability worthy of the Vicar of Bray, and was rewarded by the elevation of his dominions from the rank of a Duchy to that of an Electorate. In 1805 Napoleon crossed the Rhine, and the Elector 'was obliged', as his wife put it long after the event, 'to contract an Alliance with the Emperor of the French', and to join the Confederation of the Rhine. She adds that the Emperor 'came to Louisbourg before the Treaty was signed; and I must do him the justice to say behaved not only very politely but personally to me with great attention'. By the end of September Napoleon was writing to Frederick as one prince to another, reminding him of his promise to bring an army corps of Würtembergers to serve with the French colours. Here the Emperor, as reported by O'Meara, may take up the tale:

> When I marched upon Ulm in 1805 I passed through Stuttgart with my army, and I saw your Princess Royal, the Queen of Würtemberg, with whom I had several conversations, and was pleased with her. She soon lost whatever prejudices she might have entertained against me ... she afterwards contributed materially towards effecting a marriage between my brother Jerome and the Princess Catherine, daughter of the King by a former marriage.

In a note on this passage O'Meara remarks, 'I have been informed from a source entitled to the highest credit that the Queen of Würtemberg wrote an account of this interview to her mother, Queen Charlotte, in which she exressed very favourable opinions of Napoleon, and in describing his person concluded in the following manner, "and he has so bewitching a smile!"' 'Think', wrote Lady Bessborough in November 1805, 'of the King's eldest Daughter writing to her mother a letter full of praises of Bonaparte, saying he is much belied!' One speculates as to the amount of snuff needed to restore the Queen's poise after reading that letter.

Miss Frances Williams Wynn (the 'Lady of Quality') was in Stuttgart in October 1823, and it is to her that we owe an interesting sidelight on the Queen of Würtemberg's relations with Napoleon:

> In the midst of the incessant gossip of the Queen-Dowager, the subject of which is almost always herself and her family, some curious grains may be collected from a quantity of useless chaff. There is no topic on which she seems to me to show such good sense as in speaking of Napoleon. I heard her say, 'It was of course very painful to me to receive him with civility, but I had no choice: the least failure on my part might have been a sufficient pretence for depriving my husband and children of this kingdom. It was one of the occasions upon which it was absolutely necessary to *faire bonne mine à mauvais jeu.* To me he was always perfectly civil.'
>
> The Queen, who is always trying to puff the conjugal tenderness of her husband, told my mother that he left it to her option whether she would receive Napoleon. She said 'I could not hesitate, it was my duty'. I do not give her any credit for a determination so perfectly natural. . . . I do give her much credit for the honest candour with which she now speaks of the fallen conqueror, though perfectly aware that it is very disagreeable to most of the members of her own family, and especially to the King. The Queen of Bavaria was not as wise, and upon some occasion when Napoleon was incensed at some slight from her, he said she should remember what she was but for him, *la fille d'un miserable petit Margrave* (Baden), and imitate the conduct of the Queen of Würtemberg, *la fille du plus grand roi de la terre.*

Far from praising the charm of the Emperor's smile, the Queen told Miss Williams Wynn that 'his manners were extremely brusque, even when making the civil'. Her mother, Queen Charlotte, always a rigid economist, would have commended her prudence when Napoleon was expected at Louisbourg. '*Mon ami,*' said the Queen of Würtemberg to her husband, on that occasion, '*vous devez faire le pauvre, au lieu d'étaler vos richesses, si vous ne voulez pas avoir de fortes contributions à payer.*' When the Imperial guest admired some Lyons embroideries, and observed that he had nothing like them at the Tuileries, she boldly assured him that they were her own handiwork. Other examples of splendour she attributed to '*le Duc, mon beau père*'. 'God forgive me, that was a lie!' she added later to the 'Lady of Quality'.

Napoleon, in acknowledging the *bon accueil* which he had received at Louisbourg, begged Frederick to remember him to the Electress, to whom he was punctilious in sending polite messages from time to time.

Early in 1806 the obsequious Elector was further rewarded by seeing his Electorate transformed into a Kingdom, under the wing of Napoleon, who must have smiled in his sardonic way when signing his letters to Frederick with the inter-regal formula, '*Sur ce je prie Dieu qu'il vous ait en sa sainte et digne garde*'. Then it was that there appeared upon the roof of the palace at Stuttgart a gilded crown of such prodigious dimensions that it became proverb.

Both Napoleon's Empresses visited Louisbourg, and were successively received there with enthusiasm. Marie Louise, for whose amusement *The Judgment of Solomon* was presented in a bitterly cold theatre, wrote to her father that of the whole Royal Family she liked only the Queen, and the Hereditary Princess, her future sister-in-law.

When Princess Charlotte Augusta Matilda of Great Britain was raised to the dignity of Queen Consort by the man whom her father and his subjects identified with the Beast of Revelation, she was not above enjoying the elevation which made her the equal of her mother. 'The Queen', wrote Lady Bessborough on 10 May 1806, 'has rec'd a letter from her eldest daughter beginning, "*Ma très chere Mère et Sœur*". You may guess how it was received.' Was it perhaps at Queen Charlotte's instigation that George III decreed that no member of the Family should address the Princess Royal as 'Queen' of Würtemberg? After communications were re-established in 1813 it took the old Queen some little time to come round, and in the interim her letters to her eldest daughter had to be sent first to the Prince Regent to be 'redirected in a proper manner'.[w]

With her strong sense of justice the younger Queen abstained from vilifying the fallen Emperor, to whom she never denied the Imperial title. She assured the Regent that 'Emperor Napoleon' had ever spoken of him 'in handsome terms', and at different times expressed a wish 'to see the two countries at Peace'.[w] After Waterloo she hoped it would be in her brother's power to unite prudence with lenity and allow 'this extraordinary man' to exist as a State prisoner under his protection.[w]

In nothing does the Queen of Würtemberg appear to greater advantage than in the character of stepmother. Within a year of her marriage she had shown anxiety lest George III should be misled by accounts of 'a most vexational event' in her adopted family. A set of wicked, intriguing men, she explained, had got hold of the Hereditary Prince, and had drawn him into taking inconsiderate steps which might hereafter have made the young man very unhappy. 'The world is very bad,' commented his stepmother, 'and what I think most horrid is that people are not satisfied with being wicked themselves, but they won't allow anybody else to be good.' [w]

Promising amendment, the Prince was sent to the University of Tübingen, whence he returned a year later, much chastened and improved. To 'Trinette', who was the same age as Princess Amelia, she was affectionately attached, and upon her she tried to impress the religious principles of Queen Charlotte.

However, it was obviously the youngest of her stepchildren, Prince Paul, who occupied the warmest corner in her heart during the early years of her married life. In September 1801 she wrote to her father that she was glad Mr Wickham, the English diplomat, had given him such a good account of 'our eldest son', and adds:

> Had my little Paul been older I think he would have pleased Mr Wickham very much, as he is a very comical Boy, and in my partial Eyes his manners are like Adolphus's; but I must acknowledge that the Duke always accuses me of spoiling him and Catherine, who certainly puts me much in mind of dear Elizabeth. [w]

It was indeed a fantastic spin of Fortune's wheel which made George III's eldest daughter the stepmother-in-law of Napoleon's youngest brother. Having pleaded with the unresponsive Pope that Jerome's first marriage, with Miss Patterson of Baltimore, should be annulled, so that there might be no *fille protestante* in the Imperial family circle, the Emperor prevailed upon the Gallican Church to disolve the contract, and proceeded, with true Napoleonic effrontery, to look about him for a Protestant Princess to Miss Patterson's place.

His choice fell upon Catherine of Würtemberg. The Peace of Tilsit gave birth to the kingdom of Westphalia, and Jerome and Catherine were to be the first King and Queen.

The civil marriage was performed in the Gallery of Diana at the Tuileries, and the religious ceremony in the chapel of the palace next evening. Napoleon, observing that the bride's trousseau was not up to the Parisian standard, took the matter in hand. '*C'est l'Empereur*', wrote Catherine to her father, '*qui m'a donné des chemises.*'

Prince Paul, the 'very comical Boy', was already married to Princess Charlotte of Sachsen-Hildburghausen. This lady did not, in the opinion of her father-in-law, possess '*un bien grand degré de sensibilité*', and she allowed her husband to treat their children with something worse than neglect. The Queen Dowager of Würtemberg took charge of two of the daughters in 1819, when Elizabeth of Hesse-Homburg remarked, 'I rather believe that these poor girls have been exceedingly ill-used by their abominable father'. Paul's manners had not continued to resemble those of the ever-kindly Adolphus.

Early in 1808 there was another wedding in the Würtemberg family. The Hereditary Prince was married to Charlotte Augusta, daughter of Max I, King of

Bavaria. '*Le prince royal*', wrote his father to Catherine, '*n'a pas trouvé belle sa future, mais au reste il en paraît fort content.*' Six years later this resigned mood had passed, and the young man divorced his Bavarian wife. Queen Charlotte then wrote to the Prince Regent:

> Your sister laments, this event very much, as nothing can be alleaged against the princess but her uglyness, for she is a fine figure, mild in her disposition, talented, and uncommonly well behav'd, and with the Kg's leave and by the Prince Royal's desire, your sister is to keep up a constant connection with her.[w]

The Prince Royal's second wife was the Grand Duchess Catherine of Russia, his first cousin, widowed daughter-in-law of Peter of Oldenburg; his third was yet another cousin, Pauline, daughter of Duke Louis of Würtemberg. The despised Bavarian Princess became the fourth wife of Francis I of Austria, and incidentally the step-grandmother of the Duke of Reichstadt, *ci-devant* King of Rome.

The 'Lady of Quality' has an illuminating anecdote to relate, on the Queen's authority, which must belong to this period:

> Napoleon used to play whist in the evening, but not for money, playing ill and inattentively. One day when the Queen Dowager was playing with him against her husband and his daughter, the Queen of Westphalia, the wife of Jerome, the King stopped Napoleon, who was taking up a trick that belonged to them, saying, '*Sire, on ne joue pas ici en conquérant!*'

When diplomatic relations were reopened between England and Würtemberg the Prince Regent received from his eldest sister a carefully transcribed and obviously 'inspired' memorandum, tracing the course of events in the little dominion during the past fourteen years, setting Frederick's conduct in the most favourable light, and making a well-timed bid for English support at Vienna. The Queen did her best, and the Regent might have been glad for her sake to do his; but Castlereagh distrusted the royal weathercock, of whom Aberdeen had reported that he was abhorred in his own country, and there was no open championship of Würtemberg's interests by Great Britain.

Admittedly Frederick's position was a difficult one, and there was nothing for him to do except to adjust himself to a new situation. He notified Napoleon in October 1813 that, as the result of the alliance between Austria and Bavaria, he found himself obliged to ask for an armistice. It was tantamount to desertion in the face of the enemy, and Napoleon's comments at St Helena are not wholly unjustifiable. In the event Frederick was allowed to keep his toy kingdom, and the gigantic golden crown continued to surmount his palace at Stuttgart.

His Majesty's chief anxiety seems to have been to purge himself quickly from the Bonaparte taint. In April 1814 he was urging his daughter Catherine to follow the example of Marie Louise, and return to her family, but this the ex-Queen of Westphalia declined to do. Here, at least, the hand of England was stretched forth in mercy, though a little belatedly. In August 1819 the Queen of Würtemberg wrote to thank the Prince Regent for having ordered Sir Charles Stuart to write to the Imperial, Prussian, and Würtemberg ministers to obtain for her daughter a settlement due to her rank. 'I have', she said,' suffered very much on Catherine's account'.[w]

In December 1813 the Regent dispatched to Stuttgart his Gentleman Usher of the Black Rod, Sir Thomas Tyrwhitt, MP for Plymouth, and Lord Warden of the Stannaries of the Duchy of Cornwall, affectionately known to the Family as the Dwarf, *der Zwerg*, or his *kleine Excellenz*. The Queen was much touched, and wrote to her brother:

> One must have nine years cut off from all confidentiall correspondence with the best and dearest of relations to be able to form an idea of my happiness at being enabled to converse with a Gentleman who has been so many years attached to you and who is so thoroughly acquainted with the interior of Windsor. It has been a most melancholy comfort for me to talk over the dreadful situation of my beloved Father; my heart bleeds to think of all he has undergone, and I shudder to hear that we dare entertain no hopes of any alteration for the better. Your angelic conduct towards him, my dearest Brother, to my Mother and Sisters, is a theme Sir Thomas kindly loves to dwell on, as he sees how much it soothes my mind to be acquainted with every circumstance of your dutifull Behaviour to our Parents; and your affectionate kindness to my Sisters, whose Situation would have been melancholy and unpleasant had your good heart not induced you to step forth and have such handsome establishments settled on them.
>
> . . . Your kindness also to our poor Amelia is engraven on my Heart.[w]

Sir Thomas Tyrwhitt's diminutive stature, coupled with his grandiose deportment, amused his royal friends, and caused the Regent to nickname him 'the Twenty Third of June', which, HRH erroneously explained to Queen Charlotte, 'is the shortest (k)night'.[w] He was a discreet and sympathetic envoy, and if he did not succeed in bringing the Queen of Würtemberg back with him on a visit to England, it was not his fault. He probably helped her to draw up the clear statement of her financial situation, giving the figures of her income (derived from her marriage settlement) from 1805 to 1813, and showing how, though punctually transmitted from England, it had been reduced by the fluctuations of the Continental exchange. Out of the £5,000 due to her annually she had never received in any one year more than £1,333; in 1805 it was only

£190: 9: 6¼; and it is hardly surprising that these diminutions should sensibly have 'affected her Majesty's domestic arrangements'.

The Prince Regent was not able to do much for his sister financially, but he seems to have been anxious that she should come to England in the spring of 1814, when the Dwarf was in Stuttgart again. This plan was frustrated by the arrogance of Frederick, who was offended because the letter of invitation had been addressed to the Queen direct instead of to himself; in fact Tyrwhitt suspected him of instructing his wife to cough 'in a very painful and violent manner' in order to support his contention that she was not well enough to make the journey. Sir Thomas's count of the scene is worth quoting:

> 'I am a husband and ought to direct my wife—I ought to have been consulted, & the letter should have been addressed to me, and *possibly then much facility would have been given on my part to the object of his Royal Highness's letter*'—the Queen here (I am persuaded by order) coughed a good deal—and then said the King, '*Voyez, Monsieur, sa situation actuelle*' (more coughing) *je doute si elle pourra entreprendre le voyage même d'ici à Ludwigsberg.*[w]

Sir Thomas interrupted to remark that if the cause of her Majesty's not being able to visit her family arose from her Royal brother not having written to his Majesty, he deeply regretted that he was not the bearer of such a letter, as he was certain her family loved her too sincerely to permit etiquette debarring them the pleasure they would have in once more seeing her.

The effect of the interruption was not soothing.

> His Majesty here worked himself into such a passion that nothing could have prevailed upon him to have heard me out but the presence of the Queen. He said he could feel his own dignity as well as other Potentates—that he felt his sovereignty wounded—and as the insinuations that had been copied from English Gazettes into those of Germany respecting himself and his beloved wife (*épouse*) (here they shook hands and went thro' a scene worthy of the stage)—and here I interrupted his Majesty for the last time.[w]

This interruption, more happily worded, included a promise that when he returned to England he would send her Majesty the newspaper in which he himself had contradicted 'the whole idea'.

The 'order of the day', as Tyrwhitt shrewdly remarked, was that the Queen was too ill to undertake any journey for the moment. 'I complained', he says, 'of the *raideur* of the King towards me, which produced an expression from her which at once opened my eyes—she earnestly begged me to take as little notice of it as I consistently could, as she said, "I shall ultimately be the sufferer".'[w] Not a very comforting account of things for the Queen's friends in England, seeming indeed to confirm Castlereagh's opinion that the King was 'a tyrant both in his public and private character'; on the other hand, when the Duke of Kent was at Stuttgart in October 1816 he wrote assuring his sister Mary that he believed 'Royal' to be 'perfectly happy'. She might have been happier had her King's desire to receive the Garter been fulfilled. Its non-fulfilment rankled to the last.

The poor lady did not reach England till 1827, eleven years after her husband's death, and only one year before her own. She never wore any colour but black after he died, keeping a widow's cap in her pocket, for which she was wont to exchange 'whatever she had on her head at the time' when anyone called on her. She frequently prayed by Frederick's coffin in the royal vault, and seldom appeared without a medallion or miniature of his Majesty round her neck.

The letters written by the Queen of Würtemberg to Sir Thomas Tyrwhitt deal with a variety of topics, amongst others the rumoured intention of her brother Ernest, Duke of Cumberland, to visit Stuttgart early in 1814. She wrote urging Sir Thomas to beg the Regent to make the Duke delay his visit until after that of the Grand Duke Constantine and the Grand Duchess Catherine of Russia, 'as Ernest, having quarrelled with the Emperor of Russia, and since then with the Prince Royal of Sweden, would keep me in hot water by his imprudent conversation. . . . Besides which his dirty tricks and his freedom of speech have gone on increasing since his journey to Hanover.'[w]

The whole Continent was by this time aware that the Duke of Cumberland was wooing his cousin, the Princess of Solms Braunfels, whose second husband seemed to be on the point of following the example of her first, a Prince of Prussia, and putting an end to their marriage by a divorce. 'I dread', wrote the Queen of Würtemberg, 'that Ernest will forget what he owes to the Prince Regent, and obstinately persist in a marriage which he knows must be a source of pain to the whole family.'[w] In her anxiety to stave off the visit, she appealed to Queen Charlotte, who wrote to the Prince Regent on 8 January 1814:

> I have also received a long letter from Würtemberg, full of all the acquaintance she has made with the imperial family of Russia of which she prefers the widow of the Prince of Holstein, who she says is one of the most amiable creatures possible. . . . Her manner quite English and very desirous to cultivate English acquaintances.
>
> She has nothing but English servants about her, and begged it as a favour that they might be allowed to see your sister, which was granted, and produced a very crying meeting.
>
> She expects also a visit from the Duke of Cumberland, which it appears she would willingly decline on account of his dislike to the Emperor of Russia, of whom he allows himself to speak in a very disrespectful manner wherever he goes. She dreads therefore the consequences of a meeting between her brother

and the Duke, who is Uncle to the E. and you know easily offended. She also mentions that people in general think the D. of C. quarrelsome and dissatisfied, which would keep her in constant fear, and would not give such an enjoyment as the visit of a Brother should produce.[w]

The 'Princess of Holstein' was that Grand Duchess Catherine of Russia, Duchess of Oldenburg, who afterwards married 'Royal's' eldest stepson; and 'the Duke' was Peter of Oldenburg, who once himself nearly married the Princess Royal. Concerning the feelings of her eldest sister towards the Duke of Cumberland, Princess Elizabeth wrote, about this time, 'she has a horror of him, and is aware that he is cruelly mischievous to all those he ought to love and Honour'.[w] The visit was never paid, but the Duke of Cumberland seems to have felt no rancour. When the Queen Dowager died he had long been happily married to the Princess of Solms, who had, in his own words, known how to 'tranquillize his mind'. Of his eldest sister he then wrote to George IV, 'As I have never seen her since June 3d, 1797, upwards of 31 years ago, I have hardly a recollection of her; however, one cannot help feeling deeply when one branch of the old tree drops off'.[w]

At the time when the Princess Royal left England, in June 1797, the infant daughter of George, Prince of Wales, and Caroline, his most unfortunately chosen Princess, was only eighteen months old, but already her eldest aunt was taking an affectionate interest in the 'Little Beauty', as Queen Charlotte called her. After the death of her own baby she remarked in a letter to the Prince of Wales, 'You who have the blessing of having so charming a little girl as Charlotte will feel for my loss'; and on hearing in 1799 that he had not benefited from the waters at Bath, she urged him to take care of his health 'for all our sakes, and more particularly for that of your lovely little Charlotte'. It is clear that the fantastic vision of the Princess of Wales is hovering near when she adds: 'How painful would the thought be to Yourself were she left without Your care and protection. I always look forwards to that little Girl as being when she grows up Your Comfort and Your Companion. You little think how much I love to employ my thoughts in seeing Your future prospects cheered by her love and attentions.'[w] She sends the child small gifts, a set of doll's china, a cross of 'Ribbond Stone', and she is delighted when her brother gives her a locket with a piece of Charlotte's hair. Later Charlotte herself sent her aunt a 'Locket with a beautiful Eye and a fine Noze'.[w]

'Whenever you allow her to spend a week at Windsor,' wrote the Princess Royal on one occasion, 'all my letters are filled with accounts of the dear Child, who is, I am assured, Your Picture.'[w] She dwells often and lovingly on this small girl, and likes to imagine 'dear little Charlotte' being her father's companion at breakfast at Carlton House.

In later years, when Princess Charlotte's marriage was a dynastic necessity, her far-off Aunt was not favourably inclined towards the projected Orange alliance. 'Nothing so much I dread', she wrote in a memorandum on the subject, 'as a Prince in imitation of King William 3d, who is now cried up in every Newspaper as the only Example a King ought to follow'[w]; and she had some candidates of her own, the Hereditary Prince of Oldenburg, son of her early suitor, Peter of Oldenburg, 'the King of Prussia's nephew, Prince Frederick, the King of Würtemberg's nephew, Prince Adam, or Prince Charles of Mecklenburg-Strelitz'.[w] Any of these would, in her view, 'suit the Situation better and be less dangerous to the present Royal Family'. She does not mention the suitor whom at that moment Princess Charlotte seemed disposed to favour—William Frederick, Duke of Gloucester.

The Queen's two stepsons were in London for the official Peace celebrations in the summer of 1814, the elder as the representative of his father, the younger as an uninvited and unwelcome guest. She was glad to hear that the Prince Regent intended showing the Allied sovereigns Portsmouth, 'where', she observed, 'they must take a high opinion of the wealth and power of Great Britain. When they see the Great Fleet off the Isle of Wight they must be struck with a sight they can meet with in no other country on the Globe'; she fears, however, that the Prince, owing to sea-sickness, will be 'the Person that will least enjoy this excursion'.[w]

The unfortunate Regent had other troubles besides seasickness with which to contend. The visit of the Allied sovereigns was not a success, and Mr Creevey recorded that their host was 'worn out with fuss, fatigue, and rage'. Moreover, the engagement between Princess Charlotte and the Prince of Orange was disintegrating, and the Queen of Würtemberg had the pain of hearing from her mother of 'Prince Paul's disrespectfull behaviour at Carlton House', on the occasion when that 'savage animal', as Brougham called him, made the young fiancé 'remarkably drunk'. The news was received with distress in Würtemberg, and the Queen reminded her Family that she and her husband had warned them that for thirteen years Paul had 'done nothing but offend his father by the improprieties of his conduct'. She is obviously sincere when she adds that she shuddered 'to think of his profligacy in drawing the amiable young Prince of Orange into a scrape in the presence of Charlotte'.[w]

However deeply the Queen of Würtemberg may have been shocked by Princess Charlotte's 'inconsiderate conduct' in escaping from Warwick House in a hackney coach and seeking sanctuary with the Princess of Wales in Connaught Place, she was anxious that the Regent should not be too severe, and flatters herself that he will 'even at this very painfull moment consider Charlotte's youth'. She thinks the young Princess must have 'met with some secret ill-intentioned advisers', and urges that 'from a variety of circumstances' Charlotte has encountered 'many disadvantages in her education', and 'from not being constantly under the eye of a Parent has from her infancy been a little too much accustomed to act for herself'.[w] She has evidently heard that the Regent was inclined to severity, for she adds, 'Certainly you will soften her heart if you speak to her with the affection of a Father; your unexpected kindness will prevent her falling into fresh errors'.[w]

She was next agitated by the news of Napoleon's escape from Elba. 'His landing in France at the head of so small a body of men', she wrote to the Regent, 'would have appeared romantic to all who were not acquainted with the talents and good fortune he displayed till last year.'[w] But in one sense the break-up of the Congress of Vienna relieved her mind, for, as she confessed to her mother, she 'had feared that Vienna air and amusements might prove pernicious to the King's health'.[w]

An encouraging message from the Regent, conveyed by Lord Castlereagh, brought her some comfort, and she declared that her husband deeply felt the handsome manner in which the Regent had expressed himself concerning his 'having come forwards at this awfull moment'.[w]

An 'awfull moment' it must indeed have been, and to Frederick's apprehensive eyes never can the great crown above his palace have seemed less secure. But the Napoleonic wave rose, broke, and spent itself in vain upon Mont St Jean. On 1 July 1815, the Queen of Würtemberg was writing to Lady Harcourt:

> I am sure, dear Lady Harcourt, that you will have been delighted with the account of the glorious Victory the Duke of Wellington obtained on the 18th ultimate. I have read with the greatest pleasure all the Reports which have appeared on the subject, and followed his march on the Map.
>
> On all sides the Allies advance: four days ago my son, the Prince Royal, took possession of Hagenau. I expect much of the Duke of Wellington in Picardi, which was ever famous for the battles of Crecy and Agincourt.

Apparently the Regent did not encourage frequent letters from her, nor did he always take the trouble to reply. As his other sisters found him a constant and lively correspondent, one is forced to the conclusion that it was the eldest for whom he cared the least. She was plainly hurt that she should have learned from the newspapers the day fixed for Charlotte's marriage to Prince Leopold, and sent 'sincere wishes for their happiness' in a rather stiff tone; but before the letter ends her heart melts, and she hopes her brother 'will never quite forget a sister that loves him'. Her letter of condolence when Charlotte died has not been preserved, but it is easy to imagine how she would grieve not only for her niece but for the baby of whom Lord Eldon wrote, 'a noble Infant it was, as like the Royal Family as possible'.

The period immediately following the overthrow of Napoleon was marked by high-handed reaction all over Europe. In 1815 the King of Würtemberg, having jettisoned the constitution of 1771, offered his subjects another, more acceptable to himself, but decidedly less so to them. The Würtembergers objected, and while discussions were in progress he died, on 30 October 1816. His mother-in-law, Queen Charlotte, decreed that she and the Princesses should wear 'bombazin' for a month in mourning for him.[w]

On 7 November his widow was writing, on black-edged paper, a letter of introduction for Baron de Wimpfen, the Court Chamberlain, whom she was sending to London at her own expense. Religion alone, she declares, can give her courage to look forward to 'a life which must now ever be clouded with sorrow'. She is anxious that there should be no uncertainty as to the happiness of her marriage. 'Edward,' she writes, 'who spent some days at Louisbourg, will I am sure do justice to our attachment for each other'[w]; and this Edward had already done. The new King is 'all duty and attention'—though Elizabeth, Landgravine of Hesse-Homburg, who visited Stuttgart two years later, was not impressed by his amiability, condemned his action in selling the porcelain painted by his stepmother for the old King, and observed that the popularity of the Dowager was standing him in good stead.[w]

In a memorandum handed by de Wimpfen to the Regent the Queen Dowager mentions that she has a debt of nearly £4,000 to repay to the heirs of her late husband. The hint, however delicately conveyed, was unmistakable. The Regent's response was to send her an enamel medallion of himself, with an 'affectionate letter' setting forth very fully the reasons which made it impossible for him to offer her immediate pecuniary assistance. 'Had I been acquainted', she wrote, 'with the state of British finances or the cry for Œconomy, I should certainly have avoided being troublesome.'

She requested that General Taylor should be made joint trustee of her fortune, with Lord Grenville and Sir John Hippisley, whose original fellow-trustees, the Duke of Portland, Mr Pitt, and the Baron de Rieger, were dead. When she herself died twelve years later, her property in England was sworn at 'under £80,000 sterling'—the sum voted by Parliament in 1797—but this did not represent the whole of her personal fortune, as she had exercised her right to withdraw a certain part of it and 'lay it out on a mortgage in the King of Würtemberg's dominions'.

Though with the death of her husband the chief obstacle to a journey to England was removed, eleven years passed before, draped in inconsolable weeds, she returned to her native land. She was never again to see her father, whom she would hardly have known, with his attenuated frame and his long silver beard; or the diminutive, swarthy mother with what Stockmar called 'a true mulatto face'; or Frederick, Duke of York, whose death she bewailed as 'this severe Calamity which has afflicted not only our Family, but the Nation'. [w] The Duke of Cumberland she neither saw nor wished to see. But the Dukes of Kent and Cambridge visited her at Louisbourg; Elizabeth of Hesse-Homburg was there in 1819 and again in 1820, and in 1821 she had the pleasure of a visit from Princess Augusta. 'I know my delight', she wrote to her, some years later, 'when I drove to Bessigheim to wait for your arrival, and first catch sight of your Horses driving over the little Bridge.'[w]

Theirs was what their mother would have called 'a very crying meeting'. And when Princess Elizabeth first saw her exiled sister she could not, according to Princess Mary, 'recover herself for a long time'.

To Lady Harcourt Princess Augusta wrote:

> I found my sister very much altered at first; and had I not had the picture previous to seeing Her, I should not have guessed it was Her. . . . She is very large & bulky. Her face is very broad and fat, which makes Her features appear quite small and distended. But what strikes the most is, that from not wearing the least bit of Corset, Her Stomach and Her Hips are something quite extraordinary.

The Princess may have been prepared for the shock by Landgravine Elizabeth, who wrote of the Queen of Würtemberg in November 1819:

> . . . her person, alas, is sadly changed, for she is certainly very large, more like the Dowager Lady Ely in person, with a great deal more lower stomach. She is neat and clean, but certainly does not dress to advantage, for her hair is very thin, and combed flat upon her face, which is three or four times larger than it was . . . her hands beautifully white, and their form perfection.[w]

The thoughts of Charlotte Augusta Matilda were constantly in the unforgotten land of which for thirty-one years she had been the Princess Royal. She corresponded with the Harcourts and the Hippisleys and other old friends, as well as with the Family, and took a lively interest in the infant nieces and nephews who began to make a tardy appearance on the scene after 1818. Writing to her brother Adolphus to congratulate him on the birth of his son, afterwards George, Duke of Cambridge, she said, 'You must, dear Dolly, give him my Blessing. Only think of my remembering Your Birth as if it was yesterday!'[w] English politics she usually eschewed, though she did on one occasion exhort her eldest brother to 'put an End to the democratical Meetings which must make every British Heart blush'.[w]

Early in 1827 Princess Augusta conveyed to the Queen Dowager the reiterated invitation of that brother, now George IV, that she should visit England. The Queen wrote in reply:

> Though I am a very stupid old Being I am a gratefull one, and shall certainly do all in my power to exert, but you know I am troublesome from not being able to go in a shut carriage or walk, my breath being so short that I must be carried downstairs as well as upstairs. However I hope my dear Brother will have patience with my infirmities.[w]

She was anxious lest he should be hurt by the change in her appearance, and by her premature decrepitude. She begs him to look on her as 'an old Woman whose strength does not allow of her doing many things which would otherwise be agreeable to her'. One can only hope that, having seen the Dukes of Kent and Cambridge recently, she was prepared for as great an alteration in the looks of the King as she cannot have failed to observe in theirs.

Determined to give no more trouble than was necessary, she announces her resolution to go to Teinach and take no less than thirty medicinal baths before setting out for England; and she adds this plea:

> May I entreat you to give a little hint when the King is so gracious to send the yacht that there may be a Chair to draw me up in, as with my shortness of breath I should be quite knocked up if I was to attempt the going up the accomodation ladder. I am quite ashamed to be so troublesome, but I must do all in my power to keep tolerably, and not alarm you all with one of my Suffocations.⁽ʷ⁾

She does not mention her other brothers, but there was an eight-year-old godchild of hers at Kensington Palace to whom her thoughts turned with that peculiar tenderness which she seems always to have felt for small girls. 'I long', she exclaimed, 'to see Vicky, and hope she will take a little bit of a fancy for me.'⁽ʷ⁾

According to the *Annual Register* for 1828:

> Her Majesty had been afflicted for many years past with a dropsy, which was the cause of her extraordinary size. Her malady was one principal inducement for her Majesty visiting her native country last year, in the hope that the English faculty might give her relief. Sir Astley Cooper and others were called in to attend the Queen, and by Sir Astley Cooper's advice, her Majesty underwent the operation of tapping while residing in St James's Palace, which was performed by Sir Astley in great privacy. There were flattering hopes that the operation would lead ultimately to a perfect cure.

The Queen had suggested that she should be lodged in the room at Frogmore usually occupied by Mary, Duchess of Gloucester, so that she should always be at her brother's orders, but for some days after she was installed there she was too ill with 'St Anthony's fire' to venture out. When at last she was able to drive up to Royal Lodge, the 'Gothick' cottage built by Nash for the Prince Regent in 1814, she stayed, wrote Princess Augusta to Lady Arran, 'nearly two hours with the King, who is *enchanted with Her Company*'. For her amusement he arranged a dinner-party on the banks of Virginia Water in a large tent. 'After dinner', wrote the Princess, we ladies crossed in an Excellent Boat to the Island, where the old boat-house has been turned into a very pretty building and a habitation for one of the King's Pages, who is the first of this boat's crew, rowing extremely well, as do all His Pages, that is to say, there are *six strong Pullers*, who belong to the boat, all simply and properly dressed in blue-and-white striped jackets, white trowzers, and straw hats. [w]

In due course the King and the other gentlemen of the party joined the ladies on the Island, 'and after Coffee we took a delightfull row until after nine o'clock, by moonlight . . . my Sister and the Dear King', adds Princess Augusta, 'were as happy as it is possible to be'.[w]

Among the old friends with whom the Queen Dowager had not lost touch was Lady
Louisa Stuart. To Walter Scott this lady had written in 1815:

. . . I took it into my head to send her the song upon Mr Pitt's anniversary beginning

> O dread was the hour and more dreadful the omen
> When the brave on Marengo lay slaughtered in vain.

Not because she loved poetry when I knew her; she had the best quiet sense of them all (the Royal Family) but the gods had made none poetical. However, she dearly loved her poor father, whom she resembled in many points of character, and . . . I thought the one stanza of the song, very gratifying even to my feelings, would shed balm upon her heart.

This stanza was the fourth:

> Nor forget His grey head, who, all dark in affliction,
> Is deaf to the tale of our victories won,
> And to sounds the most dear to paternal affection,
> The shout of his people applauding his Son;
> By his firmness unmoved in success and disaster,
> By his long reign of virtue, remember his claim!
> With our tribute to Pitt join the praise of his Master,
> Though a tear stain the goblet that flows to his name.

It did shed balm upon the royal heart, and the royal hand wrote phrases of appreciation which were endorsed by Scott: 'This applause is worth having'.

Neither the delights of her sojourn in England nor Sir Astley Cooper's skill availed to arrest the progress of the Queen Dowager's malady. Throughout the summer of 1828 her health continued to wane, though within three days of her death on 6 October she entertained Lord and Lady Shrewsbury to dinner and 'kept up for nearly two hours a most interesting conversation upon a variety of topics'. The story of her last hours was told by her old friend, Lady Louisa, and is a fitting epilogue to a gracious and gentle life:

> No one of any rank ever left such sincere mourners. Her charities were unbounded, and she had so endeared herself to her husband's family, and to all his subjects, that from the present King down to the beggar, I hear, all seem to have lost a parent. In speaking of him (the King) she constantly said 'my son'. She sent for him when she felt herself dying, and had a long conversation with him, and bade him bring his wife and children the next day. By that time her sight had failed. She said, '*J'entends vos voix, je ne vous vois plus*', and was in the act of putting out one hand to him, while his little boy, on whom she doated, was kissing the other, when an apoplectic seizure ended her life. They could hardly remove the child from the body, and the young Princess Pauline, the orphan daughter of the *vaurien* Prince Paul, would not leave it for several hours. The last day I saw her she showed me a set of ornaments she had just bought at Roundell and Palmers', saying—'Don't think I wear such things myself: they are for Pauline, my spoilt child!' It was her custom on Sundays to make her English maid read her an English sermon. On the 5th of October she said, after hearing it attentively, 'There, my dear, you have done, and I thank you—you will never read me another'.

2

Princess Augusta Sophia, 1768–1840

I

When a sixth child and second daughter was born to George III and Queen Charlotte on 8 November 1768, two conspicuously dynastic names were bestowed upon her in holy baptism. Both her grandmother, the Princess of Wales, and her aunt, the Duchess of Brunswick-Wolfenbüttel, had been called Augusta; and Sophia had a threefold family association, through the Electress Sophia of Hanover, Sophia Dorothea of Zell, and the infant Princess's own mother, Charlotte Sophia of Mecklenburg-Strelitz. The little Prince of Wales wanted his new sister to be christened 'Louise', but his views were set aside.

Relations between George III and the City of London had been slightly strained about the time of Princess Augusta's birth, but it is recorded that the City Fathers 'approached his Majesty with a better grace than on some preceding occasions, steering clear of political animadversion, and confining themselves to gratulations on the happy event'. When the baby was six days old the public were admitted, according to custom, to taste the royal cake and caudle; and two young ladies so far forgot themselves as o carry off 'a large quantity of cake and some of the cups in which the caudle had been served up'. They were dealt with leniently, and allowed to escape with a severe reprimand, 'after begging pardon on their knees for so disgraceful an act'. The anonymous author of *George III, his Court and Family* observes that the delinquents had first 'drunk plentifully of the caudle', which appears to have been a heady concoction.

Lady Mary Coke, visiting Lady Charlotte Finch at Kew in December 1768, reported that the five-weeks-old Princess was the most beautiful infant she had ever seen.

Like the Princess Royal—whom Lady Mary found 'very plain'—Augusta was devoted to Mary Hamilton, to whose mother she wrote the following attractive note in 1777:

Dear Madam,
   I take the liberty to write to you for the first time. My dear Miss Hamilton is well, tell her that I hope that I shall see her when she comes to see the Cradle of

the New Child Mama is to have. Thank God she is well, and I hope she will go on so. I hope your Friends is all well.—I am Yours,

AUGUSTA

The 'New Child' was Princess Sophia.

At twelve Princess Augusta was writing to 'Dear Hamy' from Queen's Lodge, Windsor, giving her news of the Court. 'We are now come to Windsor', she says, 'and for our sins are forced on Sunday evenings to walk on the Terrace.' Here at least was one member of the royal group who did not enjoy that ritual promenade. At this time the appearance of the small girls must have been quaint, for Augusta tells Miss Hamilton, 'We now do our Hair in a new sort of fashion—we have Hats all day and no caps'. Miss Burney remarks that 'dressing heads' took two hours, and that it was 'very much the custom of the Royal Family to go without caps'.

Many years later the Princess Royal, in a letter to Lady Harcourt, spoke of Augusta's 'great shyness', but apart from the remark about the walk on the Terrace there is nothing to suggest this. If any of the Princesses were ever anything of a tomboy it was she, for when she was over sixty she talked to a small boy of cricket, football, and hockey, 'telling him when she was a little girl she played at all these games with her brothers, and played cricket particularly well'. As a child she seems to have been affectionate, impetuous, quick to repent of her little sins and adroit in coaxing pardon out of Lady Charlotte, Madame de la Fite, and Miss Hamilton. It was she who took the lead when the Sisterhood revolted against the tyranny of Queen Charlotte in 1812, and she who 'really stood forward nobly' on Princess Elizabeth's side during the negotiations for a marriage between that Princess and Louis Philippe, Duke of Orleans. This courage was matched by a gentle candour, different from the 'Sally Blunt' downrightness of which Princess Elizabeth loved to boast. 'When I was a child', Augusta wrote to her friend Mrs Dering, 'dearest Lady Cha used to say I was famous for my honesty.'

Mrs Dering, whose friendship with the Princesses Augusta and Elizabeth began when they were all three children, was the daughter of Sir Joseph Yates, Chief Justice of the Common Pleas. They continued to write to each other as long as they all lived, and Mrs Dering, the last survivor of the group, left instructions that after her death all the carefully hoarded royal letters were to be destroyed. This was believed to have been done; but many years later her granddaughter discovered a number of them tucked away in 'a curious old brass-bound, walnut-wood box, full of secret drawers and cleverly-concealed hiding-places'. By the courtesy of Mr Heneage E. B. Harrison, that granddaughter's son, several of these letters will be quoted in the present chapter, and elsewhere in this book.

Another reminiscence of Princess Augusta's childhood occurs in a passage where she mentions that 'dearest Lady Cha' had taught both her and Elizabeth to commit the following couplet to memory:

> Content is wealth, the riches of the mind,
> And happy he who can that treasure find.

It was a sadly appropriate aphorism for two girls whose lives were so to be ordered that 'the riches of the mind' would often be the only solace left to them.

Princess Augusta was seventeen when Miss Burney joined the royal household, and in the *Diary and Letters* hers is always an attractive figure. 'She has', wrote that keen though not impartial observer, 'a gaiety, a charm about her that is resistless, and much of true, genuine, and very original humour.' Of all the Sisterhood she was the most musical; she played the harpsichord to Mrs Delany when only eleven years old.

On her eighteenth birthday the Princess found upon her dressing-table a little work-box, round the centre ornament of which was written in pencil, '*Est-il permis?*' Let the modest donor relate the sequel:

> At the Queen's dressing-time, as I opened the door, her Majesty said, 'Oh, here she is! *Est-il permis!* Come, come in to Augusta', and made me follow her into the next room, the door of which was open, where the Princess was seated at a writing-desk, probably answering some congratulatory letters.
>
> Immediately, in a manner most pleasing, she thanked me for the little *cadeau*, saying, 'Only one thing I must beg—that you will write the motto with a pen!'

It is to Fanny Burney that we are indebted for a lively account of a scene between the Princess and M. de la Guiffardière (Mr Turbulent) early in 1787, when by a series of bantering questions that very unparsonical French parson reduced Augusta to a state of blushing and exasperated laughter, and revealed to Fanny that the Prince Royal of Denmark 'was in his meaning and in her understanding'. Some disparaging remarks about the sameness of the French plays read aloud every evening caused de la Guiffardière to ask what national plays had the honour of her Royal Highness's preference. Miss Burney says:

> I saw he meant something that she understood better than me, for she blushed again and called out, 'Pray open the door at once. I can stay no longer.' 'Not till you have answered that question, Madam. What country has plays to your Royal Highness's taste?'
>
> 'Miss Burney,' she cried impatiently, yet laughing, 'pray do you take him away! Pull him!'
>
> He bowed to me very invitingly for the office, but I frankly answered her, 'Indeed, Ma'am, I dare not undertake him! I cannot manage him at all.'

'The country, the country, Princess Augusta—name the happy country!' was all she could gain.

'Order him away, Miss Burney,' cried she. ''Tis your room—order him away from the door!'

'Name it, Ma'am, name it!' exclaimed he; 'name but the chosen nation!' And then, fixing her with the most provoking eyes, '*Est-ce le Danemarck?*' he cried.

She coloured violently, and quite angry with him, called out, 'Mr Turbulent, how can you be such a fool!'

The Danish project had been broached to the King as early as November 1785, but he had received it with a lack of enthusiasm which is comprehensible when we remember the tragic life of his sister, Caroline Matilda, as the consort of the imbecile Christian VII. Apparently it was still on the *tapis* fifteen months later.

Those indefatigable matchmakers, Lady Harcourt and her sister-in-law, refused to be disheartened by the unresponsive attitude of George III, and scanned the horizon for a suitable husband for Princess Augusta. One of Mrs Harcourt's candidates was Prince Frederick of Orange. She wrote of him, before the advance of the French Revolutionary armies drove the Orange family into temporary exile in England, 'he is the only man worthy of our Princesses; he even deserves Princess Augusta, all angel as she is'.

Another candidate was Prince Ferdinand, a cadet of the ducal house of Würtemberg and an officer in the service of Maria Theresa. Augusta was then, says Mrs Papendiek, 'the most beautiful creature one would wish to behold', and the Prince, who came over to woo in person, charmed everyone who saw him dancing at the Queen's birthday ball. But the King would not hear of the match; Prince Ferdinand, acknowledging defeat, retired gloomily from the field. In the diary of Mr Speaker Abbott (afterwards Lord Colchester) for March 1796 it is noted that 'the Prince of Wales has been endeavouring to persuade the Duke of Würtemberg's commissioner to ask the Princess Augusta instead of the Princess Royal'—probably a false rumour, but it suggests that the sympathetic attitude of the Prince towards his second sister was not unknown. When, twenty-two years later, Prince Frederick of Hesse-Homburg sought and obtained the hand of Princess Elizabeth, the Queen informed that Princess that he had 'proposed some years ago for one of us, and that the King gave no answer'. The unanswered proposal is in the Windsor Archives, and shows that in 1804 the old Landgrave had tried to arrange a marriage between his son and Princess Augusta. None of her sisters is mentioned.

In August 1785, two years before the Danish project was abandoned, the King and Queen, with three sons and three daughters, spent a night with the Harcourts at Nuneham, whence, in a lovely blaze of colour, they made an unpremeditated descent upon the University of Oxford. The King and the young Princes wore blue and gold, the Queen, pale lilac silk, Princess Royal and Princess Elizabeth, pale blue, and the Princess Augusta, light green.

Princess Augusta's narrative of the Nuneham visit reveals the 'genuine humour' praised by Fanny Burney:

> ... I was so Compleatly happy when I found we did not go back till the next day that My Spirits rose mountains high in half a second. . . . 'Dear Augustus' (said Ernest), 'think how amazing Good of Lord Harcourt; he has promised me that I shall sleep alone. I have seen my Room, it has a Yellow Damask Bed. I have got a toilette, too, with fine Japan boxes on it. Beautiful Lady Jersey has that Room when she is here. I suppose it is a great favor to let me have it!' 'Say what you please,' says Augustus, 'Lord Harcourt has given me a much better Room. I have got a fine view out of the window; and what signifies a damask Bed when one has not a fine view.'. . . (Adolphus) 'I suppose you none of you have seen my Room. I have got a Tent Bed in it; I should have you dare speak against a Tent Bed. It puts me in mind already that when I am an Officer, and that I am encamp'd against an Enemy, I shall have one then.'

Four years later, when the King's illness cast a heavy shadow over the lives of his daughters, it was the second whom, next to the eldest, he was most impatient to be allowed to see; and it was to her also that Queen Charlotte turned for companionship. In October 1788 Miss Burney records that while she was reading aloud the Queen several times burst into tears, and finally 'went upstairs and played upon the Princess Augusta's harpsichord'; and on the night of 29 November, when the King was brought from Windsor to Kew, we read that Princess Augusta slept 'in a small tent bed put up in the Queen's bedchamber'. The shadow of calamity brooded over the Princess's twentieth birthday, when her mother wept as she gave her 'the gift appropriate to the day' and 'the Princess received it with a silent curtsey, kissing and wetting with her tears the hand of her afflicted mother'.

Early in February 1789, during the first stage of the King's convalescence, he constrained the Queen, Augusta, and Elizabeth to join him in singing 'Rule, Britannia' and 'Heart of Oak'. His physicians and equerries regarded this as a favourable symptom. By 23 April so much progress had been made that a solemn thanksgiving service was held in St Paul's Cathedral. The three elder Princesses were present, wearing gowns of purple silk, petticoats of Indian gold muslin over white satin, and scarves of the same muslin over the high head-dress 'confined by the white satin bandeau on which the motto—God Save the King—was embroidered in gold letters'. When dusk fell, illuminations began to glow, 'transparencies' revealed their allegorical designs, and farthing candles twinkled on the counters of loyal cobblers.

It must have been a blow to the Queen and her daughters when, only a few weeks later, the duel between the King's favourite son, Frederick, and Colonel Lennox threatened to cause a relapse.

The contest, which took place on Wimbledon Common, was not a bloody one; and on the evening of the same day the Duke of York led forth his sister Augusta in a country dance at 'the most splendid ball' given in honour of the King's birthday. To the indignation of the Prince of Wales—though the Duke of York seems to have felt no resentment—Colonel Lennox 'stood up' with his partner, Lady Catherine Barnard, in this dance of which the evolutions must bring him into contact with every member of the Royal Family taking part. 'Just as she was about to be turned by the Colonel', the Princess Royal was led firmly away by her eldest brother; but Prince Frederick and Princess Augusta, who came next, 'turned the Colonel without notice or exception'. The flushed and discomposed looks of the Prince of Wales attracted the attention of his mother, to whom he remarked,

'I *am* heated and tired, Madam, not with the dance, but with dancing in such company'. 'Then, Sir,' said the Queen, 'it will be better for me to withdraw, and put an end to the ball'—which she did.

The next time we hear of Colonel Lennox at a ball, it is at Brussels on the eve of Waterloo, when, as Duke of Richmond, he was host at the 'scene of revelry by night'.

During the absence of Prince Ernest and Prince Augustus in Germany, their sisters Augusta and Elizabeth corresponded industriously with them both. Ernest—not till 1799 Duke of Cumberland and Teviotdale—was suffering From measles at the University of Göttingen when, on 20 July 1790, his second sister sent him a letter full of solicitude:

> I cannot help troubling you with a few lines, my Dearest Ernest, to say how happy I am to hear that you have got thro' the Meazles so well, and your Brothers also. . . . All your friends here thank God for it now. William is saild in Barrington's fleet, they are now at anchor in Torbay, waiting there till further orders. I never saw anybody happier than he is. It would do you good to see his zeal for the sea service. . . . (w)

Prince Ernest has never been regarded as an amiable person, and it is curious to find his sister writing to him a strain which suggests that, at least to her, he was in his nineteenth year far from unlikable:

> Pray write to me soon. I long to see you again and tell you how much I love you. Meanwhile you must believe it, as it is most true. Oh! I fancy you know it.(w)

Fanny Burney records how, in 1796, Princess Augusta related to her 'the history of all the feats, and exploits, and dangers, and escapes, of her brothers during the last year; rejoicing in their safety, yet softly adding, 'Though these trials and difficulties did them a great deal of good''.

'We have detained Madame d'Arblay between us the whole morning', said the Princess Royal, with a gracious smile. 'Yes,' cried Princess Augusta, 'and I am afraid I have bored her to death but when once I begin upon my poor brothers I can never stop without telling all my little bits of glory.' She then outstayed the Princess Royal to tell me that when she was at Plymouth at the church she saw so many officers' wives, and sisters, and mothers, helping their maimed husbands, or brothers, or sons, that she could not forbear whispering to the Queen, 'Mamma, how lucky it is Ernest is just come so seasonably with that wound in his face! I should have been quite shocked else not to have had one little bit of glory among ourselves!'

Princess Augusta's ejaculation, 'Have we not reason to be proud of our brother abroad?'—in a letter written to the Prince of Wales in August 1793—probably refers to Prince Adolphus, who about that time was wounded in the shoulder while serving under the Duke of York in the Low Countries; but it was Prince Ernest who paid the highest price for his 'little bit of glory'. There has been some doubt among historians as to the effect produced upon his appearance by 'that wound in his face' received at the battle of Tournai in 1794. Writing to their mother on Ernest's return to England in February 1796, the Prince of Wales remarked, 'his left eye is shockingly sunk, and has an amazing film grown right over it'.[w]

Miss Burney, now Madame d'Arblay, gives us a lifelike glimpse of Princess Augusta and Prince Ernest, on a certain day when she had been permitted to watch the Princess having her hair dressed:

Her ease, amounting even to indifference, as to her ornaments and decoration, showed a mind so disengaged from vanity that I could with difficulty forbear manifesting my admiration. She let the hairdresser proceed upon her head without comment and without examination, just as if it was solely his affair; and when the man, Robinson, humbly begged to know what ornaments he was to prepare the hair for she said, 'Oh, there are my feathers, and my gown is blue, so take what you think right'.

In the adjacent room a 'grand collation' had been prepared for Princess Sophia's birthday, and there suddenly appeared in the doorway 'a tall thin young man, peeping and staring, but not entering'.

'How do you do, Ernest?' cried the Princess, 'I hope you are well. Only pray do shut the door.'

He did not obey, nor move, either forwards or backwards but kept peering and peering. She called to him again, beseeching him to shut the door, but he was determined first to gratify his curiosity, and when he had looked as long as he thought pleasant, he entered the apartment: but Princess Augusta, instead of welcoming him and receiving him, only said 'Goodbye, my dear Ernest; I shall see you again at the play'.

He then marched out, finding himself so little desired, and only saying, 'No, you won't: I hate the play'.

Augusta's comment was, 'Ernest has a very good heart; only he speaks without taking time to think'.

Some forty years later the Princess wrote to Mrs Dering of the Duke of Clarence (then William IV):

> You know what dear, dear William's affection for me was. We had been each other's early friends—I had known every secret of his heart, the same when he was quite a lad, that I could believe and pity all his worries, real and imaginary, and as he grew older, all this grew into the steadiest and *firmest friendship*. Then we had the same tastes, and he was like my second self.

Miss Burney's comment on Princess Augusta's regard for him sounds tepid by comparison. 'She is very partial to him, but by no means blindly. "He had very good parts," she said, but seldom did them justice.' His opinion of her, as reported by Miss Burney when he returned from the West Indies in the early summer of 1789, was: 'Augusta looks very well—a good face and countenance— she looks interesting. . . . She looks as if she knew more than she would say, and I like that character.' He bestowed her name upon the fourth of the five daughters borne to him by Mrs Jordan, but as the other four were called Sophia, Mary, Elizabeth, and Amelia, this can hardly be interpreted as a mark of unparalleled regard.

The mutinies at Spithead and at the Nore greatly perturbed the Princess, and she overflowed upon the subject to Madame d'Arblay:

> She told me many anecdotes she had heard in favour of various sailors, declaring with great animation her security in their good hearts, however drawn aside by harder and more cunning heads. . . .
>
> In speaking of a sailor on board the *San Fiorenzino* when the Royal Family made their excursion by sea from Weymouth, she said, 'You must know this man was a great favourite of mine, for he had the most honest countenance you can conceive, and I have often talked with him, every time we have been at Weymouth, so that we were good friends: but I wanted now in particular to ask him concerning the mutiny, but I knew I should not get him to speak out while the King and Queen and my sisters were by. So I told Lady Charlotte Bellasyse to watch an opportunity when he was upon deck, and the rest were in the cabin, and then we went up to him and questioned him; and he quite

answered my expectations, for instead of taking any merit to himself from belonging to the *San Fiorenzino*, which was never in the mutiny, the good creature said he was sure there was not a sailor in the Navy that was not sorry to have belonged to it, and that would not have got out of it as readily as himself, if he had but known how.'

This picture may be thrown into higher relief by Colonel George Landmann, R.E., who was sent to Weymouth by the Duke of Cumberland in 1804 to report upon the desirability of erecting a martello tower on the spot called the Look Out. ('They are capital things, those martello towers,' said George III, 'eh? Those martello towers are capital things. We must have some here!')

One day, on the deck of the royal yacht, Landmann says:

I was accosted by one of the Princesses, who led me to walk with her, supporting herself on my arm, as the vessel was pitching a good deal in consequence of having extended our distance beyond the shelter afforded by Portland. Her Royal Highness was exceedingly inquisitive, seeking for information, but very adroitly concealing this, and left me delighted with her amiability and condescension, which greatly surpassed all I had previously heard attributed to her.

This Princess was almost certainly Augusta. Though in 1789 Princess Elizabeth had expressed 'a strong desire to see the ship's company at their dinner', there is no evidence that she ever took a practical interest in nautical matters—such an interest as inspired Princess Augusta to write to Mrs Dering in 1836, 'My heart and head have been sadly wrecked with the dreadful accounts of the shipwrecks, and I am *such a sailor* that I cannot help reading every syllable till it half kills me'.

To her third brother, the handsome but asthmatic Prince Augustus, afterwards Duke of Sussex, Princess Augusta wrote on 29 December 1790, giving him news of 'Dear William' and 'dear Dolly Dowsy' (*i.e.* Adolphus), with a passing reference to Prince Ernest not raced with any endearing word:

I shall make it my business and pleasure to write to you as often as I can, and tell you everything that goes forward in the Country. You have but to trust to me, for I have no such light as that of doing all I can to please my brothers and sisters, who are all so good to me.

Dear William returned to us last Sunday, looking both well and happy, full of the Perfections of his Ship and Ship's Company, and more good-humoured and charming than I have seen him for years. To be sure he is a dear Boy! . . . I am very happy for Ernest and Adolphus that they are to go to Hanover, as I fancy it will be a great joy and delight to them. I had a most charming letter from dear Dolly Dowsy, full of expressions of affection for you. . . .[w]

This affectionate sister is quick to tell Augustus that the new Imperial Minister, Count Stadion, had expressed to her 'in the handsomest terms' how happy the Emperor and Empress were to have made his acquaintance. 'I felt', she says, 'quite fat with pleasure when I heard it.' But it is to George, Prince of Wales, her 'dearest G.P.', that she pours forth the most ardent words of affection. On 12 May 1794, she wrote to him:

> The great point is at last decided, and we are to have a Ball next Monday. The King was so good as to name it himself, thinking it would be the amusement we should prefer, and we all very readily accepted of it. Perhaps I may see you for a moment before that day. If not, I insist upon your coming up to me the very moment you arrive, even if I am in the Midst of a delightful Dance. God bless you, my Dearest,
>
> Your Affte. AUGUSTA.
>
> Pray excuse this scrawl. The dinner is just called.[w]

Two years later she was writing to him, 'I can add no more now, my Dearest, as I am sent for to Breakfast, but had I time to cover sheets of paper they could never convey how much I love and doat upon You'.[w]

The two elder sisters of this much-loved brother must have been well aware that his conduct was causing great sorrow to their father. They knew that when the Royal Family felt themselves obliged to contribute to the national finances during the Revolutionary wars, the Prince of Wales was unable to do so 'without the leave of his creditors', and Princess Augusta, at least, was cognisant of his relations with Mrs Fitzherbert. Nothing seems to have had any effect on their regard for 'G.P.'

Out of her personal allowance of £2,000 a year—doled out by the Queen—each Princess contributed £100 to the war fund. This allowance does not seem to have been adequate to the needs of the Sisterhood. They were constantly in money difficulties and their letters to their eldest brother contain many allusions to their debts. Sir James Bland Burges says, 'The effect of this kind of life has been different according to their constitutions. Princess Augusta, soft and tender-hearted, vents her sorrow at her eyes, and cries till she becomes composed and resigned'—so little did Fanny Burney understand her 'gay Princesses'.

A great deal has been written about the attitude of all the Royal Family except George III to the marriage of the Prince of Wales and his cousin, Princess Caroline of Brunswick, and the apologists of that unfortunate lady have maintained that from the beginning she was treated with coldness by her feminine 'in-laws'. The pitch, we are told, was deliberately queered; Caroline was never given a chance. Neither the Queen nor the Princesses can have been under any delusion as to the motives for the marriage. These were ironically summed up by Thomas Ashe in his 'Political and Amatory Romance', *The Spirit of 'The Book'*, where the House of Hanover is thinly masked as the House of Edinburgh:

... the heir of the House of Edinburgh is a man of feeling and honour—he owes to his tradesmen the sum of £500,000, and his father refuses to discharge that enormous debt without the son will consent to marry; and by such means live with more regularity, and at the same time secure an uninterrupted progressive line of descent to the House. Honour, as I observed, sways this young nobleman; he has given a reluctant consent to this tyrannic proposition. . . .

The alternative of 'moderate retrenchment' suggested by George III probably seemed to his heir a proposition even more tyrannic.

These things must have been known to the elder ladies of the Royal Family, but they tried to create a hopeful, and even a sentimental, atmosphere before Princess Caroline arrived. The Prince himself joined in this game of make-believe. 'I have', he wrote to his mother, in November 1794, 'receiv'd a picture as a present, but I really am too selfish to send it away to you.'(w) 'I hope', replied Queen Charlotte, 'you and the picture continue to agree, and that this may be the case with the original.'(w) Three months later Princess Augusta was hoping that 'this thaw will hasten the arrival of *notre chère future*'.(w)

To the admiring Sisterhood, who could still see in their corpulent eldest brother only the debonair Prince Charming of fifteen years before, it probably did not occur that Princess Caroline might be disillusioned when she saw her betrothed; and their indignation would probably have been warm if they had chanced to overhear her murmured comment to Lord Malmesbury, '*Je le trouve très gros, et nullement aussi beau que son portrait*'. Queen Charlotte was promptly advised of the bridegroom's profound dissatisfaction with his hoydenish bride, but there is no hint in the letters written by his sisters during the earlier part of 1795 that they knew that all was not well at Carlton House, and that no hope of happiness for either bride or groom had outlasted the wedding night.

In May 1795, Princess Augusta, in a letter to the Prince concerning his wish to *fire a feu de joie* in honour of the Queen's birthday, adds:

> I hope you told the Princess about the dress for Frogmore—muslin and a Hat. Now that you are a married man you must be troubled with such Messages.(w)

All through the months preceding the birth of Princess Charlotte of Wales the ladies of the Prince's family were assiduous in their attentions to Caroline, and they welcomed with delight the note scribbled by him on 7 January 1796:

> The Princess, after a terrible hard labour for above twelve hours, is this instant brought to bed of an immense Girl, & I assure you notwithstanding we might have wish'd for a Boy, I receive her with all the affection possible.(w)

No baby was ever surrounded by a circle of more adoring aunts, and it may have been partly for the sake of the 'little Beauty' that they persevered in civilities to their sister-in-law even after a rupture of relations between the parents was obviously imminent. Curiously enough it was Princess Elizabeth and not Princess Augusta whom the Prince chose to convey to their mother the intelligence that he had decided to separate from his wife. Perhaps he wished to spare the feelings of his 'poor Puss', and he may also have been anxious to put himself right in the eyes of the sister to whom Princess Caroline had most inclined.

Princess Augusta, during the summer months which followed the rupture, seems to have desired above all things to comfort her agitated brother. Writing from Weymouth in August 1796 to wish him joy of his 'sweet child having cut another tooth and being quite well', she added anxiously, 'I hope you are both better and quieter than when I saw you last'.(w) There is a gap in the correspondence during the months which the Prince spent with Lady Jersey, but on his birthday in 1797 Princess Augusta wrote to him, *'Toujours présent, toujours cher*, that's what you are to your poor Puss'.(w) She was eager to let him know if any favourable words had fallen from the usually censorious lips of the King, especially if the Prince's regiment came in for a little praise.

'The King at dinner yesterday said how Superior your Regiment rides to all others', she told him in 1797; and a year later she wrote that the King had said that the Prince's regiment had 'done their Sword Exercise better than ever . . . he approved greatly of their not having rode too fast. All these things', added the gratified Princess, 'I *pocketted* for You!'(w)

It is hardly surprising that twenty years later Tom Moore should have described her as 'the favourite sister of his Majesty George IV'. In a letter to his mother, the Prince had once said, on one of the rare occasions when he had received a sign of favour from the King:

> Pray inform *dear Augusta* of my good fortune, for as she ever participates in every uncomfort that affects my heart, so I know her little soul will bound and rejoice at every event that affords me such heartfelt satisfaction.(w)

Now, during the discreditable years that lay between his separation from Caroline and his reconciliation with Mrs Fitzherbert (1796-1800), the Prince had many fresh proofs of his second sister's sympathy, though her soul had small cause to 'bound and rejoice' on his account.

Meanwhile the Princesses continued to lead their monotonous life in constant attendance upon their mother. As might have been expected, their health suffered, and their letters contain frequent allusions to 'cramps' and 'spasms'.[3] Even 'the gay Princess Augusta' did not escape, and was constrained by Dr John Turton to 'boil herself in the warm bath'. On her thirty-fourth birthday she wrote to the Prince of Wales:

I return You thanks for the beautiful Bracelets little Sophy put into my hands this morning, saying 'They come from somebody who don't love you, and who you don't love neither', and I directly guessed they came from You.⁽ʷ⁾

To her two youngest sisters, 'little Sophy' and 'dearest Emily', her attitude was always affectionate and often curiously maternal. She remembered them as babies, toddling upon the Terrace, tricked out with hoops and high head-dresses, and she had held Amelia in her arms even before that. When Madame d'Arblay brought her small boy to the Queen's House it was Augusta who, seeing that Queen Charlotte was 'not amused' by the spectacle of Alexander d'Arblay lying flat on the floor in his new muslin frock 'to repose at his ease', pleaded for him, 'He has been so very good upstairs, Mama, that nothing could be better behaved'.

That sense of humour and that quick eye for character which Alexander's mamma had marked during her sojourn at court must have stood Princess Augusta in good stead many times. Her letters to Lady Harcourt are full of vivid touches, as when she wrote of that unpicturesque refugee, Louis XVIII:

He has a very *fine manner*, and is very gracious. He is a well-informed man, speaks English very well, and understands it perfectly. He is very large, as large as Stephen Kemble. He converses in a Most agreeable manner; and generally walks up and down the Room in the hope of its keeping down His fat. His countenance is very good, and He makes a very fine Bow without any affectation. My Brothers were delighted with him.

One at least of those brothers was a connoisseur in very fine bows, and the approval of Mr Turveydrop's great exemplar would not be lightly bestowed.

Another attractive example of Princess Augusta's humour comes from the unpublished Harcourt Manuscripts, in a letter to the ever-sympathetic Lady Harcourt:

I often think of a story I heard of a poor Woman in Scotland who was visited by the famous Doctor Blair when under great *affliction*. He found her so pious and resigned that He told Her He was Edified with Her Goodness and wished to follow Her Example if sorrow should befall Him: to which She replied, 'Sir I was not so always . . . but I have read the Bible, Sir, and I verily believe David had an *Eye to Me* when He wrote some of His *best Psalms*'.

Indeed the more gloomy parts of the Psalter would have seemed sadly apposite in the early weeks of 1804. The King had been greatly agitated by the Prince of Wales's action in publishing the correspondence between them on the Prince's anxiety to be allowed to 'display the best energies of his character' in a military capacity; and a severe chill following upon this agitation had caused his reason to rock upon its already precarious throne. His recovery had never been complete, and two years earlier, during the usual summer visit to Weymouth, his behaviour had been sufficiently odd to startle onlookers and to cover the ladies of the Family with confusion. The impressions then jotted down by Sir Robert Wilson fill the reader with pity for the Princesses; as when he notes that his Majesty 'shewed once much irritation and harshness towards Pss. Augusta, who was taking care of Pss. Sophia, seized with her usual spasmodic complaint. From his countenance at that instant his appearance when in a phrenzied state might be imagined.'

The unfortunate daughters were also compelled to act as buffers between their father and mother every night, remaining in the Queen's bedroom until the King had retired, reluctantly and resentfully, to his solitary couch, and thus enabling her to adhere to her determination never again to occupy the same room as her afflicted husband—a course in which she persisted even when Addington and his Cabinet requested her to relent.

By the middle of February 1804, the King's condition was so alarming that the Prime Minister formally communicated to the Queen 'the disposition and intention of the Government to assume responsibility'. At Queen's House, on the 15th, a joint statement was drawn up in which her Majesty, together with her sons Frederick, Edward, Ernest, and Adolphus, and her daughters Augusta, Elizabeth, Mary and Sophia, set forth 'the reasons which had induced them, after duly weighing the melancholy circumstances in which they stood', to accept with thanks the offer which had been made by his Majesty's confidential servants to relieve them 'from the care and superintendence of his Majesty on this trying occasion'.[w] The occasion they defined as 'the dreadful and alarming illness with which it has pleased Almighty Providence to afflict his Majesty', and the Dukes of York and Kent seem both to have examined the wording of the royal statement, for two draft versions exist, one with the younger brother's proposed emendations on the margin.

A fortnight later the King was more composed, and though perfect quiet was still considered necessary, public recognition of his condition was again deferred, and the fall of Addington's Government in April invalidated the offer made earlier in the year. The Sisterhood breathed again, but not, it must be supposed, very freely.

In July 1804 the King was still in a parlous state, loquacious, jaunty, full of wild architectural schemes, 'altering *every House*, unroofing without end to add stories'. In August, Lady Hesketh saw him at Weymouth, and, less observant or more sanguine than Sir Robert Wilson two years before, she seems to have felt that all might yet be well. She wrote to her friend Mrs Ricketts:

> It is a most delightful sight to see him surrounded by his Sons, all such fine, noble-looking men, and all so attentive to Him . . . and when (which is however

but seldom) the sweet, amiable, truly feminine Princesses join the party on the Esplanade it is really a most charming sight.

The Prince of Wales was not among those attentive sons. Relations between him and his father were then decidedly strained. 'Vice and Virtue', remarked her ladyship, sententiously, 'Light and Darkness, can never agree.' She might have been surprised had the private sentiments of the Princesses come to her knowledge, especially those of the three eldest, who were their brother's warmest partisans.

A year later the King was sufficiently recovered to go and stay at Nuneham, accompanied by at least two of his daughters and the Queen. The arrangements were made by Princess Augusta, who wrote to Lady Harcourt, 'I am really serious about the King's bed being small, particularly as I should fear that a large one would give Him Cold'. Regarding herself and Princess Mary, she remarked, 'as for our Maids, we are not used to have them near us, therefore they will be quite as well in the Atticks'. In the interval between this visit and the final overthrow of his reason in 1810, the old, kindly, simple-minded George III came often to the surface, gladdening his daughters, but disconcerting his sons, none of whom, not even his favourite Frederick, seems to have felt much genuine affection for him.

Those daughters were now fast leaving the days of their youth behind them, but they were still held in subjection by their mother. She does not seem to have allowed them to follow the prevailing fashions in dress, for in June 1805, at a time when high-waisted, narrow-skirted 'Empire' gowns and semi-classical head-dresses were worn by every woman of any pretensions to elegance, Frances Waddington, afterwards Baroness Bunsen, described them as wearing hoops and plumes, in the manner of 1789. At Kew they 'had rooms in the attics with sloping roofs—so small that the Royal ladies were obliged to hang their hoops outside their doors', on pegs 'placed there for this purpose'.

Frances and her sister Augusta were the great-nieces of Mrs Delany, and their mother took them to visit the Royal Family in 1805 and again in 1806 and 1808. On the first occasion the elder girl—she was then fifteen thus related her impressions at the Queen's House:

> We came into a very little room, which the Princesses with their hoops almost exclusively occupied. I guessed at once which was Princess Augusta by her kindness to Mamma, Princess Elizabeth by her size, and Princess Mary by her beauty. Princess Amelia was not there, and Princess Sophia I did not much look at, as I was occupied in admiring Princess Mary's headdress which was a large plume of white ostrich feathers, and a very small plume of black feathers placed before the white ones; her hair was drawn up quite smooth to the top of her head, with one large curl hanging from thence almost down to her throat.

Her petticoat was white and silver, and the drapery and body as well as I can recollect were of purple silk covered with spangles. Princess Elizabeth had eleven immense yellow ostrich feathers on her head, which you may imagine had not a very good effect.

Three years later, Frances Waddington writes of Mary and Sophia words which would at that time have applied with equal truth to Augusta and Elizabeth. She says, 'though very smiling and good-natured, I think there is a striking appearance of melancholy in their countenances'. The lives of all four sisters were then tinged with sadness, and the life of the fifth was ebbing to its early close.

After the death of Princess Amelia and the lapse of the unhappy King into hopeless insanity, the letters of Princess Augusta to her brother are full of their father's plight. 'There has been', she wrote, in one such bulletin, 'a great deal of unpleasant laughing very early this morning, which may I fear increase in the course of the day into the same sort of irritability that we suffered so much from Yesterday.' (w) It is impossible not to feel compassion for these Princesses, spending their days within the sound of the King's wild-witted laughter, under the eye of a grieving Queen who was determined that their grief should be commensurate with her own.

II

Six weeks after the death of Princess Amelia in November 1810, Parliament met to discuss the question of a Regency, and this time no flicker of reviving sanity rendered the discussions void. Queen Charlotte was at Frogmore with her daughters, reading Thomson, Rogers, and Cowper, and planting miniature geraniums and oak-trees, and there they waited 'in a fever', feeling apparently that if the Regency Bill should become law the King would be condemned *ipso facto* to incurable madness.

Early in 1811 the Bill passed both Houses, and that summer Miss Cornelia Knight put it on record that in the event of the King's death the Regent 'meant to have his sisters' incomes increased, and to give them apartments in St James's Palace—also to keep a table for them'. He celebrated his forty-eighth birthday— his first as Regent—by riding out in the morning with the Princesses Augusta and Sophia.

On 20 March 1812, the Chancellor of the Exchequer, Mr Perceval, presented the following Message from the Prince to the faithful Commons:

> His royal highness the Prince Regent, in the name and on the behalf of his Majesty, thinks it necessary to acquaint the House of Commons that in pursuance of the powers vested in his Majesty by two acts passed in the 18th and 39th years of his reign, his Majesty was graciously pleased, by letters patent, bearing date the 2d of February, 1802, to grant to their royal highnesses the princesses Augusta-Sophia, Elizabeth, Mary, Sophia, and Amelia, an annuity of £30,000, agreeable to the provisions and subject to the limitations of the said acts, which grant was to take effect from the demise of his Majesty; and his Royal Highness being desirous, in the present situation of the royal family, to be empowered to provide for the establishment of their royal highnesses by an immediate grant, recommends to the House of Commons to take the matter into their consideration, and to enable his Royal Highness to make such provision for their royal highnesses the Princesses as in the liberality of Parliament may be thought suitable to the actual situation of the Princesses and to the circumstances of the present time.

Three days later this message formed the Order of the Day in the House of Lords, where the subject was opened by Lord Liverpool. His lordship felt confident that it must be the intention of Parliament to enable his Royal Highness to make a due and suitable provision for the illustrious persons adverted to in the message, the more so when the present peculiar situation of those illustrious ladies, and their exemplary conduct upon every occasion, were considered by Parliament, and by the country. He explained that as the sum appropriated for that purpose would not become available until the demise of his Majesty, an arrangement was pending by which each Princess should receive an annuity of between £7,000 and £8,000 a year, and in the case of a reduction in the number of those illustrious personages that income would be so divided that if three remained each Princess would have £10,000 a year, and the same sum to each, if reduced to two; but in case only one should remain, then the annuity to the survivor would be only £12,000. As it was not competent to that House to originate a measure of the kind, he would move an Address of a general nature, assuring his Royal Highness of the cheerful concurrence of their lordships.

Earl Grosvenor wanted to know out of what fund the proposed grant was to be paid, and was informed, the Consolidated Fund. The Earl of Essex, a partisan of the Princess of Wales, wished to be informed whether any arrangement with respect to a provision for that lady would be included in the proposed Bill, and Lord Liverpool replied with dignity that he had received no commands from his Royal Highness upon the occasion, and that the Message before their lordships referred merely to the Princesses.

'The question was then put, and the Addresses agreed to *nem. dis.*', their lordships having comported themselves with their wonted good breeding.

It was otherwise when the faithful Commons resolved themselves into a Committee to consider the Regent's Message. Mr Creevey began by objecting to the fresh charge imposed upon the Consolidated Fund; Samuel Whitbread characteristically suggested that the £10,000 recently added to the Queen's income had been designed for the support of her daughters, and seized the opportunity of raising the question of 'the salary of the Princess of Wales'. The Regent must have been well aware that this question would surge up, and he therefore deserved Princess Sophia's assurances that the success of the motion was wholly owing to the energy and perseverance which he had 'shewn on the occasion'.

George Tierney was among Caroline's friends who gave tongue; but a more chivalrous note was struck by Mr W. H. Fremantle,[4] the Member for Buckingham, who spoke of 'the wish the Princesses must feel to be relieved from the daily observation of domestic calamity', and added that he had lived 'in the neighbourhood of the Princesses, had witnessed their charity and had heard of the good they did'. Fin*ally the Resolution was put, and agreed to without a*

division, and ten months later the Finance Accounts of Great Britain showed
the following payments under 'Pensions':

HRH	Augusta Sophia	7,912	1	9¼
"	Elizabeth	7,912	1	9
"	Mary	7,912	1	9
"	Sophia	7,912	1	9

Why Princess Augusta should have received one farthing more than her three
younger sisters is not clear. In 1817 the Princesses were receiving £9,000 a year
each, and in 1824 £44,000 was divided between them.

Apart from his real affection for his four sisters, and apart from the streak of
chivalry in his complex character, the Regent had a personal motive for wishing
to deliver them from bondage. His daughter, Princess Charlotte, was growing
up, and he wrote to the Queen that it was 'indispensably necessary' for her to
have 'the advantage of the countenance and apparent Protection of some part
of my Family when she is to be seen in public'. It was not only to Charlotte that
such 'apparent Protection' was likely to be an advantage during the winter of
1812–13. Urged on by her eager and unscrupulous partisans, the Princess of
Wales was using her popularity as a stick with which to belabour her husband,
and there were painful scenes when his ample but not yet undecorative person
was revealed to the mob. His anxiety that some of his sisters should accompany
his daughter to the House of Lords when he opened Parliament on 30 November
1812, was probably as much on his own account as on hers. This anxiety, and
his insistence that it should be satisfied, led to a domestic crisis, the climax
of that sequence which had begun when his intention to make the Princesses
financially independent became known to the Queen.

That Queen Charlotte should have been taken aback when she saw her meek
daughters plucking up courage, and thinking for themselves, is comprehensible;
but her relentless efforts to browbeat them back into their old subjection are
painful to follow. In January 1812 Sir Thomas Tyrwhitt ('the Dwarf') told Mr
Speaker Abbott that 'the arrangements for the Queen's household would excite
great clamour, and that she was voracious, and had tormented the Prince in
his worst illness at Oatlands with a visit to prevent his giving the Princesses an
independent establishment'; and it is not difficult to imagine what her Majesty's
reactions must have been when she had to face the *fait accompli*. (The Regent
was laid up at Oatlands as the result of having injured his ankle when dancing
the Highland Fling at a ball given by the Duke and Duchess of York.)

The first open clash occurred in April 1812, when four separate letters were
handed to the Queen after breakfast by Madame Beckendorff, her Keeper of the
Robes. One was signed by all four sisters, and the other three were written by
Elizabeth, Mary, and Sophia. Their general tenor may be gathered from Princess

Elizabeth's, which is obviously intended to buttress the joint manifesto drawn up by Princess Augusta:

April 2, 1812.

My Dear Mother,

Augusta having shown me this evening a letter she has written to you it may be right that I should also say a few words, as I should be very sorry the assurances of my Affection and Gratitude should spring from any other pen than my own for no one feels more strongly than myself your Affection and Kindness from the hour of my birth.

The melancholy situation in which we are placed Augusta has explained with so much delicacy and feeling that however *painfull* it must have been to Her I trust you will with your usual generosity see that she was right in doing it, and I must assure you that all perfectly agree that you ought to be considered in everything and never left alone. I feel that she has worded this so much better than I can do that I have only to say that every mark of affection, love and duty which I can sensibly show to you, you may rely upon. . . .[w]

When Princess Augusta came in from her morning ride Madame Beckendorff handed her a letter from the Queen addressed to all four Princesses, a letter so implacable in its resentment that the unhappy quartet hastily appealed to Prince Adolphus, the only brother immediately at hand, to assure their mother that she had 'misunderstood their meaning completely'.[w]

Writing to the Regent, Princess Augusta says that she would not send him a copy of the letter, 'because in plain truth it was written in Anger, and I put a *Person in a Passion* and a *Person that is drunk* upon the same footing'; but as there is a copy of the letter in her writing among his papers she appears to have changed her mind.[w]

To say, Queen Charlotte remarks, that the perusal of her daughters 'letter gave her pleasure would be the greatest falsehood she ever pronounced, and to say that it surprised her, as great a one. She was fully aware that the happiness of an independent Establishment must carry the idea of liberty with it, and she goes on admonishingly:

as this may perhaps be the last time that any one of you may be inclined to take a mother's advice, let me beseech you well to consider that your situation is very different to that of your Brothers, who by their Situations in life must appear in Public, and have their Duties to perform in which they would injure themselves if they were not to appear. But in your Sex, and under the present Melancholy Situation of your father the going to Public Amusements except where Duty calls you would be the highest mark of indecency possible. The visits to your Brothers I will no further touch upon than to say that you never can be in the House with those that are unmarried without a Lady, and that even that Pleasure, innocent as it is, should be well considered before it is done, and, in short, every step any one of you intends to take, always to keep in remembrance that no age whatever is exempted from being criticized, and that the higher the character, the more will it be traduced. Much more should I like to say, but that would be needless, as it is very plain by the letter your part being taken and whatever I say would be of no avail. . . .[w]

Having appealed to her daughters' sense of decorum, to their affection and pity for their father, and to their dutiful obligations towards' a mother's advice', the Queen strikes a note of personal appeal on her own account:

I beg to see none of you today. If I can bring myself to see you tomorrow, I shall appear at breakfast—for I do not think I ever felt as shattered in my life as I did by reading your letter. . . . I beg not even to see Adolphus. The stroke is given, and nothing can mend it, therefore I beg that none of your brothers may even talk to me upon the subject, nor any of your friends whatever.[w]

But having once struck a blow, however faltering, for their freedom, the Sisterhood were not disposed to relapse into their old estate of servitude. They wrote a joint letter—evidently Princess Augusta's composition—to the Regent, after he had proposed that he and the Queen should meet in London to discuss 'her present and future Intentions with regard to the Line which she means to adopt'. In this letter they say, after the usual protestations of duty and gratitude to their mother:

On the other hand we most freely own that we have neither Health nor Spirits to support for any length of time the life which we have led for the last two years, more Especially the Treatment which we have experienced whenever any proposal has been made for Our absenting ourselves for a few days from the Queen's Roof, either with a view to that Relaxation which it is natural and we trust not unreasonable that at our ages we should occasionally seek, or in Compliance with the Expression of your Pleasure, repeatedly conveyed to Us.

. . . You are fully informed of the Treatment from the Queen to which Our compliance with your last invitation exposed us . . . you will therefore not be surprized that We should repeat to you our Declaration that we must abandon all thoughts of ever complying with any Invitation from you, or with any wishes or arrangements which shall require our absenting ourselves from Windsor, unless it shall be in your Power to secure us from the continuation of a treatment arising out of such compliance which is destructive alike to our health, happiness, and comfort.[w]

The critical point was reached in November 1812, when the Princesses Elizabeth and Mary came up from Windsor to accompany Princess Charlotte to the opening of Parliament. If Lady Charlotte Bury is to be believed, the presence of her Aunts did not have a steadying effect upon the irresponsible young Princess, who 'talked and laughed much, and turned her back often upon papa', but they were probably a comfortable sight to their brother, who had been received in the streets 'in dead silence, and not a hat off'.

It fell to the trusty Tyrwhitt, as Gentleman Usher of the Black Rod, to escort the three royal ladies from the Speaker's House and see them installed on the Woolsack.

When the elder Princesses returned to Windsor the Queen showed plainly by her manner that she was trying to suppress her mounting rage. 'We went on talking, just as if nothing had happened', Mary told the Regent; but—'She asked no questions about the House of Lords, and particularly said that She had not read the speech, nor did She wish to know anything that had passed'. If her Majesty had been content with this negative attitude all might have been well, but her wrath soon boiled over, and what Princess Augusta called 'a dreadfull scene' took place. The Princesses again appealed to their brother, and in the Taylor Papers there is a long and respectful protest addressed by him to their mother on 1 December 1812. 'I do implore you, my dearest Mother', he wrote, 'for your own happiness, for that of my sisters, and for the peace of the whole family, not to suffer the repetition of scenes so distressing and painful to All of us'; and he set forth the reasons which impelled him to desire the presence of his sisters in the House of Lords.

The Queen's reply is so egotistical, so intemperate, as to suggest that her character had been much warped by the long strain of the King's illness. Through all the incoherent phrases runs the abiding terror that 'the world' may think his recovery impossible. She wrote to the Regent:

> Can there be, I appeal to your own feelings, a more painful or more horrible situation than the one your Father labours under? And was it not my duty to state to your sisters that they, having no personal duty which calls upon their presence at the House of Lords, it would show more attention to female delicacy to decline it, but left it to their option to do as they pleased. For your own daughter there could be no doubt about her going. She could not have those feelings that the Aunts ought to have, and which as they did so appears to me a full declaration to the world that the King never can recover and which, you well know, not even any of the Physicians have ever ventured to declare.[w]

She is prepared to concede that the Princesses should sometimes appear with Charlotte; 'but', she adds, vehemently, 'not every week, as you must be sensible that with the small society I have here I should by that be left almost quite alone'.

She then gives her version of 'what did pass on the Sunday night' before her daughters left Windsor:

I will not deny (though I do not mean to justify my own conduct) that the answer which I received from Mary when I found fault with her for not even telling me she intended to go wounded me to the quick, for she assured me she could not longer lead the life she had led, and that Sir H. Halford was of the same opinion, and when Elizth by defending her own conduct struck in a most violent manner upon a book, saying she could take an oath she had done all in her power to please, it provoked me that I did say after that violence I should not be surprized at her giving me next a box of the ear. This gave her a hysterick fit, and they left me determined to repeat it the moment they came to town; and moreover they added that they had mentioned what had passed on Saturday to the Ladies. Whether this conduct is what a mother ought to expect from her children I leave to the judgment of those who have any.[5]

In short, this last journey of theirs has given me a Blow which cannot easily be effaced, for the coming to ask my advice, and hearing my objections and not following, is to treat me like a fool. The telling that the living with me here in my distress is disagreeable, and to repeat to everybody what concerns the interior of a family is more than imprudent.

To forgive it ever is out of my power, but I will do what I can.[(w)]

Princess Augusta, writing on the same day to the Regent, is more concerned with her sisters' distress than with her own, and declares emphatically, 'never was there a daughter more faithfully attached than Eliza to the Queen'. She goes on:

I am miserable that You, my own Dearest Brother, should have had so much vexation on our account. We are all Gratitude to You for Your most kind letter to the Queen. . . . Upon my honour, my sisters were perfectly respectful!, both in manner and words, though she was too violent to allow it, and even when she told them that she would never forgive them, Eliza said, '*May God forgive you for saying so*'. She won't allow that any of us feel for the King's unhappy State of Mind.[(w)]

And she says, with a simplicity which must have touched her brother's easily-melted feelings:

I am ashamed to have written so much on such a painfull subject, because I love the Queen with all my heart; but I *feel the injustice most deeply* with which she treats us all four. It is undeserved. And our lives have not been *too happy*, but we have never complained, nor should we if we were but quiet and comfortable with the Queen.[(w)]

Perhaps the most illuminating comment upon the episode is that made by the gentle Princess Mary, who felt a vicarious shame that the Queen should have 'exposed herself so dreadfully', and added:

It was the object of the dear King's life to keep from the world *all* he *suffered* and *went through* with *her temper*. He brought his daughters up with a most anxious wish we should assist him in that most unfortunate point, and her conduct in all this business has been *such* that by her own imprudence (excuse me for the expression) she has destroyed the poor King's honest labours of the last fifty years passed.[(w)]

On 3 December the Regent wrote to his 'Ever Dearest Mother' urging her to tranquillize her mind until an opportunity should occur for a full explanation, and assuring her that he was particularly grieved at the feelings of dissatisfaction which she had manifested towards his sisters, 'whose conduct had been so truly proper and affectionate', and whose one object had been to meet wishes expressed by himself. He also dropped a well-timed hint that he might visit her Majesty at Windsor 'very shortly'.

The Prince was adept in managing his difficult but always devoted mother, who answered that if the 'Multitude of Business' should make it inconvenient for him to go to Windsor, she would not 'make any difficulty of going to London for a day'. And go she did, to dine with him at Carlton House on 15 December. In the interim the 'great and glorious news from Russia' had created a more sanguine atmosphere, and the Queen no doubt read with perfect seriousness and some emotion the letter in which her son wrote, concerning Napoleon's defeat, that he had, 'under Providence, the Heartfelt Consolation, without unbecoming Vanity', of ascribing it in a great degree to his own 'original and indefatigable endeavours in drawing that Power to those measures which had since been pursued with such signal success'. From this to the belief that he had fought at Waterloo there is but one step, and that not a long one. His mother was in a milder mood when they met, and Princess Elizabeth wrote to him six days after that meeting:

> I now must say nothing can be more *couleur de rose* than *all has been since our dinner on Tuesday at Carlton House*. God bless you for it! [(w)]

What arguments the Prince brought forward on this occasion, with what nicely-blended cajolery and firmness he smoothed the ruffled feathers of the Queen, we can only conjecture; but during the interval she may have reflected that gentleness would serve her better than violence in dealing with daughters so full of sensibility.

Owing to a bilious attack Princess Augusta was not able to attend the *couleur de rose* dinner at Carlton House, and Princess Sophia was at Windsor, far from well; but Elizabeth and Mary went with the Queen. They were all anxious for a reconciliation, but it was Augusta who at that moment had the strongest personal motive for wishing to be on good terms with her Majesty.

Contemporary gossip declared that young Lord Tavistock had nursed an honourable and hopeless passion for the Princess Royal; allusions to a secret marriage between Princess Elizabeth and 'a Mr Ramus' have found their way into print; John Hookham Frere's brother Bartholomew was said to have languished for Princess Mary from afar; Princess Sophia's love for General Garth has received only too much ill-informed publicity; Princess Amelia's infatuation for General FitzRoy is common knowledge; but no rumour clung round the name of Princess Augusta, and no legend clings round it now. When the last baronet of the Halford creation handed over to Queen Victoria the letters written by that Princess to the first, it was suggested that these were of a sentimental tone, but there has never been any supporting evidence, and the Windsor Archives reveal that what she herself called 'the secret of her heart' was something quite different. The man she loved would appear to have been not a happily-married family physician but a bachelor Irish soldier.

Princess Augusta's own views upon her matrimonial prospects, set down in a letter to the Prince of Wales when she was twenty-five years of age, form a pathetic commentary upon the course which her fate actually followed. 'I intend', she then wrote, 'for the rest of my life to be very despotic till I have a Lord and Master, and then (unless I break the great oaths and promises I shall make when I marry) I shall give myself up to his Whims.'[w] It is interesting that she should say 'when' and not 'if' she marries.

Thomas Ashe, the author of that preposterous specimen of pro-Caroline propaganda, *The Spirit of 'The Book'*, was a vile insect, but there is some tincture of truth in the words he wrote in 1811, concerning the daughters of the house of 'Edinburgh'. And it is clear that a touch of generous indignation underlies the sententious phraseology.

> Perpetually secluded from marriage with their countrymen, however nobly and highly descended, and condemned to consume their life in the hopes of some beggarly Protestant Prince applying for their hand, they are placed on a tottering eminence, exposed to a multitude of watchful and scrutinizing eyes.
> . . .
> An insuperable line of separation is drawn between them and the nobility and gentry of their native land.
> They are immured in castles. No man but the invalids and servants of the state can enter those castles; no one must behold their faces but at Church or at court.

This was an exaggeration. At Weymouth and elsewhere the Princesses were allowed a certain measure of social intercourse with gentlemen in attendance on their brothers or on the King—as witness the anecdote related by Captain Landmann.

An inevitable death or perpetual imprisonment awaits the man who shall attempt to intrude himself into their apartments, or address a few words to them on meeting them out of doors. And the smallest instances of their affability, partiality or kindness,—such as a smile, a nod, the return of a bow, or the extension of the hand for an embrace, are interpreted into the *signs* of a passion which, if not checked, would infuse the dreadful contagion of love over the regions of the imagination and the heart.

Interpreted by whom? Perhaps by the Queen. More probably by those twin dragons of decorum, Miss Goldsworthy and Miss Gomm. It was gallant of Mr Ashe to write as if his heroines were quite young girls, but not one of them was under thirty when he wrote, and two of them at least had failed to escape the dreadful contagion.

In March 1812 Princess Augusta, evidently feeling that a new Court of Appeal had been set up in the person of her eldest brother, wrote him a long letter concerning what she calls 'the Secret of my Heart':

My Dearest Brother,
Your invariable kindness to me from my earliest infancy and the affectionate interest with which you have ever attended to my concerns when I have had an opportunity of conversing confidentially with you, calls upon me more particularly to address you now, on the subject which dwells so much on my mind, and from which *You alone* can relieve me.

You will recollect that on the King's Birthday, 1808, we had an hour of very serious Conversation after dinner, in which I took an opportunity of disclosing to you the Secret of my Heart. You kindly said that you had often remarked a gloom on my countenance which you were certain proceeded from some secret cause of anxiety and therefore had thought it *more delicate* not to notice it to me. Most kind and most delicate indeed was your Conduct, and the impression it made upon my Mind will ever be *indelible*. Untill that day I felt I could not speak to you about it. Had not the Object of my Affections been *then* abroad, and that my anxiety for His safety and welfare was put to the trial for a second time (with a greater likelihood of His Duty retaining him in a foreign Country) I do not think I should have spoken upon the subject, but my *heart was full of care*. I knew you would feel for me, and that idea cheered me!

I also mentioned his Noble Conduct in having offered *for my sake* to give up his Situation about the King, or at least to plead his being on the Staff, that he might not come too often where we *must meet* in circumstances he was aware most painful to us both. But I intreated him to remember that it was to his own Private Worth as well as to his public services that he owed the being appointed Equerry to the King, and that it was my Duty to exert every Effort not to express my feelings, both for his sake and my own. I therefore begged that He would take His regular annual waiting, and *come* as *seldom* as He could do at other times consistent with that Gratitude which He must feel for the King's marked favour towards him, and which it was His Duty to testify. To this plan he agreed fully, and he has never deviated from this line of Conduct. *A third time* he was ordered abroad, and painfull as the thoughts were of our being separated again, it was a mutual consolation to us both that you and dear Frederick (to whom I had mentioned it in 1805) were apprized of our attachment, for had He fallen He knew you would have felt for me, and have affectionately soothed my Wounded Heart, and I was certain that *both my kind Brothers* would have respected and esteemed the character which had acted in so honourable a manner towards your sister as he always has done, and have shared his sorrow, and extended your friendship to him, had anything happened to me while he was abroad.

I now beseech you, my Dearest, to consider our *Situation*. If it is in your power to make us happy I know you will. I am sensible that should you agree to our Union it can *only* proceed from your affection for *me*, and your desire of promoting my happiness and that of a Worthy Man. It is not a fancy taken up vaguely, our acquaintance having existed for twelve years, and our attachment been *mutually acknowledged Nine Years ago*. To you we look up, for our future comfort and peace of Mind. *Your* sanction is what we aspire to. And as of course it will be necessary to keep it a Secret, and as it must be quite a Private Marriage, if you think it more proper in your Situation not to be present at it, (which I need not assure you would be a sad disappointment to us both) I entreat your permission that dear Frederick may attend for you. The world, if it ever hears of this Circumstance may be astonished, but it cannot blame our conduct, especially when it knows we are supported and encouraged by my Brothers, nor can it allege any deceit to our behaviour. Our Sentiments were of too delicate a Nature for us to make them known, unless at a moment when we might hope to have our sufferings relieved. Nothing is more repugnant to my Principles or more grating to my feelings than not acting with Candour to every individual; and particularly so towards my *own* family, but this was my own Secret, and in no particular can I tax my heart with having deceived them on this occasion, for there is no duplicity in Silence.[w]

The real purpose of the Princess's letter emerges in the next passage. She dares not broach the subject to the Queen, and it is to the brother recently invested with fresh authority that she turns, hoping that he will be her mediator. Even the prospect of some degree of personal freedom has not abated her awe of that implacable little person, their mother.

Should your Answer be favourable to my Heart's Dearest and nearest wish, I shall beg of you to have the goodness to name it to the Queen. No consideration in the world (even certain of all that is *essential, Your Permission*) shall make me take such a step unknown to Her. I owe it to Her as my Mother, though I am too honest to affect asking for *Her consent, as it is not necessary*. Nor shall the most Anxious wish of my Heart ever make me unjust or unreasonable. I am certain the Queen cannot approve if She merely thinks of my birth and station. But that is the *only reason* She can object to it, and I shall never blame Her for it.

But when she considers the Character of the Man, the faithfulness and length of our attachment, and the struggles that I have been compelled to make, never retracting from any of my Duties, though suffering Martyrdom from anxiety of *Mind* and *deprivation of happiness*, I am sure that She will say long and great has been my trial, and correct has been my Conduct. . . .

These, my Beloved Brother, are the Genuine Sentiments of my Heart. I have nothing to disguise upon the subject, having once named it to You, but I will confess that I am proud of possessing the Affection and good opinion of an Honest Man and highly distinguished Character, and I am sure that what You can do to make us happy You will not leave undone.

This letter, so packed with emotion under its conventional phrasing, was written on the eve of the first rupture with the Queen. The Princess's next step was to send another letter which, if he 'should grant her Heart's wish', she begs the Regent to show to their mother 'that your Words and my own may not be perverted by an Accommodating Memory, which I am sorry to say Hers is'. And she adds with pathetic earnestness:

> I can put my hand upon my Heart, nay, even upon *the Bible*, and swear that there is not one Syllable in that letter which is not *strictly true*, and I trust you will feel equal Commiseration for *Him* about whom I trouble you as you will for *me*, when you consider all we have gone through with such Steadiness, such Correctness, and such Credit to *ourselves*.

Who was the Object of Princess Augusta's Affections? She is careful to mention no names, but she tells us enough about him to make his identification with Major-General Sir Brent Spencer, K.C.B., fairly obvious. The evidence is only circumstantial, but it is also cumulative and convincing. Let us briefly sum it up.

In 1812 *the acquaintance had lasted twelve years*. Brent Spencer, after much active service in the West Indies, commanded the 40th Regiment of Foot in the Duke of York's ill-starred Dutch expedition of 1799, and returned to England with the Duke, who had singled him out for praise in his dispatches. This puts the probable date of his first meeting with Princess Augusta about 1800.

In 1805 *Princess Augusta mentioned the attachment to the Duke of York*. In this year Spencer returned to England, after serving with distinction in

Abercromby's expedition to Egypt. He was promoted Major-General, appointed equerry to the King, and placed on the staff. It will be recollected that the Object of Augusta's affections was an equerry and a staff officer.

In 1808 *the 'Object' was abroad.* In 1807 Spencer commanded a brigade at Copenhagen. In 1808 he was with Sir Arthur Wellesley as second-in-command in the Peninsula, and fought with conspicuous courage at Roliça and Vimeiro.

'*A third time he was ordered abroad.*' This probably refers to the Peninsular war, the first and second terms of foreign service being those in Egypt and at Copenhagen.

The letter praying the Regent to sanction a secret marriage was written in March 1812. Spencer returned to England in 1811, having resigned upon being superseded by Sir Thomas Graham, afterwards Lord Lynedoch.

Corroborative evidence is afforded by the unpublished Harcourt MSS. As early as 1802 Princess Augusta, writing in response to 'an invaluable postscript' to a letter from Lady Harcourt, betrays anxiety about some unnamed person on active service, and finds comfort in ranging herself alongside a '*Soldier's Wife*' who was trying to obtain her husband's discharge. She says:

> Indeed, *if* I am a little *nervous* sometimes it is not to be wondered at—but however I know where to put my trust and I will finish with the words of a *Soldier's Wife* who gave a petition to the Duke of York some time ago to obtain her Husband's discharge from the Guards, 'Sir, we are very happy but very poor—we will do all we can for our little ones—*God knows our Wills are good*—we do *no one any harm* and if so be my poor Husband cannot rightly get his discharge now—*well, we are no worse off than before.*'

In September 1807 the Princess was in a state of pitiful suspense. 'Since the troops sailed, which is seven weeks today, I have never', she wrote, 'had an instant's comfort.' But when the Danes yielded she told Lady Harcourt that the King was 'delighted with the good news; and not a little pleased that our *invaluable friend General Spencer* took possession of the Dockyard and Citadel of Copenhagen'. On 28 June 1808, Augusta wrote:

> We have had good reports from Spain by the *Alcmene* frigate, and I trust your *fellow-Servant Genl Spencer may again shew what his great bravery and discretion can do, for He joins all these great qualities in one. I am very anxious about Him,* for He is one of my Elite friends, in the bunch with you. It is very *Small* and very *choice.*

In the interval before the intelligence reached England of the victories at Roliça and Vimeiro the Princess was 'languishing for news from Lisbon'; this, she declared, was her 'first and last thought'. And when the great news came, the

Duke of York repeated to his sister what his Aide-de-Camp, Colonel Brown, had told him concerning the behaviour of General Spencer in the field. The Duke knew of his sister's secret attachment to some staff officer on active service in the Peninsula; and if Spencer was not the man it is a little odd that he should have said so much about him, and nothing about anyone else. Princess Augusta wrote enthusiastically to Lady Harcourt:

> The dear kind Commander in Chief, *my beloved Frederick* told us that Colonel Brown, his Aid-de-Camp, had been attached to General Spencer, He says he never in his life saw anything like His *Coolness, Good Temper, Intrepidity* and *Steadiness* that he was if possible greater on the 21st than on the 17th—that his Conduct in the first day was Enough to Establish his Military Character if it had not *been often tried before* and each time with Credit to his Head and Heart. Colonel Brown was with him when it was necessary to march up a Hill which was so *dreadfully* steep that no one could venture up on Horseback, and He called out, *Never Mind! I will lead on my Men on foot.* At the top, of that very Hill he was struck on the Hand by a ball, but thank God it was only a bruise.

No other staff officer is mentioned with any particular concern in the Princess's letters of this period.

Brent Spencer, the son of Conway Spencer, an Irish country gentleman, was born, according to *Burke's Peerage*, at Tremary, Co. Down; or, according to the *Dictionary of National Biography*, following Captain R. H. Raymond Smythies' *Historical Records of the 40th (2nd Somersetshire) Regiment*, at Trumery, Co. Antrim.

There is another discrepancy between the two accounts of his family and origin. Smythies says that the first Baron Garvagh married a *sister* of Sir Brent Spencer's; but according to Burke it was Paul Canning, *father* of the first Baron, who married 'Jane, daughter of Conway Spencer, and sister and co-heir (with Charlotte, Marchioness of Donegal) of Sir Brent Spencer'. Charlotte, being then the widow of Thomas Moore of Barn, Co. Tipperary, married in 1788, as his second wife, Arthur, first Marquis of Donegal. Both sisters were dead more than ten years before the friendship between their brother and Princess Augusta began.

According to the *United Services Journal* (ii., 1829) Spencer 'descended from a most respectable family in Ireland', and was 'highly connected in the northern part of that kingdom'. In his seventeenth year he entered the Army as an Ensign in the 15th Regiment of Foot, and so began a military career followed with consistent gallantry in a surprising variety of places, ranging from St Kitts to Copenhagen, and from the Helder to the Nile and the Tagus. In *Leaves from the Diary of an Officer in the Guards* he is described as 'a zealous, gallant officer, without any great military genius; anxious and fidgetty when there was nothing to do, but once under fire like a philosopher solving a problem'.

In the landing at Aboukir Bay his philosophy was of an active rather than a reflective kind, for seeing a French soldier taking aim at him from behind a sandhill, he put the man to flight by calling out 'Oh, you scoundrel!' and brandishing his cane. Wellington seems to have thought well of him at first, but relations between the two men soon became strained, partly on account of natural incompatibility—your cool type of Irishman does not love the fiery type—and partly because of Spencer's lack of enthusiasm for the great scheme which led to the creation of the lines of Torres Vedras.

Sir Charles Oman, in his book on the *Peninsular War*, quotes a confidential letter from Wellington in which the Duke says that Spencer was apt to give his opinion on every subject and change it with the wind; but if he was the 'Object of Princess Augusta's Affections' he showed in love a steadfastness for which he was not conspicuous in war.

Two motives led to Brent Spencer's resignation in 1811. The first was 'that in consequence of Sir Thomas Graham's appointment as second-in-command (having held that high position himself for so long) he could not reconcile his feelings to accept a lower post, such as remaining in command of the First Division, which had been offered him by Lord Wellington'; the other was the confident expectation that he would be 'employed elsewhere'—namely, in succession to Sir George Prevost, then Commander-in-Chief in America. This expectation was not fulfilled, and Sir Brent—no doubt to Princess Augusta's relief—bought a small estate at the Lea, three miles from Great Missenden, where, within an easy drive of Windsor, 'he passed his time in perfect retirement, enjoying the pleasures of a rural life and the society of a few chosen friends'.

Three years after this 'highly distinguished character's' death, Wellington, in the course of a conversation at Walmer with John Wilson Croker, described him as 'a very odd sort of man', and, with additions by Sir Henry Cooke, gave a vivid impression of him in the Peninsula.

> Spencer was exceedingly puzzle-headed but very formal; he one day came to me, and very slowly said, 'Sir, I have the honour of reporting that the enemy has evacuated Castello Bono'. It was not Castello Bono but Carpio, as indeed, we could all see, and his aide-de-camp whispered the right word, upon which Spencer began again, as slowly and solemnly as before, 'Sir—I—have—the—honour—to—report' etc., ending once more with *Castello Bono*, and though he made three several attempts, he never could get rid of *Castello Bono*. He would talk of the Thames for the Tagus—eh, Cooke? Cooke. Yes, Sir. He told me one day to get my horse and just trot down to the Thames and see what they were doing there. I told him that I wished with all my heart I could!

Did the Regent fulfil the petition of his sister, and sanction a private marriage between her and the man of her heart? We shall probably never know for certain. But there are some scattered pieces of evidence which, taken in conjunction, make it seem likely that he did.

In June 1812, only three months after the Princess's letter was written, the Duke of York held an Installation of Knights of the Bath, among whom was Brent Spencer. Queen Charlotte was prevented by illness from being present, but Princess Augusta was there, as well as her sister Sophia, and her niece, Princess Charlotte. If the Regent had rejected her petition, would she have had the heart to go to Henry VII's Chapel that day? In 1814, five of the older Knights having died, five of the Extra Knights 'became part of the constituent body', and among the soldiers thus advanced in the Order were Spencer and his old Peninsular rival Sir Thomas Graham. In 1815 Spencer was one of the forty-four Knights constituted by the Prince Regent, 'Military Knights Grand Crosses, composing the First Class of the Most Honourable Order of the Bath'; and he was one of the thirty who were present at the Coronation of George IV.

There is in *The Taylor Papers* a letter from Queen Charlotte *à propos* of a rumour that Sir Brent was proposing to enter politics, and her Majesty's allusion to his 'known attachment' to the Family may perhaps have some significance.

But it is Lord Sidmouth who unconsciously provides the most powerful argument not only in favour of the hypothesis that Brent Spencer was Princess Augusta's *ami de cœur et d'âme*, but also in support of the theory that they were secretly married. In relating to Lady Harcourt the manner in which the news of Princess Charlotte's death had reached Windsor, Princess Augusta says:

> Lord Sidmouth wrote the most kind and feeling letter to Sir Brent Spencer to announce the sad tidings to us. He [Spencer] had witnessed and shared, as well as the Excellent Lord Winchilsea, in all our trouble and suspense the preceding day; so that besides really loving poor Charlotte very sincerely, you may suppose what it was to Him to come and put an end to all our hopes.

At no time after his retirement from the Army did Sir Brent Spencer hold any post or office at Court. Why, then, should Sidmouth have chosen him as his messenger, unless he was aware of the relationship between him and Princess Augusta? In the letter of March 1812 the Princess speaks of her friend's 'Noble Conduct in having offered for my sake to give up his Situation about the King, or at least to plead his being on the staff, that he might not come too often where we must meet in circumstances he was aware most painful to us both'. It seems improbable that five years later he should still be in the foreground, unless either the circumstances, or his sentiments and hers, had changed.

And if during those five years he had not been fairly constantly at Windsor, how could he have seen enough of the young Princess to love her 'very sincerely'?

Still more significant is the passage in which Princess Augusta describes the breaking of the news:

> He came to my door; and His step was so heavy, and his knock so short it was really like the Knell of Death. But when I saw His face, I called out, 'Oh! that look kills me'. We could neither of us speak a Word; but after a little while He put Lord Sidmouth's most distressing but humane letter into my trembling hand. . . .

None of the letters written by the Princess in 1828—the year of Sir Brent Spencer's death—seems to have been preserved; but there may be a note of personal reminiscence in her condolences when Mr Dering died in 1836: '*I respect grief.* I have had my share, and know the spirits ought not to be hurried.'

The marriage, if it ever took place, was kept a secret. That William IV nicknamed Miss Clitherow 'Princess Augusta' because she was 'the Old Maid of the Family as the Princess was of his own' is not conclusive. His sister had said that 'she knew every secret of dear William's heart', not that he knew every secret of hers; or it may be that he regarded an unavowed widow as the equivalent of an old maid.

On 24 August 1813, Ralph Heathcote, a close friend of the Taylor family, wrote from Sanguessa concerning the future Sir Herbert:

> Taylor's brother is now a Major General. He still remains about the Royal Family at Windsor, and I am told the *chronique scandaleuse* will have it that he is married to Pss M.

He certainly was not married to 'Pss M.'. But the *chronique scandaleuse* may have got hold of a rumour to the effect that a Princess was about that time secretly married to a Major-General—and if so, the romantic couple were probably Princess Augusta and Sir Brent Spencer.

There remains one more piece of corroborative evidence: a letter from Schiller's widow, *à propos* of the marriage of the Hereditary Prince of Hesse Homburg and Princess Elizabeth, quoted by Mr Philip Yorke in his edition of that Princess's letters. Frau Schiller writes of the bride, 'She was the only one who could have been sought in marriage in England; for one has been privately married to an Englishman, the other is too much of an invalid'. Mr Yorke thinks this second clause is a belated reference to Princess Amelia, already eight years in her grave; but it seems more likely that its subject is Sophia, and that the 'privately married Princess' was Augusta. The small German courts seethed with gossip—as Princess Elizabeth was to find—and the poet's widow was in close touch with the Hesse Homburg circle.

Among the problems which faced the Prince Regent in 1812 not the least delicate was the public and private situation of his sisters, and he dealt with it in a manner which in the jargon of the time—did equal honour to his head and to his heart. It would be interesting to know, and it may yet come to light, whether he consented to a private marriage between his second sister and Brent Spencer; but one thing at least is certain. She was not that unique creature, a daughter of George III who had never been in love.

The Prince, having created a *couleur de rose* atmosphere about his womenkind, spared no pains to keep the cheerful tint from fading. He invited the Queen and the Sisterhood constantly to Carlton House and to the Pavilion, he poured forth humorous and affectionate letters, full of banter and gossip, and even took the trouble to impart the rules of new round games which he thought might enliven the tedium of candlelight at the Queen's House or at Windsor. His associates seem to have adapted themselves to the rarefied air which the Queen and Princesses brought with them to Brighton, and it is with some surprise that we find those decorous ladies expressing the pleasure they had derived from the society of Lord Hertford and Captain MacMahon. Lord St Helen's, nicknamed 'The Saint', was another unexpected favourite.

The admiring Sisterhood believed that the downfall of that 'indigenous devil' Napoleon, as Princess Augusta called him, was in a large measure due to the exertions of the Prince Regent, and this belief made their rejoicings peculiarly personal when the crash came. They sympathized with their brother's efforts to control his daughter, and they grieved without restraint when Princess Charlotte and her baby died.

To Lady Harcourt, Princess Augusta wrote on 8 November 1817:

> I had *loved, pitied*, and been all anxiety about Dearest Charlotte from the hour of Her birth, and flattered myself that I might say I was easy and happy about Her *now*. But why do I say *now*, when *She is no more!*

Etiquette forbade Charlotte's aunts to be present in St George's Chapel when the young Princess and her child were laid to rest; but they heard 'the dreary, heavy sound which is sad and melancholy to the Ear and most painfull to the Heart'—the sound of mourning coaches slowly lumbering up the hill. Princess Augusta wrote to Lady Harcourt:

> We had a most dreadfull Evening; but I contrived to get out of the Queen's room just to hear the last bell for poor dear Charlotte, that I might have the comfort of repeating, while it was sounding, *God rest Her Soul in Peace.*

It was not long after the death of this only legitimate grandchild that the health of the indomitable old Queen began to cause anxiety. More than thirty years before, Mrs Papendiek had put it on record that the dropsy which had been floating in the Queen's constitution since the birth of Prince Alfred had 'made its deposit and caused her at times much suffering'; and in 1807 Mrs Waddington described her Majesty's figure in terms which suggest that the malady was in its early stages not dropsy but emphysema. 'The Queen', said Mrs Delany's niece rather brutally, 'is grown so enormous that she looks as if she carried all the fifteen Princes and Princesses before her.' Early in 1818 she suffered from fits of depression, and her daughters tried to amuse her 'talking over old-time stories'. She was loth to give up her usual habits, and almost made herself believe that it was her dress that caused her breathlessness. Princess Elizabeth wrote to the Regent in January:

> ... seeing her breathe so uneasy really frightens me so that I cannot possibly stand it, and thank God she cannot bear us with her. ... I entreat her to cry, as I am sure when her spirits are in that state it is better to give vent to tears than to choke herself by swallowing them.[w]

It must have been with a heroic effort of will that Queen Charlotte braced herself to endure the fatigues and emotions of the four weddings—those of Elizabeth, William, Edward, and Adolphus, which were solemnized in her presence during the spring and summer of 1818.

Autumn found her at Kew, in the charming red-brick house which she had purchased in 1772. The Princesses Augusta and Mary were with her, and the Regent paid frequent visits to his much-changed mother.

As the year waned the Queen's vitality ebbed. On 12 September she sent for Sir Henry Halford to ask him whether he did not think that her constitution was giving way, but his blandly evasive replies failed to satisfy her, and about a month later she charged Princess Augusta to request General (afterwards Sir Herbert) Taylor, her Private Secretary, to obtain the honest opinion of her two physicians, Halford and Sir Francis Milman. On 17 October the Princess wrote to the Regent an account of what had passed between her and the Queen after Taylor had carried out his commission:

> As soon as I came into the room She held out her hand and cried a little, but with a sort of catch which proceeded from difficulty in the flow of tears. After telling me She had slept well She said, 'Have You seen Taylor?' I said, 'Yes, and would You like me to repeat to You what I said to Him?' She said, 'I should like it of all things'. I then related it to Her, and She observed it was exactly what She had wished me to say. I then told her that General Taylor thought it very natural for herself, or any person who had been ill for many months, to be anxious to know the real opinion of the physicians, though She had every reason to be satisfied with them: that he had faithfully stated to them what I delivered to him as Her commands, and that he was very much struck with the candid and handsome manner in which they received the communication.

General Taylor has written in a letter to me—that I could relate it to her if She wished it, but it appeared to me as more likely to do justice to their feelings and integrity and more satisfactory to herself if I read the letter to Her. She said, 'My dear, you are quite right'. I then read the whole of it. When I came to the conclusion, She said 'I had not thought it would have come to this. But pray read it again, and read it very slow.' I did so. And then She cried and said, 'I had hoped to get better, but nobody knows nor can know what I suffer. They don't name immediate danger. Did they name it to you?' I said, 'When you are under a spasm the physicians have always told us candidly that you are in great danger'. She then asked whether they talked of danger now? I answered 'This morning they both together told Mary and myself that they thought they could ensure you not being likely to have a spasm and they judged of it by your pulse. But they could not deviate from the daily expression that you are very ill.' She said 'So'! Then she laid her head on her pillow and cried, but with the same difficulty and after a few minutes of continued silence she said, 'I had hoped to see you all happy, and now I fear I shall not arrive at that wish of my Heart'. I said 'Indeed we are all sensible of your Affection and most gratefull for it'. She added, 'I have caused a very dull summer to you all, for the Prince would have given his Brothers balls and parties on account of their marriages, and poor I have been a bane to everything'. . . .(w)

There is something ironical as well as pathetic in these tardy scruples of the mother who had caused so many dull summers—and winters—to her daughters, and to whom the political marriages of her three middle-aged sons represented a pretext for 'balls and parties'. Princess Augusta assured her that nothing could be further from the thoughts of any of her children, and then, after dwelling for a moment on her sons, and on the two daughters who were near her, her thoughts took flight to 'dear, dear Windsor' where the King, oblivious of her and of all things, was still to drag out his ghostly existence for two more years:

She said 'I wish to God I could see *your Brothers*—tell them I love them— but I am too ill. I can only see you and Mary'. She then said, 'I pray from night till morning and from morning till night. I think a great deal, I assure you. I wish I was near the dear King. I ought to be at dear, dear Windsor.' I said 'That is most Natural; and as for praying and thinking, it is the moment to think and reflect when one sees what you suffer, and with what forbearance and patience you submit to it all'. She said, 'My dear, I reflect a great deal'. She then mentioned her legs, and said they were very bad, and that they hurt her as much as the drag in the chest, and added 'I wonder what it can be'. I said, 'Have you ever asked the Physicians whether they think the swelling of the legs is connected with the complaint on the Chest?' She said, 'No, I cannot plague them with my foolish fancies and questions'. I replied, 'Believe me, no question can be foolish after such a long illness, and the Dutifull Affection and solicitude of Sir Francis and Sir Henry demands that you should not keep back any of your feelings or ideas respecting your health'.—She often put her head on the Pillow whilst the conversation was going on, and at last she gave me her hand and said, 'Dear Augusta, I thank you for having executed my Commission so exactly and faithfully': and she cried very much indeed and then she was silent again—and I thought was asleep, but I saw her hands move up and down gently as if She was in prayer.[w]

On 17 November the Queen died at Kew, sitting up in a horsehair-covered armchair and holding the hand of her eldest son. A week later Princess Augusta wrote to the Prince:

My Dearest Brother,
    Your most kind letter has just reached us, and both Mary and myself are very much obliged to You for your kind enquiries. We are really tolerably well to-day, and have had a walk. Mary's cold is much better, and I have not any symptoms of jaundice, though Mary says I am still Yellow. . . . Perhaps it is as well that you did not see us to-day, as we are a little low.[w]

By her Will, made only a day before her death, Queen Charlotte bequeathed the house and farm at Frogmore to her daughter Augusta, and Lower Lodge to her daughter Sophia. It was not, however, until after the death of George III that Windsor Castle ceased to be the headquarters of the second Princess, and that what had been a sort of plaything house became her country home, the delight of her life, 'this dear, dear place', she calls it in a letter to Mrs Dering, 'more to be loved and admired every day'.

Formerly the residence of Horace Walpole's elder brother Edward, Frogmore was reconstructed by Queen Charlotte, with the aid of Wyatt, and 'converted into an elegant villa'. The floral paintings executed by Miss Mary Moser still remain, but the two rooms 'japanned' by Princess Elizabeth, one in red and gold, the other in black and gold, are no longer as they were when Princess Augusta entered on her heritage. The island still nods its green plumes in the centre of the lake, but the hermitages and temples have left not a rack behind.

At the suggestion of the Queen's Executors, Sir Herbert Taylor and Lord Arden, the Regent ordered a public auction of her effects, with this stipulation:

All the Books in the late Queen's library which have any of her Majesty's writing or annotations upon them, or are otherwise particularly distinguished as objects of her Majesty's attention are to be reserved: and a special List made of them, so that the Princesses may have the option of selecting themselves those which they wish to keep. . . . [w]

Of the papers all that were immaterial were destroyed, including (with their Royal Highnesses' permission) the letters from the Princesses, only those of Princess Elizabeth being 'reserved for HRH's pleasure'.

Many of Queen Charlotte's personal belongings were 'bought in' by her daughters, but it was necessary for Princess Augusta to replace most of the furniture and the ornaments at Frogmore. 'For the shortness of the time', wrote Princess Mary in April 1820, 'it is wonderful how very comfortable she has made the House . . . all the furniture very handsome and what it ought to be.'(w) And the Queen of Würtemberg wrote to Lady Harcourt that she was 'trying by degrees to pick up pretty trifles in China and Bronze' to replace the ornaments which were to 'fall into other hands'.

Princess Augusta was present when the Regent divided the Queen's trinkets into four equal portions for distribution among her daughters, and it was then, by a curious chance, that the missing swordhilt, star, loop, Garter, and other jewels of George III came to light. The disappearance of these possessions had been the subject of a correspondence between Princess Augusta and Lord Liverpool in June 1815, from which it appears that the King had packed them away when his wits began to unsettle in 1804, and had forgotten where he had put them. All the Sisterhood recollected that on St George's Day 1805, when the King wished to wear the jewels at the Installation of the Knights of the Garter, 'his Majesty was much distressed' at not finding them. Now, early in 1819, when receptacles were required for Queen Charlotte's trinkets, 'one of the female attendants' suggested that they might be put in some of the empty boxes in an adjoining lumber-room; and in one of these were revealed these baubles which the King would never need again.

When, in 1820, Princess Augusta moved from the Castle to Frogmore, she was so depressed by the prospect that she asked the Dowager Lady Harcourt to spend the first days of settling-in with her. Dearly though she loved the place, it could not but be haunted by many memories of bygone picnics and garden fêtes; of the Jubilee of 1809 when Tritons gambolled in the lake, and loyally blew their wreathed horns; of King George himself enjoying Mrs Billington's performance in *Acis and Galatea*, in the Colonnade; of Queen Charlotte's feast to the Eton boys in July 1817, when the lawn was shadowed by 'Asiatic tents' (formerly the property of Tippoo Sahib) 'in each of which tables were spread with elegance and abundance', and the air was rent by the 'animated huzzas' of the guests.

Painful though the *déménagement* proved when the old King died, the Princess had cheered up sufficiently in June 1821 to enjoy the new King's juvenile ball, and to assist Croker in arranging 'some quadrilles for the little folks'. Her visits to Stuttgart, Hanover, and Homburg must have been exciting adventures for an elderly lady who had never journeyed further afield than Cheltenham. It was after her stay in Homburg that her sister, the Landgravine Elizabeth, wrote to Sir William Knighton, 'Yesterday I parted from my dear, generous and good

Augusta—believe me, she is sterling worth'. In 1830, and again in 1835–36, the Landgravine visited her, in the snug cheerfulness of Clarence House, St James's, and the leafy seclusion of that 'loveliest of all places', Frogmore. The younger sister was then delighted to see the elder 'valued and beloved' as she deserved to be, and installed as befitted a daughter and sister of Kings.

History, music, gardening, and a little theology whiled away the quiet days. When she sent to Homburg some prayers 'written by Mr Henry Thornton', the Landgravine's comment was:

> They are thoroughly orthodox by her sending them, for she has a horror of all sects as well as myself—but I am not to compare with my excellent Augusta as to religious knowledge. I believe few people are so well and so thoroughly right upon such subjects as her. I have a weaker head, but those books she sends me I stick to.

It may have been that weaker head which prevented her from perceiving that a horror of all sects is no true mark of orthodoxy. But Princess Augusta was certainly not narrow-minded; she once shocked a Windsor clergyman by telling him that the sky was her parish.[w]

On 15 July 1819, she gave Madame d'Arblay a taste of her quality as a musician, and the gratified Fanny notes:

> A message from HRH Princess Augusta, with whom I passed a morning as nearly delightful as any now can be! She played and sang to me airs of her own composing, unconscious medley reminiscences, but very pretty, and prettily executed.

In May 1824 it was Tom Moore's turn to hear the Princess perform her artlessly derivative compositions. This was at Lady Donegal's, where Mary Duchess of Gloucester, and her sister-in-law, Princess Sophia Matilda, were also of the company. Moore relates that Princess Augusta sung and played for him, among other things the new airs which she had composed for two of his own songs, 'The wreath you wove'—'rather pretty' remarks the poet, in parenthesis—and 'The Legacy'. She also played a march which she told him she had 'composed for Frederick', and a waltz or two, and some German airs. Later she reverted to the Irish melodies, and produced some variations on 'Love's Young Dream'.

It is a pleasant theory that Brent Spencer may have been responsible for her Irish predilections, but we know that the Duke of Clarence y *était pour quelquechose*. In a letter to Lady Arran, from St James's, in December 1812, the Princess says:

> . . . on Thursday *William dined with me* . . . we had some of my favourite Irish melodies and simple Ballads, which I like better than anything else, and

then I played, to amuse *William*, every Paddy tune I could think of, *O'Carrol*, *O'Rafferty*, *O'Carey* all his *delights*! [w]

In the same letter, written on a foggy December afternoon, she remarked that 'William' had just been with her, and pulled down her blinds with his own hand, and had the candles lighted, 'for he said it was *too melancholy*'.[w]

Always, as she wrote to the Duke of Sussex, 'truly anxious and interested' in her brothers, it was Princess Augusta's fate to see two of them crowned, and the daughter of a third on the throne. Even with the morose Duke of Cumberland her relations were cordial, and he wrote from Brighton Pavilion at a time of much political unrest, 'the stories afloat are very alarming, but Augusta and I keep up the spirits of our neighbours'. It was she whom he had to thank for the eventual recognition of his wife at the English Court, though the two exiled sisters had accepted the inevitable some years before. Earl Grey wrote to Princess Lieven in August 1829:

> There has been a negotiation through Sir H. Taylor with the Princess Augusta, and she has consented to receive the Duchess of Cumberland. This, I suppose, means the whole family, the Princess Augusta taking the lead as the senior Princess.

In February 1821 Princess Lieven told Metternich how George IV had interrupted a long after-dinner harangue to turn to Princess Augusta and exclaim, 'Sister, I drink to you. Long live wine, I say, long live women.' The phrasing of the toast is unexpected. Fifteen years later William IV at his birthday dinner raised his glass to Augusta and then, swinging round to the demurely-ringleted Princess Victoria sitting on his other hand, observed, 'And now having given the health of the eldest I will give that of the youngest of the Royal Family'.

Throughout George IV's reign the Princess remained steadfast in her belief that it was only necessary for him to be understood in order to be loved and admired. It was at Frogmore with her that the King found sympathy and seclusion while his wife was scandalizing decent opinion by going in public procession to St Paul's to thank Providence for the break-down of the proceedings against her in the House of Lords; and when he died, an odd but not a craven figure of a King, she wrote to Lady Arran:

> I am as composed as I can be, though I have met with a very heavy affliction, and time will with God's mercy soothe my *feelings*; and if it pleases Him that dear *William* keeps his health, and that his good intentions, his good sense, and perfect determination to fulfill the great trust which is reposed in Him to the utmost shall be *valued* as it ought to be, I shall then be happy again.[w]

Mr Greville was rather shocked at the new King's deportment immediately after his accession, when 'he drove all over the town in an open *calèche* with the

Queen, Princess Augusta, and the King of Würtemberg'; but in the eyes of the Princess 'dear William' could do no wrong. 'You would', she told Lady Arran, 'esteem and love both Himself and our most loveable and perfect Queen if you could see the real Modesty with which they bear their new Honours. All their arrangements are done in such a delicate Manner.'[w]

When William IV died, the Landgravine Elizabeth wrote that 'dearest Augusta had lost everything', but the first three years of the new reign brought happy hours to the senior Aunt. She loved Victoria and described her as 'a dear, good little creature, and so affectionate and kind to us all'. Her interest in the young Queen had begun before her birth, when the Duke of Kent was hustling his wife across France to England. Princess Augusta then wrote, 'I am outrageous with Edward, for he is behaving like a fool and a madman'. Of all the brothers he and the Duke of Cumberland seem to have been the least loved; Wellington told Creevey that the Duke of Kent's sisters called him 'Joseph Surface'.

The first winter after King William's death, Princess Augusta spent at St Leonards with Queen Adelaide. Not until the following year did she summon up courage to revisit Brighton, staying at the white house on the Steyne which she had had twelve years before, and missing 'William' painfully. She wrote of him to Mrs Dering:

> When I came to Brighton he was either at the door to receive me, or I was at my window to kiss my hand to him and the dear Queen Adelaide. Now, my dear Mrs Dering, I come to a door where I only met *then* for a kind face my own servant, and I walked up to my room, and was thankful I got upstairs at all, and that I had *two hours* to be *quite alone.*

The Princess was greatly perturbed by the struggle between the young Queen and Sir Robert Peel over the question of replacing the Whig Ladies of the Bedchamber by Tories, and wrote anxiously to her old friend:

> ... it is a very trying moment for an *old stager* like myself. To see my poor *innocent child* made a tool of ... quite kills me, but I hope people will be gentle to her, and *pity* more than blame her, poor thing.

Of all the consolations which remained, the greatest was to be found in the children of her kinsfolk and friends 'a very great delight, let me tell you', she wrote to Mrs Dering.

She did not live to see Queen Victoria's nursery fill up almost in the manner of Queen Charlotte's, but she took the liveliest interest in the attractive children of the Duke of Cambridge—'little angel George', and the charming Princess Mary Adelaide by whom, to her great delight, she was described as 'a capital Aunt', after a scene during which the little girl had been recalcitrant and the old lady had abstained from 'telling tales'. Her kindness of heart was known outside the circle of her own family, and she was constantly assailed by petitions, with which Sir Herbert Taylor would often help her to cope. None of these can surely have been more absurd than the one addressed to her in 1819 by a Mr J. Mackrell Poulden, who dropped into poetry, apostrophizing the fifty-one year old Princess as 'thou bright Nymph, thou soother of distress', and urging her to 'clasp his trembling infants in her arms'. 'Yes, yes,' concludes Mr Poulden hopefully, 'I know thou wilt their little wants supply, nor suffer them and me in misery to die.'

The death of 'our dear, invaluable Sir Herbert Taylor' early in 1839 grieved but did not surprise Princess Augusta. To Mrs Dering she wrote, wrestling valiantly though ineffectively with the name of the fatal complaint:

> I had, though, to tell the truth, given him up sooner than any of my family, for I well knew that over ten months ago he grazed his leg against a Rock, and that it produced in Sir Herbert an Erycepalus that he has not had a day's health. . . . He had giddiness then, coughs and bowel complaints. All, you may depend upon it, *Erycepilus checked*.

The death of 'dearest dear Eliza' in January 1840 was a far heavier blow. The two sisters had written to each other every day for many years, 'to go twice a week by the foreign post,' and writing these letters had been Princess Augusta's 'daily pleasure, comfort, and occupation'. It is easy to imagine with what tearful sensibility the elder Princess received the ring with a portrait of their father bequeathed to her by the younger. Yet the last months of her life were made happy by the attentions of her young couple, as she called Victoria and Albert. In April 1840 she and Queen Adelaide attended the opera, when 'the principal ballerina made such ridiculous antics and jumps', and the young Queen and her husband came into their box between the acts, to have 'a delightful chat'.

Five months later Prince Albert, receiving the freedom of the City of London, intimated that owing to bad reports of the health of Princess Augusta he could not dine with the Lord Mayor and Aldermen after the presentation, having promised the Queen to return. The Duke of Cambridge, who was of the company, apparently took a more hopeful view. According to Greville, the Duke said that the Princess was better than she had been for some time and that, while Prince Albert could please himself, he personally could not make that excuse to the Lord Mayor.

All through the summer Princess Augusta's failing health had distressed the young Queen, to whom Leopold, King of the Belgians, wrote on 22 September— the actual day of the Princess's death—'I pity poor Princess Augusta from all my heart. I am sure that if she had in proper time taken care of herself she might have lived to a great age.' But according to the ideas then current seventy-one years was a very tolerable span of life; and the frequent allusions in her letters to the ministrations of Sir Henry Halford and Sir Matthew Tierney, as well as to the leeches, blisters, and potions with which they plied her, suggest that she did not neglect her health.

Queen Victoria was at Windsor in the last weeks of September 1840. Her first baby was expected two months later, and Prince Albert may have wished to spare her the pain of seeing her 'good, excellent Aunt Augusta' die. Etiquette prescribed the attendance of the greatest possible number of family witnesses at such a scene, and the *Annual Register* records that 'all the Royal Family in town' were with the Princess at the end. The Dukes of Sussex and Cambridge were there; Mary, Duchess of Gloucester, and the pathetic, sightless figure of Princess Sophia; but it was the Dowager Queen Adelaide who held the hand of the old Princess and, when all was over, closed her eyes. Mr More, the apothecary, had been sending a bulletin to Windsor every morning, and the Queen told her Uncle Leopold with obvious *attendrissement* that almost the last words spoken by her Aunt were, 'Have you written to my Darling?'

Escorted by a detachment of the 9th Lancers, the remains of 'the late most Illustrious Princess, Augusta Sophia' were removed from Clarence House, St James's, to Frogmore, and on 2 October 1840, the funeral ceremony took place in St George's Chapel, to the light of flambeaux held by Life Guardsmen. Five heralds walked in the procession, and the Duke of Cambridge brought his boy, Prince George, both of them draped in mourning cloaks of great length.

Princess Augusta died intestate, and her modest personal fortune, 'sworn under £30,000,' was divided among her brothers and sisters. A short time before her death she sent tokens of remembrance to the various members of her family, and gave a lithograph portrait of herself to each of her servants. One of her dressers, Wright by name, 'the most attentive, attached, worthy, best of creatures', had been with her thirty-four years.

3

Princess Elizabeth, Landgravine of Hesse-Homburg 1770–1840

I

In the summer of the year 1780 Queen Charlotte was, as not infrequently happened, expecting another baby; and three of her children spent the months of June, July, August, and September distributed with governesses, governors and sub-governors, among the group of modest dwellings known as 'Sea Houses, East Bourn'. Lady Charlotte Finch and Mary Hamilton were in charge of the Princesses Elizabeth and Sophia, and three gentlemen, one French and two English, were occupied in looking after Prince Edward.

Sea-bathing was the vogue, and in addition they walked on the sands, went for drives over the Downs, and played in the garden of Lady Betty Compton's house—now Compton Place. Writing from that garden, Miss Hamilton said:

> Princess Elizth and *my sweet engaging Child*, Pss Sophia, are playing about like Butterflies in the Sun, and culling wild flowers on the Grass whilst I am watching them. . . . Adieu, the wind blows my paper about, and my Dear children wish me to play with them.

With their golden hair and their white muslin dresses the two little girls, one ten years old, the other only three, must indeed have resembled both butterflies in the sun and wildflowers on the grass; but Sophia was perhaps the more flower-like of the two, for of Elizabeth Mrs Papendiek records that 'she was born fat, and through every illness, of which she had many, she never lost flesh'.

On 23 September 1780, Princess Elizabeth wrote to her 'dearest Papa':

> This morning I was made very, very happy by receiving a letter from you. I was made glad to hear that my dear Mama was so well, and that I had got another Brother.
>
> Sophia says she has got a little Granson: Octavius she calls her Son. . . . The Cannons fired from the Ships and from the Beach both yesterday and to-day. I was so overjoyed when I had your letter this Morning, my Dear Papa, that I could not settle myself to write.[w]

To the third daughter of George III, born at the Queen's House on 22 May 1770, was given the name of his long-dead second sister, the delicate, deformed little Princess Elizabeth of whom Horace Walpole wrote: 'I saw her act in *Cato* at eight years old (when she could not stand alone, but was forced to lean against the side-scene) better than any of her brothers and sisters . . . she had learned the part of *Lucia* by hearing the others study their parts'.

Upon the infant son whose birth had set the cannon thundering off the Sussex coast the name of Alfred was bestowed. He did not live to bear it long.

Like her two elder sisters, Princess Elizabeth was educated under the eye of her intelligent and indefatigable mother. Though she had more taste for music than the Princess Royal, and 'sang very prettily in point of voice', she congratulated herself in later life that she had never become 'a performer', remarking a little sententiously that 'it leads people to be so enthusiastic that it is quite unpleasant'. Her talent was for drawing, and this she was encouraged to develop in every sort of medium, crayon, pastel, water-colour, charcoal, mezzotint, gouache, and lacquer.

Letters and memoirs of the English Court in the last two decades of the eighteenth century contain many allusions to her frequent illnesses. In 1785 Mrs Delany was in a state of constant apprehension about the Princess, who, in addition to 'an inflammation on her lungs' (Fanny Burney calls it 'a complaint on the chest'), was suffering from the inevitable 'spasms'. Mrs Papendiek, less reticent, adds the information that Elizabeth had 'a scrofulous abscess on her left side'. Bleeding and blistering were the methods employed by Sir George Baker, and it is not surprising that the patient's spirits 'became so low that 'whenever she saw those whom [*sic*] she knew felt for her and loved her, she invariably shed torrents of tears'. She seemed, records Miss Burney, 'so extremely delicate in her constitution, and so sweet and patient in submitting to her destiny, that I was quite affected by her sight'.

During this illness the Princess was at the Lower Lodge, where the King and Queen 'deeply afflicted', visited her two or three times a day, but might not speak to her. Later, after the expedition to Nuneham in the summer of 1786, she was again prostrate, and between that time and the autumn of 1788 her illnesses were so frequent and so severe that Lord Bute's former residence on Kew Green (now known as 'the King's Cottage') was assigned to her as a sort of sick bay.

According to a persistent legend, this Princess was secretly married to an obscure member of the royal household, and the 'chest complaints' and 'spasms' which necessitated her occasional withdrawal to the little house by Kew Church were in reality so many babies. Mr Childe Pemberton, in *The Romance of Princess Amelia*, says categorically of Elizabeth, 'this Princess in early youth had made a secret marriage with a Mr Ramus, by whom she had children, but the circumstances were not romantic'—a curious verdict if we remember the Squỳèr of Low Degree 'that loved the King's daughter of Hungarie', or, even more appropriate to the circumstances, the Lady of the Strachey, who 'married the

Yeoman of the Wardrobe'. It was whispered that George III had grandchildren of whom he and the *Almanach de Gotha* took no cognizance, and Princess Lieven reported to Metternich Caroline, Princess of Wales's characteristic threat to 'give a little historical narrative of the behaviour of each member of the Royal Family, not forgetting the offspring of the unmarried Princesses'; but it seems more probable that in each instance some secret ceremony had taken place, regarded as binding in the sight of God, though recognized to be void in the eyes of man. It is perhaps not without significance that the Marriage Registers of Kew Church for the years 1783–1845 are missing, having disappeared, with their iron chest, in the latter year.

Crisp, in his monumental and usually accurate *Visitation*, puts it on record that a Mr James Money was married to Eliza, 'daughter of George Ramus, *Page of George III* by Princess Elizabeth *his wife*, daughter of George III'. But as far as can be ascertained the King never had a Page whose name was *George* Ramus.

The Ramus family, which was numerous, may have come over with Queen Charlotte. W. Ramus was a Page of the Bedchamber from 1763 to 1789; in 1775 Charles Ramus was a Clerk of the Kitchen, and Joseph Ramus, assistant Clerk to the Spicery. Three years later William (probably the son of 'W.') and Nicholas Ramus were Pages of the Backstairs, and in 1797 John Ramus was Gentleman of the Ewry. George Ramus certainly existed, but he appears in the household records only at Midsummer 1774, when he signed a receipt on behalf of his brother, the Page of the Bedchamber; and he held no post in the royal household where his kindred held so many.

In 1778, when the King visited Portsmouth, one of this family—'W.', no doubt—went to and fro between that town and Windsor. Queen Charlotte then wrote to his Majesty:

> Ramus did not return till ten o'clock last night. He finds the House at Portsmouth extreamly neat, all rooms furnish [*sic*] with *Elegant Cotton Beds* (this is his expression) but no bedding for servants' beds. . . . Ramus also wishes to know whether the *Epergne* from Windsor is to be sent or not.[w]

Of greater significance, as showing the status of the Ramus tribe, is this passage from Mrs Papendiek:

> The eldest daughter of Mr Ramus, one of the senior pages to the King about this time (1778) was married to Sir John Day. On its being notified, according to the usual form, that Lady Day would be presented at the next Drawing Room, the Queen objected to it, on account of the position her father held in the household; but when, shortly after, Sir John Day was appointed Governor of one of our East India Settlements, the right of presentation could no longer be disputed.

Thirty-two years later Princess Elizabeth was writing to Princess Amelia's nurse, Mrs Williams, concerning the death of 'poor Lady Day':

> She will be a sad loss to Isabella Ramus, who is with her. They tell me she had £160 a year. The half must go to Sir John Day's brother, the other is in her own power, and it is supposed that she will leave it to her niece.[w]

In a note to the *Lousiad* Peter Pindar called 'Billy' Ramus 'one of the Pages who shaves the Sovereign, airs his shirt, reads to him, writes for him, and collects anecdotes'. This coarse but lively satire grew out of the incident when the King, having caught sight of 'an offensive insect' in a dish of green peas, decreed that every cook, scullion, and kitchen-boy in the royal household must have his head shaved. Pindar represents his Majesty as much annoyed at the levity with which the ladies of the Family treated the episode, and thus gallantly apostrophizes the Princesses:

> Sweet Maids! the beauteous boast of Britain's isle,
> Speak—were those peerless lips forbid to smile?

His description of the functions of 'Billy' Ramus forms an interesting commentary on the legend—it has almost attained the dignity of a tradition—that one of the 'Sweet Maids' was secretly married to a member of the 'trusty Page's' family:

> Now to the crowded kitchen Ramus springs,
> Ramus, call'd' Billy' by the best of Kings:
> Who much of razors and of soapsuds knows,
> Well skill'd to take great Caesar by the nose;
> Much of his Sovereign lov'd, a trusty Page,
> Who often puts great statesmen in a rage;
> Poor Lords! compelled against their will to wait,
> Though ass-like laden with affairs of state,
> Till Page and Monarch finish deep disputes
> On buckskin breeches or a pair of boots.

In the *Morning Post* of 3 March 1789, there is an allusion to a current rumour that four of his Majesty's Pages had been dismissed 'because the Pages in question were thought to be men of indifferent conversation and had been detected in observing his Majesty's looks and gestures during the absence of Dr Willis with a curiosity very offensively minute'. The newspaper declares that 'Mr Ramus *only has been dismissed*'; and it is significant that in 1790 his name is missing from the list of the royal household given in the *Court and City Register*.

In the copy of the *Book of Common Prayer* which Princess Elizabeth used up to the time of her death she wrote:

> This Prayer Book was given me by Genl Goldsworthy in 1786, during my great illness, and has ever proved my truest and most comforting friend in all my distresses.

It seems improbable that the gift would have been made, or the inscription written, if there had been anything ambiguous about the 'great illness' in question.

The preposterous Thomas Ashe, in *The Spirit of 'The Book'*, introduces a story concerning 'the Lady E——— and 'the elegant M———e', an officer in the Guards, by whose 'constant assiduities' her heart had been 'much affected'. 'M———e', paying a clandestine but strictly decorous visit (in full regimentals) to the apartments of the Lady, was overpowered by the sentries, who carried him, faint and bleeding, into the august presence of her father. 'The wretched E———', says Mr Ashe, 'rushed out . . . shrieked, and fell prostrate to the ground.'

> The agonies of a parent, the terrors of the spectators, cannot be described. The amiable father sunk beneath this load of distress. He strove to recover his daughter; promised her his blessing and forgiveness and only required of M———e that he should travel on the Continent during the term of six years.

This episode, if it ever happened, must have taken place towards the period 1788–89. Ashe stresses the honourable character of the attachment, and gives this remarkable sketch of his heroine:

> As to the form of the Lady E———, without being thin and taper it is limber and elegant, elastic and well-contoured, and those attractive properties, joined to the softness and fairness of her skin, to the freshness of her complexion, and the carnation of her frame, render her one of the most interesting women of her age.

A puzzling feature is that between 1795 when she described herself as a 'single woman', and 1818 when she married Prince Frederick of Hesse-Homburg, Princess Elizabeth constantly reiterated her desire to 'settle', her anxiety to be 'a perfect wife'. She must have regarded herself as free from matrimonial commitments when she wrote to the Prince of Wales in September 1796:

> I trust that the Pss R's being determined upon may open the way for others, for times are much changed, and every young woman who has been brought up as

we have been through the goodness of Mama must look forward to settlement, which was I to say *I* did not, your own good sense must tell you is false.[W]

It may be that George Ramus was dead, and that she had taught herself to keep the whole interlude in the background of her mind. Certainly no whisper of an infant had reached Fanny d'Arblay when she took her son Alexander to the Queen's House in 1798, and 'almost sighed' that the Princess who romped so charmingly with the little boy should have 'no call for her maternal propensities'.

The financial position of the Princesses was at this time difficult. Mr (afterwards Sir) James Bland Burges wrote in November 1794:

> . . . Lady Elgin also told me that these poor Princesses were in a terrible state with respect to their finances. The three eldest have each had for some time past an allowance of £2000 a year, out of which they are obliged to furnish themselves with everything—clothes, servants' wages, and even jewels, for neither the King nor the Queen have ever given them any. The two eldest are very prudent, and contrive to live tolerably within their allowances; but Princess Elizabeth is a bad economist, and, as she says herself, must go to gaol very soon.

In July 1796 Princess Elizabeth was in a more than usually tight corner, and turned to that impecunious eldest brother whose affection for his sisters seems to have been almost the only stable element in his nature. She wrote to him:

> Your great goodness at all times to me, my dearest Brother, makes me trouble you with this letter, though I will own my conscience & my feelings can scarcely bear doing so, but my confidence in the best of Brothers is such that I can only apply to Him, & *Him alone, in distress*; it is cruel when you are so severely worried in every way to plague you during your quiet, but alas, a very disagreeable circumstance has happened to me which makes me fly to You. You shall hear what I have to say, though it makes me really miserable to teaze you.

> At this moment, owing to many, many unpleasant things, I have been very much plagued to pay a sum of money which is totally out of [my] power, if I do not entreat you to lend me some, which I will most solemnly promise to pay off by one hundred a Quarter till it is quite discharged to You. If you can lend it me it would be an obligation never to be forgotten as my mind is upon the Rack from never having allowed myself before to have a difficulty. The truth of how it happened shall be told to you honestly, but I must entreat you never to name it to any of my family upon any account whatever, excepting my oldest Sister, who found me in a most woeful situation, and to whom I said the only friend I could look up to for assistance, if it was to be had, was Yourself.

The sum, I must now tell you, is £600. I am shocked with horror at it and when if I ever get out of this difficulty, you may depend on my honour I shall never fall into it again, as I have [never] suffered so much in my whole life. Pray, Pray, forgive me this petition and judge by your own excellent heart what I must feel in troubling you with this. I really can write no more, I am so agitated, only to say our dear mother is, thank God, well, my eldest Sister all happiness, and the rest of the family quite in health.

(P.S.) If you write to me, direct it to Gooly, to be given me alone, as it is private for myself. I would not have Mama know it for the world.[w]

Less than a fortnight later she was writing to the Prince of Wales, 'Indeed it is impossible for me ever to find words strong enough to give you the slightest idea of the fulness of my heart when your letter arrived. The more I think of it, the more I think it a dream, this sudden change in my heart from the deepest distress to the joy and gratitude you have created.'[w] Somehow 'G.P.' had contrived to lay his hands upon £600. Surely it should be accounted unto him for righteousness that at a moment when his own distresses, domestic and financial, were exceeding great he should have made a point of answering his sister's appeal so promptly and to such good purpose.

If Princess Elizabeth was a bad economist, her predicament may have been the aftermath of some imprudent expenditure; but it is also possible that the money may have been needed for something different—something that would be better explained by word of mouth. Her brother would have been the last person to blame her if she had been buying too many yellow plumes for her hair, or lacquered cabinets for her 'apartment', and there seems no reason why she should hesitate to write to him of such things.

Bland Burges was no doubt correct in his estimate of the Princesses' financial position, but it is with surprise that we find him telling his wife that Lady Elgin had enlisted his aid to procure for those devoted sisters 'private accounts of what would be interesting to them about their brothers, of whom they were never allowed to hear anything'. Though no communications from any of the brothers to their sisters seem to have been preserved, the Windsor Archives contain many long and affectionate letters from the elder Princesses to the elder Princes, most of which, even the earliest in date, suggest a constant exchange. The sisters were certainly able to write undetected, and to dispatch what they had written; and with the friendly connivance of 'Gooly', they must occasionally have received replies.

It is possible that these much supervised young ladies may have desired to judge for themselves just how much reason their father had to burst into tears, rise up and walk about the room, and then kiss his daughters while thanking God for giving them to him to comfort him for the misdeeds of his sons—a proceeding by which we are told 'the Princesses were variously agitated, and sometimes so much so as to go into fits'. Princess Augusta was aware of the

Prince of Wales's relations with Mrs Fitzherbert; and if Prince William did indeed, from the first, tell her all his troubles, a great many of these confidences must have been made—as Miss Pinkerton would have said—'epistolarily'. The fact that many of the private accounts of the doings of the Royal Dukes would have been *pas pour les jeunes filles* explains Queen Charlotte's desire to exclude them. It is significant that in the secret jargon of the Family a 'shewable' meant that sort of letter which might with safety be shown to Mama.

Princess Elizabeth's epistles to her brothers, Frederick and Augustus, do not suggest a life of invalidism and gloom. They are so full of balls and betrothals that she tells the Duke of York that she is 'affraid' he will take her letter 'for an old newspaper'[w] and to Prince Augustus, said by Madame de la Fite to have been her favourite brother, she declares that her joy at finding a letter from him on her dressing-table caused a general laugh, as she 'quite skrimed'.[w] One of the two absentees sent her some china (of which she was for a time an impassioned collector) but it was lost in transit. She received a present of some coral with enthusiasm, as it was the thing she 'most wished to have'.[w]

In July 1791 she describes how the Queen, Princess Augusta, and herself go down to the 'cottage' at Frogmore, recently purchased from Lady Egerton:

> Mama sits in a very small green room which she is very fond of, reads, writes and Botanizes. Augusta and me remain in the room next hers across a passage and employ ourselves much in the same way. Of a Saturday my younger sisters have no masters, so they also come down.[w]

Two years later Madame de la Fite was assuring Fanny Burney that she would have some difficulty in recognizing Frogmore.

> *On y construit des ruiner, et bientôt on aura achevé un vieux bâtiment Gothique; ici s'élève un petit temple octagone dont le plafond est dessiné par la Princesse Elizabeth; là on découvre un hermitage dont elle a donné le modèle.*

Rumour had declared in the summer of 1786 that Princess Elizabeth had been sent to Mr Walpole's *bâtiment gothique* at Strawberry Hill 'for two days, for the air'; and nine years later she was one of the bevy of royal ladies, led by the Queen, who honoured his pie-crust castle with a visit. Lord Orford, as he then was, does not mention her specifically when describing the 'invasion of royalties' to Field-Marshal Conway; but it was when attempting to dictate his catalogue to Kirgate 'for Princess Elizabeth' in July 1796 that the old gentleman alarmed his secretary by a sudden confusion of speech, which he himself ascribed not to excitement or fatigue, but to excessive indulgence in raspberries and cream.

All the Princesses seem to have enjoyed their visit to 'Twit'nam', and Elizabeth wrote to Lady Harcourt:

If My time would allow me I could run on in raptures about everything; but I will not leave the subject without a few words concerning the owner of this curious and interesting mansion, whose pleasing manners thoroughly gained the whole company. We hope that he will not have suffered from his great civility to us; it pained me to think that we were the cause of his exerting himself as he did. . . . I wish I could be housekeeper there for a fortnight. In case of your hearing that Lord O. is in want of one, send to such a No., in such a place, near such a street, by such a Castle, in such a Lodge, you will find a discreet, steady young woman, who bears a tolerable good character, with the advantage of speaking a little French, who will be willing to enter into such a Capacity. She is a single woman.

As it was at this time that Lady Harcourt was bestirring herself to find husbands for the elder Princesses, this last remark is not without significance.

The infirmities of age—he was seventy-eight—may have made their host feel that he was unequal to the obeisances proper to the occasion, but certainly did not cripple his wit, for Princess Elizabeth wrote to the Prince of Wales that their eldest sister desired her particularly to tell him that, whatever *he* might think, they had made a conquest, 'of no less a person than Lord Orford, who says that he does not wish himself to be turned into *one* Emperor but *into three*'.(w)

It was in this same year—on 17 January 1795—that P. W. Tomkins, 'Historical Engraver to her Majesty', published a series of twenty-four plates with the following title-page:

To the Queen
This book representing
The Birth and Triumph of Cupid
In her Majesty's Collection, from Papers cut by Lady Dashwood
Is with permission most humbly dedicated by
Her Majesty's most devoted and very much obliged servant

P. W. Tomkins
Historical Engraver
to her Majesty

In a letter written four years earlier to one of her brothers, Princess Elizabeth had remarked that she would send him some more of her 'cuttings', adding, 'and as you like them I will set my wits to work, and invent some new ones. . . . Lady Dashwood is going to make a collection for me of the cuttings I make, and if she succeeds I will get her to give some for you.'(w) Hence probably arose the idea of attributing the Princess's work to that attached friend of the Family who figures in Fanny Burney's diary as 'Lady D.'.

Eleven months after the publication of *The Birth and Triumph of Cupid*, Bland Burges (now Sir James) wrote to his sister concerning certain poetical exercises upon which he was at that time engaged:

> I caught it from some drawings of Princess Elizabeth, and I am writing the poem for her Royal Highness. It will in all probability be published. . . . Don't be surprised at my having this sort of intercourse with so exalted a personage. I have already had the honour of being concerned in a joint work with her, with which the King was so pleased that he had it printed at his own expense.

What was this earlier 'joint work'? The *Dictionary of National Biography* assumes that it was *The Birth and Triumph of Cupid*, from which Bland Burges says he 'caught' the poem which, in November 1795, he was writing for the Princess; but it seems a little curious that he should speak of catching an idea with which he was already familiar. At all events this pleasant Scotsman was responsible for the lyrical letterpress of *The Birth and Triumph of Love*, published in 1796 by T. Egerton of Whitehall, who mentions in his foreword that 'the plan of the work was taken from a Series of Plates entitled *The Birth and Triumph of Cupid*—the superior merit of that performance is sufficiently known and acknowledged. Nothing can surpass the Delicacy of the Idea on which it is founded, or the Elegance of the Manner in which it is executed. 'Egerton was the publisher of the poem only, but the plates were obtainable from him as well as from Tomkins by those persons who 'will be inclined to bind up the plates' with it. Neither the Princess's name nor Lady Dashwood's is mentioned.

James Bland Burges, as well as being himself of a poetical turn, was a cause of 'poetry' in others. It was an early attachment of his which inspired Lady Ann Barnard to write 'Auld Robin Gray', and Princess Elizabeth addressed him in galloping stanzas, bidding him

> . . . believe when we mention your name
> That we always do think you a favourite of Fame.[w]

He was a friend of the Cumberland family, and, as a Member of Parliament, an associate of Edmund Burke, whom he is said to have supplied with the actual dagger dramatically flung down in an astonished House of Commons in 1792.

It will be noticed that in the second edition of the *Birth and Triumph* the name of the 'hero' has been changed from 'Cupid' to 'Love'—perhaps out of deference to the wishes of Queen Charlotte, who had read the poem in manuscript. Lady Elgin, who was the poet's ambassadress at Court, reported to him that the Princess was 'absolutely ashamed that her little amusement, as she humbly calls it, should have drawn out such a work 'which does not look as if the original idea had been the result of a previous collaboration—and the admirable Mr

Smelt, who had come up from Yorkshire to visit his royal friends, declared that 'there was more real poetry' in Bland Burges's composition than had appeared 'these many years'.

To obviate misunderstanding as to the character of the work, the poet declares in the opening lines:

> Of Love I sing—not of that treacherous Boy
> To whom the impure Venus erst gave birth.

The distinction is a nice one, made all the more so by the pagan appearance of the *amorini*, who might have flown straight out of one of those Pompeian frescoes with which the archaeological zeal of Sir William Hamilton had recently familiarized the polite world. 'Ah!' exclaims Sir James,

> ... who can tell the charms of Infant Love,
> His mild, transporting beauties who can speak!

Elizabeth's 'cuttings' are uncoloured, but the imagination of the reader is thoughtfully stimulated in the letterpress:

> Pure silvery curls his polished forehead deck,
> Skirt his encrimsoned cheeks with modest grace.

It was some twenty-six years before a second impression of the work was called for, but in the interim Dr Vincent, Dean of Westminster, had chosen what he described as the *roseique Cupidinis ortum* as the subject of his election verses at Westminster School, congratulating the *nitidissima nympha*, the sweet *progenies regum*, upon her skill.

Tomkins published in the same year, 1796, seven 'proofs before subscription' of a series entitled *The Birthday Gift or the New Doll*, 'from Papers cut by a Lady'—the British Museum ascribes them to Lady Templeton, but the work was Princess Elizabeth's, and her ladyship had no more to do with the *Birthday Gift* than Lady Dashwood had to do with the *Birth and Triumph of Cupid*.

The Print Room at the British Museum contains several examples of royal industry: water-colours, lithographs, mezzotints and etchings, including the original sketch of a little girl with a bundle of faggots on her head which afterwards figured as 'The Wood Girl' in a series called 'The Seasons'. In all these the execution is amateurish, but they are not devoid of intelligence and imagination. In artistic matters she was the product of her age. Dimpled infants teem upon her drawing paper, and her notepaper was embossed with doves, quivers and similar devices. Her seal bore an arrow and the motto *Je blesse en secret*.

In 1804, inspired by the patriotic fervour of the time, she 'designed' twelve plates, engraved (and perhaps touched up) by W. N. Gardner, and 'illustrated' with verse by the earnest Mr Thomas Parke, FSA. Here we see Cupid supplicating Minerva to let him become a British Volunteer, taking the oath of allegiance before the altar of loyalty, doing musketry practice, beating a drum, and finally depositing his banner in the temple of Minerva. As an example of Mr Parke's poetical fervour the first stanza may serve:

> Rous'd by the threat which rouses all
>   To arm in Albion's patriot cause,
> The vaunting threat of frantic Gaul
>   That she will pare the lion's paws,
> And with her locust-band despoil
>   Britain, the heav'n protected isle!
> Thus rous'd, e'en Love, the archer-boy
>   Who wings Idalian-tempered darts
> Which, while they wound, give wounds of joy,
>   And only pierce to rivet hearts,
> Love drops the bandage from his brow
>   That he may face this threatful foe;
> He spurns at every boyish fear,
>   And the sage goddess of the gorgon shield
> Implores to let him try to wield
>   The weapons of a *British Volunteer*!

The drawings are worthy of a more grammatical and less incoherent commentary; some of them are charming, especially the frontispiece, which shows two cupids supporting the fur-trimmed headgear of the Volunteers. The Princess was never well served by her librettists.

For the Jubilee of 1809, celebrated upon the threshold of the King's final breakdown, his gifted third daughter again enlisted the aid of her favourite *putti*, this time to flourish roses, shamrocks, and thistles instead of muskets and flags. Three years earlier had appeared *A Series of Etchings Representing the Power and Progress of Genius*, dedicated to the Queen and signed *Eliza invent & sculp*[t.] The subsequent history of these productions is curious. A new edition appeared in Hanover in 1833, lithographed (not etched) by J. Gieze, the eighteen plates having been '*gezeichnet*' by J. H. Ramberg, '*nach Entwürfin Ihrer Königlichen Höheit der verwitwetten Frau Landgräfin von Hesse-Homburg, Geboren Prinzessin von England*'. In the same year the lithographs were issued again, under the title of *Genius, Imagination, Phantasie, Ein Bilder und Sonnetten Kranz*, dedicated, not by Princess Elizabeth but by Minna Witte, the poetess who provided the sonnets, to Adolphus, Duke of Cambridge and Viceroy of

Hanover—*Digno Gubernaculus* he is called on his medallion portrait. In a facsimile letter to her brother the Landgravine writes:

> Mademoiselle Minna Witte . . . kindly has made the sonnets to each print from the Original, which was (tho' intended for both our adored Parents) dedicated to our invaluable mother. Wishing to be of some trifling use to the Town of Hanover, the Native Land of our Family, I took courage to employ Mr Ramberg (who travelled under the auspices of our Father) to ixert [*sic*] his wonderful genius in improving what was originally done merely for the amusement of the moment. . . . Your own manner of acting has served me as an example to throw my *Widow's Mite* into the general Poor Box.

Mr Ramberg, with nicely balanced ruthlessness and tact, transmuted the amateur etchings into smooth lithographs, and Minna Witte (later Frau Maedler), a poetess so obscure that *Meyers Lexikon* will have none of her, adorned them with Petrarchan sonnets which, if not of the first quality, are at least less absurd than the meanderings of Mr Parke, FSA.

The rather strained allegory shows how two sisters, Fancy and Imagination, find a baby—Genius—in a laurel grove, and, not without difficulty, bring up and educate him, at the same time giving rise to the arts of poetry, music, sculpture, and to such useful inventions as the boat, the windmill, and the plough. Fräulein Witte thus describes these sisters in her opening lines:

> Entsprungen aus dem Urquell ew'gen Güte,
>   Bergrüsset mit Himmelslächeln, mild und klar,
>   Die Welt ein holder Zwillings Schwesterpaar
>   Sich ähnlich wie die Blätter einer Blüthe.

Interpolated explanatory matter, in English, is expanded from the brief notes which accompanied the original etchings. We are informed that

> The Frontispiece represents the Homage of the Arts, Poetry, Music, Sculpture and Painting, descending from Heaven, placing themselves before the bust of George III, who was ever their Protector. Charity joins them, begs to be admitted, and is supposed to say to them, 'Those beloved and valued features, which you have by your talents imprinted on the world, are by me stamped upon all hearts.'

Three years later another edition of the original etchings appeared in England, and an autographed copy presented by the artist to her niece, the Princess Victoria, is in the royal library at Windsor.

Let us go back to the month of October 1810, when H. D. Thielcke published an oblong volume of plates bearing no general title, but dedicated, 'by Permission', to Queen Charlotte. These are six in number, and show, in the would-be-classical style of the period, the Father's Return; Faith and Charity; Pleasures of Childhood; Affection and Pleasure; The Warrior's Tale; Resting after Travelling. These are the engravings alluded to in the title of William Combe's *Six Poems Illustrative of Engravings by HRH the Princess Elizabeth*. The name of the author of Dr Syntax does not however appear in the edition published in 1813 by R. Ackermann, who in his foreword observes:

> The following series of engravings was originally published by Mr H. Thielcke without any Illustration. But as they are now come into my possession I am influenced by the Beauty of the Designs, the Interest of the Subjects, and the profound Respect due to the Royal Personage whose superior Taste and leisure Hours produced them to republish the whole with original and appropriate verse.

The verse, considering the feeble character of the engravings, was indeed appropriate, as witness these lines from 'The Warrior's Tale':

> To arms, to arms, the hero flew;
> No soft repose the hero knew.
> His dauntless heart, 'mid martial storms,
> Sought danger in its direst forms.

It is startling to read in the *Dictionary of National Biography* that Princess Elizabeth' collaborated' with Combe, who spent the last forty-three years of his life mostly within the rules of the King's Bench debtors' prison.

Bound up in the same volume with the six engravings as published by Thielcke there is, in the royal library at Windsor, another series without title, brought out by the same publisher on 1 December 1816. These bland and woolly prints represent Pylades and Orestes before a rose-decked urn, 'the tomb of Agamemnon' (there is a coloured version of this in the British Museum); Plato when a Child, with the traditional swarm of bees hovering over him; a Family escaping, gracefully, from a Fire; a Roman Lady showing her Jewels to the Mother of the Gracchi; and the Curiosity of Aglaura and Herse.

Painting, engraving, and japanning were not the only resources of the Muse, as Elizabeth was called by the Family. 'I have', she wrote to Miss Madeleine de Soyres, great-niece of Mademoiselle de Montmollin, 'the prettiest little tiny cottage which joins my own garden and field', at Frogmore. In the grounds of this toy dwelling she loved to give *fêtes champêtres* in honour of birthdays and other anniversaries, and in her toy farm she nurtured a breed of especially succulent pigs. Friends, headed by the Prince of Wales, sent her various objects for the adornment of the place, and 'beautifull bell-ropes' from Miss de Soyres were welcomed, because they would 'look so very pretty at the cottage'. It seems to have been the daughters, not the sons, of Farmer George who inherited his bucolic instincts. Writing on behalf of the Queen to Lady Mary Pelham, daughter of Lady Holdernesse, the Princess said that, as her Majesty

> understands that the physical people have allowed Lady Holdernesse to eat anything She likes, She has ordered two Pigs which have been born and bred at Frogmore to be sent up by tomorrow morning's early stage for her. She flatters herself that dear Lady Holdernesse will like them; you may laugh, my dear Lady Mary, but I am not a little proud of receiving this commission from Mama, for the farm is my Hobby Horse . . . the Pigs are of the Chinese breed, which makes them look so small.

All the Family, except its august Head, took a hearty German interest in the pleasures of the table, and some of them suffered accordingly; as when Princess Elizabeth wrote to the Prince of Wales, 'I was taken exceedingly ill in the night, violently sick, and so swelled that they think I must have been poisoned, and that owing to a remarkable large lobster which I had eat of at supper'.[w] Harriet, Countess Granville, gives us an engaging glimpse of Princess Augusta in 1820, 'good humoured and jolly, stuffing *filets de sole* and veal cutlets', and the ailing Princess Amelia was able to enjoy green peas and panada of chicken to the last.[w]

It does not appear that the Muse made any 'cuttings' to celebrate the marriage of her eldest brother to Princess Caroline of Brunswick, but, acting as the Queen's secretary, she helped in the preparations, and gave directions that royal guests were to have silver favours, and the officers of the Household white trimmed with silver. 'I give you my honour,' she wrote to the Prince,' my mind has been quite tortured about you, for your happiness I have so much at heart that you are scarcely ever out of my mind I beg that if you are ever in want of a friend that you will remember the corner room at the Queen's House'.[w] When the ill-assorted union cracked he may have remembered, for it was Princess Elizabeth whom he chose as his messenger to the Queen in the hour of crisis.

At the outset relations between Princess Caroline and the Sisterhood had been cordial enough, though it is significant that in a letter to his father written after the separation the Prince of Wales accused his wife of 'odious endeavours to vitiate the principles of his innocent sisters'.[w] Princess Elizabeth seems to have been rather a favourite, and Caroline made a point of writing to wish her joy upon her birthday, which fell in the May following the marriage. This letter of hers, even if disingenuous, belies her later allegations that during the first months of her married life 'the only woman apart from herself was Lady Jersey', and that the men were blackguard companions of the Prince, 'sleeping and snoring in boots on the sofa'. This is what she wrote to Princess Elizabeth on 23 May 1795:

Ma charmante sœur, je me trouve bien contente et heureuse à la campagne, et nous faisons tout ce que nous pouvons pour ne pas nous ennuyer. Je ne monte plus à cheval cependant, le Pr nous mène en voiture ouverte, ce qui me fait grand plaisir.[(w)]

A curious statement coming from anyone so outspoken as Princess Caroline, especially if, as she afterwards declared, her husband was at that time treating her with cruelty, forcing her to smoke a pipe, and denying that her unborn child could be his.

It is Lady Carnarvon, not Lady Jersey, who is the snake in the grass. Princess Caroline has '*beaucoup de choses*' to tell her sister-in-law concerning this lady's efforts to make trouble between her and '*le Pr*'; and she goes on:

J'ai pris le parti de lui en parler immédiatement pour prevenir les suites, et votre Cher l'a traité avec la même bonté qui lui est naturelle pour tout le monde.[(w)]

Surely not written ironically? Princess Elizabeth sent a copy of the letter, and a copy of her discreet reply, to her brother on 24 May, together with some comments which sound strangely in our ears, so long habituated to Caroline's later description of these early days of her marriage:

I am extremely happy that you have taken no notice of the extraordinary conduct of Lady C. to *my sister*. I think the latter has showed herself in a very *amiable point of view*, and if she goes on in everything as she has acted in this [I] think you must be pleased & as I am more anxious about your happiness and your feelling more comfortable in your mind than you have done, I must say this has given me pleasure, as it shews the Princess to have an open character, which is a very necessary *virtue* in her situation, & I trust will prove a comfort to you. I really must do her the justice to say that she spoke very openly to all parties concerning her present happiness, & wishes that it should be told, which is very pleasant for us and particular for myself to hear, & having the appearance of perfect good temper I flatter myself that you will have her turn out a very comfortable little wife.[(w)]

Two months later Princess Elizabeth met Lord and Lady Carnarvon on the Terrace, when her ladyship 'enquired much after the Princess and how she was going on. I was most happy', adds the loyal sister, 'in having it in my power to say she was both *comfortable* and *going on well*, which I said as loud as I could.'[(w)] When Lord Glenbervie sat next Lady Carnarvon at dinner at the Bishop of Cashel's in 1797, he noted that she 'asked a thousand questions on delicate subjects', as her custom was. At a later date she became Lady of the Bedchamber to the Princess whose honeymoon she had endeavoured to mar.

In January 1796 the Family were anxiously awaiting the arrival of the child concerning whose paternity they, at least, seem to have felt no uncertainty. 'When at Frogmore', wrote Princess Elizabeth to her brother, 'the House Bell makes me jump and fly to the window, in hopes of being the person to bring news of the happy event to Mama, who thinks much of you, for we are sure you are upon the *high fidgets*, walking about the room, pulling your fingers and very anxious'.[w] The baby was welcomed with delight by all her relatives, not least by the King, who not only drank her health at dinner on the night of her birth, but also 'went into the Equerries' room and made them drink it in a bumper'.[w]

Six months later all pretence of harmony at Carlton House was at an end. In a letter probably written towards the middle of 1796, Princess Elizabeth said to the Prince of Wales:

> You may easily conceive, my beloved Brother, the distress and misery your letter occasioned in my breast this morning on reading the contents which indeed is *shocking* adding no other words to agravate your distress of mind. Before 8 o'clock I gave it to Mama, who desires me to say with her kind and affectionate love that she will do everything that lays in her power to serve you when the King tells it her, but that you well know there are many things that she cannot say she knows, as she thinks the bounds of *Decency* should never be put aside even between Man & Wife. . . .
>
> Mama thinks she knows the K so well that She is full persuaded he will be against an open rupture if *he* does anything.[w]

An open rupture, or, as Elizabeth preferred to call it, a 'resignation', was soon perceived to be inevitable. 'We are one and all very miserable about you', she told the Prince in June 1796, and she kept him *au courant* with the comings and goings of Ernest and William, who were apparently pleading the cause of their eldest brother with the alarmed and slightly resentful King. The three elder Princesses were in a state of dismay at this crisis in the life of the Heir Apparent, though they derived pleasure, chequered with pain, from the sight of his 'beloved infant'. At the New Year, 1797, Princess Elizabeth wrote to him, 'If my poor prayers are granted you would never have a moment's uneasiness, and was it in my power my broad back should ease you of your afflictions'.[w]

On Charlotte's first birthday her aunts gave her a variety of gifts. From the Princess Royal she received a necklace; from Princess Augusta a pair of bracelets; from Princess Mary a doll; from Princess Sophia a silver rattle; from Princess Amelia a fan; and from Princess Elizabeth a Chinese toy. Each aunt in her own way was devoted to the child, and they combined to keep alive that fatherly interest which the good-natured Prince of Wales could not but feel before his wife and her friends began to use her as a goad with which to torment him. 'I flatter myself', said Princess Elizabeth to Fanny Burney—then Madame d'Arblay—'that Aunt Libby, as she calls me, is a great favourite with her'. And there is a charming glimpse of the baby, in a letter from that particular aunt, dated 'Weymouth, August 2, 1797':

> I must tell you an anecdote of Charlotte which has amused me much. When she goes to Bed she always says, 'bless Papa, Mama, Charlotte & friends', but having been cruelly bit by fleas the foregoing night instead of *friends* she introduced *Fleas* into her prayer. Lady Elgin being told of it, she said we must make her say *friends*. Miss Hayman, with much humour, answered, 'Why, Madam, you know we are told to pray for our enemies, and surely the Fleas are the only ones HRH has'.[w]

And again, in a letter written at Windsor in March 1798:

> She behaved like an angel yesterday and shew'd such pleasure and thankfulness on the King's giving her a very large Rocking Horse, we all were hurt you was not present to see her dear little happy Countenance.[w]

II

It might have been supposed that Princess Elizabeth, having so many resources in herself, would be less irked than her sisters by their existence, but she chafed more than all the rest, and never seems to have lost sight of her objective, marriage. On 3 August 1804, she wrote to her 'dearest G.P.' that she could conceive no joy equal to that of seeing those one loves made happy, and added:

> I believe we feel that sort of thing more than many people from knowing it so little ourselves—it may in the long run be of use to us, but do not say I have said this—a time may come when—but no, I better hold my tongue—why plague You! There is no use in it. I am certain You will ever be a true friend. Burn this pray—but I am too sincere not to grow sometimes a little imprudent, particularly when writing to a person I love as sincerely as I do You.(w)

In September, 1808, she wrote:

> We go on much as usual, very quietly, as You know—vegetating. . . . I have begun my early walks at eight in the morning for the sake of not losing the use of my legs—for as all my amusements keep me at my desk & not having a famous head, I always think of poor Genl Goldsworthy, who used to say 'I fear a visit from Poll', meaning an apoplexy. However, since this wise determination of mine it has pleased God to send a perpetual rain for the last four or five days, yet it has not disturbed my temper, which I try to keep good by drinking sugar & water at night, never touching vinegar, which I hate. For You are sensible that it requires not only a great flow of spirits to follow up a day's duty (which however I really ever wish to do with pleasure) but a degree of submission which seldom falls to the lot of any but a *R.H.* which, to make You smile, I tell you a *secret* is the *Cannister to my tail*, but that is for yourself, for these truths don't do at Court, but when scribbling to You I blow all my stiffness away, and write *comme une bourgeoise*, or why may I not say the Cottager, whose comforts have been so much owing to your unparalleled kindness. I agree with the old song, 'It is good to be merry and wise', & how many people think Wisdom consists in swallowing a poker! (w)

The Princess begs that her brother, in answering this letter, will 'allude to nothing of all this', as a letter from him always provokes questions, and if he has anything private to say he had better send 'a little enclosure'.

But the Prince's friendship went beyond listening to her laments and sending her comforts for her cottage. On 25 September 1808, she wrote to him at great length concerning a scheme which appears in the first instance to have emanated from the Duke of Kent:

> . . . at the moment it is better to state facts than to plague you with expressions of affection: . . . having heard that a *letter* of *confidence* has been written to *You on my Subject* by a person who shall be *nameless*—on Thursday I was asked whether I knew *this*, and if my Brothers had spoke to me—the whole detail You will see in a letter enclosed which Augusta gives my mother to-day. All I beg is that You will not think me impertinent, childish or silly in what I have done, for I had flattered myself that from my constant steady attendance upon my Mother, with my natural openness of character, I had hoped she would have had confidence in me at my time of life, but finding alas to my grief that was not the case I thought it more honourable by *her* and just towards myself to let her know I was *not ignorant* of what had passed, with my sentiments and feelings upon it. If there is no possibility of the thing *now*, I only *entreat of You* as the person, both from *inclination, Duty and affection* we *must* look up to, that You will not dash the Cup of Happiness from my lips. Yet believe me, whatever I may feel at present, and flattered at having been thought of, if I did not hope I flatter myself I might make them happy I would not think of it, and being without any soul near them that might worry & plague on the *Score of Religion* I do not fear it, for You know I hate meddling, have no turn for Gossiping and being *firm to my own faith* I shall not plague them upon theirs.
>
> I hope this proof of confidence to my Brother will not give offence, but should it, promise me your present support and your *future protection*. You shall never see an ill-humoured look or anything to offend *here*, and I faithfully promise that however I have been *wounded* that I will with *pleasure continue* my *attentions* towards *her* as if nothing had happened.
>
> I only hope You remember that You ordered me if I had anything upon my mind to tell it you, and You solemnly promised me to keep it to yourself. So pray say not a word to your companion, for no soul knows anything of it here but Augusta and Sophia. You know sweet dear Mary is most amiable, but I have not breathed it for fear of its coming out *elsewhere*. But all that when we meet You shall know.
>
> *Burn this*, and send me back the enclosed which Augusta has copied as I was so worried that at last I hardly knew one letter from another. And all I wish You is a *shewable* to ask me if my Mother has not told me, which at my age

you supposed she had—if You do that it will prove to Her that we all think alike.—

   Yrs very affe

E.

We are all well. Direct your letter under cover to my maid Miss Brawn, Windsor Castle.[w]

With this letter is another, endorsed 'to be read last', from which it is plain that Queen Charlotte's reactions to the subject were what might have been expected; but the Prince of Wales had no intention of waiting—if he could help it—until he had the power to grant his sister's wish. He alone of Queen Charlotte's children could manage her, and persuade her to rescind some of her apparently immutable decrees. From the next letter in this group—dated October 2, 1808—it is clear that, while urging Princess Elizabeth to be patient a little longer, he had expressed his willingness to continue the negotiations with the mysterious 'them'. And now we get a clue as to 'their' identity. The plural pronoun is merely the royal 'we' transferred to the third person, and the candidate is none other than Louis Philippe, Duke of Orleans, whom the Duke of Kent had met in exile in Canada in 1794–95. Despite his own chronic impecuniosity, the English Duke had lent the impoverished French one £200, 'to eke out his salary as an American schoolmaster'; and the friendship thus inaugurated had continued when in 1800 Louise Philippe came to England and established himself in an unassuming manner at Twickenham. The Duke of Kent even had a special bedroom furnished for him at Kensington Palace, and on Christmas Day 1807 he and Madame St Laurent entertained him to dinner at the house which he had taken for Madame in Knightsbridge.

Here obviously is the 'D—— of O——' to whom Princess Elizabeth refers in her next letter:

October 2, 1808

My Dearest Brother,

No words can ever express what I feel towards you for your unbounded goodness to me—you have eased my mind beyond belief, and I trust my conduct will ever be such that Your good opinion of me may never change.

I own this has been the wish of my heart *so long* and *my esteem has been gaining ground for so many years that it has* truly *been my prayer*—therefore I feel that Providence has done *more for me* than I deserved and merit, and all I wished was your *friendly attention to my petition* and that you *would but say* be *prudent* and *silent,* and I trust happiness may yet be your lot that you have said, so *with* that I am on my knees with gratitude, and what promise you make *me* must be *secreted* in *my own heart,* and *that* you may depend on.

When I wrote I was in such an agony of mind no poor wretch was or has been more miserable than I have, yet if I told You there had been a coldness between the Madre and me it was *not the case*, but all I wished was that she had named it, that I might have acted by her with the degree of honesty . . . I thought she would have desired, which was, 'let me accept it'—but never mention it whilst life is preserved to us. Do You think, my dear Brother, I would have wished it brought forward, after all I have seen? Good God, no—and I think that by the whole manner of the D—— of O——'s conduct they would have agreed to what *may be* unfortunate *to us* but which will make everything *couleur de rose* afterwards, by considering my *Father* before Ourselves. I said that day on which my Mother spoke with me You shall never see a wry face and believe me she never shall, for I have gone on just the same and will do so to the last, for without being a *perfect* good Daughter I *never* can *make a good wife*.[w]

Princess Elizabeth is not going to say a word of this letter, or of his, to which it is a reply, to anybody but Augusta. 'The others' knew that she had written, and she begs him to convey to them how sensible she is of their affectionate anxiety. They were all sure, she declares, that he would 'never put a negative' to what had really been her earnest desire ever since it was mentioned to her. The 'others' are Princess Mary and Princess Sophia. Princess Amelia, already sick unto death and painfully preoccupied with her own unhappy love affair, was left out, 'from delicacy'. The letter continues:

Mary has written to beg You to see her before You go *elsewhere*. She has been most angelical, but Augusta has really stood forward nobly for me, in short, I cannot say enough *for all*. Sophy also, for the state I was in made them see I was all but wild, and they have behaved so very amiably that I hope You will express your approbation. The reason why not a word has been said to the youngest was from delicacy, which I will explain when we meet, but Mary must see You, for the Madre has dreaded my saying a word to any of my Brothers, and I said if they spoke to me, which I would almost swear they would, I should to them, and therefore You must manage seeing me before Her—and many things I will then tell You which determined me at once to say I would *never give it up*—for it was hinted many, many things had been brought forward and rejected without a word from us, and therefore we all felt the Sun of our Days was set—if You are only kind and good as You have always been and ease my mind and one other person's, *Mum* will be the word of the day. . . . [w]

'One other person' was, of course, the 'D—— of O——': and he, too, is the 'person in question' of the closing paragraph:

You have delighted *me* with all you have said of the person in question, for I believe them everything that is good, attached to You and all their family, and their character has never varied, and that has ever pleased and delighted me. Volumes would not suffice to express what I feel towards You, and You may be certain that I never can be thankful enough for your advice and all that your invaluable letter contains.—Yr affe

E. (w)

Nine days later Princess Elizabeth is still sufficiently sanguine to write to her brother concerning her suitor's anxiety as to the legal status of any children born to them, from which it would appear that some sort of private marriage was in contemplation, otherwise 'the least doubt' could not have arisen upon this subject. It did not seem at that time as if Louis Philippe would ever come to the French throne; Napoleon was almost at the peak of his power, and a Bourbon restoration, actually a mere six years distant, seemed remote and improbable. The Duke of Orleans, in any event, was not the next heir, as the future Louis XVIII and Charles X stood nearer in the line of succession. Concern as to the legitimacy of his children was therefore a personal rather than a dynastic sentiment, and Princess Elizabeth's anxiety that the subject should be frankly discussed by him and her brother was made keener by her knowledge that Louis Philippe was on the eve of quitting England.

November 3, 1808

. . . I beg you will not think me tiresome or troublesome in again writing upon the subject *nearest* my heart—but I think it right to inform you that in consequence of Edward's having seen the D. of O. and mentioned the kind manner in which you had spoken to me, of wh. he acquainted him by your permission, *He wishes*, in justice to Himself as well as out of delicacy to me, that you would merely insure the legitimation of children should there be any—for that subject, once clearly decided upon His mind will be at ease, whereas if the least doubt should arise, as to their legal situation, He should feel that he was *scandalizing* the world, ruining me, and entailing misery on his children, all of which he is certain your good Heart would revolt at.

I must now make one request to You—from myself, which is that you would send for Him before He goes, and not feel shy in talking the Subject that once over with Him—for of course it must be an ease to his mind as well as to mine to hear what You have said to me from your own mouth, and that he would swear never to reveal what passes.

I think it right to tell You that in examining the business more closely I find no marriage whatever can be looked upon as valid without the sovereign's consent, which alone makes the law.(w)

Whether this obstacle proved insurmountable is not clear. Two months later Princess Elizabeth, with the concurrence of the Duke of Cambridge, was borrowing £4,000 from the Prince of Wales, and in March 1809 she was sending a message through him to someone who was probably Louis Philippe, and 'would like to know how it was taken'. But after that a curtain falls between her and the portly Frenchman who, with his simple domestic tastes, might have made her so excellent a husband; and on 25 November 1809, the Duke of Orleans was married to Marie-Amélie, daughter of Ferdinand, King of the two Sicilies.

Twenty-eight years later, when Elizabeth was a widow and her quondam suitor was sitting, not too comfortably, upon the throne of France, she had the generosity to speak of Marie-Amélie as an angel, and to say of the French King, 'His greatest misfortune is having been the Son of a Monster; and that is his misery, and he wisely never will utter a word which he ought not, but his conduct has been perfect since he has been where he is'. As she mused by her German fireside, 'which is, tho' lonely, very comfortable', the Dowager Landgravine must surely have reflected sometimes that but for the obduracy of Queen Charlotte she might herself then have been sharing the throne of France. She did not live to see one of Louis Philippe's daughters the wife of Charlotte's widowed husband Leopold of Coburg; and she had lain eight years in her German grave when the King of France, with his whiskers shaved off and wearing huge goggles, took refuge for a third time upon the hospitable shores of England.

In 1810 Princess Elizabeth still dreamed of having a home of her own, but the dream is now of a spinster existence, in which the outstanding male figure will be that of her eldest brother, to whom she wrote in the summer of 1810:

> Whenever it pleases God to grant me a *chez moi* I will certainly have *un bon table* in hopes of Your being one at *the board*, when You are sure of being the *most* agreeable Guest in every sense of the word—mais le bon tems *not* coming and yet time going on I fear all my bright Castles in the air (which have so entirely failed in this world and left I fear a deep scar *not to be effaced* tho' *smothered* in my *own breast*) are nearly at an end, if not quite so . . . I have been well tried in my *Spring* and *Summer of life*; I expect my Autumn and Winter to be free from chilling cold, and whilst I have kind and good friends, a Great chair, a pinch of Snuff, a Book, and a good Fireside, with a *kind Brother* I think I shall in the end rest very quietly.[w]

The remark about 'a pinch of Snuff' is a curious epilogue to what this Princess said to Fanny Burney in 1786, 'I hope you hate Snuff? I hope you do, for I hate it of all things in the world.'

In the same month that witnessed the nuptials of Louis Philippe and Marie-Amélie—November 1809—Princess Amelia returned from Weymouth to

Windsor to die. Caroline of Wales, who had long forgotten the affection she had once felt for her *charmante sœur*, wrote to Lady Charlotte Bury:

> I heard the other day from a lady who lives a good deal at Court, and with courtiers, that a most erroneous opinion is formed in general of the Princess E., and this is exemplified in her conduct to the poor Princess A., who is dying. ....
> The Princess M. and S. are devoted to her, but Princess E. treats her with the most cruel unkindness and ill-temper.

Princess Elizabeth may have been the least sympathetic of the Sisterhood, and Amelia may have been right in regarding her as the Queen's adherent in the struggle which raged between the youngest Princess and her mother during the years 1809-10. But it was Princess Elizabeth who gave a memorial engraving of Princess Amelia, in an ebony frame surmounted by a gilt coronet to Mr Battiscombe, the Windsor apothecary who often figures in the correspondence, and who walked in Amelia's funeral procession; and sixteen years later it was Elizabeth who wrote 'the loss of a sister I know too well how to feel'.

Princess Amelia at Weymouth in 1809, sick in body and in heart, certainly entertained no very affectionate feelings towards her third sister. 'Don't tell the Queen', she wrote to the Prince of Wales on the eve of her return to Windsor, 'that I can feel any pleasure in seeing her, for I can't, and Eliza some day or other shall hear my mind.'(w)

Elizabeth betrays no consciousness of this mood of Amelia's in any letter written at this period, and there is an unwontedly tender note in her words to Lady Harcourt when the poor King sank again into madness after Amelia's death. Against hope the remaining members of the Sisterhood were hoping that when the first violence of sorrow had spent itself their father's mind might recover its poise.

> Aggrivating subjects have been the causes of his former illnesses; this one is owing to the overflowing of his heart for his youngest and dearest Child, a child who had never caused him a pang and who he literally doted on.

She trusts that all who love the King 'will but give us time', and the same note is struck in the letter written to Mrs Adams, the devoted nurse of Princess Mary and friend of the Family on 16December in the same year. The 'events of the day in town' were keeping them all 'in a fever'; but 'if the worst should happen', she would humbly submit, 'still looking up to heaven for comfort'. The 'events' were the Parliamentary debates on the sovereign's mental condition, and 'the worst' was the setting-up the Regency.

However well we understand the reluctance of George III's womenkind to see him superseded in his lifetime by the eldest son who had caused him so much distress, it is curious that the Princess should have dreaded the step which led to her emancipation from her long bondage to Queen Charlotte, and indirectly to the 'settlement' round which she had built her 'bright castles in the air'.

'Your kind intentions towards us', wrote Princess Elizabeth to the Prince Regent in January 1812, 'is en-graven on my heart, and though I do not expect to be happy, believe me, I shall be content'.[w] The 'kind intentions' were mainly financial, and their fulfilment has been related in Princess Augusta's chapter, where Queen Charlotte's own account of Princess Elizabeth's behaviour during the domestic crisis of December 1812 is also given. Concerning what her mother had called her 'hysterick fit', the Princess then wrote to her brother:

> As the Queen has mentioned the seizure I had I think it right to state that it was of that kind to give me *serious alarm*, and I own fairly I look forward to what I had always thought with horror of a sudden death—but I trust in God's mercy my future conduct may be such that if it pleases the Almighty to end me thus I may be in that state of mind that may make me deserving of happiness in another world which for many years I have not experienced in this.[w]

Later in the same letter she exclaims, 'I own the blow of being thought unfeeling and wanting in duty to the King haunts me', and she speaks of parting from the Queen and settling in her cottage, 'for I really feel I could not bear our present daily affliction; with her constant look of dissatisfaction'.

Like the rest of the Sisterhood, Princess Elizabeth was convinced that the Prince Regent was largely responsible for the course of events in Russia which he used so adroitly to sweeten the temper of the Queen. 'You have certainly', she wrote to him in November 1813, '*sans flatterie*, put your Shoulder to the Plough!' And with a fine 'derangement of epitaphs' she ejaculated seven months later, 'The Monster dethroned is quite a *balm to our hearts*'.[w]

The Princess became more cheerful as the years passed. When the Dowager Lady Harcourt paid a visit to her royal friends in January 1814 it was inevitable that her presence should awake memories, as well as reviving hopes. 'She comes', writes Princess Elizabeth,

> and sets with me of a morning—we build castles in the air which amuse us, or rather she builds them for me, and when she has worked my imagination to the summit of bliss I still find myself in my own room, by my own fireside, with my comforts around me, for which I am thankful, but I don't disown that like an infant my card-house is fallen to the ground.[w]

Relations between the Princess and her mother were so good in the autumn of 1817 that when the Queen was ordered to try the Bath waters for her *estomac*, it was she who went with her. It was a strange season for Queen Charlotte to be far from London, with her granddaughter's confinement expected at any hour. Indeed, if Croker is to be believed, there was a certain amount of comment, as it was felt that a lady so experienced in such matters might well have been of use to her granddaughter, and ought to have remained within call at Windsor, even if she did not actually establish herself at Claremont.

She and Princess Elizabeth, however, stayed at 93 Sydney Place, Bath, and there, just as the elder Charlotte was having her diamonds adjusted 'for the reception of the Mayor and Corporation' they received the news that the younger Charlotte's labour had begun. Characteristically the Queen decided to go through with the reception, and both she and Princess Elizabeth were 'a blaze of jewels' when the City Fathers bowed before them.

The next intelligence that reached Bath was that the child had been born dead. Princess Elizabeth's account of what happened when the news of the young mother's death arrived is an interesting pendant to Princess Augusta's description of how Brent Spencer broke the news at Windsor:

> . . . just after we had set down to dinner, at six, Gen. Taylor was asked out. Our hearts misgave us, he sent out for Lady Ilchester, which gave us a moment for to be sure that something dreadful had happened; the moment he came in my mother said, *I am sure it is over*, and he desired her to go upstairs.

With remarkable fortitude, considering her age and the state of her health, the Queen hurried back to Windsor; but by 24 November she and Princess Elizabeth were again in Bath, with the Duke of Clarence, staying a few doors away.

On the morrow of their return to Sydney Place the Princess wrote to the Prince Regent:

> . . . after the dreadful blow you have had we greatly fear that you will not so readily get the better of it—the suddenness of the event stunned me—it is afterwards that it will work upon the feelings, and knowing Your heart I tremble lest You should be seriously ill—but I hope now that You are at Brighton that You will begin Your riding, for there is nothing like air when one is in affliction.[w]

She tells him that she has kept back thirty or forty letters of condolence from various people, including one from the Dowager Princess of Orange, mother of Princess Charlotte's one-time suitor, because 'there is no use in tearing open so recent a wound'.[w]

With what anxious haste the Family fell to discussing the dynastic repercussions of the event is shown by Princess Elizabeth's letters from Bath only a month later. The question of finding wives for Princes William and Adolphus was already on the *tapis*. The Queen, says her daughter, will talk to William':

But she is quite convinced he will never run the chance of such a thing without being sure that his large family will be provided for, and when his mind is eased in feeling that he can make them comfortable he will rejoice (as I have often heard him say) in having a companion who, he trusts, will make his home what he wishes it to be.[w]

Very creditable to William. But the Princess could little imagine, as she sat driving her pen over the black-edged paper that winter morning in Bath, that in the matrimonial rush the following summer the first marriage would be her own.

On 28 January 1818, the Princess received a letter which the next morning she showed to the Queen, before confiding it to Princess Mary to forward to the Prince Regent. 'I give you my word of honour', wrote Mary, 'not one of us have been in Eliza's confidence (if she did not know of it), for she has *declared* to Augusta, Sophia and me on her *word of honour* it was as great a surprize to herself as it was to us'.[w] Why Princess Elizabeth should not herself have sent this exciting letter to the Prince Regent is not clear, for she wrote to him at great length and its purport is stated in her opening words:

My Dear Brother,

I received last night after my letter was closed to You one from Count Münster informing me of the Hereditary Prince of Hesse-Homburg's arrival, and his purpose of coming here to ask me in marriage. You may easily conceive the sort of flurry it through [*sic*] me into. I instantly went to Augusta and Mary, and we agreed that I must instantly inform the Queen of it in the morning, which I did before my sisters. She answered, upon my reading the letter, 'You always wished to settle and have always said that you thought a Woman might be happier and more comfortable in having a home'.

I answer [*sic*] I have ever thought so, and add that a time may come when I shall bless God for a home. In our situation there is nothing but character to look to, and Count Münster says that the Prince's is excellent. I therefore candidly own I wish to accept this offer. I am no longer young, and fairly feel that having my own home will be a comfort in time, tho' it causes me a degree of pang which I feel *deeply*—more than I have words to express—but God knows our lives have been lives of *trial* and ever will be so. I have tried to the utmost of my power to do my Duty as a daughter and sister. I pray the Almighty to strengthen me in those of a *wife*: for did I not feel that I should in every sense *try* to make my husband happy you may depend upon it that I should think myself very wrong were I to wish to change my situation.[w]

She mentions that the Queen had told her that the Prince of Hesse-Homburg 'had proposed some years ago for one of us' (this was the proposal of 1804, when only Princess Augusta was named); but she does not mention, perhaps she did not know, that he had come to London in 1814, with the Allied Sovereigns, when he probably had a glimpse of both of them.

On the same day—28 January 1818—that this letter was written, Lord Castlereagh wrote to the Prince Regent that he felt it was his duty to apprize his Royal Highness confidentially that he had just been made acquainted with the arrival in London of the Prince of Hesse-Homburg 'for the purpose of soliciting *the hand* of the Princess Elizabeth'. No tentative negotiations can have been made through the normal diplomatic channels, for the Foreign Secretary is evidently surprised, and expects the Regent to be the same. The wooer had probably been warned by some well-wisher that unless he went secretly and rapidly to work the obstructive tactics of the old Queen would bring everything to naught.

It was perhaps natural that Princess Elizabeth should have steeled herself against her mother's tears, but Queen Charlotte was so visibly breaking up that it is difficult to understand how her daughter could have found it in her heart to leave her at that last hour. The soft-hearted Mary reported that the Queen was 'really overcome and crying dreadfully', but Count Münster, who was Hanoverian Minister at the Court of St James's, had done his preliminary work well, and we find the elder Princess writing firmly:

> After all Count Münster said of the Prince of Hesse's character I cannot but think myself most fortunate. He kindly told my mother this, which Augusta repeated to me, and after a long conversation with her (who had been all kindness), she said 'look at the bright side of the measure, and don't you kill yourself with pining over my mother's manner. It is hard upon you, but tell my Brother that he must a little prepare the P. of H. for fear of her not receiving him well—that my mother is a spoilt child, for my father spoilt her from the hour she came, and we have continued doing so from the hour of our birth, and she is vexed that she cannot manage this her own way. 'I am sure you will smooth and soften her.[w]

Both Princess Augusta and Princess Mary were kindness itself to their agitated sister, though the younger Princess did write to the Regent that when she 'reflected the manner in which the whole had been carried out', it really went to her soul; and added that 'Eliza and the Queen would be *better parted*'.[w] It was probably this conviction which prompted her to intervene on behalf of 'H.H.', whom she met at the Opera, full of gratitude for the Prince's kindness but '*much hurt at the Q.'s manner*'. He also 'went out of his way to say he *hated writing*' but hoped that the Prince would 'make the Q. see the necessity of his seeing Eliza'.[w]

Alone of all the daughters of George III Princess Elizabeth—'Sally Blunt' as she sometimes called herself—was wont to assume credit for her candour. It is therefore with surprise that, remembering Princess Mary's words on the subject, we find her revealing to the Regent that the Hesse-Homburg project had been suggested by 'Royal' some months earlier, when certain unnamed brothers, probably the Dukes of Cumberland and Cambridge, had 'wished it', though the Duke of Cambridge had approved Elizabeth's conduct in declining herself to mention the matter to Count Münster. This hardly tallies with her assurances to Augusta, Sophia, and Mary about her 'surprize'. And Schiller's widow was under the impression that 'the idea came from England'.[6]

Whatever the Prince Regent's personal feelings may have been as to the suitability of the candidate, or the manner in which 'the whole had been carried out', he exerted himself to obtain their mother's consent. One day he thought she was coming round, the next day the Queen was as obdurate as ever. 'No sunshine,' wrote Princess Elizabeth gloomily, on 6 February, 'and the clouds are as thick, if not thicker, than when you arrived on Sunday.'[(w)]

Three days later, however, it was clear that the Prince's visit had had a soothing effect, and Princess Augusta reported that their mother was softening a little towards the delinquent. Finally, on St Valentine's Day, 14 February we find this note in General Goldsworthy's old Prayer Book, in which Princess Elizabeth used to enter important events in her life, 'Saw the H.P. of Hesse Homburg for ye 1st time at the Queen's House'.

Contemporary English opinion was severe upon the suitor's looks and habits, and it is significant that on the morrow of their first meeting the Princess should have written of his 'extreme honesty and integrity' without making any allusion to the outward man. Mr (afterwards Sir) W. H. Fremantle, the chivalrous MP who had spoken up for the Princesses in the debate on their allowances six years before, was shocked, and wrote to the Duke of Buckingham and Chandos:

> It is impossible to describe the monster of a man—vulgar-looking German Corporal, whose breath and hide is a compound between tobacco and garlic. What can have induced her nobody can guess: he has about £300 per annum. The Queen is outrageous, but is obliged to submit. It will be a dreadful blow to her, and I should not wonder if, after the Princess is gone abroad, she sinks under it. She is much altered, and I think breaking fast.

Another of the Duke's correspondents, Mr C. W. Wynn, wrote about the same time, 'I have just seen H.H. at the levée; and an uglier hound, with a snout buried in hair, I never saw'. None of the critics surpassed Lady Jerningham, according to whom 'they immersed him several times in a warm bath to make him a little clean; and they kept him three days from smoking [before his wedding day] which, as he smoked five pipes a day, was a great forbearance'. No wonder Mr Fremantle said that the marriage was 'universally quizzed and condemned'.

Far away upon his dreary island Napoleon heard the news, and commented on it to O'Meara with characteristic malice. 'The English royal family', said he, '*va incanagliarsi* with little petty princes to whom I would not have given a brevet of *sous-lieutenant*.'

Frederick Joseph of Hesse-Homburg may well have seemed an uncouth object in the eyes of Englishmen, led by Beau Brummell to esteem personal spruceness and crisp linen. He wore a moustache and whiskers *à la* Blücher, whereas with the inauspicious exception of the Duke of Cumberland the sons of George III were clean-shaven. He smoked in an age when drunkenness was regarded as a more gentlemanly indulgence.

The House of Hesse could trace its descent in an unbroken line from the eighth century, and had produced more than one Prince of considerable courage and intelligence. Among these was Frederick of the Silver Leg, who had lost a limb when fighting for Charles X beneath the walls of Copenhagen in 1658. The father of Princess Elizabeth's Frederick, whom he succeeded as Landgrave two years after their marriage, was a person of some culture, an amateur poet and playwright, who had visited Voltaire at Ferney and hobnobbed with Encyclopaedists in Paris. His son, like Rawdon Crawley, 'was not literary and that'; only with extreme reluctance did he give up his military career at the old Landgrave's request. But he had a taste for genealogy, and encouraged his English wife to make family trees, gay with bright coats of arms and adorned with legends in 'Gothick' lettering.

'H.H.' was first and foremost a soldier. He had been wounded at the battle of Leipzig, as the admiring Princess Elizabeth noted in General Goldsworthy's Prayer Book on the anniversary of the event. In point of character, if not of deportment, he was the superior of the wags who rejoiced when, by stooping to retrieve Queen Charlotte's fan, he 'created a parlous split in his breeches'; and there never was a more unjust nickname than that of 'Humbug', which they bestowed upon him.

The person most concerned remained well pleased with her choice. During the weeks that elapsed between her first meeting with him and their marriage at the Queen's House on the evening of 7 April 1818, she seems to have felt, and even to have looked, like a young woman in love. The gift of a diamond necklace from the Queen on 16 February had been rather chillingly accompanied by a request that the recipient should not go to her; but Princess Augusta and Sir Herbert Taylor interceded, and the reunion which then took place 'went off on the whole very well'.[w]

The Prince Regent, in the throes of an attack of gout, was not present when his sister, clad in rich silver tissue with flounces of Brussels lace, her head plumed with ostrich feathers, was married by the Archbishop of Canterbury; but Queen Charlotte was there, wearing conspicuously a large miniature portrait of the King, and moving among the guests with a graciousness which warmed the democratic heart of the American Minister, Mr Rush. 'The conduct of the Queen', remarked his Excellency, 'was remarkable.' It was more remarkable than he knew.

The trousseau, appropriate rather to a young and graceful girl than to a substantial bride of nearly forty-eight, included dresses of white satin, Pomona green satin, lilac-and-white striped satin, fine Indian muslin and white kerseymere. For the drive to Windsor in 'a landaulet and four' the bridegroom exchanged his General's uniform for full ball dress, and the bride donned a white satin pelisse, with a veil over her head. Providence seemed resolved to put Princess Elizabeth's happy temper to stern tests, for on the road the bridegroom, 'through not being used to a closed carriage', was so sick that he had to get out and climb into the dickey, his place being taken by his gentleman, Baron O'Nagten. At the Royal Lodge, the Regent's cottage, he spent most of his time in the Gothic conservatory, wearing dressing-gown and slippers, and smoking vigorously.

To spare the Queen's feelings she was not told the date fixed for their departure from England, and it was represented to her that when they went down to the Sussex coast early in June it was merely in order that the Prince should bathe in the sea. The honeymooners were cheerful in Brighton, staying at the Pavilion, visiting places of interest in the neighbourhood, and going for sea trips. One day a loyal procession in honour of Sir Godfrey Webster, the local True Blue magnate (son by her first husband of the amazing Lady Holland), halted outside the Pavilion to sing 'God Save the King'. Princess Elizabeth came to the window and curtseyed to them, at the same time noting the legends on their banners, 'The Plough and the Fleece', 'Webster and Independence', and 'The Good Old Constitution of England'.[(w)]

As the day drew near when they were to board the royal yacht and cross the Channel the Princess found her fortitude wavering, and she had a struggle to conceal her feelings from her husband; 'but', she wrote to the Regent, 'do not think that I am not grateful to God and You for having given me so excellent a Being, whose one thought is to make me happy'.[(w)]

They went to Hastings on 27 June, and when in 1822 she heard that her friend and former governess, Dame Margaret Meen, was staying there she wrote to her:

> I am happy to think that I know where you are, for I slept the night before last four years ago there on my way to the Continent. This day four years I quitted dear old England, and stepping onto the boat to quitt the shores of Great Britain gave me a pang which as long as I exist I shall never forget. . . . But I feel so thankful that I am placed where I am. I am so contented with my lot that I can never be too thankful. For believe me, single I should have been wretched.

At Calais, where they arrived on 'the most lovely day that ever was', they paused to pay their respects to the even more recently married Kents. The

Duchess they found 'very pleasing but neither pretty nor handsome'.[w] At Mayence they were cordially received by the Emperor of Austria, Marie Louise's father, who made a point of telling the bride that her sister was adored in Würtemberg. 'At dinner', wrote the Princess, 'he spoke most openly to me of all that he had suffered at his daughter's marriage, and said, 'My face shows it'— and truly it did, for a more careworn countenance I never saw.'[w]

The travellers then proceeded to Schaumburg, where the Empress received Princess Elizabeth 'as an old friend', and where they found the Queen Dowager of Würtemberg, the Duchess of Cumberland, and Prince Peter of Oldenburg. The Princess wrote to the Regent begging him to send her a miniature of himself for her to wear. The Duchess of Cumberland was wearing one, and people had noticed that she herself was not. In the same letter she says:

> In England we have no idea of the magnificence of the dress on the Continent, particularly pearls, which they have in enormous quantities, all hanging about them, but the instant dinner is over they undress, and then look horrid.
>
> ... the day I went to pay my respects to the Empress of Russia I shall never forget the scene of bustle and confusion I was in; the Dss of C——d doing the honors to perfection, but from eleven in the morning till nine at night the room was full. I must make You laugh at her asking me, with my ugly figure, to put on one of her gowns. I could not help saying 'Do look at Your beautiful figure and look at mine. You mean it kind, but thank God I am not a Fool.'[w]

And so, at last, 'H.R.' and his English bride reached Homburg, where she was welcomed by the portraits of her father and mother in their Coronation robes, which he had purchased in London without her knowledge and had had hung in her apartment. This may have been suggested by the action of the Hereditary Prince of Würtemberg twenty-two years before. There were, however, many comforts which the fastidious though long-suffering Elizabeth missed in her new home. She wrote to Lady Banks, 'You would be astonished at the extream filth and dirt one meets with—it drives me near wild, but I have a regiment of females who I keep to sweep, to wipe, to clean'. To the same correspondent she confessed that she was now a perfect stranger to the good things of this world, 'as our Table, that is to say the Landgrave's, for we always dine with him, is abominable'.

She sought, and soon found, solace in building a one-storeyed hut, supported on columns of fir, which she fondly thought might give the Homburgers an idea of an English cottage. It had 'a real cottage garden', with thyme, rosemary, rue, roses, and 'common flowers', and a little kitchen garden for the caretaker and his wife. Another hobby was collecting curious fragments of stone, and she confessed to Lady Banks that her room looked like a quarry. 'Bluff', as she nicknamed her husband, continued to deserve her good opinion, and certainly won that of Miss Cornelia Knight, who visited Homburg more than once, and was much pleased with his 'noble frankness of character'. Miss Knight adds the unexpected testimony that 'he was remarkably neat in his person, and never came into company without changing his dress if he had been smoking'. This may have been his wife's influence at work. His lack of beauty would seem less conspicuous in a country where, as Princess Elizabeth told Mrs Adams, all the gentlemen looked 'as if they had been picked out to prevent the dear Landgrave being jealous, for I do declare such a frightful set of men never was seen Monsters!'

The occasion for this interjection was a visit paid to Homburg by Mrs Adams's grandson, the Rev. Frank Fulford, afterwards Bishop of Montreal—'much too beautiful for a clergyman, my dear friend!'

When Queen Charlotte died, only seven months after Princess Elizabeth's departure, she left affectionate messages for the absent child, who wrote to the Regent, 'my beloved husband is kind enough to say that he can well understand what my Mother felt at parting from me now, knowing me as he does'.[w] A long visit to the Queen Dowager of Würtemberg at this time helped to distract her thoughts, and gave her an opportunity to pour forth reams of affection, in very bad French, to her '*cher et adoré Fritz*', then at Vienna, though she knew that his comment would be '*Voilà des phrases!*'[w]

To her mother-in-law, after the death of the old Landgrave, the new Landgravine showed a tolerant amiability which her English relations found excessive. Princess Elizabeth wrote to her eldest brother:

> You would have died had you seen her agony—poor soul, at losing her dignity, which at first I was fool enough not to understand, but when she fell back upon her couch saying She had lived too long as She now was nothing, and that I was first, I told her I never would walk before my Husband's Mother she jumped up like a girl, embraced me, and said, 'I am not disappointed in you'.[w]

Princess Mary's comment to the head of the Family was 'As to the old Mother-in-law I feel just like you, out of all patience with her, and I own I think Eliza *lowers* herself in giving way to such a Woman, and it is wrong in Bluff to allow of all that Nonsense'.[w] King George IV, as he now was, does not seem to have been mollified when Elizabeth wrote of his portrait, sent to her by the hand of Augusta in 1821, 'it even roused my poor old Mother-in-law, who is so sensible of your angelic recollection of me that she desired me to have the picture with her for some hours that she might study your lovely countenance'.[w]

Partly from real family sentiment, and partly, perhaps, from a desire to extract the last ounce out of the picturesque and emotional possibilities of the ceremony, George IV desired to assemble the whole surviving Sisterhood, widow, wife, and spinster, at his Coronation. When Elizabeth hesitated on grounds of expense, he even offered to help towards the cost of the journey; but this Bluff would not allow, and the Landgravine had to wait to see her brother until he went to Hanover to receive the homage of his faithful lieges later in the year.

Among the gentlemen in attendance on the King during the visit was the often disparaged medico, Sir William Knighton. His Majesty told his sister to look upon Knighton as a friend, and within a short time of their meeting she was using him as her agent in an attempt to raise money to relieve the financial situation in which the late Landgrave had left his son.

Tardy justice has been done to Knighton by Roger Fulford in his book on George IV, and it is clear that Princess Elizabeth found him a faithful intermediary in her efforts to raise a £50,000 loan through the London and Frankfurt branches of the House of Rothschild; it was to be paid off in yearly instalments of £5,000, four-fifths being taken from her jointure and one-fifth from the Landgrave's revenues. The details of the transaction are complicated, and several alterations were made in the original plan, but what happened when the Landgravine embarked upon direct dealings with the Frankfurt financier ('Our great Man' she calls him sarcastically) is best told in her own words to her brother, who afterwards stood guarantor for the loan:

> By a debt of His [Bluff's] father's which he knew nothing of He had been particularly pinched, so unknown to him I sent my jewels to the Shylock until we could be assisted by the money we had hoped that through your kind interest we could obtain. Conceive that this morning he sent Fritz word that he would not let Him have the money—or rather me, I ought to say for three months, and if I could not pay Him He would buy the jewels for his wife, who would like to have them . . . if you had seen Fritz's face of horror—for he said—'The idea that I should be such a R——l, for no one will believe that you did this unknown to me!'[(w)]

'Fritz's' language must normally have been of an almost painful moderation if his wife felt that 'Rascal' was a word too violent to write in full. He wanted to sell his woods, but she would not hear of it. 'How', she asks, 'can we trust such a Jew?' She will send her jewels to England if the King desires it, but she 'cannot bear the thought of Shylock's wife wearing them'. In January 1822 she wrote in agitation to Knighton, suggesting that she should transfer some money to George IV for him to give *as if from himself* to the Landgrave, who never wished anything from him but his interest with the Rothschilds.

By the Treaty of Vienna the old fortress of Meissenheim had been ceded to Homburg, but Princess Elizabeth, who was restoring and beautifying it, preferred to think that she had 'given it to Bluff', and felt that it was sufficiently her own to be offered as security for the desired loan. Finally Baron de

Langsdorff, the Hessian Minister in London, was able to write in July 1824 that he had succeeded in raising the sum of £120,000 in the City at 5 per cent. In the interval her brother had given her another proof of his affection. She wanted to borrow—unknown, as usual, to Bluff—£1,000 towards the expenses of repairing Meissenheim, and the King sent her £1,500 as a gift.

The Landgravine's assurances of her happiness ring true. 'I thoroughly believe', she wrote to Mrs Adams in 1826, 'that few in my situation of life are as happy as I am. My dear Landgrave dotes on home, and we hardly ever quit it.' But her heart veered often to her own people in England, and when the Duke of York died in 1827, 'in the purest state of mind that ever was known', she trembled for the consequences to Princess Sophia, 'for all she most valued and loved is gone'.[w] In April 1829 she herself was bereaved by the death of her Bluff, who fell a prey to influenza, complicated by the breaking out of the old wound in his leg.

The kindly Duke of Cambridge attended his brother-in-law's funeral in the small hours of an April morning. '*C'est pourtant beau à lui*', wrote the Landgrave's sister, Amelia, Hereditary Princess of Anhalt Dessau, appreciatively.

Princess Elizabeth was grief-stricken. But even from a distance, and at a time when his own health was giving him concern, George IV was able to comfort her. It was at his wish that further repayments to the Rothschilds were to be made only with the sanction of her trustees, Count Münster and Sir Herbert Taylor, and he himself sent 'a most liberal and generous donation' to make her position easier. 'No woman', she wrote to Sir William Knighton, was ever more happy than I was for eleven years, and they will often be lived over again in the memory of the heart.'

The first anniversary of her loss found the Landgravine at Hanover with the Duke and Duchess of Cambridge, planning to accompany 'Dolly' when he should return to England, and cheered by a warm invitation from the King. On St George's Day 1830 she wrote to George IV:

> Only promise that when I am with you you will look upon me as a quiet old Dog, to whom you can say 'Now, leave me for a month, go away to Mary'— and so on—without an idea of offending—In the way I shall not be, for once in my own Room and not with You I have employment enough never to annoy anyone.[w]

But on 3 May alarming accounts of the King's health reached Hanover. He had had a severe heart attack in April, and though his physicians comforted themselves with the reflection that they had 'a Herculean constitution to deal with', it was generally recognized that his condition was grave. Tapping gave him temporary relief, and he rallied a little, but Knighton cannot have shared his royal patient's momentary flicker of optimism, for on 1 June 1830, the

Landgravine wrote to him, 'I so longed to see the dear King again, until last week I had hoped to press him to my heart again'. She begged Sir William, if the dear Angel should be taken from them before she saw him, to 'put by a glass, or a cup, or any trifle, ever so small, that he has used, even a pocket handkerchief', for her. She would have been 'too happy to be his nurse, or do the most menial service to soothe and soften his sufferings'.[w]

King George IV died, with a courage not unworthy of that other exemplar of deportment, Charles II, on 26 June 1830. In the autumn of the same year Princess Elizabeth came to England, and it was from the Pavilion, 'that magnificent castle ... his own formation',[w] that she wrote to thank Knighton for the two snuff-boxes which he had conveyed to her. They would, she said, 'be taken the greatest care of, and the snuff never taken out, so dear it is to me'.

When Knighton's widow published his *Memoirs* eight years later she included some of the letters written by the Landgravine to him, and the Princess 'nearly wept' at seeing herself 'in print'. In a long epistle to her friend Mrs Dering she makes the *Memoirs* the text of an interesting comparative analysis of the characters of her eldest brother and their father, George III:

> My eldest Brother was *all heart*, and had he been left to his own judgment would ever have been kind and just. But people got hold of him, and Flattery did more harm in that quarter than anything. I hate to say it, but I will not write what is not sincere. To you often have I cried over him; he was so little understood, and was received from his good looks his captivating manners, but so young, and admired, and made much of, that it was ruin to him—and to whom would it not—[be] A more generous creature never existed, and had his talents been properly called out he would have been very different from what he was. He showed when he was urged into action that he had very excellent good sense, and he certainly was the man who was the great instigator of the Duke of Wellington attending in Spain & Portugal, which occasioned in the long run the fall of that Monster who had been a scourge to us all for such a number of years. My father ever acted on the finest of feelings, and as an honest man, and with his ideas of justice would never have done what a man of the world would do; but different characters always must act differently. My Father was a man after God's own heart, the finest, purest, and most perfect of all characters: the other God made perfect but the world spoilt him. . . . My Brother was always in a dazzle. My Father was always seeing things composedly, sensibly and seeing much further into the danger of what such and such things would produce. And who knows if many things which may have done us so much mischief may not have come from *overdoing* what would never have been done by so solid a mind as my father's.
>
> All this is written by a great *ignoramus*, but so I feel it.

George IV had suggested, and the new King, William IV, warmly concurred, that Princess Elizabeth should make Hanover her home, but though she spent a great deal of her time there, she never uprooted herself entirely from the place where she had passed those eleven happy years. Her affection for the Duke of Cambridge and his family added to the enjoyment of her Hanoverian visits. In January 1834 she stood godmother to the Duke's second daughter, Princess Mary Adelaide Wilhelmina Elizabeth, whom she held at the font, 'for the dear Queen' (Adelaide) and herself. 'The child's dress amused me', she wrote, 'a *drap d'argent*, all tied *with pink* bows, and an enormous long train of the same, all trimmed with fine Brussels lace; two cushions of the same, so think what a weight to carry.'

The Duke's birthday was celebrated with *tableaux vivants* and masquerades, which nobody enjoyed more than his widowed sister.

At Homburg the Landgravine continued to reside at the Castle, as the guest of the new Landgrave, Prince Louis, a gaunt, taciturn man whose unhappy marriage had ended in a divorce. Among the other members of the family established there were a younger brother, Gustave, his deaf, rather 'difficult' wife, and their three children, with all of whom the widowed Landgravine contrived to remain on excellent terms. She retained her old suite of rooms on the first floor, looking towards the Taunus mountains, and furnished with fine 'pieces' in lacquer and ebony. Among her *bibelots* was a silver model of a man-of-war presented by William IV; and among the steel-engraved portraits in her dining-room was one of the Duchess of Kent with the infant Princess Victoria in her arms. In her bedroom, near the clock with the name of a Windsor maker on the dial, was a miniature of George III in his last days, wigless and bearded, 'in a purple gown,—the Star of his famous Order still shining idly on it'.

At Frankfurt the Dowager had what she called 'a miserable *pied-à-terre*' in the Zeil, grimly furnished with black horsehair-covered chairs—in contrast to the splendours of the Rothschild mansion where she condescended to attend a reception, and was much impressed by the objects she saw. 'Who can have them', she wrote, 'if they have them not, who are *all gold*!'

The Landgrave Louis died in 1839, and for the last year of Princess Elizabeth's life the holder of the title was the next brother, Philip, a sickly man who had contracted a morganatic marriage with a certain Frau von Schimmelpfennig, otherwise the Countess of Nürnberg. How his royal sister-in-law dealt with the problem of this lady's existence and her arrival at the Castle may best be related in her own words:

> You may believe his family did not like the connection, & his brother Louis gave, *entre nous*, a reluctant consent, as he was sent for by the Emperor of Austria to entreat him, as they thought Philip dying; instead of which we lost my invaluable brother, and *he* is now Landgrave—the most amiable, dear, &

beloved of beings, yet they all felt that he should [not] have done this. I was asked what I should do. My answer was—'Remember, all is changed. Philip is Landgrave and how can this sister-in-law whom he allows to live in his house say to him, or to any married man so nearly connected,' You shall not bring your wife'?'

Mindful of these things, and also of Philip's poor health, Princess Elizabeth decided to make the best of it.

> The moment he came in I embraced him, and upon his saying, 'My wife', I saluted her as I would any other Countess. And to do her justice all I see pleases me, for she never pushes, and behaves with tact and good sense and is very pretty. The men rave, and say she is the most beautiful woman that ever was. That is not so. You may believe me, as I have ever been a great admirer of beauty in my own sex. She has what surpasses beauty in my eyes, for she has something so pleasing and you feel that she talks herself handsome. . . .
>
> I will do all in my power to make her happy, for Philip's sake, and I should be very wrong if I was to say a word that was not in her praise, for she plainly sees my object is her comfort. . . .
>
> I have made all visit her—and I went the other evening, to please the *natives*, upon the *Salle* being opened for the first time near the well, which is a great event, and I made her sit next to me to let them see how very well I was with her.

The Landgravine's life pursued a pleasant train; she had her card parties, her drives, her hobbies, and the society of young as well as of elderly people. 'I hate rookeries of old gossips!' she wrote to Mrs Dering, and she was glad when the nightingales' softened the clappers of the ill-natured'. In dealing with the young she observed, 'the first thing is never to forget one was young oneself, by which means young people don't fear you'. When she was in England in 1835 she wrote to Mrs Dering that she was taking Mr Henry Wheatley's daughter to a ball at Devonshire House 'in aid of the Scotch Children', and added, 'There is nothing to me half so delightful, "now that youth and beauty both are flown", as to have a young person, for then I feel useful: otherwise I feel nothing of the kind, when alone, and rather a dead weight. But I have taken upon me the character of a chaperon famously.' In Germany she loved to go to the children's fair where the cheap toys were sold at Christmas. She wrote, in December 1838:

> My list is large, and it is a great pleasure and amusement, for you must manage to please all, and at the same time to have some comical things, tho', privately, I do not think that the Germans have much humour. They are a sedate, quiet people, whereas you know what a cheerful being I am & now

and then excuse a laugh when little expected: but to see fun received with a [illegible] Bow and Curtsey turns the cream sour.

When Gustave's daughter Caroline was married to the Prince of Reuss, the widowed Landgravine 'took all upon herself', owing to the Landgrave Philip's 'shocking state of health', and decorated the corridors and salons with candles, evergreens, and 'Gothick skreens'. She was never without simple pleasures; making a 'Rose Tent' in her little wood, which in a few years she hoped would be 'quite a *Lion*'; cultivating a new plant, 'exactly a laburnum in purple bordering on blue'; giving nosegays and ribands to the Tyroleans, on whom she 'doated', and from whom she bought all her gloves; and going out 'when the heavens were studded with stars'.

Her last visit to England in 1835–36 was a happy one, though the 'improvements' in London 'drove her wild', for, she wrote, 'all is gone of what formerly was familiar to me, so that I came home not knowing where I have been, or what I have seen'. At Windsor she found it difficult to summon up sufficient courage to enter 'the Cathedral', as the Family called St George's Chapel, where her father and mother, the Duke of Kent, and the Duke of Gloucester had been laid while she was far away in Germany. When she did make the effort it was in order to see Prince George of Cambridge confirmed.

To Mrs Dering, whom she had invited to visit her in Sussex, she wrote:

> I find everything much dearer—one ought to have the *Mint* to live here . . . and as I am new-roofing at home I must take care when new-roofing my old head not to do it too often, otherwise the candle would be burning at both ends—so expect to see me very dowdy at Brighton.

In July 1836 she was regretfully making ready to go, and on the eve of her departure Mrs Fitzherbert came to see her, 'looking as handsome as possible, quite astonishing for her years'. 'Last days are sad things', she wrote to Mrs Dering; but when she got back to Homburg she was greeted with illuminations quite in the Pumpernickel manner, and 'all sorts of pretty sentences of contentment' at her return. The worthy Homburgers may have found her high spirits and her infantile jokes hard to understand, but her charities and her virtues were in another category. At Hanover too her goodness was known, and the *crèche* founded by her for the small children of 'those who go out to work for the day' flourished exceedingly.

Visits to various German spas kept her amused during the years 1837–39, though she was careful to point out that what she went in quest of was *her legs*, and not a husband. Indeed her mind dwelt constantly upon her dear Fritz, and every year she remembered that February the 14th was the anniversary of her first meeting with him. 'I can go on', she wrote, 'hour after hour, thanks to the blessing and pleasure of memory, to look back at the sun beginning to shine upon me, as it did when he arrived, and I am sure it never set afterwards.'[w]

In the spring of 1839 Sir Henry Halford and Mr Keate received cheering accounts of her from Dr Dennie (the *Gentleman's Magazine* calls him 'Dr Downie'), a physician who had gone out to Frankfurt with Sir Thomas Cartwright, the English Minister, and proved himself to be so clever that Sir Thomas prevailed upon him to establish himself there. In May she had a relapse, but rallied so promptly that her maid of honour, Mademoiselle Veronica de Stein, was able to write hopefully to Princess Augusta; and the patient soon followed with a letter 'full of her own natural charming fun', comparing herself not only to Mother Hubbard's dog, but also, because of the weakness of her legs, to 'the late Earl of Huntingdon, whose knees were so bent *outward* that he appeared as if he was making a minuet curtsy'.

The old pain in her side had returned—the pain to which Sophia, Amelia, and Charlotte also were prone—but through the summer and autumn of 1839 she continued to write so cheerfully that Princess Augusta could not 'see it in the light of a disease likely to terminate her precious life'. As the year waned her strength and her eyesight both failed her. To write her Christmas letter to her elder sister was the laborious effort of three days, and Princess Augusta thought that when she wrote again on the last day of the year she must have been 'very low' as she ended with the words '*now I am useless*'.

The Landgravine's old quarters at Frankfurt, where she spent her last Christmas, had been smartened up with new wallpapers, and with 'linnen from England', and her English maid was still with her, the trusty Brawn who forty years before had been wont to smuggle 'G.P.'s' letters to his sister. And so, in this place of exile, but not without some touch of home about her, the lady who had loved to sign herself 'born Princess of England' breathed her last on 10 January 1840.

At her earnest desire the Anglican burial service was read when her dust was laid in the family vault at Homburg. Five English parsons followed her thither, in her coffin sent from Hanover—a last link with the cradle of the dynasty to which she belonged. The House of Hesse-Homburg was represented by the Landgrave Philip and his brother Gustave.

On 22 January her sister-in-law Amelia of Anhalt-Dessau, quoted an eye-witness as having said of the dead Landgravine: 'I saw her only the day before, and I can say with truth that I have never seen a dead person whose face looked so calm; she seemed only to be asleep. There was no distortion of the features, not even that lengthening which almost always occurs after death.'

The Landgravine's will had been made on 12 February 1830, and by the time she died it became necessary for her to execute a codicil concerning her funded property, all of which she had bequeathed to the Landgrave Louis, and her jewels, destined originally to be heirlooms in the Hesse-Homburg family for the use of future Landgravines. After the death of Louis she so altered her dispositions that the capital sum she had destined for him should remain in England, and her jewels were to pass to Gustave's wife, the deaf Princess Louise. The terms of the codicil apparently did not include certain small personal trinkets mentioned in the body of the will. All her own brothers and sisters had been remembered, though George IV did not live to receive the gold snuff-box she always used. To her 'beloved and dearest sister Mary' she bequeathed the bracelet she always wore with her father's picture, given to her 'by dear Augusta when at Homburg'; to the Duchess of Cumberland, 'Ernest's picture as a child, worked with his hair'; and to the Princess Victoria, the gold toothpick which had belonged to the Duke of Kent, sent to the Landgravine by the Duchess after his death. To her 'excellent and valued Brawn' went all her linen, clothes, gowns, shawls, and £100 a year. Apparently the shawls would normally have been the perquisite of the maid of honour Veronica de Stein, for it is specifically stated that the five hundred florins bequeathed to her, in addition to a coral necklace and a pair of ear-rings, were 'instead of shawls'.[w]

England has completely forgotten this kind-hearted garden-loving Princess who was in some ways the most typically English of George III's daughters; but in her adopted country she is not forgotten. A Quell and a street in Homburg bear her name, and her bust, handsome and matronly, outside the English Church reminds the passer-by that in this pleasant place an exiled but unchanging Englishwoman lived and died. This memorial, unveiled in 1908 in the presence of King Edward VII by his nephew Kaiser Wilhelm II, was erected at the suggestion of the Empress Frederick, who would often talk with familiar and almost personal affection of her 'dear Great Aunt, Elizabeth'.

4
Princess Mary,
Duchess of Gloucester,
1776–1857

I

By common consent it was the fourth of George III's six daughters who was the beauty of the Family, 'the first', ejaculated Miss Burney, 'of this truly beautiful race!' She was only a year and four months old when she appeared on the Prince of Wales's birthday in 'a lace frock over a blue silk coat', and Mary Hamilton remarked that she was 'a lovely, elegant-made child'. On the same occasion the three elder Princesses wore 'blue and silver polonaises, with the hair dressed upon high cushions, with large stiff curls powdered and pomatumed'; and it is easy to imagine how much more natural and charming their little sister looked.

In a letter to the King—then at Portsmouth—written in April 1778, Queen Charlotte gives a glimpse of their fourth daughter:

> Mary is very anxious to see your Majesty. She desired me to call *dear Papa*; but after telling her that could not be, she desired to be lifted up, and she called for at least half-an-hour, *Papa coming, Papa comes!* But seeing she was disappointed by not receiving any answer, I desired her to tell me what I should say to the King in case I should write, and she answered, *Minny say Goody Papa, poor Papa!* (w)

Four days later the Queen wrote:

> Dear little Minny remains quite uneasy about not finding you anywhere in the House. Every coach she sees is Papa coming, and nothing satisfies her hardly but sitting at the window to look for you.

Rumours of Princess Mary's beauty reached Holland when she was five years old; and her young cousin, Princess Louise of Orange, wrote to the pushful and pedantic Madame de la Fite, then newly installed at Windsor, '*la Princesse Marie est-elle aussi jolie qu'on le dit?*'

The City Fathers of London, finding themselves called upon in April 1776 to congratulate their sovereign upon the birth of another daughter, 'begged leave to assure him that there were not in all his dominions any subjects more faithful, or more ready to maintain the true honour and dignity of the Crown'; they added meaningly that 'they would continue to rejoice in every event which might add to his Majesty's domestic felicity, expressing at the same time a hope that every branch of the August House of Brunswick would add further securities to those sacred laws and liberties which their ancestors would not suffer to be violated with impunity, and which, in consequence of the glorious and necessary Revolution, that House was called upon to defend'. It is not clear how this fresh sprig was expected to add security to their laws and liberties, but she never did anything to blot the Protestant 'scutcheon of the dynasty.

The King returned a curt answer to these civic admonitions. It was, as Miss Martineau pointed out many years later, 'a time at which King George did not want to hear anything about liberties and revolutions'. Two months later the Americans published the Declaration of Independence.

We owe an early glimpse of Princess Mary to Mrs Delany, who had made the acquaintance of the Family in 1776, and who became almost a cult with the King and Queen. Why this should have been so may be a little difficult to understand; but Bishop Hurd, from the eighteenth-century angle, gives the root of the matter in the inscription he composed for her monument in St James's Church, Piccadilly: 'She was', says the Bishop, 'a lady of singular ingenuity and politeness, and of unaffected piety. These qualities endeared her through life to many noble and excellent persons, and made the close of it illustrious by procuring for her many signal marks of grace and favour from their Majesties.' These marks of favour Mrs Delany received gratefully but not obsequiously; and the simple friendliness of her intercourse with the royal children is repeatedly shown in her correspondence.

Here is her picture of the Family as she saw them on the Princess Royal's birthday in 1779:

> The Queen was dress'd in an embroidered lute-string; Princess Royal in deep orange or scarlet, I could not by candlelight distinguish which; Princess Augusta in pink; Princess Elizabeth in blue. These were all in robes without aprons.
>
> Princess Mary, a most sweet child, was in cherry-colour tabby, with silver leading-strings; she is about four years old: she cou'd not remember my name, but making me a very low curtsey she said, 'How do you do, Duchess of Portland's friend; and how does your little niece do? I wish you had brought her.'
>
> The King carried about in his arms by turns Princess Sophia and the last prince, Octavius. I never saw more lovely children, nor a more pleasing sight than the King's fondness for them, and the Queen's; for they seem to have but one mind, and that is to make everything easy and happy about them.

On the death of the Duchess of Portland six years later, Mrs Delany, who had long lived with her as lady-companion, was left stranded. The King and Queen then came forward with the offer of a little house in the garden of Queen's

Lodge and a pension of £300 a year, and so began a gracious intimacy that did equal credit to both sides. Mrs Delany's sundial naturally recorded only the bright hours; her memoirs reflect a serene home life at Windsor, the benignity of the King combining with the charm of the Queen to create a paradise for their smiling young. While accepting the picture with gratitude we must not be unduly surprised if we find from other sources evidence of occasional strain below this smooth surface.

To this strain Princess Mary seems to have been the most sensitive. She was the gentlest of the Sisterhood and perhaps the best-loved 'the dear, perfect Miny',[7] the 'sweet, dear Mary', of the Family letters; but the others sometimes hesitated to take her fully into their confidence, 'for fear', as Princess Elizabeth said, 'of it coming out elsewhere', and she was at one time unjustly suspected by Princess Amelia of being 'the Queen's tool'. There is nothing in her correspondence to suggest that she was weak or disingenuous, and she showed candour and initiative on more than one occasion.

As a child she was lively and well-mannered. We catch a glimpse of her in Miss Burney's pages, 'just arrived from Lower Lodge . . . capering upstairs to her elder sisters', but stopping to enquire how Fanny did 'with all the elegant composure of a woman of mature age'; and in her earlier letters, some in English and some in French, we see her conning her lessons with Mademoiselle Montmollin and playing dominoes with Mrs Delany. She was particularly fond of her baby sister Amelia, whom she describes coming up on her bed to receive the gifts sent to them both by the King, when she was lying ill at Kew in 1788.

A year later the Duke of Clarence was on leave, after a twelve-months absence in the West Indies with his ship the *Andromeda*, breezy, friendly, and loquacious, and quite ready to impart his impressions of his sisters to Miss Burney. He said 'he had been making acquaintance with a new Princess, one he did not know nor remember—Princess Amelia. "Mary, too," he said, "I had quite forgot, and they did not tell me who she was; so I went up to her, and without in the least recollecting her, she's so monstrously grown, I said, 'Pray, Ma'am, are you one of the attendants?'"'

Two years later, when she was 'introduced' at Court, the Princess may perhaps have wished that her sailor brother had been at sea, and therefore not available to lead her out upon that rather trying occasion. According to Mrs Papendiek:

> The Princess was anxious to take a few lessons from Desnoyer in a court hoop and train, in order that all might be perfection in appearance, for the beauty of Princess Mary was exquisite, both in figure and grace, with a very handsome face and a sweet expression of countenance.

The Duke of Clarence seems to have been elated at being chosen to partner his prettiest sister, but unfortunately his elation led him to ply the equerries—and himself—with champagne at the preceding dinner. He concentrated his efforts upon the Queen's equerry, Mr Stanhope, a rather solemn man with conspicuous dentures, and when his victim pleaded that he would be 'apt to be rather up in the world' if he went on at that rate, the Duke retorted gaily, 'Not at all! You can't get drunk in a better cause. I'd get drunk myself if it was not for the Ball. Here—champagne—another glass for the philosopher! I keep sober for Mary!'

But he did not keep sober for Mary. He got, in fact, so drunk that he kissed the hand of Madame Schwellenburg. All Desnoyer's efforts were wasted on a pupil whose partner was incapable of going through the movements of any complicated dance, whether hornpipe or *minuet de la cour*. Princess Mary afterwards told Miss Burney 'the history of her dancing at the Ball, and the situation of her brother and partner . . . with a sweet ingenuousness and artless openness which are marks of her very amiable character'.

Like the other members of the Sisterhood this Princess regarded the annual summer sojourn at Weymouth without enthusiasm. The solemn promenade upon the sea-front was only a variant of the tedious 'Terracing', and the evenings spent in a small theatre reeking of lamp-oil cannot have been pleasant, even when the performers were 'stars' from London and the play worth seeing. Captain Landmann may have been right when he said that 'the Queen and Princesses were very fond of sea-bathing'; but he was wrong in thinking that they all enjoyed the daily excursions on the royal yacht, for the Queen was 'much afraid of any motion', and the Princesses were often glad to beg off both bathing and boating.

The picture drawn by Landmann increases our sympathy for them:

> The royal family were called from their beds every morning at five o'clock so that they might be out by six. It will be readily imagined that such early hours at Gloucester Lodge produced equally early movements throughout the population . . . the shops were opened regularly at half-past five o'clock, for by six the streets were thronged with all the fashionables at Court.
>
> The great attraction was to see the Queen and Princesses walking from Gloucester Lodge to their bathing-machines, or to cheer them on their embarkation with the King and a select party on board the royal yacht.

Indeed, the one person who really seems to have been happy was the King himself. The air suited him, though it did not suit Queen Charlotte; the inhabitants were loyal; they even stationed brass bands in bathing-machines to play 'God Save the King' when he took a dip, and erected an enormous equestrian statue of him on the cliff. Such dutiful attentions were particularly grateful at a period when ill-conditioned persons on the Continent were overthrowing ancient monarchies, while others were uttering disloyal cries and printing seditious libels at home.

Writing to the Prince of Wales in September 1798, Princess Mary said:

This Place is more *dull* and stupid than I can find words to express, a perfect standstill of everything and everybody, except every ten days a very long Review, that I am told is very *fine*, but being perfectly *unknowing* in these things come home less amused than before I left home.[w]

The interest in the military career of her cousin, Prince William Frederick of Gloucester, ascribed to the Princess by sentimental persons many years later, does not seem to have been sufficiently strong to include any other military activities. To while away the days at Gloucester Lodge she wrote gossiping letters to the Prince of Wales, telling him that 'poor Chassy'—Lady Charlotte Bruce—wished to be agreeable but that her health and spirits at times quite failed, and that Frederick, who has grown very fat, does not like to be told so—'but it is so very visible that I could not help making the remark'. In another letter written at Weymouth in the autumn of 1798 she observes, 'As for General Garth, the Purple Light of Love, *toujours le même*'.[w] The allusion was to the portwine-mark which disfigured the countenance of that dapper little soldier, but which apparently did not impair his charm. Princess Mary cannot surely have realized that about this time the General and her sister Sophia were falling in love with each other.

Both Princess Mary and Princess Amelia now began to address the Prince by the affectionate nickname of *Eau de Miel*, because he sent them gifts of honey-water; and Mary, although the distance in age between her and her eldest brother was only fourteen years, more than once signs her letters to him 'Your affec sister, and I may almost say *child*'. The Prince always contrived to hold the balance true between the five sisters who looked to him for comfort and kindness, never seeming to favour one at the expense of any other, and distributing to all alike his jokes, his gifts, and his sympathy. The Princess Royal was too near him in age to get the full flavour of his elder-brotherliness, which was reserved for her five grateful juniors.

Princess Mary being the acknowledged beauty of the group, it is curious that we should find no hint of any early romance in her life. Had not the Queen of Würtemberg written, at the time of their marriage in 1816, of the 'steady attachment 'which the Duke of Gloucester had shown the Princess 'for near twenty years', it would seem not impossible that their love-story had been belatedly invented to lend a touch of sentimental grace to the occasion. Mary certainly does not allude to her cousin in letters to her brother before 1811, even when she was staying in the house at Weymouth which had been his father's, and where he himself had spent part of his childhood. She may have felt that reticence was the better part; and pride may have intervened when the Duke was a candidate for the hand of her niece, Princess Charlotte. As for the rumour, which reached the ears of Thomas Ashe, that John Hookham Frere's younger brother Bartholomew (Bartle) Frere had fallen in love with Princess Mary at the Eton Montem one year, and had carried a broken heart with him to his diplomatic posts in Spain and Turkey, there is nothing to substantiate it unless it be the fact that he died a bachelor.

Frances, Lady Shelley, notes that in 1801 her future husband (Sir John Shelley) 'was the favourite partner of Princess Mary (afterwards Duchess of Gloucester), then remarkable for her beauty, grace, and the perfection of manners which still distinguish her'; but there is no hint of any romance between the Princess and the dashing Coldstreamer. At twenty-nine she must have been in her fullest bloom, for it was 'by her beauty' that a youthful visitor to the Queen's House recognized her in 1806. Lord Malmesbury does not mention her looks, but he records a few years earlier that she was 'all good humour and pleasantness; her manners perfect'; and that he never saw anyone so exactly what she ought to be'. Lord Glenbervie, whose scurrilous pen left her unscathed, said of her about the same period, 'The Princess Mary is perfect, a very pretty small face, full of sense and sweetness'.

Unlike their three elder sisters, the Princesses Mary and Sophia were slenderly built, and delicately modelled. Allusions to their health abound in the correspondence of the Family, but the terms 'cramp' and 'spasm' are used to describe so many different shades of illness that it is impossible to narrow down the definition. With Princess Amelia the case is different; she was undoubtedly tuberculous. When in the late summer of 1809 she was sent to Weymouth, it was Princess Mary who went with her. Most of the letters written by the elder Princess between August 1809 and January 1811 will be found in Princess Amelia's chapter. Queen Charlotte disapproved strongly of the arrangement, and would have brought it to an end before Princess Amelia's death had she had her way. She seems to have been the only person to realize that Princess Mary's own health might suffer. The King, on the other hand, delighted that his beloved Amelia should have so kind a companion and so faithful a nurse, wrote to 'dearest Mary' in October 1809:

> Your conduct through life has amply proved how much my satisfaction and comfort have been your object, and every act of yours has tended yet more to endear you to me, none more than the tender love and attention which you have bestowed on a beloved suffering sister, and the cheerfulness with which you have devoted yourself to her service.[w]

When everything was over Mary collapsed, and the Duke of Cambridge wrote to her former nurse, Mrs Adams, on 16 December 1810, 'Dearest Miny has not had a quiet night, which I believe is partly owing to her seeing Sir Henry Halford late last night'; and writing to the same correspondent on the same day, Princess Elizabeth expresses the opinion that 'dear Mary's' indifferent night was owing to her 'talking over late the events of the day in town', which looks as if Sir Henry Halford had discussed with his royal patient the Regency debates then taking place.

No sooner had the Regency been set up and the Queen given the custody of the King's person than Princess Mary began the task of writing a daily bulletin to the Regent concerning their invalid father.

Here and there the reports contain allusions to other matters, and as they cover the years 1811–13 they give Princess Mary's reactions to the domestic crises of January, April, and December 1812. Usually the gentlest of the sisters, she is apt at times to write with a sharper pen than any of them.

The King was lodged in a suite of ground-floor apartments, now the lower rooms of the Royal Library, on the north terrace of Windsor Castle, and the Princess's expression for visiting him is 'going down'. On one occasion she wrote to her brother, 'I went down with the Queen, and it was shocking to hear the poor, dear King run on so, and her unfortunate manner makes things so much worse'. This manner the Princess ascribed partly to 'extream timidity' and partly to an inborn deficiency in 'warmth, tenderness, affec", and that soothing manner which could alone be of any use 'in enabling the poor King to make up his mind to this long confinement'.

King George's change of feeling bore with crushing severity upon the Queen, to whose good qualities he himself bore witness in a letter written to the Prince of Wales in 1780. He then declared that 'her conduct as Wife as well as a mother even malevolence has not dared to mention but in the most respectable terms'; adding, 'I can with truth say that in nineteen years I have never had the smallest reason but to thank Heaven for having directed my choice among the Princesses then fit for me to marry'.[w] She certainly had that charm which transcends beauty. Nobody looking at the smiling Gainsborough portrait in the Victoria and Albert Museum can feel any surprise that Lord Harcourt should have said that she was the most captivating woman he had ever met. Her rigid Lutheran orthodoxy and her inflexible sense of duty would appeal to her husband's normal judgment; but his normal judgment was now in eclipse.

To meet the tragic circumstances Princess Mary made a new suggestion to the Prince Regent:

The Queen I am sure will never do *but her Duty*; it is in trifles that she always contrives to *fail*, not only by the King but, if I may say so, by us all. It therefore strikes me that if the *power* was given us either by the Phy[ians] or proposed by the Council, that we might go down two at a time we might do both the K. and the Q. good, save the Q. much fatigue, and it would enable us to speak kindly of her to the K. and agreeably so of the K. to the Q., repeating all that could do good and give comfort to both.

I fear we can never make them a *real comfort* to each other again, as all confidence has long gone, but I am sure they have a *great respect* for each other, and that the Q. loves him as much as she can love anything *in this world*, but I am clear it is in the power of their daughters, if they are allowed to act, to keep them tolerably together . . . so far as to make no compleat separation, which I own I dread *now*, if great care is not taken.[w]

Sir Henry Halford's persuasive powers were invoked, and the Queen was prevailed upon to accept the proposed plan. The Princesses, who were assuredly not lacking in warmth, tenderness, and affection, were always able to submerge their natural terror in the depths of their compassion for their father.

Even in this period of gloom there were interludes of cheerfulness. The Queen had an unfailing sense of humour, and on one occasion the Duke of Clarence was able to amuse her by 'keeping up a constant conversation and making her die of laughing with some of his most wonderful stories'; another time we get an engaging glimpse of her with her little granddaughter, when Princess Mary writes:

> Fortunately Charlotte is not at all afraid of the Queen, as she runs on from subject to subject and into all her jokes with the Q., just as she does with us, and stands over the Queen's chair, and yesterday afternoon kept the Queen laughing from 8 o'clock till 10.[w]

Her daughters entered into innocent little conspiracies to amuse her, as when in the summer of 1812 Princess Mary suggested that the Prince Regent might bring Colonel Congreve to 'show off some of his Rockets' at Eliza's cottage at Frogmore for the Queen's amusement; but the Prince was exhorted not to mention the source of the idea, for 'she does not like anything any of us propose'. The Princesses were further delighted when she suddenly suggested a visit to Ascot, and Princess Mary wrote to the Regent:

> . . . the weather beautiful, and the whole thing most gay from your Stand, which the Queen took full possession of and enjoyed it as much as anybody. This drive to Ascot was quite an idea of the Queen's, for we none of us could believe our ears when she said last night that she had a great mind to go.[w]

Such interludes were brief and few, mere breaks in the prevailing sombreness; and the clouds darkened again when the question of a separate establishment for the Princesses was brought forward.

The Queen's Council did not find her easy to deal with, and Mr Perceval had difficulty in persuading her even to consider the plan which he and the Cabinet drew up, and which the Duke of York read and expounded to Her Majesty and the Sisterhood. 'For Godsake', wrote Princess Mary to the Regent,

> don't let us be the cause of any *mischief* or *distress*. We have so long submited [sic] to a thousand disagreeables, and are so used to our *situation* that we are all quite prepared, I assure you, not to be disappointed . . . and we shall be miserable if we hear that you are vexing yourself and making yourself ill.[w]

She wants it made plain to Mr Perceval that she and her sisters had no wish to leave their parents beyond the comfort of enjoying more of the Prince's society, and that of 'some few friends' whom they could not expect to visit them at Windsor. Maternal distaste, it appears, was reinforced by frugal instincts. When the Queen felt sore that Mr Perceval had not met her own desire for such an establishment, Sir Herbert Taylor reminded her that she had 'expressed a horror of any responsibility, and had said she had not health or spirits to undertake any, and had added that she wished for no personal advantage'.[w] In fact, if Princess Mary's account is correct, Sir Herbert had used plain language, saying

> that this was done to enable her to put so much more money in her pocket, and to enable us to begin by degrees an Establishment which, if we managed well, we ought to save now, that should anything happen to the poor King we might have money in hand to fit us out properly, without calling any more upon You or the country. All this did not make things go better.[w]

Satirists were not slow to fix upon this idiosyncrasy of the Queen's. In March 1792 Gillray had published a cartoon entitled 'Anti-Saccharites, or John Bull and his Family leaving off the Use of Sugar'. This represents the five well-liking Princesses at breakfast receiving with resentful looks an exhortation from their cadaverous mother at the head of the table: 'O, dear creatures, do but taste it! You can't think how nice it is without sugar! And then consider how much work you'll save the poor Blackamoors by leaving off the use of it! And above all remember how much expense it will save your poor Papa! Oh, its charming, cooling drink!'

The frugal mind of the Queen seems to have been a source of particular regret to Princess Mary, and she comments on it with some sharpness in her letters to the Regent. Perhaps because their mother became more difficult as years passed— no matter for surprise—perhaps because the elder daughters grew up more immediately under her influence, the three younger Princesses are certainly more critical than their seniors had ever permitted themselves to be, at least in writing.

Only two years after Queen Charlotte's death, Princess Mary wrote to their brother that she wished he could have heard Sophia 'take off a conversation that she witnessed taking place between the poor Queen and Dr Pope that I know would have killed you, and really brought the poor Queen completely back to my memory, that had I shut my eyes I should have thought she was in the room'.[w] And the Queen's guttural German voice, her trick of interjecting 'So!' and her passion for snuff were all mentioned with rather malicious humour by Princess Amelia.

There is something pathetic about this progressive alienation of Queen Charlotte from her daughters. 'The prejudices', wrote Princess Mary, 'which belong to all those who do not live in the world are most strongly marked in the Queen's character'; [w] and it may have been these prejudices, as well as her

naturally possessive disposition, which made her resentment so strong when
the question of a separate establishment arose. Her allusions to the Princesses
in her early letters to the King are often affectionate, and this gentler mood
is still manifest sometimes up to Princess Amelia's death and the King's final
breakdown. An undated letter, referring to some royal jubilation and addressed
jointly to her daughters, Mary and Amelia, illustrates this contrast:

> Accept, my dearest Mary and Amelia, my congratulations upon this happy
> day. I am sure our Prayers will be in Unison for the preservation of our beloved
> Kg, and to whom can his life be more precious than to myself and children?
> For his unremitted Piety and Virtue he will be blessed by his Exemple. I trust
> that every blessing will attend his family, and that you may all be equal sharers
> in such a father's blessing is not only the sincerest but the most unutterable
> wish and fervent prayer of your ever most affectionate mother and friend.
>
>   CHARLOTTE
>
> Adolphus shares in all this, but you must excuse my not writing separately—
> my heart is so full that I am ready to cry. Adieu.

Surely not the letter of a woman totally deficient in tenderness? It is none the
less impossible to doubt that Princess Mary was speaking the sad truth. If she
had wished to malign her mother, would she have chosen the Prince Regent
as her auditor? And there is corroborative evidence in the letters of the more
reticent sisters as well.

Life must have been hard enough for the Sisterhood even when their father's
authority stood between them and their mother's despotism, but when he was
swallowed up by the prison-house on the North Terrace their plight must have
been dreary. Princess Amelia had less to endure than her elders, for Worthing
and Weymouth were three days' journey from Windsor, and she was seldom
at home. 'Little Sophy', too, had a way of escape—to her own apartments,
where she was able to enjoy an invalid's privileges for months at a time. 'You
know', this Princess wrote to the Regent in 1818, when their mother's health
was breaking up, 'I am not so much with her as my sisters are.'[w] It was upon the
Princesses Augusta, Elizabeth, and Mary that the burden pressed most heavily,
and this may have spurred their brother on when at last it was in his power to
help them.

The year 1812, so memorable in the history of Europe, was marked by three
crises in the lives of the four remaining Princesses. The first arose in January,
when the intentions of the Prince Regent to give them separate establishments
became known to the Queen; the second in April, when, on the initiative of
Princess Augusta, the sisters stated their views in writing, and placed them
before her; the third in November–December, when their determination to be

guided by the wishes of the Prince led to the sharp and painful clash already described in Princess Augusta's chapter.

'My own private opinion', wrote Princess Mary in January 1812, 'is that she is ashamed of owning it, but that the *great* distress is jealousy of *your* kindness towards us.'[w] She was probably right. When the Regent sprained his ankle while staying with the Duke of York at Oatlands, she wrote to him, 'I long, I perfectly *die* to come and see you. Could you not make Frederick or somebody write in your name to the Queen to beg she would send us to Oatlands, only *for an hour?*'[w] This the Prince did; but the Queen eventually announced that if any of the Princesses went, she would go with them. She may have been anxious that they should not have too many opportunities for confidential talks with their champion, and we know from Lord Colchester's *Diary* that she took the occasion to have a conversation with the invalid, hardly calculated to raise his spirits or charm his ears. A decree was issued that Augusta and Sophia should proceed to Oatlands first, the Queen following two days later with Elizabeth and Mary. This last Princess wrote to the Regent:

> As the Queen knows poor Sophia is in a most delicate state, and *really* quite unfit to undertake so long a drive as to Oatlands and back again it is the more provoking that she would not out of charity spare her and send me.[w]

In spite of all the Queen's manoeuvres the Regent's tact prevailed once more, and Parliament and Mr Perceval translated his good intentions into concrete facts. When, in April, the second clash came, Princess Mary wrote to the Prince:

> I hope you will give us the *comfort* of *assuring* us that you approve of *all our letters* and likewise of Dolly's good nature and kindness on the occasion. I certainly expected a storm when we made known our *decided* wishes and ideas as to our future plans in life, but I own I did not suppose it possible she *could* have *misunderstood* Augusta's letter as *compleatly* as she *has* done.
>
> Great allowances must be made for a Woman who has had her own way for so many years, and that we *all* have *reason* to know has *not* a good temper.[w]

The good-nature of 'Dolly' was all the more to his credit as he was recovering from a sharp twinge of gout. Care was taken that neither the Duke of Cumberland nor the Duke of Clarence should be aware of what was going on.

By the end of May the Princesses Augusta, Elizabeth, and Mary had so far gained their point that they all went up to London together, without the Queen. Mary wrote to the Regent:

> We gave up your kind invitation of being at Carlton House *not* because *we saw* the smallest *impropriety* of being in your House (which was the Queen's reason) but because we felt as the Q. offered us to go to the Q.H. perhaps at

this moment, when you must have so many people to see, we had better be out of the way, and as the great object is to break the ice, we have made up our minds to be at the Queen's House. . . .[w]

She adds that, in consequence of their obduracy, they had 'lived upon very cross words and sour looks'.

Not being allowed to stay at Carlton House was a hard thing, for the Sisterhood admired its splendours, enjoyed its comforts, and entertained a grateful sense of the Regent's charm in the character of host. There were occasions, however, when the ban was partly lifted; and in February 1814 the Grand Ball at Carlton House was opened by the Duke of Cumberland and Princess Mary to the tune 'Gang nae mair to yon town'.

The third crisis, that of November–December 1812, is also reflected in the daily reports of the fourth Princess. Anxiety about the Regent's health contends with joy that 'Russia by the grace of God has compleatly succeeded in humbling the Monster'. She exhorts her brother to take care of himself, keep as quiet as possible, and not to 'set late after dinner and drink wine to *drive care away*'. At Windsor she is able to tell him that they have 'gone on tolerably', though it appears that the Queen's fires were only banked. To the young Princess Charlotte her aunts said plainly, 'the kindest thing you can do by us is never to provoke the Q.'[w]

In June of this year Princess Mary was writing to the Prince Regent:

> Charlotte is in poor Amelia's rooms; it half killed me to go and see her in that apartment, and she really is so like her that it turned me quite sick—I do assure you I thought it was her, as she stands by her dressing-table and walks about, just as she used to do.[w]

But, as we know from a letter written by Princess Amelia in 1802, it was Mary herself whom of all his sisters the Regent most wished his daughter to resemble.

All the daughters of George III were kind-hearted and charitably inclined. 'Royal' was loved in Würtemberg for her many acts of beneficence, public and private; Princess Elizabeth, after founding at Windsor a spinning school for children and a society to provide marriage portions for poor girls, flung herself vigorously into good works at Homburg; both Augusta and Sophia concerned themselves with the fate of old dependents and subscribed to many benevolent objects; and Princess Amelia, by her undiscriminating generosity, came to be not only exploited but misunderstood. It was Mary, however, who seems to have been the Almoner of the Family, and to have made it her especial care to bring cases of hardship quietly to the notice of the ever-generous eldest brother.

Owing to her carelessness in dating her letters, it is sometimes difficult to fix incidents; but all through the correspondence there persists the anxiety to do kind things and to get them done. Now we find her visiting and consoling Thielcke, the engraver, on his death-bed; now interceding for 'that excellent creature Bott', whom to see comfortably provided for 'would take a weight off Sophy's mind'; now begging 'a little Hanoverian pension for poor old Godbächer'.[w] She took pains to smooth the path of Mademoiselle Julie Montmollin through the customs when that excellent woman returned to her native Neuchâtel, and devoted her skill to making a 'lovely waistcoat in pale grey ribbed silk with pockets beautifully embroidered in fine chain-stitch and sequins' for the Duke of Gloucester's surgeon-equerry, Mr Charlton.

An example of the private benefactions of three of the Princesses occurs in some undated letters to Sir William Knighton.[w] Five years earlier, Princess Mary and Princess Sophia, then staying at Brighton, had taken some drawing lessons from a Mrs Cook, 'who taught in a peculiar stile', thereby supporting six children and an aged mother. Two of the daughters were said to be 'interesting and full of talents', and only wanted 'funds to bring them forwards'. Encouraged by royal patronage, Mrs Cook and her family migrated from Brighton to Brompton, where her cottage was 'twice robbed, and all her drawing-materials, as well as everything most valuable to her stolen'. Why burglars should have thought it worth their while to pay two visits to a small dwelling in that district of nursery-gardens is not clear. A clue may be found in the drawing-materials, to replace which Princess Mary assured Knighton no less a sum than £250 would be required. Mrs Cook's 'peculiar stile' seems to have demanded costly media.

Her royal patronesses rallied to her aid. Princess Mary headed the subscription list with £50, and reported that Augusta and Sophia 'had already been most kind', Sophia having undertaken to make good 'a great deal of the first Robbery'. Etiquette forbade George IV to make a public donation to the 'distressed family', but he gave a private one so generous that Princess Mary declared it 'would nearly be the saving of them'. Sophy, she added, was going to 'manage the money, and lay it out for their advantage'.[w]

Princess Mary seems to have been the least accomplished, though not the least intelligent, of the four eldest sisters. Sophia and Amelia were less carefully educated, chiefly on account of their delicacy, and partly, no doubt, because their mother was too much preoccupied with the King personally to supervise their lessons. Indeed Mrs Papendiek records that in 1788 the Queen remarked, 'I pity my younger daughters, whose education I can no longer attend to'. How well qualified her Majesty was for her self-imposed task Lady Harcourt bears witness when she says:

> Her understanding was indeed of the first class; it was equally quick and solid. Her mind was highly cultivated; she was fond of reading, and well acquainted with the best authors in the English, French, and German languages.

Apart from the Cook incident, there is little evidence that Princess Mary cared for drawing; nor do we find her playing any instrument. In Robert Fulke Greville's *Diary* it is recorded that in January 1789, when the King was taking a turn for the better, Princess Mary, to please him, sang 'Wind, gentle Evergreen' and 'Deil tak' the Wars' 'most prettily', but we hear no more of this. Her chief accomplishments were social, and the memoirs of the time abound in allusions to her exquisite manners. Among those whom she charmed was Lord Chancellor Eldon, nicknamed 'Bags' by the Family, who used to relate that Queen Charlotte accused him of flirting with her daughter Mary, but that he assured her Majesty she need not be alarmed, that he was neither a King, nor a Prince, nor an Emperor; and moreover that he had a wife already.

As a letter-writer she was discursive and ejaculatory, but she was an amusing correspondent none the less, and even the daily reports from Windsor during the Regency are enlivened by family gossip. When in 1813 Caroline, Princess of Wales, took herself off, Princess Mary wrote to the Prince Regent:

> I congratulate you on the prospect of a *good riddance*. Heaven grant that she may not return again and that we may never see more of her. Should a storm blow up and the ship go to the *bottom* I shall send you a *small Fashionable* Pocket handkerchief to dry your tears. It will be the only black gown I shall ever put on with pleasure.[w]

Princess Mary and her sisters took a friendly interest in the young FitzClarences, especially George and Sophia. When George Fitz Clarence (afterwards Earl of Munster) was wounded during the campaign that preceded Napoleon's first exile, he wrote a reassuring letter to Lady Harcourt 'to *relieve the Minds* of the dear Psses, who he was sure would be all anxiety about him the moment they heard he was wounded. These', Princess Mary told the Regent, 'are his own words, and he really did us but justice.'[w]

In the premature jubilations of the summer of 1814 the Queen, Princess Augusta, and Princess Mary had some share. They were present at the great fête given by the Regent to Wellington at Carlton House, when Princess Mary opened the ball with the young Duke of Devonshire to the tune of 'Voulez-vous danser, Mademoiselle?' and her Majesty stayed until half-past four in the morning. At that hour the sedan chairs (still to be seen at Windsor) of herself and the two Princesses were carried back to the Queen's House, while the birds sang in the grey morning light among the trees of St James's Park. At Carlton House night's candles were not yet burned out, and the orchestra was still performing in its bower of artificial blossom. 'It is quite impossible', wrote Princess Mary, 'to tell you *how very* much I have enjoyed myself, and how I do delight in everything, small and great, that is done at Carlton House. . . . I am sure we all talk of nothing else but all your kindness, and all those I have seen are full of *gratitude* and delight with your manners and great good nature and kindness to every soul. I never saw the Queen more pleased.'[w]

Negotiations for the marriage between William Frederick, Duke of Gloucester, and his cousin Princess Mary were on foot in the December of 1815. This is clear from a group of letters addressed to the Prince Regent by his sister, who was staying at Brighton at the end of that year and evidently relying on him to conduct the negotiations. Her *soupirant* had arranged to keep tryst with her there, though his visit was to be ostensibly to the Prince. 'I think', wrote Princess Mary anxiously, 'it would annoy him much if he did not find you at Brighton, as his visit is really to *you* and not to *me* upon this *occasion*.'(w) She adds that the Prince's people 'are all kindness and attention, but still the Master is wanting'; and she roundly wishes his Government at the bottom of the sea for calling him away. Two days later, on 5 December, she is 'hoping and trusting' that her brother will be able to come down at the end of the week. 'I have', she says, 'had a letter from the Duke saying he shall come and see me either Friday or Saturday . . . and all I trust is you will be at Brighton before he comes; it will be a great mortification to me if you are not at Brighton when he arrives, so do try all you can to get away. . . . I don't mind waiting any hour for dinner if you do but come.'(w)

She was evidently well aware of her wooer's intractable nature, as well as of his notion of his own importance. She bombarded the Regent with urgent appeals. 'Pray do come before the Duke arrives—I am so anxious you should', she wrote on 6 December; and on the 8th she was 'begging and praying' him 'to try *hard* to come'. Her long-suffering brother paid a flying visit to the Pavilion between 8 and 16 December. 'It appeared to me', remarked his sister, 'as if you went away the very moment after you arrived'; but apparently all had gone well for she looks forward to his eating his Christmas dinner with her at Brighton; and on the 23rd she was expecting him the next day, and would engage a whist table for the Duke the following night.(w) Undeterred by snowy roads, the royal negotiator dashed to and fro between Carlton House and the Pavilion, and by the dawn of the New Year matters were so far advanced that when sending him his *étrennes* she is able to speak definitely of her 'intended marriage'. She is looking forward to the '*unspeakable comfort*' of enjoying more of his dear society than she has done, and of finding her way into his room 'occasionally of a morning when in town'.(w)

. . . If I might feel empowered to do this, and that you promise to come *when* and as *often* as you please to my House, it will be the jóy of my life to *see you*. I have taken every opportunity of telling the Duke of Gloucester how compleatly and *entirely* my happiness depends on my remaining on this Blessed footing with *You* and all my Family, and he enters so warmly into my feelings that I have the greatest satisfaction in assuring you that I *trust* and *hope* my intended marriage will rather *add to* and *increase* my affec, my attachment, my *devotion* to my Family, and that as a Married Woman I can come forward and be *of more use to You all* than I can now. . . . Therefore, my beloved Brother, I rely on your calling upon me on every *occasion*, either Town, Cottage, or at Brighton. Nothing but illness will prevent my coming, barring the D. of Gloucester is ill, or there should be any illness at Windsor that requires my share of attendance with my *Sisters*.(w)

To Lady Harcourt the Princess wrote a long letter which shows that she was not free from misgivings, and realized the difficulties ahead. Apologizing for not having written sooner, she says:

> . . . The real truth is that though the Q. and Prince gave their consent on Saturday, and felt satisfied all was settled, I was not so myself untill *last night*, because I *started* a subject to the D. of Gloucester that required a very decided answer before I could make my mind up to change my situation. I got a satisfactory answer last night from the D. of York, therefore I can *now* say we compleatly understand each other. . . . I don't know what other people feel when going to be married, but as yet I have done nothing but cry.

Apparently the final discussion between the Princess and her fiancé took place at Windsor, the helpful Frederick standing by. She writes to the Regent that this conversation had perfectly satisfied both her and the Queen; and to do the Duke of Gloucester justice he seems never to have placed any obstacles between his wife and her relations, nor done anything to thwart her desire to be with them in times of family trouble.

This time Queen Charlotte behaved handsomely. The Princess's letter to Lady Harcourt, her '2d mother', continues:

> I have been half killed by the kindness of the Queen and all my Brothers, and such a day as I passed at Windsor yesterday I never can describe—that dear Castle that contains all I revere in this world, in which I have passed many happy days, that spot in which my most *valuable* and *respectable* Father is encircled. That alas! I am not to receive his Blessing and Approbation with that of all the rest of my Family kills me.

The Princess reiterates that the Duke has entered most kindly into her feelings, and says that she has convinced him that it will be in her power 'to add the duties of a Wife with all those at Windsor (to a certain degree)'; and she is cheered by the thought that Bagshot is an easy drive from the Castle, so that she will be able to stay with Sophy 'whenever the Q. goes to town or to Brighton'.

The Regent's consent does not appear to have been what King Claudius called a 'smiling and unforced accord', and the Duke of York's presence at the decisive interview suggests a certain amount of apprehension on the part of the Family. But Queen Charlotte's acquiescence is curious. She cannot have forgotten how strongly the King had disapproved of the marriage between his brother, the Duke of Gloucester, and Sir Edward Walpole's illegitimate daughter—father and mother of her prospective son-in-law, Prince William Frederick.

II

In Gillray's cartoon 'The Bridal Night', inspired by the nuptials of the Hereditary Prince of Würtemberg and the Princess Royal, there stands in the right-hand foreground a lank, uncouth figure with large, flat, out-turned feet, said to represent Prince William Frederick of Gloucester.

This youth, then twenty years of age, had been gazetted at the early age of thirteen to the first regiment of Foot Guards, and after an academic interlude at Cambridge, where he was given his degree of M.A. in 1790, he served under Sir William Erskine in the Flanders campaign of 1794–95. He also served in the expedition to the Helder in 1799. George III, who had violently disapproved of the clandestine marriage between his favourite brother, William Henry, Duke of Gloucester, and Maria, Countess Waldegrave, never looked with any particular favour upon either of the two surviving children of that union. On the other hand the Prince of Wales, either to annoy his father or out of genuine good-nature, took a friendly interest in his cousins, encouraged William Frederick to write to him during his absence in the Low Countries, and called him home to be present at his wedding.[w]

The King naturally demurred at his brother's alliance with the illegitimate daughter of Dorothy Hammond and Sir Edward Walpole. The Walpoles were a Norfolk family of respectable antiquity, though in the matter of pedigree Sir Robert's children were not of uniformly patrician descent, for Lady Walpole had been born plain Catherine Shorter, and her grandfather, Sir Henry Shorter, Lord Mayor of London, had been an importer of Baltic timber. This was a negligible impediment compared with the lineage of Sir Edward's mistress, whose parents had been of the humblest labouring class, and who had herself been employed driving a rag-and-bone cart in Holborn and selling old clothes in a shop in Pall Mall.

The romance did not turn out altogether happily, she proving *exigeante* and he unfaithful. But when the Duke died in 1805 he left his Duchess everything he had, and they vied with each other in their affection for Prince William Frederick and Princess Sophia Matilda.

When the small Prince was one year old his great-uncle, Horace Walpole, described him as 'a pretty boy'; and when he was five, his half-sister, Lady

Charlotte Maria Waldegrave, thought his looks 'divine'. But he resembled his father too closely to retain these early graces, and neither he nor Sophia Matilda inherited any of the beauty which had been Maria's legacy from the lovely, tuberculous Dorothy Hammond.

In Flanders, Prince William Frederick proved an earnest and gallant officer, and early in 1794 he was gazetted Colonel. Upon this occasion he wrote anxiously to his cousin, the Prince of Wales, 'I hope you will approve of my Choice in my Uniform. I have fixed on Black Velvet Facings, with gold-laced Button Holes, the Hat and Sword to be the same as the 1st Regt of Guards.'[w] A year later the Prince, now a Major-General, wrote to his kinsman a letter which may be interpreted as further evidence of his early attachment to the Princess Mary, though he was such a persistent hunter of promotion that the '*Subject*' in question may have been nothing more romantic than his elevation to the rank of Field-Marshal, for which he had to wait thirteen years longer.

June 12, 1795

. . . I cannot resist writing a few lines to request the Continuation of those Marks of Friendship I have ever been Proud of receiving from You. . . . I therefore hope I do not take too great a liberty in begging You to continue your Interest and Assistance upon a *Subject* you know I have so truly at heart. And I own it will be a great comfort to me, during my long Absence, to know my Case is in such safe hands.[w]

It is not always a proof of a man's popularity that he is given a number of nicknames. William Frederick rejoiced in at least three, and at no time was his a very engaging figure. Two of his sobriquets, 'The Cheese' and 'Slice', derived obviously from 'Gloucester'; the third, 'Silly Billy', had a more personal application. His grateful Alma Mater made him Chancellor in 1811, but when he was in residence he failed to give any tokens of unusual intelligence. Miss Cornelia Knight records that a visitor to Trinity College, seeing a violin on his table, asked his tutor if the Prince played much. 'Not much,' said the other, 'only God save his Uncle, and such little things.' It was amiable in the young man to invoke divine protection for an uncle who had proved so lukewarm in that role. No son of George III was more conscious of his dignity than was this semi-royal nephew. Frances, Lady Shelley, met him at a house-party at Croxteth, in 1805, when he was commanding the Lancashire district, and made these shrewd comments:

The Duke, in common with all persons who are not quite sure of their position—for he was not then a Royal Highness, a title conferred on his marriage with Princess Mary—exacted more than royal respect and attention. He never allowed a gentleman to be seated in his presence, and expected the

Above, left: King George III in coronation robes; a portrait by Allan Ramsay, *c.* 1765. *Art Gallery of South Australia*

Above, right: Queen Charlotte, (1744–1818), in her coronation robes, 1762; a portrait by Allan Ramsay. *National Portrait Gallery*

Above, left: Queen Charlotte before her marriage when she was Princess Sophia Charlotte of Mecklenburg-Strelitz; a portrait by Johann Georg Ziesenis, *c.* 1761. *The Royal Collection*

Above, right: Queen Charlotte, a portrait by Henry Robert Morland. *Private collection*

Above, left: Queen Charlotte, *c.* 1762. A portrait from the studio of Allan Ramsay.

Above, right: Queen Charlotte with Princess Charlotte Augusta Matilda; a portrait by Francis Cotes, 1767. *The Royal Collection*

Above, left: Queen Charlotte; a portrait by Benjamin West *c.* 1776. *Denver Art Museum*

Above, right: King George III, an early profile portrait by Allan Ramsay.

The two eldest brothers of the princesses as young boys; George, (1762–1830), later to become the Prince of Wales and Frederick, (1763–1827), later to become the Duke of York; a painting by Johan Zoffany.

Queen Charlotte with her brothers Ernest, (1742–1814), (*left*) and Charles, and of her children; probably Edward, Augusta and Elizabeth. Lady Charlotte Finch 'Cha' is in the background, holding the baby. A group portrait by Johann Zoffany, *c*. 1771–72. *The Royal Collection*

Above, left: Mary Delany, *née* Granville, (1700–1788); a portrait by John Opie. *National Portrait Gallery*

Above, right: Fanny Burney, (1752–1840), a portrait by her relative Edward Francis Burney. In 1793, she married a French exile, General Alexandre D'Arblay. Fanny Burney achieved fame through her writing, her most ffamous works being: *Evelina: or The History of A Young Lady's Entrance into the World*, 1778; *Cecilia: or, Memoirs of an Heiress,* 1782 and *Camilla: or, A Picture of Youth*, 1796. *National Portrait Gallery*

Windsor Castle, 1793; an aquatint by Joseph Constantine Stadler after a painting by Joseph Farington.

George, 2nd Earl Harcourt, (1736–1809); his wife Elizabeth, (1746–1826) and brother William; a group portrait by Joshua Reynolds. *Ashmolean Museum*

A distant view of Oxford from the Harcourts' estate at Nuneham Courtney, 1793; an aquatint by Joseph Constantine Stadler after a painting by Joseph Farington.

George III, Queen Charlotte and their six eldest children. A group portrait by Johann Zoffany, *c.* 1769. *The Royal Collection*

Queen Charlotte with Charlotte, Princess Royal; a double portrait by Benjamin West, 1776. *The Royal Collection*

Above: Princess Augusta,
Princess Elizabeth, Prince
Ernest, Prince Augustus,
Prince Adolphus and
Princess Mary by Benjamin
West, 1776. *The Royal
Collection*

Right: The three youngest
daughters of George III—
Princess Mary, Princess
Sophia and Princess Amelia;
a group portrait by John
Singleton Copley, 1785.
The Royal Collection

Above, left: Charlotte, the Princess Royal; a portrait by William Beechey, 1797. *The Royal Collection*

Above, right: The Hereditary Prince (later, 1806, King Frederick I) of Württemberg (1754–1816). A portrait by Johann Baptist Seele. *Schlossverwaltung Ludwigsburg*

Above, left: An irreverent cartoon by James Gillray, April 1797.

Above, right: The Queen of Württemberg in later life. *Private collection*

Another irreverent cartoon by James Gillray, May 1797. Lord Salisbury holds the door, while the king leads the way holding two candles accompanied by Queen Charlotte. William Pitt holds a money sack containing £80,000. The Hereditary Prince leads in his blushing bride, face hidden by a fan. They are followed by the Prince of Wales, the royal dukes and the Prince of Orange.

Left: Jérôme Bonaparte, King of Westphalia and Queen Catharina, Charlotte's step-daughter; a double portrait by Sebastian Weygandt. *Private collection*

Above: The three eldest princesses, Charlotte, Princess Royal; Augusta and Elizabeth; a group portrait by Thomas Gainsborough, 1784. *The Royal Collection*

Above, left: Princess Augusta; a portrait by William Beechey, 1797. *The Royal Collection*

Above, right: This portrait of Princess Augusta forms part of the series of fifteen portraits commissioned from Thomas Gainsborough, probably by Queen Charlotte. They were painted at Windsor in September and October 1782. *The Royal Collection*

Above, left: Princess Augusta; a portrait by William Beechey, *c.* 1802. *The Royal Collection*

Above, right: Princess Elizabeth, another of the fifteen portraits commissioned from Thomas Gainsborough in 1782. *The Royal Collection*

Above, left: Princess Elizabeth; a portrait by William Beechey, *c.* 1802. *The Royal Collection*

Above, right: Lady Charlotte Finch née Fermor, (1725–1813), Governess to the children of King George III; a portrait by William Hopkins. Lady Finch was known as 'Cha' to the children.

Above, left: Princess Mary as a child, another of the fifteen portraits commissioned from Thomas Gainsborough in 1782. *The Royal Collection*

Above, right: Princess Mary; a portrait by William Beechey, 1797. *The Royal Collection*

Above, left: a later portrait of Princess Mary portrait by William Beechey. *The Royal Collection*

Above, right: Princess Mary in later life, a portrait from the studio of Sir Thomas Lawrence, 1817. *The Royal Collection*

Above, left: Princess Sophia as a child, another of the fifteen portraits commissioned from Thomas Gainsborough in 1782. *The Royal Collection*

Above, right: Princess Sophia, *c.* 1792. A portrait miniature painted by Richard Cosway, believed to have been commissioned by George, Prince of Wales. *The Royal Collection*

Above, left: Princess Sophia; a portrait by William Beechey, 1797. *The Royal Collection*

Above, right: Princess Sophia; a portrait by Sir Thomas Lawrence, 1825. *The Royal Collection*

Above, left: Princess Amelia as a child; a portrait by a young Thomas Lawrence, 1789. *The Royal Collection*

Above, right: Princess Amelia; a portrait by William Beechey, 1797. *The Royal Collection*

Above, left: Princess Charlotte, the daughter of the Prince Regent; a portrait by Sir Thomas Lawrence, 1817. *The Royal Collection*

Above, right: King George IV depicted wearing coronation robes and four collars of chivalric orders: the Golden Fleece, Royal Guelphic, Bath and Garter. A portrait by Sir Thomas Lawrence, 1821. *The Royal Collection*

Windsor Castle; the Round Tower, Royal Court and Devil's Tower from the Black Rod. A painting by Paul Sandby, *c.* 1767. *National Gallery of Victoria, Melbourne*

Frogmore House; the Green Pavilion, by Charles Wild, 1817. *The Royal Collection*

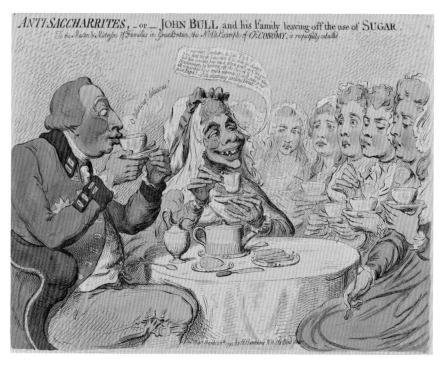

Anti-saccharites, or John Bull and his family leaving off the use of sugar. A satirical cartoon by James Gillray, 27 March 1792. The King, Queen, and six Princesses, three quarter length, are seated round a frugal tea-table.

Above, left: King William IV, by Sir David Wilkie, 1837. *National Portrait Gallery*

Above, right: Adelaide Amelia Louisa Theresa Caroline of Saxe-Coburg Meiningen, (1792–1849), Queen consort to William IV; by Sir William Beechey, *c.* 1831. *National Portrait Gallery*

Above, left: Edward, Duke of Kent and Strathearn, (1767–1820), by Sir William Beechey, 1818. Edward was a brother to the princesses, and the father of Victoria. *National Portrait Gallery*

Above, right: Queen Victoria in her early years. A portrait by Franz Xaver Winterhalter, 1842. *Osborne House*

ladies of the party to hand him coffee on a salver, to stand while he drank it, and then remove the cup. He always travelled in great state.

It is fair to add that in a dissolute and cynical age, when the virtuous example of the Sovereign was but little followed, Prince William Frederick led a life of unblemished decorum, was punctual in the public performance of his religious duties and munificent in his private charities. 'From all I can learn', noted Lady Charlotte Bury in 1812, 'he is a good man, and has the upright, solid basis of religion and virtue which distinguished the poor, fallen monarch.'

Of his personal appearance there exist two descriptions. Stockmar wrote that he had 'prominent, meaningless eyes; without actually being ugly, a very unpleasant face, with an animal expression; large and stout, but with weak, helpless legs. He wears a neckcloth thicker than his head.' Greville gives us a glimpse of him in 1830, after an inspection of the Coldstream Guards by William IV, 'bowing to the company while nobody was taking any notice of him or thinking about him'; and adds, 'Nature must have been merry when she made this Prince, and in the sort of mood that great artists used to exhibit in their comical caricatures. I never saw a countenance which that line in Dryden's *MacFlecknoe* would so well describe—

And lambent dullness plays around his face'.

In *Collections and Recollections* G. W. E. Russell preserved two anecdotes of HRH, one illustrating his ideas upon geography, and the other his taste in dress. At a levée the Duke one day caught sight of a naval friend with a weather-tanned face, and thus accosted him: 'How do, Admiral? Glad to see you again. It's a long time since you have been at a levée.' 'Yes, Sir. Since I last saw Your Royal Highness I have been nearly to the North Pole.' 'By God, you look more as if you had been to the South Pole.' Sir Charles Wyke told Mr Russell that he was walking down Piccadilly with the Duke of Cumberland on one occasion when Silly Billy came out of Gloucester House. 'Duke of Gloucester, Duke of Gloucester,' roared Cumberland, 'stop a minute, I want to speak to you.' Quite pleased at being an object of attention, Gloucester 'ambled up smiling', only to be asked 'Who's your tailor?' 'Stultz.' 'Thank you,' returned Cumberland, crushingly and characteristically, 'I only wanted to know because, whoever he is, he ought to be avoided like the pestilence.'

An example of Gloucester's conversational felicity is given in the *Croker Papers*. The Duke of Grafton, who was sixty-six, plumed himself upon looking some fifteen years younger, and was nettled when Silly Billy, in the presence of a large house-party, enquired how old he was.

Some time after the two Dukes met again, and the Duke of Glo'ster repeated the question, to which the Duke of Grafton replied dryly, 'Sir, I am exactly three weeks, two days, older than when your Royal Highness last asked me that disagreeable question'.

At a later date the Duke of Gloucester involved himself in a quarrel with the Duke of Wellington, who did not suffer fools gladly and resented being harangued and interrogated upon political and military subjects. This state of things, noted by Croker in 1823, was still in being seven years later, when Greville comments on the ball to be given by the Duke and Duchess of Wellington in July 1830:

> The Duke of Cumberland won't go to Apsley House either, but sent the Duchess and his boy. The Queen said at dinner the other day to the Duke of Cumberland, 'I am very much pleased with you for sending the Duchess to Apsley House', and then turned to the Duke of Gloucester and said, 'but I am *not* pleased with you for not letting the Duchess go there'. The fool answered that the Duchess should never go there; he would not be reconciled; forgetting that it matters not twopence to the Duke of Wellington but a great deal to himself.

To have evinced a temper even less conciliatory than that of the Duke of Cumberland was something of an achievement.

Wellington's regard would not be heightened by the Duke of Gloucester's attitude to Caroline, Princess of Wales. It was natural that when he seemed to be a candidate for the hand of the Heiress Presumptive to the throne, Prince William Frederick should have frequented the tawdry courts at Blackheath and Kensington; but it was after Princess Charlotte's death that he abstained from voting at her mother's trial and is said to have declared his belief in her innocence.

During the earlier part of his career, after he had left the army and taken up his residence as Ranger at Bagshot Park, the Duke of Gloucester was a strong Whig, an abolitionist, and emancipationist, and a friend of the most progressive member of the Family, the Duke of Sussex. Creevey recorded in 1821 that at a dinner-party at Holkham 'Slice of Gloucester had with royal solemnity declared himself a Radical'; but the Reform Bill proved too much for him, and in 1834 he gave a dinner to signalize his 'formal junction' with the Tories. His Whiggery had been offensive to some of his royal relatives. Even Princess Amelia had written to Lady Harcourt in 1808, 'Was there ever anything so wrong-headed as the D. of Gloucester's conduct in politicks—not to say worse! What wld his poor Parents say!'

Such was the man whom the Prince Regent escaped having as a son only to have him as a brother-in-law. The Duke's attitude to the Princess Charlotte project had been enigmatic. His ambition might have triumphed over his attachment for Princess Mary; and the young Princess certainly seemed to incline to him, though this may have been a screen to hide a passing fancy for the young Duke of Devonshire. The Duke of Cumberland wrote in March 1814, when the Dutch Prince was in the field, that he had been 'very much afraid she would prefer the *Cheese* to the *Orange*'. But Prince Leopold of Coburg carried off the prize, and the Cheese proceeded to sue for the hand of his still-charming cousin, Princess Mary.

As the spring of 1816 advanced towards Princess Charlotte's marriage, preparations were also going forward for the wedding of Prince William Frederick and Princess Mary. If the older bride had been the younger she could hardly have been in a greater flutter. Her reactions to a suggestion from the Duke of Cumberland, then out of favour at the Queen's House on account of his own marriage, that he should come there one morning in order to see her, are characteristic. She wrote to the Regent:

> It strikes me it would be much better *let alone*. I am quite certain the Queen would be greatly [*sic*] offended if he came *into her House* and 2ly was he to say anything against the Duke of Gloucester—it would place me in a most awkward situation. I can only follow the Q's line of conduct towards the Dss of Cumberland, married or unmarried, that alone will not make him wish to see me, and therefore I believe for all parties it is better to have no interview at all.[w]

Two letters describing the wedding at the Queen's House on 2 July 1816, have been preserved by the descendants of Princess Mary's nurse, Mrs Adams, by whose kindness they are quoted here. The writer was Mrs Adams's daughter, Louisa, and the recipient was her cousin, Miss Kitty Mayow.

At four o'clock in the afternoon the Adams ladies found the Princess 'just beginning the duties of her more important toilette'. She wore a profusion of diamonds on her head, though no feathers, and her gown and train were 'a mass of silver, very elegant yet light'. Her chief care in dressing seemed to be 'of a sentimental kind—that she should wear on this awful day the present of each of her Brothers and Sisters and the Queen. Her arms were loaded with bracelets, and her fingers with rings. . . . Then she took a ring with the King's hair, and cried poor soul, sadly as she put it on, and said, "This I would not for the world omit. I have a superstitious dread of misfortune if I did."'

At the Princess's request Miss Adams kept her watch in her hand so as to 'send her down at the right moment'. But before that came a tearful scene with 'all the Female servants, pages' wives, etc.', who had come for a glimpse of her in her bridal array, and whose 'well-meant but injudicious expressions of regret, and good wishes for her happiness, overcame her a good deal'.

By half-past eight the company had assembled, and the doors of the saloon were thrown open. The temporary altar was 'very magnificent, of crimson velvet and gold the Communion plate of gold, richly wrought—the room brilliantly lighted to give the best effect to the whole scene'.

On the right was the King's vacant throne, on the left, the Queen's chair of state. Royalties, English, French, and German, ambassadors, great officers of state, the ladies of the Family, 'blazing with jewels and towering with plumes of feathers', added to the riot of colour. The Duke of Orleans and his Duchess were there, as Princess Elizabeth can hardly have failed to observe.

The Archbishop read the service 'most impressively', using the same book that had been in the hands of Archbishop Ker when he had married the King and Queen. Louisa Adams records:

> I stood just behind the Prince of Coburg, my mother on one of the steps of the throne, and I heard her calling out *rather too audibly* 'Poor child! poor dear child!' At one time I feared Pss Mary would have fainted; the Prince Regent was exceedingly affected, and had several times recourse to his Pocket handkerchief. The Duke of Gloucester looked very serious, and pronounced his vows with right good will—the Queen, tho' much agitated, restrained her tears, but Pss Elizabeth and Sophia of Gloucester cried (almost) aloud. Just as the Archbishop had pronounced 'whom God has joined together let no man put asunder' the Park guns began to fire, and continued to do so during the exhortations that follow; it was not intended to be so soon, but I thought it added to the solemnity of the feeling.
>
> As soon as it was over Princess Mary went to the Queen and kissed her. Lady Ilchester stood close to them and told me she never saw anything so affecting as the tenderness, respect and grace of Princess Mary's manner.

Lord Eldon wrote to his daughter Frances that 'dear Princess Mary's behaviour was so interesting and affecting that everybody was affected. Even the tears trickled down my cheeks; and as to Mamma she cried all night and nine-tenth parts of the next day': but if the anecdote-book of 'Bags' is to be believed, 'some persons' in the crowded saloon conversed together so loudly as to be disturbing, and were thus admonished by Lord Ellenborough, 'Do not make a noise in that corner of the room—if you do, you shall be married yourselves!' After making due allowance for the traditional wedding tears, it looks as if the bride's relations and friends were unable to regard the union without misgivings.

The Duke and Duchess took up their abode at Bagshot Park, which was Crown Property. Lord Albemarle, in *Fifty Years of My Life*, relates that George II had made a grant of this residence to his (Albemarle's) father, and his uncles, Augustus and William, for their respective lives:

> At the death of my grandfather in 1772 Bagshot came into the occupation of Admiral Keppel, but he, wishing to make over the residence to George III's

brother, Henry Frederick, Duke of Cumberland, applied to his Majesty for a renewal of the grant. The request was peremptorily refused. According to a family tradition the King was so rejoiced at thus defeating the wishes of two persons so obnoxious to him as his brother and my uncle that he burst into a paroxysm of laughter which lasted so long as to constitute the first symptoms of that mental malady of which the unhappy monarch soon gave such unmistakeable proofs.

It is to be hoped that this tradition was not known to Princess Mary, or the Keppel portraits gazing at her from the panelling of the house may have carried painful associations.

On 26 July 1816, the bride wrote contentedly to her eldest brother:

The House is comfort itself, and to crown all, the Duke all affec and kindness, and has no object but my happiness . . . therefore let me take this opportunity of expressing my gratitude to you for giving your consent to a marriage which promises every comfort, as the more I see of the Duke, the more I am convinced of his honourable character and excellent heart.[w]

This conviction was not shared by the Regent, for one day later the Princess heard from the Duke of Cambridge that their eldest brother was vexed at having had no news from her. She answered that, 'knowing his affec Anxiety', she would not write till she had been long enough at Bagshot to assure him that she not only *was happy but certain it would last*. 'The assurances of a day or two after marriage, I felt would not satisfy your anxious mind, and that alone made me delay writing.'[w]

Three days later the Regent and Queen Charlotte visited Bagshot, and 'quite overset' the Duchess by their kindness. The Queen's verdict on the *nouveaux mariés* was that they were 'most rationally Happy and Comfortable'; and on the house, 'tho' not large, it is convenient'.[w]

Sanguine though she may have been as to her own prospects, Princess Mary was less confident as to those of her recently wedded niece. After a visit to Claremont in September 1816, she wrote to her brother that it had gone off very well—

considering that we went to see two people compleately engrossed in each other, but anxious to be *kind*, and do all they could to make it go off comfortably, I doubt that the sort of life they are now leading *can last*, but I wish it may with all my heart.[w]

'You know', wrote the Duchess, after Princess Charlotte's death, 'I always loved poor Charlotte and looked upon her quite as my own Child, and she never for one moment of her *short life* ever altered towards me.'[w] She was at

Weymouth when the tragic accouchement took place at Claremont, and hurried
to Bath to join the old Queen. Three weeks later she and the Duke visited the
widower, whom they found 'very much affected at times, but perfectly calm and
composed', ready to talk about Charlotte, anxious to keep the house just as it
had been in her lifetime, and to carry out the little alterations she had planned.
He told them that 'he meant to return to the apartment he had inhabited with
her but had not done so yet, but made it a rule to walk into there every day'.[w]

The first impulse of the good-natured Princess Mary had been to express
delight at the charms and comforts of Bagshot: but this happy mood her husband
would not allow to persist. We soon find her writing apologetic notes hinting,
and even praying, that improvements might be made in the house. The Duke,
she explains, will make no application to the Government, 'not wishing to put
them to any unnecessary expence', and trusting that the Regent will 'represent
their *real situation* to Lord Liverpool'.

> From the Duke's appartments and mine being so compleat people who don't
> know the House run away with the idea that it is a larger house. *Now* the
> fact is barring *our rooms* there is not another place in the House fit to be seen
> and those Gentlemen who belong to the Duke are lodged in the garrets, and
> nothing but the number of years they have been attached to the Duke would
> make them put up with being placed among the servants. [w]

No application had been made to Parliament for an increase in Princess
Mary's allowance, and it may have been on that account that the Duke felt
justified in pressing for some improvements to the Crown Property of which
they were the occupiers. The kindly Regent could not remain deaf to these
appeals. He sent his architect, Nash, to see Bagshot House, and himself tinkered
in a friendly manner with the plan which was drawn up, *his* 'very pretty plan',[w]
as his gratified sister called it, for the proposed alterations. It now, she declares,
contains every comfort they can possibly wish.

Like her sisters Augusta and Elizabeth, Princess Mary was an enthusiastic
garden-planner, and at the end of ten years she had done wonders with the
neglected grounds at Bagshot. In the summer of 1826 Princess Augusta wrote
to Lady Arran:

> It is a constant pleasure to see that lovely place improve so fast. In fact it
> only wanted the woods to be cleared when the Duke of Gloucester got the
> place many years ago, but as Shooting was his greatest Object here he naturally
> simply attended to what would increase shelter for game. Now within these ten
> years Mr Curry has cleared the ground, which was in a very bad state, taken
> down frightfull hedges, but no beautiful trees by taking down dead ones, and
> now the Park is getting neat. . . . The flower-garden is really unique. The Duke

of Gloucester gave Mary a piece of a *wood*, with magnificent forest trees, and with Mr Curry's taste she has made all the walks lead to these fine objects.[w]

Through the domain that she and Mr Curry had thus refashioned Princess Mary took her sister 'in the Chair drawn by her two Ponies, which she manages very well'.

Princess Augusta seems to have liked her brother-in-law. In July 1818, when Queen Charlotte's health began to cause alarm, she wrote to Lady Arran:

> It is a very great consolation to me that Mary is with us. The Duke of Gloucester has been most kind in allowing her to stay with us, and nothing can exceed the delicacy of His feeling in going abroad, which He will do the third week in this month. He feels so thoroughly that *undivided Duties* are those that ensure happiness. He leaves dearest Mary with us while He is away. . .
>
> He absolutely goes that she may remain with us. It is an act of kindness which we can never forget. And if He staid at Home and Mary was *at Kew* the ill-natured World would certainly say that they had a quarrel, therefore it is the *true, Sensible, Kind* and *Prudent* line of Conduct He has taken.[w]

To Lady Harcourt the Duke wrote from Paris, 'It will always be a great satisfaction to me to have enabled my dearest Wife to perform her last duties by her Mother, which she did in such an exemplary way'. Princess Mary, with her sympathy and experience, must have been a comfort to her sisters. 'Sir Henry will tell you', she wrote once to her eldest brother, 'that I am a capital nurse.' When all was over she accompanied Princess Augusta from Kew back to Windsor, and remained there for a time. 'Your own good heart', she told the Regent, 'will be a judge of what we felt on first coming into this Castle and seeing Sophy': and three days later, on 7 December 1818, she wrote to him:

> Our going to Prayers yesterday was dreadfull—the passing the Queen's empty Chair was quite a *trial*. Thank God it is over, and we are getting used to everybody and everything, and much more composed. . . . We are *fumbling* into our old ways and doing all we can to exert, and be of use and comfort to each other.[w]

On 22 March 1819, just two months before the birth of the future Queen Victoria, the Duke of Kent wrote to the Duchess of Gloucester emphasizing his intention of coming to England without delay, 'if he could raise the ways and means through *Friends*'. He felt it a duty he owed to the Duchess, his 'dearest Victoria', to apply for the Yacht; 'but', he added firmly, if that cannot be managed, I shall bring her over in the Packet'. Mary viewed the whole proceedings with misgiving. 'I wish', she wrote to the Regent, 'I may be wrong, but I fear it is a *deep—very* deep—layed plan.'[w]

The Regent's humane feelings would not tolerate the idea of his unfortunate sister-in-law being 'brought over in the *Packet*'. The yacht was made available. All went well; and before the end of the year Princess Mary was able to send him this lively picture of the now augmented Kent family:

> The Kents passed two nights at Windsor, bag and baggage I mean by that besides the baby she brought her daughter, and Mlle de Spate [Spaeth]—and they *all retired to rest* both evenings at 9 o'clock, the Duke and Dss of Kent, Baby, Nurse, the Pss Fedora, and Mdlle de Spate *all* wished them good Night at the same time and actually *went to bed*, to the very great amusement of the whole society at Windsor.[(w)]

January 1820, with its two royal deaths, brought much agitation to Princess Mary. 'Thank God,' she wrote, poor Edward died easy and sent his love to all his family.' It was to her that the widowed Duchess and her brother Leopold turned for practical sympathy, and through her good offices that they obtained the permission of the Regent for the widow and her baby ('also suffering from a cold') to take up their quarters in Kensington Palace.

Three days earlier Princess Mary had reported the Duke of York—official guardian of his father since Queen Charlotte's death—as being 'struck with the prodigious alteration in the poor King's face and countenance'.[(w)]

After the death of George III on 29 January the Duchess gravitated naturally to Windsor and found Princess Augusta 'mild and less hurried than I had any idea of', and 'Sophy still without spasm, but I fear we shall not put it off much longer'.[(w)] She kept her sisters company while they were 'making great exertions to get their things all packed up to leave the Castle', commended Princess Augusta's action in asking the Dowager Lady Harcourt to go with her for the first few days to Frogmore, and was anxious to see Princess Sophia safely established in London. In April 1820 a paragraph appeared in the *Gazette* announcing that the new King would henceforth celebrate his birthday on 24 April instead of on the actual anniversary, 12 August. Lord St Helens, *alias* 'the Saint', much puzzled, went round to Gloucester House to ask the equally puzzled Duchess what it was all about. Knowing her brother's dread of 'the black-glove period'—as he had called it at the time of Princess Charlotte's death—Princess Mary hastily wrote to him that if there were any chance of his sisters seeing him on that day (24 April) they 'would *of course* make a point of taking off their black gloves. But', she adds, 'if You are not to be within reach of any of us then I suppose You would not expect any of us to *take off our deep mourning*.'[(w)]

'My dearest Soul, *how can You*?' wrote George IV in reply.[(w)] The paragraph, though it had appeared in his own *Gazette*, was baseless; and by 12 August it was expected that the worst rigours of Court mourning would be over. But on 7 August the Duchess of York died at Oatlands. On the morrow of her death the Lord Chamberlain's office issued the *Orders for the Court's Going into Mourning for her late Royal Highness:*

> The Ladies to wear black silk, plain muslin or long lawn, Crape or love hoods, black silk shoes, black glazed gloves, and black paper fans.
> Undress—Black or dark grey unwatered tabbies.
> Gentlemen to wear black cloth, without buttons on the sleeves or pockets, plain muslin or long lawn cravats, and weepers, black swords and buckles.
> Undress—dark grey frockcoats.

The King refused, none the less, to let his first birthday after his accession coincide with a 'black-glove period'; for the Court was not to mourn for his sister-in-law till 13 August.

Princess Mary was now established with the Duke at Gloucester House, on the corner of Piccadilly and Park Lane. It had been Lord Elgin's town house, 'the stone-shop', as Byron had called it when it was filled with

> Misshapen monuments and maim'd antiques;

and was purchased at the time of the Princess's marriage by her bridegroom. A near neighbour was the faithful 'Bags'—Lord Eldon—who lived at the south end of Hamilton Place.

Not long after the death of George III and the departure of the Princesses Augusta and Sophia from the Castle, Princess Mary wrote to the new King:

> Judge of my joy yesterday when the door (of G.H.) opened, and who should walk into the room but dear Sophy, the first visit she has made, and she actually came up to the top of the house, and *really* did not appear the worse for it, went all over it, and set with me nearly an hour, *quite herself* and in cheerfull spirits.[w]

This letter provides corroborative evidence in support of a passage in the *Creevey Papers*:

> You will be affected to hear that the dear Duchess of Gloucester is not happy, and that tho' Slice is in politicks a Radical in domestic life he is a tyrant. Some lady called on the Duchess (indeed it has happened to two different ladies) and being admitted, was marched up quite to the top of the house; where being arrived out of breath, the Duchess apologized with great feeling for the trouble she caused her in bringing her up so far, but that in truth it was owing to the cruel manner in which she was treated by the Duke—that he had taken it into his head that the suite of rooms on the drawing-room floor was not kept up in

sufficiently nice order, and on that account he had locked them up, and kept the keys himself.

Creevey's comment is, 'It is no wonder the King treated Slice the last time he was at Court with the same sauce that he did Leopold. The Radical has declared he will never go there again.' Princess Mary's letters to her brother do not suggest any estrangement, but diplomacy was evidently needed to obtain her husband's permission for her to visit the Pavilion. Princess Augusta wrote to George IV on 25 January 1821:

> Dearest Mary is all gratitude for your Message, and we both agree that You should write to Her. I trust and cannot doubt that there will *not* be any questions on the Subject, only pray don't write any *word* that may be taken up. She never does Shew Her letters to the Duke, but as You must ask Him I think She will be quite right to Shew Him the letter: it will be advisable and do good.
>
> She assured me upon her honour, and Charlotte Belassyse said the same when alone with me, that all is as comfortable as possible at Bagshot Park. Politicks *we never talked upon*, and all has been as chearfull as possible. I asked Charlotte if I might really say so with truth to You, and she said, Upon my Word and Honour you may, for I would not say so if it was not true.[(w)]

The reassuring Charlotte Bellassyse, nicknamed by Princess Amelia 'Charlotte Belly', was Princess Mary's lady-in-waiting. Without throwing doubt upon her sincerity, it may be questioned whether everything was always 'chearfull' at Bagshot. The Duke imposed his will upon the Duchess with an obduracy which must have been trying at times. His Sabbatarian scruples would not let her travel—even to visit the King—on a Sunday, nor were the King's wishes to determine the date and duration of her absence. In one letter concerning a proposed visit to Brighton she writes:

> Yet after all I thought it best to tell you the *truth*, that in case I cannot continue to stay the length of time your great kindness purposes, that you will not take it ill of me, or in ill part of *him*, for Man is Man, and does not like to be put out of his way, and still less by a *Wife* than anybody else.[(w)]

How greatly the Duchess enjoyed her visits to the Pavilion comes out in her letters again and again. She describes herself, on her return, following the King from room to room in imagination, 'like a true Dog', and fancying she sees him at dinner, 'offering the Punch and the Brown Bess all round the table'. Her heart 'fills with delight' at the recollection of the happy days she passed under his roof. Her chief care was to maintain friendly relations between the King and her husband. She sought leave for the Duke—an excellent shot—to shoot sometimes in the

Great Park, all the game that fell to his gun to go to the royal table; but when he permitted himself to solicit the governorship of Guernsey, vacant through the death of Lord Pembroke, she seems to have held aloof. Her name is not invoked by the Duke in his letter to the King,[w] nor mentioned by Wellington in his remarks on the proposed appointment. In the event Sir William Keppel was gazetted to Guernsey and Slice received the governorship of Portsmouth.

In the summer of the same year, 1827, the Duchess had borne her part in the Family reception of the long-exiled Princess Royal. Writing to Lady Arran from Frogmore in July, Princess Augusta gives a glimpse of herself and her younger sister during the visit:

> Since last Friday my sister Mary has joined us, so that the House is literally what the common people call *chockfull*. Our sitting-room every morning after breakfast is the Colonnade, which is *lovely*. Mary and I have each our table opposite each other, our book, writing-box, and a good large *Couch*, in the middle of which we sit, making a second and third table of each end of it, for all our superfluous articles of Baskets, Dictionaries, trays for the Wafers and Wax etc.[w]

All the aunts took an interest in the little Princess Victoria of Kent. 'Poor Edward', Princess Mary had written, during the last days at Sidmouth, 'God knows may have his faults, but he has ever been a most affec Brother to me',[w] and she repaid that affection to his daughter, who looked upon her as a 'sort of grandmother'. 'Aunt Gloucester' comes charmingly upon the scene during the visit of Princess Victoria to Windsor in the summer of 1826, when George IV said 'Give me your little paw', and bent down his old, painted, but still kindly face for her to kiss. The next day, walking with a group of companions towards Virginia Water, the eight-year-old Princess 'met the King in his phaeton, in which he was driving with the Duchess of Gloucester, and', she records, 'he said "Pop her in", and I was lifted in and placed between him and Aunt Gloucester, who held me round the waist (Mamma was much frightened)'.

The Conyngham family, some of whom helped to entertain this important young visitor, were much in evidence at Royal Lodge during the last years of George IV's life. With what complacency Princess Mary accepted the installation of the elderly and pious Lady Conyngham under her brother's roof is shown by an undated letter of this period in which, after dwelling with much sympathy on the circumstances which cause her to defer a visit to the Lodge, she reveals that what makes her anxious 'not to vex or worry' the King is the illness of Lady Conyngham.[w]

Meanwhile the health of the Duke of Gloucester had been giving cause for uneasiness, and Earl Grey was unkind enough to observe to Mr Creevey, 'Well, if he dies all I can say is he won't leave a greater fool behind than himself'. The

Duke's complaint, according to Croker, 'began with a bilious inflammation but ended in the *family* complaint, and the immediate cause of death was the bursting of a scrofulous swelling in the head'. The Duchess nursed him devotedly, while, 'having given himself over from the first moment', he spent his hours in 'good nature, charity and piety'. Nearly sixty years before, his father, William Henry, Duke of Gloucester, had obtained George III's permission to build a new vault under St George's Chapel, and there the bodies of an infant daughter, Caroline Augusta Maria, William Henry himself, and his beautiful widow had been laid in turn. With them William Frederick, Duke of Gloucester, was buried privately on 11 December 1834, the chief mourner being, at the King's express desire, Augustus, Duke of Sussex.

The details of Slice's will do him honour. 'He left legacies to all his attendants to the total amount of £80,000; the rest to the Duchess. It turns out', adds Croker, 'that he and the Duchess have habitually given above £6,000 a year in charity.' And he desired that one of the Duchess's rings should be put upon his finger.

A month later Princess Lieven wrote from St Petersburg to Earl Grey:

> The news of the Duke of Gloucester's death seemed to me at first rather like a weight taken off my chest—the poor man used to bore me so terribly. . . . You will see the Duchess of Gloucester will now get perfectly well. There is nothing so bad for the health as small daily worries, and nothing so trying as continual ennui.

And indeed, Elizabeth, Landgravine of Hesse-Homburg, who came over to England 'with the good intention of dedicating herself to dearest Mary', was able to assure Mrs Dering in March 1835 that her sister was 'wonderful, considering the shock she has had, and the constant business she has had ever since the poor Duke of Gloucester's death'. In the summer of the following year the Duchess took courage to visit the Landgravine, from whom there is a letter in the Taylor MSS., dated 20 August 1836, saying, 'To my sorrow dearest Mary quitted me yesterday. I took her to Franckfort, where we parted. . . . God knows parting is misery.'

Little imagination is needed to picture the sorrow of Princess Mary when George IV died, only ten years after she had wept with emotion to see him crowned. During the last year of his life she was as constantly with him as the Duke of Cumberland would permit her to be. Greville notes her complaints that the Duke thrust himself in whenever she was alone with his Majesty, but she seems to have known and realized the seriousness of the King's state when she told Princess Lieven only a month before the end that 'the wounds in the legs had been closed by the doctors for fear of gangrene supervening'.

William IV, like his predecessor, loved to have 'dearest Mary' about him in times of stress; and it was she to whom, according to Greville, he unburdened himself 'more than to anybody else'. She told Lady Georgina Bathurst that 'he was in a most pitiable state of distress, constantly in tears, and saying that he felt his crown tottering on his head'. After King William's reign ended, Princess Elizabeth wrote to Mrs Dering from Homburg:

> Dearest Mary is a proof of what affection will do, for ill as she was in the winter, and so unwell before my brother's death, Augusta's state of agony was such that she roused herself to support her.

This is indeed the Princess Mary of Weymouth and of Windsor, the sister of whom the Duke of Kent had written, 'as to dearest Miny she is as usual everything that is heavenly'.(w)

Princess Mary had one foible which is seldom met with in the self-forgetful. 'She is unfortunately', wrote Princess Augusta in 1840, 'timid about her health, in which she is totally unlike the rest of her family.' Yet Augusta herself had then only five more months to live, and Mary, in whose constitution the elder sister 'feared the seeds of dropsy', was destined to survive her by no less than seventeen years.

The affection of the Duchess for the Duke of Cambridge, her last surviving brother, was very great, and was extended to his Duchess, his two charming daughters, and his son. The Duke always made a point of spending his sister's birthday with her, and on the first anniversary after his death, his widow and Princess Mary Adelaide (afterwards Duchess of Teck and mother of her Queen Mary, consort of George V) took his place. 'You enabled me', wrote the old Duchess to her sister-in-law, 'by your kindness and dear Mary's very delightful spirits to pass the day chearfully.'

The pretty Winterhalter group of children multiplying round Queen Victoria and Prince Albert was a great source of happiness to their Aunt, always a lover of children. The Duke of Argyll records in his *Passages from the Past* that one of the most hospitable of the hostesses in Park Lane during his childhood was the Duchess of Gloucester:

> who lived at the corner of Piccadilly in a house subsequently occupied by the Duke of Cambridge. A crowded ball for children, held in a large upper room, was always attended by all the Stafford House children, a very numerous contingent: and the Duchess of Gloucester, with grey curls on each side of her head and a small cap above her good-natured face, was most kind and attentive to us all.

Ventriloquists, or '"little wonders" of about six years old who played the violin and piano', entertained the Duchess's young guests.

From the opening of her reign Queen Victoria was kind and attentive to 'dear Aunt Gloucester'. Lady Lyttelton relates how in October 1838 Queen Victoria, the Duchess of Kent, Lady Mary Stopford, 'a nice little red-haired old maid', and herself drove off at a great rate to pay a morning visit to the Duchess of Gloucester at Bagshot Park:

> The Duchess of Gloucester was delightful, and it was a very pleasant visit. The Duke of Cambridge staying there. There is such heartiness and seemingly endless good temper about all the Royal Family, to judge from manner and look, it is nice to see them.
>
> We of the household staid in one room while the Queen was with her family in another, and staid long, and sang to them, and seemed quite snug.

Visits to Brighton, where she stayed at the Bedford Hotel, and to the Isle of Wight alternated with longer sojourns at Gloucester House, White Lodge, and Bagshot.

The Duchess kept in touch with her old friends in every degree, and many of them brought children and grandchildren to see her. When one of Mrs Adams's granddaughters was introduced at Gloucester House a large wax doll with eyes that opened and shut was waiting for her, and a special pudding was provided for her at lunch. More than eighty years later Miss Adams remembered making her curtsey—as instructed—as soon as she entered the drawing-room, and the kindly laughter of the Duchess when she later asked, 'Where's *my* pudding?'

In December 1847 the Queen, writing to thank her aunt for the 'pretty gifts' sent to her children, mentions that 'Alice was quite *beside herself* at her first earrings and is all anxiety to have her ears bored'. Five months later, when the baby Princess Louise was christened, her Majesty wrote to her Uncle Leopold:

> The poor Duchess of Gloster is again in one of her nervous states, and gave us a dreadful fright at the christening by quite forgetting where she was, and coming and kneeling at my feet in the midst of the service. Imagine our horror!

An undated birthday letter to the Prince of Wales, written probably in the last November of 'Aunt Gloucester's' life, betrays a touch of vagueness—she was nearing her eighty-second year—but in kindliness and cheerfulness recalls the 'Miny' of fifty years earlier:

Nov. 9, G.H.

My Dear Nephew,

I beg you to accept my most affte congratulations on this dear day, and trust you will live to enjoy many, many happy returns of the 8 of Nov. [sic] and the older you grow, be a greater comfort your [sic] dear Parents, and continue to be as much beloved as you are now, by attending to all your studies and various Duties that must aid to endear you more and more to *them*. I beg you to accept a telescope that I trust you will find usefull, and if it sometimes recalls

me to your recollection it will greatly gratify Aunt Gloucester. I rejoice you
have good accounts of dear Alfred and that the journey was so *prosperous*.
The act of parting with him must have [been] painfull to you all, but I hope he
will not be very long absent, and the pleasure and joy of seeing him again will
repay you all for all you suffered in parting with him.

    Love to all your Brothers and Sisters, and believe me always.—Your affe Aunt
MARY

I send you the Key for the Box that accompanies these few lines.[w]

She was a good judge of character, discerning already two characteristics of
the future King Edward VII—a gift of winning affection and a disinclination
for intellectual effort; but she died too soon to perceive how much the boy had
inherited of that *joie de vivre* which none of his great-uncles lacked.

Another undated letter, probably of the same period, celebrates the first
occasion when the Heir Apparent 'went out with the guns':

> I can well believe how delighted you must have been at being allowed to go
> out shooting for the first time, and the being so fortunate as to have killed two
> Rabbits gives every hope that you will be a good sportsman by and by.[w]

Her great-nephew sometimes supplied her table from the bag, for another
time she tells him, 'I made an excellent dinner yesterday on one of the fine Birds
you kindly brought me from Osborne, and I have another to-day'.

In August 1856 the Duchess had 'an attack of faintness and oppression' on
returning from a drive; a month later she wrote to the Duchess of Cambridge,
'I am happy to be able to tell you that I was up, and dressed, and in my room
yesterday from half past two till near six o'clock—I am improving in a quiet
way and beginning to employ myself'.[w]

In the spring of 1857 Queen Victoria, who had been awaiting the birth of her
first child when Princess Augusta died, was expecting that of her last. Princess
Beatrice was born on 14 April, and a few days later the *Illustrated London News*
noted that 'the Prince Consort and the junior members of the Royal Family
have been out daily, generally calling at Gloucester House to enquire after the
illustrious and venerable Princess whose dissolution is hourly expected'.

The last frail link with the vanished Family, with all its splendours and
sorrows, its romances and eccentricities, was wearing thin. Princess Mary's span
of life stretched from the London of Gillray to the London of Cruikshank. She
had been born into a world which laughed at the wit of Sheridan; she died in a
generation that wept at the pathos of Tom Taylor. The whistle of the locomotive
had superseded the gay flourish of the mail-guard's horn; pompousness had
ceased to be fruity and had become oleaginous; and by imperceptible degrees
raffishness had glided into respectability.

25 April was the Duchess's eighty-first birthday, and her niece, Princess Mary of Cambridge, wrote in her diary, 'Alas! we dared not keep it except sacredly, as it were'. During the days that followed, the Duchess of Cambridge and her daughter were constantly at Gloucester House. Two days later, as they left the dying Duchess's room, Princess Mary relates:

> she put up her hand as if to kiss it to me. Hawkins next went in, and she said to him, 'The Queen is coming to-day', which much startled him. Her eyes were wide open, and she looked round the room very much as dear Papa used to do in his last illness.

In the early hours of 30 April the two young Princesses of Cambridge were summoned to join their mother at the bedside of the Duchess.

'There was no consciousness', wrote the younger Princess, 'and the doctors assured us no suffering, but the struggle with death was most distressing . . . and lasted till 5.15, when, with another stretch and a momentary convulsive contraction of the face, all was over, and with the dawn of day the gentle spirit returned to God who gave it.'

'Her loss', wrote this Princess a fortnight later, 'can never be repaired, as she was the centre around which we moved, and there is a void in our hearts and daily life which we shall realize by and by more fully than even now. . . . We drove over to the White Lodge to see everything as she had left it. Alas! how sad it made us. We went over the house and garden, and my heart ached to see it all so desolate.'

Princess Sophia,
1777–1848

I

On 3 November 1777, when the sister next in age to herself, that 'lovely, elegant-made child', Princess Mary, was only one year and seven months old, the fifth daughter of George III and Queen Charlotte was born at the Queen's House. She was christened a month later by Archbishop Cornwallis in the Great Council Chamber at St James's Palace, and her godmothers were the Duchess of Brunswick and the Grand Duchess of Mecklenburg-Schwerin. Her godfather, Prince Augustus of Saxe-Gotha, was the brother of Augusta, Princess of Wales, so it would have been a family reunion had the illustrious sponsors stood in person by the font.

During the following summer the baby was at Kew with her nurse, Mrs Williams, from whom she was severed almost as suddenly as was Paul Dombey from Polly Toodle. Knowledgeable old women at that time, and for long after, were convinced that an abrupt weaning was inimical to an infant's health; and Princess Sophia was always delicate. Mary Hamilton relates the circumstances:

> July 11, 1778. I have volunteer'd to superintend the 2 Rockers and take charge of ye Dear infant Princess Sophia, as her Wet Nurse, Mrs W., was so affected on hearing of the illness of her Mother that it was proper to wean the child, & she (Mrs W) went to her Mother. Princess Sophia's nursery is in this House where I lodge (viz. Prince Ernest's) & I shall sleep in her room till either Mrs W returns or some other arrangement is made.

Mrs Williams reappears later on as Princess Amelia's nurse. Like Mrs Adams and Mrs Cheveley ('Chi-Chi'), she remained on affectionate terms with her foster-children after they were grown-up.

Princess Sophia remained Mary Hamilton's 'little favourite', her 'sweet, engaging child', and Miss Burney, though less lyrical, was obviously charmed eleven years later by the shy Princess, who blushed as she curtseyed, and insisted on carrying away in her own arms the basket of the Queen's pet dog, Badine, which she was sent to fetch. In November 1787 the small girl had been ill for some time, and kept her birthday in bed, receiving 'very prettily' the offerings which Miss Goldsworthy ushered Fanny in to present. The quick sympathy of the Princess's character is shown in two anecdotes recorded by Miss Burney. Hearing that a lady, discreetly alluded to as 'Mrs——', had lost a baby, 'Dear me,' exclaimed Princess Sophia, 'how sorry I am for poor Mrs ——. I'm sure I hope she'll soon have another.'

The second anecdote is delightful. The Queen, who had always a kindly regard for the feelings of dependents, thought it wise to warn 'little Sophy' not to laugh or stare at the exceptionally prominent nose of her new music-master, Mr Webb. This warning the child bore in mind, and one day when Lady Cremorne, who had never seen him, was with her at the moment of his arrival, 'she coloured very red and ran up to Lady Cremorne and said to her in a whisper, "Lady Cremorne, Mr Webb has got a very great nose, but that is only to be pitied—so mind you don't laugh"'.

Sixty years later, when Princess Sophia, old, blind, and stricken, had just died in seclusion at Kensington, the *Illustrated London News* graced its obituary notice with this story:

> On one occasion at breakfast, whilst the King was reading the newspaper to his family, the Princess Sophia, then very young, said, 'Mamma, I can't think what a prison is'. Upon its being explained, and understanding that the prisoners were often half-starved for want, the child replied, 'That is very cruel, for the prison is bad enough without starving. I will give all my allowance to buy bread for the poor prisoners.' Due praise was given for this benevolent intention, which was directed to be put into force together with an addition from the royal parents, and many a heart was relieved that knew not its benefactor.

An early undated letter to George III, in French, shows that the accomplished Swiss lady, Charlotte Salomé Montmollin (or de Montmollin), taught the little Princesses French and ancient history as well as needlework and purse-netting:

> *Vous apprendrez avec plaisir que ma chère Marie a fait la meilleure leçon qu'elle a prise de sa vie avec Melle Montmollin, et je fais de même, car je ne voudrois pas reculer; au contraire je ferai toujours de mieux en mieux, et surtout ce qui me plaît le plus c'est l'histoire des Grecs.*[w]

Another missive of the same period mentions her regret that a cold from which she is suffering prevents her from reading aloud with 'Melle' Montmollin, 'et cela', adds Princess Sophia, '*me fait de la peine parceque nous lisons tant de jolies choses ensembles*'.[w]

The friendship between the Family and Charlotte Salomé extended to the younger generation of the Montmollins, and Princess Sophia seems to have been particularly fond of them all.

The father of the original 'Melle' was a pastor and professor of Belles Lettres and Philosophy who kept a boarding-school at Neuchâtel. For the modest fee of 450 Dutch francs a year, he provided his pupils with *'la table, le bois, les chandelles, chambre chaude et blanchissage'*. The subjects taught included Greek, Latin, Heraldry, all branches of Philosophy, theoretical and practical, Natural Law and Civil Law. One of the pupils, Jean Louis de Sperandieu (*Espère-en-Dieu*), fell in love with the dominie's eldest daughter, Charlotte Salomé, who was sent to the Imperial Court of Russia to act as governess to the young Grand Duchesses. It is an interesting reflection that she must have seen the Prince of Würtemberg, who was afterwards to marry the Princess Royal, and also his flighty first wife, niece of George III. Her next *étape* was Windsor.

When, in 1791, the pertinacious de Sperandieu renewed his suit, Charlotte Salomé married him, and her place in the royal household was taken by her cousin Julie, described by Miss Burney as 'agreeable and sensible'. Julie's sister Marianne followed her to England, and we shall meet her later in Princess Sophia's company. A brother, Georges, was one of Louis XVI's Swiss Guard, and his name is engraved with those of his comrades upon Thorwaldsen's Lion Monument at Lucerne.

Unlike their pupils, the governesses of George III's daughters tended to find husbands. Suzanne Moula, Charlotte Salomé's friend, colleague, and contemporary, married a Captain Allen Cooper of the East India Company, and remained on cordial terms with the Princesses. The knot was tied by the Reverend Charles de la Guiffardière, otherwise 'Mr Turbulent'. In the public library at Neuchâtel there is a collection of faded and almost indecipherable letters from Suzanne Moula and her sister Marianne to Madame de Charrière, and in one of these we get a glimpse of the wedding of 'La Mont'—*i.e.* Charlotte Salomé—to whom Suzanne Moula was to act as bridesmaid. '*La Reine*', remarks Marianne rather acidly, *'fait autant de "fuss" de ce mariage que si c'etait une de ses filles. Les cadeaux lui pleuvent d'autre part.'*

More interesting, and also more difficult to unravel, is the letter of 30 April 1798, in which Marianne Moula describes a visit to Frogmore with the 'Guiffs', and to a review in a camp seven miles from Windsor. She is full of admiration at the evidences of royal art and industry in Queen Charlotte's retreat; curtains, chair-covers, tablecloths, pictures, all the work of the Princesses' own hands. 'If', remarks Marianne, 'they had been great geniuses, or had revealed much taste for study, it would be a pity to see them occupied with needles and paint-brushes. But those things are better occupations than gaming, novels, and intrigues. They have none of those tastes, and are, I assure you, excellent young persons.'

Mademoiselle Moula then proceeds to sketch the 'excellent young persons' one by one. The least likeable, though perhaps not the least worthy of being liked, was the Princess Royal. 'They say she is adored in her new home, but the others seem a little more gay since she departed.' Princess Elizabeth '*a pris un petit air de conséquence; elle est une personnage dans la maison'*. Princess Augusta is, as she has always been, the most unassuming; Mary is very cheerful, rather inclined to gossip, but so good and so easy of approach that everyone likes her. Princess Sophia, who had always been Marianne's favourite, is the least *'douce'*. Her nerves are sensitive, and she is *'sujette aux "low spirits"'*— these ladies love to show off their English. None the less it is she who has more sensibility, energy, and imagination than all the rest put together. Her features are the least regular, but her face is the most *'élégante'*—a good touch.

The review at Windsor was a fine sight, and the seven or eight thousand cavalry, wheeling, glittering, and thundering, thrilled Mademoiselle Marianne. Among those present was the Prince of Orange, who followed the troops in *'une bien mesquine chaise de poste'*. The night before he had been at the play, seated between his two pretty cousins, Mary and Sophia; *'et je le vis dormir la plupart du tems, malgré que Sophie cherchait à le tenir éveillé en lui donnant l'étui de son éventail'*.

It is curious how often we find Princess Sophia mentioned as somebody's favourite among the Sisterhood. She was Mary Hamilton's; she was Marianne Moula's; and, if Fanny Burney is to be believed, she was the Duke of Clarence's— at least when he returned from the West Indies in the summer of 1789. She was then, says Fanny, his 'professed favourite', and he was boisterously delighted when he 'had had the honour of about an hour's conversation with that young Lady, in the old style; though', he added hastily, 'I have given up my mad frolics now. To be sure I had a few in that style formerly!' The 'old style' must have been his, and not hers, for his sister was at that time not quite twelve years old, and he had been absent from England for more than a year with his ship, the *Andromeda*. Fifteen years later the Duke of Kent is writing of her to the Prince of Wales as 'my little favourite, Sophy'.[w]

Both Princess Elizabeth and Princess Sophia have suffered severely from the scandalous pen of that 'clever, voluble, sort of cunning Scotsman', Sylvester Douglas, Lord Glenbervie, the questionable source of whose anecdotes was the Court of Caroline, Princess of Wales. It does small credit to Glenbervie's acumen that he should have accepted as even approximately true the gossip of Kensington Palace and Blackheath, and smaller credit to his decency that he should have recorded it with Boswellian precision, salving his conscience with occasional interjections of 'How strange and how disgusting!' A typical example of his unreliability is his allegation that the Family, while outwardly affable, 'cordially hated' the Dowager Lady Harcourt. His lordship might have felt some surprise if he had had an opportunity of seeing the *Harcourt Papers*, with their strong evidence of enduring regard on both sides.

Nothing pleased the younger Princesses better than a visit to Nuneham, of which even the austere John Wesley said that it was 'the pleasantest spot he had ever seen'. The house had been rebuilt in 1782, crowned with a tower designed by William ('Scroddles') Mason, Horace Walpole's parson friend, and embellished with painted glass, supplied by Walpole himself. In July 1791 Queen Charlotte wrote from Weymouth to Lady Harcourt:

> I take the earliest opportunity of thanking you and My Lord for your very unbounded goodness and attention to my youngest Daughters; they are perfectly drunk with the pleasure they have felt, and are still feeling, of being with you, and will, like me, retain an everlasting remembrance of your kindness.

A year later, and again in 1793, Princess Sophia suffered from a tedious illness, which included trouble with what she called her 'swallow'. She wrote to her father from Kew in August 1792: 'I can with truth say my swallow has improved within the last few days, though not yet arrived at perfection'.[w]

Whatever the nature of her malady, it was such in the summer of 1793 that she could not hold her pen steadily. The writing in this birthday letter to her eldest brother is significantly shaky:

> *July* 29, 1793
>
> My Dearest Dear Prince of Wales,
>
> You are so good to us at all times that notwithstanding my trembling hand I shall venture to trouble you with these few lines without making an apology, as I am sure you will forgive me. Miny and me beg your acceptance of the little box which accompanies this note—it is but a trifle, but I can with truth say it comes from two hearts which never can forget your goodness.
>
> God bless you, my dear Angel—I would write more if I could.—Your affecte sister,
>
> SOPHIE [w]

Another letter of the same summer, written with a firmer hand, shows that to 'little Sophy' as well as to all his other sisters the Prince of Wales had been both father-confessor and comforter. She begins by telling him that she had seen Sir Lucas Pepys, who forbade the Sunning Hill water 'as it is too Cold'. He has ordered her a new medicine, and if it agrees she is to go to Tunbridge Wells.

There had evidently been trouble both in Upper and Lower Lodge:

> Many more unpleasant things have passed since we met. Princess Royal and Lady Cathcart I strongly suspect are at the bottom of everything. I should not say this unless I was quite sure. My reasons I will give you when we meet, which God grant may not be later than the end of the week. I have very good ones, and now I have heard many a story that Princess Royal has repeated to the Queen. I have not forgot your advice and fear at last I must have recourse to it, as things are very so-so here.[w]

It has already been pointed out that the Princess Royal was the sister for whom the Prince of Wales's affection was the least warm. If in spite of her good qualities she really was a tale-bearer, that may be the reason. An allusion in a letter written by Princess Mary from Weymouth about the same period supports this theory, and perhaps explains Marianne Moula's remark that the younger sisters 'seemed a little more gay' after the eldest had departed. Princess Sophia continues:

> I am sure, my Dearest, you will not be displeased at this when I tell you that nothing could have made me happier than your permitting me to open my heart to you—our conversation on Sunday night was quite a cordiall to my heart. One thing I must beg and pray is that you will not mention to any of my sisters what I said to you at the Lower Lodge, as I well know what a fuss it would make.
>
> The Dear King is all kindness to me and I cannot say how grateful I feel for it. Mama, Adolphus, and all my sisters are gone to Oatlands.[w]

Evidently the new medicine prescribed by Sir Lucas Pepys did agree, for in October the Princess was at Mount Pleasant, Tunbridge Wells, and writing to the King:

> What words to make use of I do not know for to express my gratitude to my dear, dear Papa for his Angelic letter with which I was agreeably surprised this morning. . . . How good you are, my dearest Papa, to be so anxious about me! . . . My Faintings are less, though not as much diminished as I could wish—as to my swallow, with your leave I will not mention that, but I assure you I am not impatient—it came quite Right before, and why should I despair? Nothing can be so bad for me as impatience.[w]

So begins the long story of Princess Sophia's precarious health, her 'cramps', 'spasms', and recurrent attacks of 'pain in the side'. At the time of Princess Charlotte's death a writer in the *London Medical Repository* remarked, 'We have been informed that the whole of the Royal Family are liable to spasms of a violent description'; and as late as 1857 the enigmatic term was used to describe the closing stages of Princess Mary's illness. In the interim it had sunk in the social scale, and Mrs Crupp had used her 'spazzums' as a stratagem whereby to obtain brandy from the ingenuous David Copperfield.

In the intervals between her attacks Princess Sophia emerged from time to time, a rather elfin, elusive creature. Her eldest brother nicknamed her the 'Sea Nymph', and Lord Melbourne told Queen Victoria that 'he always thought Princess Sophia (when young) very pretty, though very like a Gipsy'. None of Queen Charlotte's children inherited her dark colouring, and the Gipsy quality noted by 'Lord M.' was probably a matter of expression and demeanour, for the fifth Princess was not the least fair. She was a good horsewoman, and we get glimpses of her riding with the King at Windsor and at Weymouth. On 21 May 1811, the *Annual Register* noted that his Majesty 'rode out on his favourite horse, Adonis, accompanied by his daughters Augusta and Sophia'. It was his last appearance in public, and on 12 August of the following year the same two Princesses shared the Regent's birthday canter. After Princess Sophia's severe illness in 1814 one of the medical bulletins stated that she had 'been on horseback for a short time', and that 'it was pleasant to her Royal Highness, though she was a little fatigued by it'.[w]

Music does not seem to have been among Princess Sophia's accomplishments, but she was skilful with her needle and her paintbrush, embroidering pole-screens, netting purses, and painting cherubs' heads on parchment with a deft hand. As a letter-writer she is often amusing, though in later life rather prone to pious ejaculations.

A few letters to Lady Harcourt and some scattered allusions in those of her sisters are all that remain to bridge a gap between 1793 and 1801 in Princess Sophia's correspondence.

A great deal of stress has been laid upon a letter written by this Princess to Lady Harcourt from Weymouth, in August 1794. It is clear that her ladyship, not for the first time, had been admonishing her, though on what grounds it does not appear.' I shall ever remember with pleasure the last conversation we had together,' says Princess Sophia, 'and I shall do all I can to follow the good advice you gave me.' And then, further on in the same letter, quite distinct from this passage, comes the paragraph upon which certain biographers and novelists have focused their gaze:

> Dear Prince of Wales arrived yesterday, and leaves us again on Tuesday; he is as charming as usual and a great comfort to us. Dear Ernest is as kind to me as it is possible, rather a little imprudent at times, but when told of it never takes it ill.

In the mind of anyone who has gone through the correspondence of the Family there can, I think, be small doubt as to the nature of Prince Ernest's 'imprudence'. Even as a young man he was an inveterate mischief-maker, with a bitter, mocking tongue; and Princess Sophia was what was then called a 'quiz'. Mr Roger Fulford, while effectively demolishing a sinister imputation, suggests that there may have been 'a certain amount of irresponsible foolishness between the Duke and his sister', and cites as an analogy the 'almost fantastic admiration' professed for Princess Mary by the Dukes of Clarence and Cambridge. But Prince Ernest alone of all the brothers avoided exaggeration. The diction of the Heir Apparent was ecstatic to the point of absurdity; his sisters addressed him in language which was so affectionate as to verge upon the amorous. There was not one of the Brotherhood who was not apt, upon occasion, to indulge in gush—except the Duke of Cumberland. His whole personality was harder than that of any of the others. It is not very easy to imagine him being affectionately irresponsible; his irresponsibility, when he condescended to any, was rather of a crude and derisive kind. And the crisis of Princess Sophia's life came six years later.

In December 1800 Princess Sophia wrote to Lady Harcourt a letter of more tragic import, for by that time her child, the 'Thomas Garth' of her subsequent miseries, had been born. She begins by telling her 'very dear Lady Harcourt' that she may easily believe how often their *private conversation* has occurred to her mind, and goes on:

> . . . how happy I am now that I had courage to begin it, for the excessive kindness of your manner has, I assure you, greatly soothed my distressed and unhappy days and hours. Be assured my dearest Lady Harcourt, that I will do all in my power to prove I am not ungrateful! for all your kind concern about me, by the prudence of my conduct; but you will allow, I am sure, that I require time to recover my spirits, which have met with so severe a blow.
>
> I have no doubt that I was originally to blame, therefore I must bear patiently the reports, however unjust they are, as I have partially myself to thank for them. . . . It is grievous to think what *a little trifle will slur a young woman's character for ever.*

This last is a curious remark, and, on the face of it, a brazen one. A liaison resulting in the birth of a baby cannot be called 'a little trifle'. But an interpretation suggests itself which sets the Princess's words in another light. If she was, as tradition avers, secretly married to General Garth, either before the birth or before the conception of her child, she may have felt that morally her position was unassailable, and the 'little trifle' may have been some incident which threw into too clear relief her infatuation for the elderly equerry. 'However imprudent I may have been,' she says to Lady Harcourt, in promising to try to regain her own 'slurred' character, 'it has, I assure you, been injured unjustly.'

When Princess Mary died, Miss Martineau made some observations in the *Daily News* which certainly support the 'secret marriage' theory:

> All that long series of heart histories was closed. The wretched avowed marriages, or chequered secret marriages, and the mere formal state marriages which took place in consequence of the Princess Charlotte's decease, had been alike dissolved by death. What a world of misery could this survivor have told of, arising from the law-made incompatibility between royalty and the natural provision for the domestic affections. . . . Those various love-stories are hidden

now in the grave; and she who was the depository of so many of them has followed them thither.

The 'chequered secret marriages', the 'various love stories'—what did Miss Martineau know, that made her write in the plural at a time when the only secret marriage generally suspected was that between Princess Amelia and General FitzRoy? Princess Augusta and Brent Spencer, Princess Sophia and Thomas Garth—theirs were surely among the romances of which 'dearest Miny' was 'the depository'.

Nearly thirty years later, when the Garth scandal exploded, Charles Greville found in it the material for some characteristic passages in his diary. Sir Herbert Taylor told the diarist that there was 'not a doubt' that 'Old Garth' was the father of Princess Sophia's son, thus removing—one assumes—Mr Greville's uncertainty on that point, an uncertainty which had been produced by a rumour that Young Garth was the son of 'some inferior person, some say of a page of the name of Papendyck'.

> The old King never knew it. The Court was at Weymouth when she was big with child. She was said to be dropsical, and suddenly recovered. They told the old King that she had been cured by roast beef, and this he swallowed, and used to tell it to people, all of whom knew the truth, as 'a very extraordinary thing'.

Glenbervie, whose evidence, however suspect, must sometimes be heard, was writing in 1801 of 'Princess Sophia's extraordinary illness at Weymouth last autumn', when she was attended by Sir Francis Milman. In January 1804 he noted that 'the foundling which was left at the Taylors at Weymouth about two [three?] years ago is now in a manner admitted by the Court to be the Princess Sophia's, and, as the story generally goes, by General Garth'. In November 1810 he described the child as 'nine years old—and most strikingly like the Royal Family'. During the previous summer it had been on a visit to Datchet—within easy distance of Windsor. 'General Garth acknowledges him', adds Glenbervie.[8]

The old tatler's informant was the Princess of Wales, who declared that she thought that Princess Sophia was 'so ignorant and innocent as really not to know till the last moment that she was with child'. Whether or not this unhappy episode was the 'little trifle' of which Princess Sophia wrote to Lady Harcourt, it is practically beyond question that Garth was her lover, and that the son she bore was his. Whether a secret marriage ceremony at Ilsington, actually Puddletown, to which Mr Childe Pemberton refers in *The Romance of Princess Amelia*, took place before or after, and even if it took place at all, is likely to remain unknown. But it is at least possible that at some time the curiously assorted couple entered into some sort of pseudo-religious contract, and that theirs was one of the 'chequered secret marriages' hinted at by Miss Martineau at the time of the Duchess of Gloucester's death.

Between 1801 and 1804 the hideous legend had emerged associating the Duke of Cumberland with Princess Sophia's disaster. It seems to have originated, as so many other horrible stories originated, with the Princess of Wales, who was by this time more than a little crazy, and who took a delight in shocking her auditors. 'How horrid!' interjects Glenbervie, as he notes the tale in his diary, not forgetting to put on record that the Princess gave as her authority no less a person than the Duke of Kent. That he should have retailed such a story about the sister whom at that very period he was calling his 'little favourite, Sophy', seems impossible. It happened to suit his book to hobnob with his disreputable sister-in-law, and he may have been foolish enough to indulge in a little head-shaking, *à la* Joseph Surface,[9] over the young Princess's 'imprudence'; but it is difficult to imagine him charming the willing ear of Caroline with a whispered tale of horrors within the precincts of the Family.

Evidence of the friendly relations between the Duke of Kent and Princess Sophia is not lacking. In February 1801 he was the bearer of a letter from her, thanking the Prince of Wales for the gift of a chain. In August 1804, when tension between George III and his eldest son was acute, it was the Duke of Kent who paid Princess Sophia this kindly tribute in writing to his agitated brother:

> ... her conduct when she rides with the King, whenever the P of W's name has been mentioned, is beyond any praise, for the spirit with which she has spoken out, and the real, genuine, unaffected attachment she has evinced towards you—and I should be very deficient in what I feel for you both did I not name it to you as it merits.[w]

On the Prince of Wales's birthday a year later, Princess Sophia, by the hand of her 'best and kindest friend', viz. her 'dear Edward', laid 'a trifle' at his feet; and in 1814, during her long illness, no one was more assiduous in sympathy than he. Is it conceivable that he could have smirched the name of that affectionate sister with the legend which the Princess of Wales was so happy to hand on?

Princess Sophia no doubt had some special reason to describe Prince Edward as her 'best and kindest friend', but during her 'distressed and unhappy days and hours' after her illness at Weymouth it was the Prince of Wales who seems to have exerted himself to comfort her. The beauty of the chain he gave her in February 1801 exceeded, she told him, anything she ever saw, and she declared that she would never wear it without thinking of the donor.[w] Writing him a birthday letter that August, she thanks him for sending her his love by Colonel Cartwright. 'God bless you', she exclaims, 'for thinking of little Sophy, who will ever love you dearly!' She will drink his health most heartily; 'and I wish', she says, 'that I could give you a Kiss, for you are a Dear'.[w] And to his sisters he certainly was.

On her birthday in November 1802 he sent her a kind letter, accompanied by a trinket in the form of a pansy, in gratitude for which she poured forth her heart on yellow-edged notepaper embossed with a medallion of George III:

My Dearest G.P.,

If you are so good as to say that your words fall short of what you feel towards me, how very, very unequal, my dearest, are any expressions of mine to express my gratitude and thanks for the kindest of letters you have sent me, and for the beautifull present which accompanied it. . . . I am in ecstacies with my lovely Pensée, yet, dear love, I will not disown that the contents of the dear letter is what I prize most, as it contains the assurance of your affection. Everything that comes from you is *valuable to Sophy*, but how far more than I had reason to expect is your great kindness in remembering this day. . . . God bless you again and again—I shall read your dear letter a dozen times over, for I am so happy and gratified by it that my words fly, which shows you the impatience of your faithful and affec

SOPHY (w)

The Prince of Wales was constantly sending her little gifts. In July 1803 he sent her a feather which he himself had worn. 'Believe me', she wrote, 'it will be highly valued by your own Sophy.' On her birthday in 1803 he sent her a jewel in the form of a heart, and her response was, 'If I may hope that I have a little corner in the *original* heart of which this dear one is a representative, it will make me happy, for I do love you, *de cœur et d'âme*'.(w)

A little exaggerated, perhaps; and yet it was natural that her heart should brim over with gratitude to the dazzling elder brother, the idol of the Sisterhood, when he descended from his pedestal and held out his hands to her, the most unhappy of them all.

Not the least curious feature in the story is the cordial attitude of the Family, including Queen Charlotte and the Prince of Wales, towards Garth himself.[10] Glenbervie says that the Queen believed Garth to be the father of Princess Sophia's child, and no doubt she did. Appreciation of the General's kindness in helping to cloak a scandal can hardly have accounted for her amiability; nor is it likely that she and her eldest son would have given him a place in the household of Princess Charlotte if he had been either the custodian of a terrible secret or the chief actor in a clandestine intrigue. They would have been more likely to give him some lucrative employment in some remoter place.

There is evidence that Princess Sophia was genuinely in love with Garth, and if he loved her he may well have felt that a secret marriage might mean her salvation. The Prince of Wales may have agreed with him, remembering the Princess Royal's plight in 1795.

Everything that is known about Thomas Garth suggests the upright officer and gentleman. He was born in 1744, son of Sir John Garth, Recorder of Devizes and MP for that borough, and great-nephew of Sir Samuel Garth, Physician in Ordinary to George I. There were two elder brothers, Charles Garth, who succeeded Sir John as MP for Devizes, and died in 1784; and General George Garth, Colonel of the 17th Foot, who died in 1819.

Thomas Garth entered the Army as a Cornet in the 1st Dragoons in 1762, and served in the Allied Army in Germany under Prince Ferdinand. Lieutenant in 1765, Captain in 1775, he went in 1779 to the West Indies with the 20th Light Dragoons. Back in England on half-pay in 1792, he was successively Major in the 2nd Dragoon Guards and Lieutenant-Colonel in the 1st. He next saw active service in the inglorious Flanders campaigns, and became Colonel of his original regiment. Major-General in 1795, Lieutenant-General in 1805, he was promoted full General in 1814.

Two years later the name of 'Thomas Garth' is again found in the Army List, this time as a Lieutenant on half-pay in his father's old regiment, the 1st Dragoons; but he was transferred in 1820 to the 37th or North Hampshire Regiment of Foot. This young man never rose above the rank of Captain; but that he rose so far must have been an embarrassment to his cousin, Captain Thomas Garth, RN, with whom people were apt to confuse him. It was, for example, the sailor and not the soldier whom Captain Gronow met at Tortoni's and described as 'the kind and excellent Tommy Garth'.

Captain Landmann saw a good deal of General Garth at Weymouth in 1804. 'A little man', he calls him, 'with good features, but whose face was much disfigured by a considerable purple mark on the skin, extending over part of his forehead and one eye.' (Glenbervie, however, described him as 'a very plain man', and Charles Greville as 'an ugly old devil'.) The General lent one of his own horses to Landmann, a beautiful and spirited animal, which 'had not been out of the stables for a few days', and was so frisky that the unfortunate engineer was forced, as he says, to avail himself of the length of his legs to cling with his feet under its body. Riding thus along the cliff-edge at the King's side, Landmann met with a mishap which might have been fatal both to himself and to his borrowed mount. Lord FitzRoy approached, and in returning his salute George III, after his fashion, 'swept off his hat to the full extent of his arm', slapping General Garth's horse across the face. The horse immediately plunged over the cliff—only to land unhurt upon a ledge nine or ten feet from the top.

Mrs Papendiek tells a story of 'Generals Garth and Manners' who, when travelling to Bath, stopped at the inn at Devizes (Garth's birthplace) kept by the father of Thomas Lawrence. They were much struck by the boy Thomas, who marked for them during a game of billiards, but had a little table in a corner, with books and drawings. When they left they took some of his drawings away with them, and gave him their names and their addresses in town. Not long after, the elder Lawrence went bankrupt, and the younger called upon the two equerries in London. It was at the period of George III's first illness, and they could not do much at Court for the youth, who had entered himself as a student at the Royal Academy; but they introduced him to Lady Cremorne, who sat to him, and whose patronage stood him in good stead.

Garth, like Brent Spencer, stood well with the King; indeed his nickname of 'the King's Garth' suggests that he was the favourite equerry. Landmann records that on one occasion at Weymouth in 1804 the General 'remarked that the sash his Majesty had on was an exceedingly handsome one; upon which the King with his left hand taking up the ends that were hanging down, observed, "Yes, yes, this is a very handsome sash—very handsome—very handsome—quite new. Charlotte makes all my sashes all my sashes—she always makes 'em."' Garth's praise of the sash, and the circumstance that it was he who headed the 'great scramble of officers' when the King let fall in turn his gloves, his cane, and his hat, suggest that he was a man likely to please his Sovereign by assiduous attentions. But it was during this Weymouth visit that George III's mind showed those signs of returning instability noted by Sir Robert Wilson, and the General may merely have been anxious to keep things running smoothly.

Among the agitations of 1804 was more than one quarrel between the Dukes of York and Kent. The younger brother suspected the elder of having been instrumental, as Commander-in-Chief, in procuring his recall from Gibraltar; and he also resented his intervention in the court-martial of a certain General Burton 'on some charge about a duel'. The feud smouldered, with occasional outbreaks, until the Mary Anne Clarke scandal of 1809, which the Duke of Kent undeniably helped to bring to a head. It was upsetting for Princess Sophia, who was attached to both brothers, and who had the further pain of seeing their dispute produce alarming reactions in the King. After one of these clashes Princess Mary wrote to the Prince of Wales:

> Our dear Sophy . . . was taken with one of her worst spasms yesterday. . . . All that past in her room last Monday was more than her delicate little frame could stand, therefore I own I expected this attack would follow. It is the more provoking as I must do Frederick the justice to say he did all he could to avoid seeing Edward but he actually *would* force himself into Sophy's room to have this conversation with Frederick.[w]

The Duke of Kent continued for some years after this episode to write with great affection of his 'dearest Sophy', but her allusions to him tend to become less enthusiastic, and as he loses ground with her, the figure of the Duke of York comes forward to fill the vacant place. That agitating conversation in her rooms may have marked a turning-point in her relations with both Dukes.

There is little evidence as to Queen Charlotte's attitude towards this daughter. Princess Sophia in her letters to the Prince of Wales seldom refers to their mother, and any allusion she makes is tinctured either with awe or with a faint tinge of mockery. Alone of the Family that adamantine personage seems to have felt small tenderness towards 'little Sophy'. Princess Mary was indignant at the lack of compunction which she showed during the domestic crisis of January 1812, when her sister Sophia was packed off to Oatlands in the middle of winter, on a double journey to which she was quite unequal; but two years later her Majesty did occasionally give the Prince news of his ailing sister, in a perfunctory sort of way. This detachment, coupled with her gracious attitude towards General Garth, suggests that the Queen may have felt that the impetuous girl was more to blame than the elderly equerry. Princess Sophia's words to Lady Harcourt on one of the occasions when the King's health seemed to be failing again, are significant:

> . . . though God knows I always adored my dear, dear Father, yet his sore illness has endeared him to us beyond the power of expression; his health is our only object; life, indeed, would be a burthen to us poor Girls without him.

And a 'burthen' it was indeed until the Prince Regent rode forth, an elderly Knight-Errant, to rescue the four damsels in distress.

When the Princesses Mary and Amelia went down to Weymouth together in August 1809 they broke the journey at General Garth's country house, Ilsington, in the ancient village of Puddletown—sometimes alternatively known as Piddletown—six miles from Dorchester. More than sixty years later the place figured as 'Weatherbury' in Thomas Hardy's *Far from the Madding Crowd*. The fine church, with its Norman font, rood-loft and musicians' gallery, is said to have been the scene of the secret and illegal marriage between Garth and Princess Sophia. The Vicar from 1790 to 1805 was the Rev. John Gibbons, M.A., so he presumably officiated, though it is improbable that the services of the Puddletown choir, in which Hardy's grandfather played the bass viol, were enlisted upon that occasion.

Ilsington was leased by Garth from the Earl of Orford, and Princess Mary thus describes the house and its tenant in a letter to her father from Weymouth, on 31 August 1809:

> We left Woodgatestone this morning at 9 o'clock, and got to Blandford soon after 11, when Amelia was so faint and unwell that we rested half-an-hour, when we proceeded to General Garth's, who received us with the greatest kindness, and nothing could exceed his attentive wish that Amelia should find everything comfortable at his House, and everything I must say was quite perfection, all in the most compleat order, and just as one would expect to find his house.
>
> I am sorry to say he looks very ill, and is still very lame, and appeared in his large cloth shoes, and I fear must have fatigued himself with all the trouble he

gave himself, as he would Hobble up and downstairs much oftener than was necessary, and would not let anybody attend at breakfast but himself.[w]

Only six years have elapsed since we saw the General riding spirited horses at Weymouth, and plying the King with courtly attentions. Invalidism was not, however, to be his portion for the remainder of his days, for five years later we find him in active attendance upon Princess Charlotte.

Princess Mary, knowing that her father will be interested in all she can tell him about the home of the 'King's Garth', goes on to give a detailed description of Ilsington. It is, she says,

> quite an old-fashioned Mansion—it stands in a courtyard, and the approach up to it is under an old avenue of fir-trees. You come into an emence [*sic*] old large Hall, up a very large staircase, which brings one into the most delightful, comfortable, long library I ever saw, which has three windows, and one in a long kind of recess with a Balcony, which is quite charming and this room is the General's constant living-room, summer and winter. His bedroom is next to it, which is likewise a very large good room. Below I saw a very good dressing-room, and a Drawing Room, all equal large rooms, very lofty and well-proportioned.[w]

Both during her stay in his house and later when he was in attendance on her at Weymouth, Garth was exceedingly kind to Princess Amelia, by whose altered looks Princess Mary noticed that he was 'much overcome'. Nine years earlier he may have been even more moved by the frail beauty of Princess Sophia, 'sujette aux "low spirits"', and suffering from the Queen's insensibility. Watchful attentions from a man whom her father honoured would be likely to make an impression upon a sensitive girl, and it is difficult to blame Garth if her gratitude became immoderate. Nothing that we know of him suggests the libertine, and now in his own environment he sustains his character as a courtly old soldier. Ten years later Captain Gronow was at Windsor and noted that 'the equerries present were Generals Garth and Gwynne, both fine gentlemen of the old school in powder and pigtails'.

Though it is unsupported by either documentary evidence or contemporary allusion, the tradition in the Corry family that Princess Sophia was secretly married to Isaac Corry cannot be left unmentioned here. Corry, who was Chancellor of the Irish Exchequer before the Union, is described by Thomas Ashe as 'possessing from nature a very pleasing exterior, he lost not that advantage by a slovenly neglect of it, but instantly impressed strangers with a favourable opinion of him by the gracefulness of his manner and the unaffected propriety of his deportment'. Glenbervie wrote of him, 'He was called to the Bar, and he once acted as a sort of Groom of the Bedchamber to the late Duke of Cumberland'—George III's brother, not his son—and gives the further information that he was '*un peu intrigant en politique et en amour*'. There was apparently some mystery as to the mother of his three children; for her name is mentioned neither on the monument to two of them, Charles McNeill and Selena, in St Mary Abbotts, Kensington, nor on his own monument in St Mary's Church, Newry, Co. Down. The descendants of his daughter Catherine, one of whom is said to have resembled Queen Victoria, were convinced that the unnamed ancestress was none other than the Princess Sophia. But many ladies resembling Queen Victoria might trace their descent from the House of Hanover without the daughters of George III furnishing the point of contact, and the only traceable connection between Isaac Corry and that monarch is his Majesty's remark at the time of the Union that 'Corry was a person of no consequence, but Pitt had said that he must be made easy'.

During the years 1804–12 Princess Sophia seems to have remained in the background. Her 'delicate little frame', as Princess Mary called it, grew yet more ethereal, and her face took on that look of sadness which impressed Frances Waddington at the Queen's House in 1809. In 1808, when the Prince of Wales was endeavouring to arrange a marriage between his sister Elizabeth and Louis Philippe, Princess Sophia wrote to her brother a letter in which she makes one of her infrequent allusions to Queen Charlotte. 'I feel sure', she says, 'that you will do all you can to support and comfort our amiable Eliza. . . . I must add that Eliza's conduct to my Mother is *perfect*, and I lament her total want of confidence in her children.'[w]

A year later it is Princess Amelia upon whom Sophia's sympathy is focused. In spite of her 'bad and unintelligible' writing, the Prince of Wales entrusted 'little Sophy' with the task of keeping him advised of Princess Amelia's condition, first at Weymouth and later at Windsor. Extracts from these letters will be found in Princess Amelia's chapter, and they offset the assertions of the dying Princess that she was unaccustomed to receiving kindness from her family. Nothing could be more tender or more comprehending than Princess Sophia's attitude to 'this dear Child', as she calls her, and that she herself was in need of sympathy at that time is shown in this letter of 6 October 1809:

> All goes on much as usual *chez nous—un peu triste* I do not deny, and I feel like a wanderer without my beloved Miny: but as I told you when we met last, I keep very much in my own room, where thank God I am never at a loss for employment.[w]

The Mary Anne Clarke scandals lent a note of excitement and indignation to what was otherwise a year of gloom, and it is apparently to the *dénouement*, resulting in the Duke of York's exculpation, that Princess Sophia refers in an excited letter of this period to the Regent. 'As you know what nerves are', she wrote, 'you will know how I am at present, for I am in a Shake of Happiness from Top to Toe.'[w] Her affection for her brother Frederick deepened as time passed. He seems to have acted as an intermediary between her and Garth in matters concerning her graceless son, and if he had lived two years longer he might have been able to make the young man see reason, and so have averted the public unfolding of that unhappy history.

When the Regency was brought into being and the Regent immediately set about making plans for the benefit of his sisters, Princess Sophia wrote him a characteristic letter in a most uncharacteristically clear hand, between carefully ruled lines, dated 'From the Nunnery, No. 3, Castle Court, 12 December, 1811':

> As I know how difficult it is to You, My dearest Brother, to read my scrawls I was determined to send you a few lines in a legible hand trusting to your kindness to forgive my troubling You at this busy time, but my heart *overflows* with gratitude for all Your noble and generous intentions towards us, which should You succeed in or not, our gratitude must *be the same*. The only thing that frets and worries me is the idea that your kindness to *four Old Cats* may cause You any *désagrément* with the Ministers; I could forfeit anything sooner than that we should be the cause of this.
>
> How good you are to us which however imperfectly expressed I feel most deeply. *Poor old wretches* as we are, a *dead weight* upon You, *old Lumber* to the *country*, like *Old Clothes*, I wonder you do not vote for putting us in a *sack* and drowning us in *The Thames*. *Two* of us would be fine food for *the Fishes*, and as to *Miny and me* we will take our chance *together*. Thank God that you got safe to Town—how vexed I am that I did not see you before you left Oatlands.
>
> All here goes on the same—quiet days do us no good—it only shews the mind more completely gone. God bless You, My dearest G.P.—Ever Your unalterably attached
>
> SOPHY[w]

Princess Sophia was in her thirty-fifth year when she wrote that whimsical and yet quaintly pathetic letter. Neither sorrow nor spasms had dimmed her sense of humour, though we might not have suspected this from Glenbervie's description of her only a year earlier, when he remarked that 'the Princess Sophia, if a sinner, has the demeanour of a very humble and repentant one. She has something very attentive and kind and even affectionate in her demeanour.' In conversation with Lady Glenbervie at the Queen's House, the Princess often talked of the King's 'misfortunes', more especially his blindness. 'She takes', says the diarist, 'a great interest in comparing Lord Guilford's case with his, and in inquiring the particulars of his blindness of his daughters.' There has been no hint as yet of any trouble threatening in Princess Sophia's own eyes, but this preoccupation with her father's loss of sight is interesting, because she was the only one of his children to die blind.

Owing to her delicate health the Princess was not actively involved in either of the crises of 1812, though when she was sent to visit the Regent at Oatlands at the beginning of the year, her looks and her words were probably enough to confirm him in his view that something must be done. There was no suggestion that she should accompany Princess Charlotte to the opening of Parliament on 30 November, but when the Queen's wrath had been appeased, the Princess wrote to her brother:

> Could you but know what I have suffered since this unfortunate misunderstanding your own good heart would tell you better than my words can convey the gratitude I feel towards you for having restored Peace between the Queen and us.[w]

All through 1813 Princess Sophia remained ailing in seclusion at Windsor. News of her bad health reached the Queen of Würtemberg, who wrote to Sir Thomas Tyrwhitt in March 1814, 'I fear that you will have found poor Sophia sadly altered. I understand she continues growing weaker, which makes me dread a decline.'[w] The optimism of the physicians—Halford and Milman—who had assured Queen Charlotte three months earlier that the patient was 'going on much better' was not justified.

Insomnia seems to have been part of the trouble. 'Sophia', wrote the Queen to the Regent in January 1814, 'has had two good nights, which is a happy circumstance, and God knows a blessing which seldom falls to her share.' Although it is not until this period that regular bulletins indicate anxiety, she had already been confined to her own apartments for nearly a year. In April Princess Mary wrote to the Prince that she really thought that their sister was recovering better than she usually did 'after one of her spasms', and in May she was able to send this cheerful report:

> I am sure you will be glad to hear that dear Sophy has been in the Queen's room for an hour this evening and I hope is not the worse for it, though dreadfully fatigued and overcome with finding herself once again out of her own appartments after a confinement of a *compleat year and a half*.
>
> It is impossible to describe the joy and pleasure Her appearance among us has occasioned. She went to bed the moment she returned into her rooms Sir Henry cannot tell till tomorrow if this trial has done harm or not.[w]

Sir Henry Halford apparently kept the Dukes of Kent and Cambridge informed of the Princess's progress, and both brothers were effusive in their expressions of gratitude to him and sympathy for the patient. The Duke of Cambridge wrote from Hanover in December 1813:

> Most anxious do I feel concerning her, and I wish to hear that she is beginning to recover her strength. Till then I shall not feel comfortable, which is very melancholy at the distance I am from her. My last visit at Windsor on the 28th November has, I fear, done her harm. I am very sorry for it, but I really was so much affected at taking leave of her that I could not hide my feelings, and with her delicate frame it is no wonder that she should have suffered from it.

The Duke of Kent, who possessed less sensibility, was not less emotional in his allusions to his 'poor suffering Sophy', and he shows a gleam of insight in this paragraph from a letter to Halford dated 28 January 1814:

> I perfectly understand all you say about the difficulty of making a certain quarter [*i.e.* Queen Charlotte] understand the real state of things, but where there is a natural want of warmth it is difficult in the extreme to make a proper impression. Thank God! all are not alike on this head.

And again, in sending Halford the present of a riding horse about this time, as a mark of gratitude for that tactful physician's services to himself, he added:

> I have long wished for an opportunity of expressing to you how deeply I feel your unremitting attention to that dear little angel, my younger sister, who, I may say to you, is one of the greatest comforts of my life.

There was, one feels, more of the elf than of the angel about her.

During the visit of the Allied Sovereigns to London in the summer of 1814, Princess Sophia was too ill to take any part in the festivities; but the Regent sent her gifts of fruit from London to console her for missing the sights there,[w] the pagoda and the Temple of Peace in St James's Park, and the fireworks after dusk.

By the end of 1814 the Princess was mending, able to get on her pony for quarter of an hour, 'and most highly delighted', notes Princess Mary, at finding herself once more on its back.[w] A year later the Duke of Cambridge wrote to Halford, 'Dear Sophy is, thank God, wonderfully better. She will, however, I fear be more or less of an invalid, though I trust she may lead a very different existence than she has done, poor thing, for the last three years of her life.'

II

General Garth had a niece, Frances Garth, whose name figures rather prominently in the reminiscences of Lady Charlotte Bury, Lord Glenbervie, and the Regency diarists. When in 1795 the young lady was given a minor post in the household of the baby Princess Charlotte, the Queen wrote to the Prince of Wales, 'her appearance is neat and clean, not offensive in her manners but modest and pleasing, not befeathered, nor any inclination to get into the great world. . . . She has been brought up by her grandmother in a very plain and solid way.'(w) The Queen adds that she believes 'it is the poor Colonel, not the rich General, who has been her protector'.

The 'poor Colonel' was George Garth, Colonel of the 17th Foot, who died in 1819; so, presumably, Frances was the child of Charles Garth, MP for Devizes, who died in 1784. She formed a natural link between her Uncle Thomas and Carlton House.

'Miss Garth', says Lady Charlotte Bury, 'is a very estimable character, simple-minded and very downright in all she says, and little suited to a court, except for her high principles and admirable caution.' Glenbervie noted that she seemed 'proud of the supposed royal connection', but, knowing more about the circumstances than his lordship did, she may have felt that there was little cause for shame.

When in 1814 General Garth, to the regret of his royal friends, relinquished his post in Princess Charlotte's household, he recommended as his successor Colonel Addenbrooke, a kinsman of Lord Rivers, whose estates the Colonel managed. Queen Charlotte herself intervened to make sure that these two gentlemen should have a preliminary conversation, and some correspondence took place between her and the Prince Regent on the subject.

The Regent also was anxious that Colonel Addenbrooke should have a full and frank conversation with the General, whose conduct he was to take as his model,

as I am sure nothing can answer my wishes more thoroughly than the exemplary Line of Conduct which has been observed by the General since he has been placed about Charlotte, and for which, as I cannot unfortunately be at Windsor when he takes his Semestre or leave of absence, I shall feel myself under the greatest possible obligations to you if you will endeavour to express to him not only my most unqualified Approbation of his conduct but my warmest thanks for the cheerfulness and extreme attention with which he has met and at the same time defeated many little difficulties. . . .[w]

Queen Charlotte promised in reply that when she saw General Garth she would not fail to read what concerned him in the Prince's letter, by which she was sure he would be 'much flattered'.[w]

When these changes were afoot in the *entourage* of Princess Charlotte, Princess Sophia was beginning to revive after her long illness, but there is a blank in her correspondence until January 1818, when we find her fulfilling a promise to supply 'dear Miny's place as soon as she left Windsor as a faithful reporter of the Queen's state'.[w] The Regent was apparently anxious about his mother's reactions to the arrival of a suitor for Princess Elizabeth in the person of the Hereditary Prince of Hesse-Homburg, and Princess Sophia tells him how, on the evening following 'the first blow', the Queen 'did not dine in company, but entirely alone in her own Room, nor did she go to the party in the evening, but allowed me to be her companion till my usual hour of retiring'. For the second time Sophia is sympathetically watching her elder sister struggling to 'settle'—this time with success. The Queen, she writes, was 'flurried and vexed' at the abruptness of Elizabeth's resolution:

> At times she cried bitterly, but took in good part my attempts to soothe Her, and to palliate by stating she knew this was always Eliza's object. . . . I am sensible that she requires watching without appearing to observe her, and that the utmost tenderness is necessary in our attentions to her.[w]

On 5 February the Princess, taking her role of correspondent seriously, reports that 'good humour and all our prospects of being able to bring the Queen round vanished as your carriage drove off', and adds that Halford thought her Majesty looking pale, 'and came out quite astonished at the perturbation and distress of feelings which she manifested'.[w] When, at last, the Queen was brought round, and the marriage took place, Princess Sophia's occupation was gone. The Princesses Augusta and Mary were with their mother at Kew during the last months of her life, and Sophia remained alone at Windsor, whence she forwarded to the Queen's Council the daily report of the physicians on the condition of the King. 'This was by her own special order', wrote the Princess to the Regent on the day of the Queen's death; and she goes on:

> Now, alas! the Mouth that gave that order is shut for ever!!! As this has lately passed through *my* hands to our dear and venerable Parent, and has continued one day more by the attention of the Physicians now in waiting to find its way to me, and feeling that I have no longer that charge now the care of

the King's Person has devolved to the Council, I think I ought to send it to You, who will give me ready credit for not presuming beyond my proper Sphere.

I own it will give me great pain to live in future without the daily comfort of an authentic report of the King's state, and that it would gratify me as far as I am capable of pleasure under our sad loss if you would allow the account you receive every day to be transmitted through mine or Augusta's hands.

Upon this last severe blow I dare not trust myself to express what I feel, or to aggravate your regret by dwelling on the sad scene you witnessed this morning—yet I fancy that to have witnessed it will always be a melancholy satisfaction to you, for *I confess I could envy it You*, who have not had the comfort in any part of this long protracted illness of administering to our dear Mother, or of alleviating her sufferings by any of the tender kind attentions which You shewed her so incessantly and indefatigably.[w]

Although the bulk of the Queen's jewels were sold by auction, the Regent retained a few trinkets, which he distributed among the Sisterhood. To Princess Sophia he sent, by the hand of Halford, the watch which had been a present from himself, and from among other jewels she chose a ruby and diamond bracelet for the upper part of the arm, 'being compelled from necessity to wear such an ornament'—she does not explain why; perhaps it may have been to hide a scar or because her arm was what would then be regarded as slender to excess. In his choice of gifts for 'little Sophy' the Regent seems often to have been guided by his idea of her as a sort of fluttering sprite. At one time he sent her a jewelled butterfly; at another, a keepsake in the form of a bee. 'My Dear little Bee she then wrote,' either lives on my Finger or in my Pocket, and it puts me in *mind* that I would rather be a *Drone* than a Wasp.'[w]

Among Sir Herbert Taylor's papers there was a letter[11] from General Garth to the Duke of York, written about six weeks before Queen Charlotte's death. It is of interest not only as showing that Garth and the Duke were corresponding upon military matters, but also as containing an allusion to the General's 'Protegee'—young Thomas Garth—so worded as to indicate that upon this subject also there was an exchange of correspondence.

The King's Mews, *October 6, 1818*

Sir,

I had the honour to receive your Royal Highness's letter, together with Mr Becket's opinion just as I was leaving Dorsetshire to come to town. I immediately transmitted the opinion to Mr Durand at Weymouth, pointing out to him, at the same time, how impossible it was for Yr Rl Highness to order any revival of the court-martial or to alter any part of the sentence.

I have not written on the subject of my Protegee, fearing to intrude on the anxious moments so lately occupied by the melancholy intelligence daily received from Kew. As I received a report of his being ill at Sligo with a Fever,

I became greatly alarmed, and therefore applied to Sir George Beckwith for leave of absence for him as soon as he was able to travel which was kindly granted till December, and he is now in Dorsetshire in perfect health.

I should esteem it a great favour, if Your Royal Highness would grant me an Audience e'er I leave town the latter end of this week.

I have the honour to subscribe myself Your Royal Highness's most dutiful and obedient humble servt

Thos: Garth

Young Garth was at that time a Lieutenant in the 1st Dragoons; two years later he was gazetted Captain in the 37th or North Hampshire Regiment of Foot. There is something curiously pathetic about the old General becoming 'greatly alarmed' at the report that his 'Protegee' was suffering from a fever at Sligo. Nothing that we know of the graceless fellow suggests that there was much to love in him, though his father seems to have been fond of him, perhaps more for his mother's sake than for his own. In her seclusion at Windsor it may have comforted the Princess to know that her son had so careful a guardian.

The death of her father 'overwhelmed' Princess Sophia, and there is a note of shyness in her first letter to the new King, who would, she was sure, 'continue to be a Parent' to them all. But his Majesty soon put her at her ease, and by his interest in her plans for the future, and his invitations to her to come and see him *en intimité* at Carlton House, removed any qualms she may have felt as to their altered relationship.

An undated letter from Princess Mary seems to belong to this period:

I find I was quite correct in assuring you to-day that Sophia had no wish or intention of *ever making herself a permanent inmate* in the Duke of York's House. She told me much as she loves them both she *never would think of such a thing*—that she hopes to live much with them and see more of them than she has done yet, but will never be upon any other footing than as a visitor—and Sophy is anxious and ready to enter into any plans You may *advise*, and is most anxious to *go hand-in-hand with me*.[w]

Princess Mary wished her sister to settle in London, and Sophia offered no opposition. There were indeed several reasons why she should agree. With Princess Augusta at St James's Palace, the King at Carlton House, the Duke of York in South Audley Street, and the Duchess of Gloucester in Park Lane, London was obviously the most convenient centre. But Princess Sophia preferred to live in the comparative seclusion of Kensington Palace, where the future Queen Victoria was then housed with the Duchess of Kent. If the service-staircase tradition handed on by Mr Childe Pemberton is to be believed, she had her own reasons for wishing to live in an inconspicuous spot. Her son, it seems, came to see her sometimes, and such visits might have caused tongues to wag if they had been paid in the West End.

Soon after she was installed at 'K.P.', she wrote to the King in reply to his 'kind and most amiable expressions' towards her:

> I assure you that the hopes of being able to see so much more of You and to be near at hand was an Essential inducement to me to fix upon the *Little City* as my permanent home—and whenever I can be so indulged as to see You, and the more frequently that happens, the better pleased I shall be.
>
> I am very well satisfied with my new abode, and am trying to look at all around me in a favourable light; if *I know myself*, which is a doubt with me, as so few people do, I am not very difficult to please, having very few wants, and only wishing for a quiet, snug home. Of course some thoughts of a serious and painful nature will at times occur to cast a gloom for a moment, but when I consider, as I really do, how much I have reason to be grateful for, the prospect soon has a more chearful appearance.[w]

The King no doubt knew, while we can only conjecture, just what construction to place upon 'thoughts of a serious and painful nature'. In his reply he invited her to walk in the grounds of the Queen's House, adding that he did not 'mean to alarm' her about coming to Carlton House. But she repudiated the idea of feeling any alarm at such a prospect:

> The moment I can venture out I shall take advantage of Your most kind and welcome proposal of going out in the Gardens at the Queen's Palace—but while I say this I must do away an Expression of Yours which runs thus—'I do not mean to alarm You about coming to Carlton House'. I trust you never can suppose that going to You can *alarm me*, and I do hope when Spring comes in I may ere long have the delight of once more finding myself in Your room, where I have ever been so kindly received that Gratitude alone would take me there *blind fold*.[w]

She did not, however, wait till the spring before she went to Carlton House. On 26 January 1821, when thanking the King for a 'valuable little ring', she wrote:

> From your note I conclude you will be much hurried tomorrow ere you depart for Brighton, otherwise I should have called (wind and weather permitting) to enjoy the pleasure of another *as comfortable* a visit as you indulged me with on Monday.[w]

An engaging trait common to the whole Family was their fidelity to their old friends and retainers. Among the pleasures of Princess Sophia's later years were visits from Mrs François Jourdain de Soyres, *née* Marianne Montmollin. Mr de Soyres, pastor of the French Protestant colony in Bristol, was one of the royal chaplains, and met his future wife when on duty at Court. After Marianne was married and settled at Bristol, several of the royal ladies went over from Bath to see her. Queen Charlotte and Princess Elizabeth made that excursion when they were staying there in November 1817, and it is probable that Princess Sophia was with them. She is not mentioned in the Family letters as having been there, but she did call on the de Soyres at Bristol about that time, and Prince Leopold wrote on 2 November of that year, 'Grandmamma goes to Bath tomorrow for the birthday of her youngest and sickly daughter, and for the anniversary of the death of another who died some time ago'. These anniversaries fell on the second and the third of the month, and Prince Leopold's words suggest that Princess Sophia was already at Bath when 'Grandmamma' betook herself there.

By that time Mrs de Soyres had already been ten years a widow, and none of her eleven children was in the nursery. When she came to London in the late 'twenties, she brought her daughters to pay their respects to the Duchess of Gloucester and to Princess Sophia, and at Kensington the cake was handed at tea by the future Queen Victoria. Princess Sophia was very fond of Marianne de Soyres, and by way of *étrennes* in the New Year of 1837 she gave her a pocket-book in which she had written:

> *Les années s'écoulent mais l'amitié et l'affection ne saurois changer—les paroles et le cœur vous le répète, ma toute chère amie, de la part de votre dévouée et reconnaissante Sophie. 1 Janvier, 1837.*

One of her daughters, Madeleine, was a great favourite with the Princess, to whom she acted for a time as companion after she became blind. She married Charles Bowles Fripp, a partner in a Bristol firm of soap manufacturers and an early promoter of railways, who poured forth poetry in her honour in the local press with a fervour worthy of Mr Snodgrass.[12] In one of his lyrical outpourings Mr Fripp draws an imaginary picture of his fiancée quaffing 'ruby wine' at Kensington in 'gilded halls', and 'treading the mazy dance'. But it is improbable that the reality was anything like so gay. Princess Sophia, especially after her blindness became absolute, led a very secluded and uneventful life, and what Mrs Fripp's recollections of those visits were is clearly and touchingly shown in the inscription written by her on the back of the miniature which she had received from the Princess's own hands, and gave to her daughter and namesake, Madeleine:

For Madeleine Gifford De Soyres.

May she try to be as humble and meek as this Princess, who was thoughtful and kind to all; never idle; ready to learn from all; became blind, and even then was always busy and thoughtful for others.

Madeleine Fripp De Soyres.

Both Princess Elizabeth and Princess Augusta were affectionately anxious about the possible effect upon their sister's health of the death of the Duke of York in January 1827. The Landgravine wrote to George IV:

> ... poor Sophy has been mercifully supported to the last, and will ever have the consolation of feeling that God in his mercy has supported her in a most wonderful manner, so that she has through the whole illness been the constant soother and comforter to him in his hours of misery and pain. Yet I tremble for the consequences now, for all she most valued and loved is gone.[w]

The Duke of York's health had begun to fail in the summer of 1826, when he sought relief first at Brompton, in the house of Taylor's friend, Greenwood, and then at Brighton. At the close of the year he was established at the Duke of Rutland's where, 'unless prevented by indisposition', Princess Sophia came to see him every day at two o'clock. She found him always propped up in a crimson chair, wearing a grey dressing-gown, and ready, if not willing, to die. As he grew weaker, those about him noticed that the presence of his sister seemed to give him fresh force, while she on her side 'supported herself wonderfully'.

On 28 December the Bishop of London came for the second time to give him the sacrament, which Sir Henry Halford, Sir Herbert Taylor, and the Princess received with him. Sir Herbert writes:

> Part of the prayers for the sick were read; but the service was, at the suggestion of Sir Henry Halford, the short service. The Bishop was very much affected, particularly when pronouncing the concluding blessing. The Princess Sophia supported herself wonderfully throughout this trying scene, and the Duke was quite free from agitation.
>
> After the service was over, he kissed his sister and shook hands most affectionately with the Bishop, Sir Henry Halford, and me.

By the 31st he was perceptibly weaker, but when his sister came in, 'the manner in which he roused himself ... was very striking'. On New Year's Day 1827 the Dukes of Clarence and Sussex came:

> ... he received them affectionately, but did not speak, and they left him immediately. The Princess Sophia then went to him: he kissed her and said, 'God bless you, my dear love—tomorrow, tomorrow', and she left him.

A day later she saw him for the last time. He recognized her, but could not speak. Indeed, that benediction was almost his last coherent utterance.

From Kensington Palace, Princess Sophia released a flood of agitated epistles, of which these two are typical. Writing to the King on 16 January, she says:

I think of you, and of your sad, sad loss till my head turns for in how many years you will miss him! . . . Your dear letter made me shed tears for the first time since the blow *was struck*, and thus relieved my poor head, for I am still a piece of marble, and can catch myself for ever inclined to call out, 'And is it all true?'[w]

To Lady John Thynne she also uses the marble metaphor, and then continues, a little incoherently:

. . . dearest Ly John, what a *loss He is*! both Public and private, to me individually. Then, but what was to me *everything*!—so kind a Brother, so affecte and sincere a friend, always the same when once he professed a regard, and I *can glory* in the feeling of his being so convinced of my devotion and attachment to himself. . . .

I have witnessed such proof of his excellence of heart, I have watched him during months of the severest sufferings, and never heard him utter a complaint.[w]

From Würtemberg the eldest of the Sisterhood, then eagerly planning her long-awaited visit to her native land, wrote sympathetically on 2 April 1828, to the Princess Augusta:

Thank God that dearest Sophy has so well got over her last spasm, and has not suffered from paying you a visit, which must have agitated her, being the first time she has been in that part of London since our dear Frederick's death. It was fortunate that you had company, which made her in some measure forget her own feelings, and the situation of your House.[w]

The unfortunate 'Father of the British Army' died fathoms deep in debt, and by his will, dated 26 December 1826, he entrusted Sir Herbert Taylor and Colonel Stephenson with the task of settling his affairs, expressing the hope that his property would supply a fund more than sufficient to pay his debts, the residue, if any, to go to Princess Sophia. The Princess, greatly touched, wrote in the same letter to Lady John Thynne:

Alas—all his property, you know too well what must become of it! He orders *all* for the mere paying of his debts and kindly adds, 'if there be anything over I name my beloved sister Sophia as residuary legatee'. Of course there is nothing to inherit, but the naming me in such a manner has made me feel I am Heir of his *affection*, which is the most precious gift I could receive.[w]

The Duke's horses, carriages, and dogs were sold at Tattersalls; his wines, linen, china, plate, guns, and other personal belongings at Christies'. Among the 'lots' was an inkstand, a birthday present from one of the Princesses, with a finely-modelled figure of a female in mat gold, kneeling while she attaches a wreath to an Ionic column of burnished gold, having within the wreath the inscription *Vous la méritez.*

It is not improbable that Princess Sophia was the donor, and she the 'member of the Royal Family' who bought it back at the sale. Sir Herbert Taylor sent her, at the King's request, a list of articles to distribute 'with some aid from dear Miny', among the Family; and to his Majesty she allocated the last opera-glass which their dearest Frederick used. The Princess was slightly embarrassed by the 'list of Persons' enclosed by Taylor 'to whom he states these things'—*i.e.* the remainder of the various objects—'should be given', and discreetly forwarded the list to the King, with a copy of her reply to Sir Herbert, adding:

> I feel persuaded, my dearest dear Brother, that you will enter into my feelings on this subject, and sanction my confining myself to *be only* the distributor of your most feeling recollections in Your own Family, for the reasons I have assigned, as I conceive the list not one for me to be mixed in.[(w)]

A little less than two years later, on 17 November 1829, General Thomas Garth died in his house at 32 Grosvenor Place, at the age of eighty-five. Sir Herbert Taylor's friend, Mr Charles Greenwood, wrote to him on the following day this interesting letter, which is here published by courtesy of Sir Herbert's great-nephew, Mr Ernest Taylor, the editor of the *Taylor Papers*:

> Craig's Court, *Nov.* 18, 1829
>
> My Dear Taylor,
> The name of Garth must be hateful to you, and I know not whether the Event which I have to communicate to you will be productive of relief to you, or of more trouble. I should fear the latter.
> Genl Garth died last night in his son's house in Grosvenor Place, and expired in his son's arms. He was perfectly aware that he was dying and embraced his son with the greatest tenderness, told him that he had left him all he had, and was sorry that it was no more. This intelligence comes to me from a person that was present at the scene, but nothing seems to have been said relating to the Captain's particular situation—at any rate, I have stated all that has been told to me.—Ever, my dear Taylor, Truly and Affectionately Yours,
>
> Cha: Greenwood

This Event will I conclude be the means of a summons to you, and I shall soon see you in town.

The *Gentleman's Magazine*, at the close of its obituary notice, remarks:

Recent unfortunate circumstances have made the marriage of Gen. Garth with a lady of illustrious birth much more notorious than the parties desired. The issue of the marriage was one son, who bears his father's name, and is a Captain in the Army. He was the chief mourner at his father's funeral, which took place at St Martin's in the Fields on November 27.

The 'recent unfortunate circumstances' had occurred in the previous March, when Captain Thomas Garth of Melton Mowbray, 'a military officer on half-pay', filed an affidavit which produced a crashing detonation. According to this affidavit the deponent came into possession of 'certain documents of very great value and importance, relating immediately to his fortune, station, and affairs', and Sir Herbert Taylor wished to obtain possession of these documents, agreeing in return for them to pay Captain Garth's debts, and to settle an annuity of £3,000 on him for life. It was further stated that these documents had been deposited, on 28 November 1828, with Messrs. Paul and Co., bankers, who gave two receipts for them, one to Sir Herbert Taylor and one to 'C. M. Westmacott Esq, a friend of Captain Garth'. In case Taylor should not carry out his part of the agreement, Garth retained the key.

By March 1829 nothing had been done towards paying the debts of which the young man had forwarded a list, and he therefore chose this spectacular way of revoking the authority he had given jointly to Taylor and Westmacott. The motive of the affidavit was obviously to prevent Sir Herbert from laying hands upon the box till the agreed price had been paid in full; but *The Times* cynically suggested that Garth suspected Westmacott of double-dealing, and took this method of preventing any collusive action between him and Taylor. Charles Greville here takes up the tale:

March 22, 1829.—Met Taylor yesterday, and talked about Garth's business. He says that he shall, as far as he is concerned, be against paying the money, as the object of payment was to avoid publicity, and that now is impossible. Garth is an idiot as well as a scoundrel. Taylor was to have paid him £1,500 a year and half his debts, and General Garth the other half. He kept attested copies of the papers in the box, and these he showed to anybody who would read them. Westmacott has abstracts of all the papers, which he offered to give up to Taylor: he says Westmacott has behaved well to him, and he has never given him any money (money, however, of course he has had, for he is the Editor of the *Age*, and a great villain). The papers prove that old Garth is the father, of which Taylor says there is not a doubt. Old Garth has assured the Duke of York that they were all destroyed.

It was indeed impossible to avoid publicity. Already on February 4 Princess Lieven mentions 'a horrible business talked about in the matter of the Duke of Cumberland': and on February 14, the very day when the Duke returned to England from the Continent, Creevey was revelling in rumours of 'a hurry scurry' at Windsor, and great agitation in the Family. Of Princess Sophia he remarks 'the poor woman has always said this business would be the death of her'. Mr Creevey, of course, believed the Cumberland legend. It was an idea for which Byron's matrimonial troubles, to say nothing of his *Giaour*, had prepared a certain section of the public mind. According to Creevey's version, General Garth had consented 'at the suit of the King' to pass himself off as the father of Princess Sophia's son—the child of whose existence Greville declared that George III was unaware. There is, however, probably an element of truth in the statement that when the General was 'extremely ill and thought himself quite sure of dying', he wrote to the young man, 'telling him who he was', and putting him in possession of corroborative documents. 'Upon his unexpected recovery he applied', says Mr Creevey, 'for the return of the documents; but I thank you! they had been seen and read, and deemed much too valuable to be given back again.'

One of Creevey's most incredible assertions is to the effect that among the Garth papers was a letter from George III dealing with this secret in the Family. The mind that could picture the King writing such a letter would have no great difficulty in imagining the General keeping it for years, and then placing it in the hands of his adopted son. Yet it must always remain a matter for bewilderment that any documents susceptible of a sinister interpretation should have been 'released' in the way suggested. Can it be that the General did not realize their potentially explosive nature?

Princess Lieven, with her habitual shrewdness, saw what lay behind the publicity given to the sensational affidavit. It was all part of a plot to discredit the Royal Family and force the Duke of Cumberland out of England. She wrote to her brother at the time:

> The much-desired outcome, however, will not happen. The Duke of Cumberland remains, and all the more will remain, for his honour obliges him now not to have the air of being intimidated by this terrible charge.

The newspapers were soon in full cry, the loud baying of *The Times*, the *Globe*, and the *Morning Chronicle* mingling with the shrill yelping of Leigh Hunt's *Examiner*. The *Chronicle* made one interesting statement. 'The deep and painful interest' excited by the affair had, it said, 'led to an investigation which had assumed a form almost entitled to the appellation of semi-official'; and the adherents of the 'Personage in question'—*i.e.* the Duke of Cumberland—then asserted that 'not only has no proof of the alleged criminality been discovered, but that the imputation which forms the gravamen of the charge was clearly established by the stubborn evidence of facts and distances to be a *physical impossibility*'. But this did not satisfy *The Times*, which clamoured to know what secret was to be kept, and out of whose pockets the price of silence was to be paid.

The Duke of Cumberland, though his position made it impossible for him to grapple openly with the slander, refused to budge. He sent for his wife and son to join him in England, and *The Times* commented grimly that they were to reside in that part of Windsor Castle commonly known as the Devil's Tower.

The most deplorable aspect of the whole story is the readiness of young Garth to exploit, as an instrument of blackmail, the legend of his doubly royal origin. He was utterly worthless, unscrupulous and unstable, 'an idiot as well as a scoundrel', and it seems odd that his dying father should have embraced him 'with the greatest tenderness'. Mr Greenwood's informant was in error, however, when he said that it was in his son's house that the General died, and also when he added that he had left that son 'all he had'. By his will dated 12 September 1829, he left to his nephew, Captain Thomas Garth, RN, the estates in Northamptonshire devised to him by his sister, Elizabeth Garth—was it by virtue of those estates that Queen Charlotte had called him 'the rich General'?— and to his niece, Frances Garth, spinster, an annuity of £300.

The *Gentleman's Magazine* adds that Miss Garth was one of the King's Herbwomen at the Coronation procession in 1821, and that she had died on 17 January, 'in Baker Street, Portman Square', just two months after her uncle. In 1821 Princess Augusta had written to George IV asking him if he could give three or four rooms at St James's to 'poor Miss Garth', and what follows shows both the General's affection for his niece and the regard of the Family for him:

> I give you my Honour I have *not* been desired to name her, but I know it was General Garth's intentions to have spoken to the late Queen on her behalf, and then to have applied to You before the King's death. After which he was so very ill that he was only in London a week, and too infirm to call *here* on his way out of Town. But I am very certain as Miss Garth has lost *everything owing to her own integrity* it would gratify poor old Garth, and send him in peace to His grave.[w]

The clauses in General Garth's will concerning his 'son, Thomas Garth', are rather curious. A moiety of an annuity of £3,000 granted by Charles II, which the testator by a deed of settlement dated 17 November 1820, had settled on himself and 'in certain events' on his son, is to be paid by the trustees to his son and that son's lawful issue. Failing issue it is to go to Thomas Garth, RN. His house, 32 Grosvenor Place, 'lately purchased from Sir Henry Hardinge', together with plate, household furniture, and personal effects 'in the said house and in and about the estate at Piddletown', he left to his son. Each of his servants was to have a year's wages; to a certain Mary, wife of Thomas Legg—perhaps she had been his son's nurse—an annuity of £30 was bequeathed; and 'to William Lovell of Piddletown, £1,000 in 3 per cents'. It is surely not too fanciful to imagine that this Lovell may have been some discreet and faithful retainer or tenant, related to the woman of the same name whom at Princess Sophia's earnest suit the Regent appointed housekeeper at the 'Great Lodge' in July 1814. 'I can feel sure', the Princess then wrote to her brother, 'that you will be faithfully served, for she is an excellent creature.'[(w)]

The General left the residue of his property to his naval nephew and namesake. It would obviously have been impossible for him to leave any token of regard to Princess Sophia, even if their old affection remained after many years and much sorrow. Besides Mary Legg, only one woman is mentioned in his will. 'From the great regard and affection I have entertained for the late Charles Boone Esq.,'[13] wrote Garth, 'as well as for his daughter, Lady Drummond, I beg her Ladyship's acceptance of 100 guineas, for the purchase of a ring, or anything she may chuse, as a memorial of my affectionate regard for her.'

Insubstantial as the Cumberland myth has been shown to be, it still clings. Its very flimsiness makes it difficult to destroy. But on one point at least it is possible to discount the remarks of Charles Greville concerning Prince Ernest's deportment to his sisters. 'It is notorious', says Greville, 'that the old Queen forbade the Duke's access to the apartments of the Princesses.' In the MS. the apostrophe is a fraction beyond the 's', but this does not necessarily indicate a plural noun, for it was Greville's habit so to place his apostrophes after an unequivocal singular. The balance of probability is here in favour of a singular Duke. From the letters of the Princesses the fact emerges that all the brothers, not excluding the Duke of Cumberland, were constantly in and out of their sisters' quarters. For example, we find Princess Mary writing to the Regent when he was expected at Windsor, 'I shall take care to be in my Room to receive You. Should Ernest happen to be with me, pray find any excuse to get him away, for *alone* I can say anything to you'; and in the closing chapter of the present book will be found a letter written by Princess Amelia in 1806 to the Prince of Wales in which she says that she does not think Ernest 'has been more, if so much', in her room as in her sisters', and that she is grieved to think that there should be a necessity for avoiding being alone with him. The context shows plainly that these words refer merely to the Duke's well-known mischief-making propensities, but read out of their context they are rather dangerously ambiguous. If this letter had been written by Princess Sophia instead of by Princess Amelia, and if a few carefully detached phrases had been quoted, it is not difficult to imagine with what glee the Glenbervies and Grevilles, Creeveys and Crokers, would have fastened upon them. It may be that among the 'documents' which Sir Herbert Taylor tried to retrieve, Princess Sophia had written to General Garth some such sentence as 'You know I dare not be alone with Ernest for a moment'. To a mind coloured by the scandal already started at the Princess of Wales's Court, such a sentence would be confirmation enough.

One more piece of evidence may be cited to show what was Queen Charlotte's attitude towards her daughters in relation to her fifth son. In June 1810, after the murderous attack made on Cumberland by his demented valet, Sellis, she wrote to Princess Mary:

I need not, my dearest Mary, repeat what your sisters have already informed you of, namely our visit to your poor brother Ernest. Suffice it to say that, independent of one's feelings towards him, one cannot but lament to see so fine a Creature so disfigured—but thank God he is most miraculously saved to us. . . . He was uncommonly flurried when we came, but the meeting being over calmed him.[w]

'Your sisters' probably meant Augusta and Elizabeth. Princess Sophia was no doubt considered too delicate to pay so harrowing a call. But the unwontedly affectionate tone of the letter is in itself eloquent.

More need not be said about this tragic chapter in the life of 'little Sophy'— too much has been said already by writers who have found better 'copy' in the Cumberland myth than in the Garth history. It is a pity that their reactions were not of the colour of Princess Lieven's when she exclaimed, 'It must be an infamous calumny, for I shall never give credit to unnatural horrors'.

After 1830 Thomas Garth vanishes from view. He probably lived abroad to escape the attentions of his creditors, returning to England occasionally to pay those stealthy visits to his mother for which she prepared by telling her attendants to leave her absolutely alone. If he resembled the Family he may have been handsome; but of any decency of character he seems to have had no trace.

In March 1830, just a year after the affidavit was sworn in Chancery, Sir Herbert Taylor, to whom the name of Garth must by then have been more hateful than ever, received the following letter:

45, Wigmore Street, 18th *March* 1830

Sir,

In consequence of a circular letter I attended a meeting of Captain Garth's creditors yesterday, where a representation was made that he was successfully prosecuting his suit against you, and which was being done for their benefit, but that some of his creditors were proceeding to outlawry against him, the consequence of which would be to put an end to the suit against you, and of course prevent the possibility of his ever being able to pay any of them a single shilling. The creditors appeared willing to consent, but I proposed an adjournment for a few days to consider the question. The parties—at least two of them—who are proceeding with the outlawry are friends of mine, and I should feel most happy if at the next meeting I could turn them the way which would be most agreeable to your wish and which should be done if I knew what that wish was.—With great respect, I am, Sir, Your very humble Servt

William Connell

To this communication Sir Herbert replied coldly that he 'could not interfere in any matter respecting Captain Garth or his concerns'.

It was in 1838 that the Princess underwent the operation—then known as 'couching'—for the removal of a cataract on one eye. The Duke of Sussex had already passed through the same ordeal with success, and she may well have hoped that some measure of sight would be restored to her. The tremulous letter in which she describes to the Duke of Cambridge the sudden failure of vision in her right eye is dated only '27 Jan', but an allusion near the end to 'Augustus' having seen his son and thinking him 'altogether not quite so ill as he expected to see him', suggests some date anterior to 1832, when relations between the Duke of Sussex and Sir Augustus d'Este became permanently strained:

My Beloved and Dearest Dolly,

   I have no doubt that our dear Miny will have mentioned to you the *affliction* with which the Almighty has thought fit to try me with [*sic*] in the total loss of my right Eye. I could not bear that you should not receive a line from me as your affectionate heart would I am confident enter into my anxiety. I was so [indecipherable] that dear Mary happened to enter my room as the servant announced Mr Alexander, for I had been away for some time from seeing so ill, and on Monday morning in the last week I awoke blind of the right eye. I bore it that day, still bearing up with the *uncertainty*, but when on Tuesday I awoke and found I remained the same, I sent for Mr Alexander, and he came just as dear Miny came in from Bagshot.

   I said to him, 'Pray, treat me like a rational being and tell me the *real truth*, for I assure you I am prepared for the worst'.

   He examined it, and said it was decided *cataract* come on abruptly: that he saw no reason at *present* for fear of the left eye failing me, and that *unless* it did he was not for advising an operation.

   I am grateful indeed for many, many blessings, and if Providence will be so merciful as to spare me my left Eye then indeed I am more than blessed! (w)

The letter ends on a more cheerful note, thanking the Duke of Cambridge for a gift of delightful books and trusting that he will find the little whist-markers she encloses 'up to all that is required'. She also gives him news of the Duke of Sussex. 'Augustus looks well, but he is odd, as usual, with his vile whiskers.'

Early in 1838 Elizabeth, Landgravine of Hesse-Homburg, wrote to Mrs Dering:

   My great anxiety is dear Sophia, who has gone through the operation of couching wonderfully. God grant she may be rewarded, but the cold weather has, I fear, caused much inflammation and pain, which has, we are to hope, retarded the power of vision to be as quick as we could wish.

The Landgravine's diction is never lucid in times of stress, but it is evident that the oculist had been blaming the weather for the failure of the operation. It was not until three months later that the pain and inflammation subsided, and there was no consequent improvement in the sight of the eye. Not long after this Princess Sophia became totally blind.

Princess Augusta now turned with particular tenderness and compassion to her unhappy sister. The senior Princess was installed in Clarence House, St James's, whence she wrote to Mrs Dering, after being confined for several months to her room:

I have seen all my family except *dear Sophy*, but she is fearfull of coming here, therefore I must let her *feel her way*. She knows the steps of my old house, but these are new to her, particularly those in the lilac garden. . . . I so long to see dearest dear Sophy. Since October *I have not got a sight of her*. She is well in health, but miserably blind, and, poor thing, she says if she gets even quite darkened she will still be resigned and happy.

Someone had told Princess Sophia that pillows filled with torn-up paper were comfortable for the sick, and she now set herself to work to tear up old books. Princess Augusta wrote in April 1840:

Dear Sophy is wonderfully well, and so sweet-tempered and resigned to her affliction of blindness, which is the greatest of all trials. She bears it with such calmness and piety, and even cheerfulness, now that her mind is made up never to be any better, but it is painful to witness the poor dear, who used to be so often and so well employed, reduced now only to open books and tear up paper for couch-pillows.

The Princess had moved from Kensington Palace to York House, a modest Georgian building in the quiet alley connecting Palace Green with Vicarage Gate. A watercolour in the Kensington Public Library, made just before the house was demolished in 1904, shows a large old tree screening the windows of the lower floors so effectively that it is rather difficult to see the plan of the place. Here were reassembled her collections of bibelots, ranged where she would be able to find them by touch. One of her attendants, who bore the delightful name of Phoebe Kift, preserved the two large beadwork bags, dark crimson and lemon yellow, bordered, tasselled, and festooned with white tubular beads, which used to hang by their white satin ribbons on either side of the Princess's chair, one to hold letters recently received, the other, letters ready for dispatch. These bags were later in the possession of the family of Phoebe's cousin, Mehitabel Kift, together with other little relics of which the most pathetic is the fire-screen of metal gauze beautifully embroidered by the Princess with a wreath of pink roses and purple and yellow pansies encircling a large 'S' surmounted by a coronet.

Princess Sophia had been one of Mademoiselle Montmollin's best pupils, and as late as 1832 the youthful Princess Victoria recorded that Aunt Sophia's Christmas present to her had been a dress worked by herself. Three years later we catch an almost cheerful glimpse of this aunt at a drawing-room concert by Grisi and Lablache. Princess Victoria sat in the front row with Princess Sophia and the Duchess of Cambridge, and 'quite close to the piano', and 'Aunt Sophia, who had never heard any of these singers before, was delighted'. Two months later—in July 1835—the young Princess was confirmed in the Chapel Royal, and among the relatives who watched that diminutive figure in its white lace dress and bonnet were her Uncle Ernest and Aunt Sophia, he still upright, soldierly, and whiskered, she now a frail shadow of her former delicate self.

This is not the only occasion when we see those two under the same roof. The year before the Garth scandal exploded, when the Duke of Cumberland alarmed his political and personal enemies by coming over to England to visit George IV, Miss Cornelia Knight noted in her diary:

> *June* 16, 1828.—In the evening at Princess Sophia's Sir J. C. came in and gave a droll account of the magnificent breakfast given by the Duchess of St Albans at the villa near town. . . . The Dukes of Cumberland and Sussex, and Prince Leopold were there.

'Sir J. C.' was Sir John Conroy, Princess Victoria's *bête-noire*, 'whose person', says Lord Esher, 'was odious to her'. As Comptroller to the Duchess of Kent he acquired over her Royal Highness a degree of influence which her daughter considered excessive, and it will be remembered that one of Victoria's first acts as Queen was to dismiss him. 'It is supposed', wrote Greville, 'that the Duchess of Kent used to meet him there'—at Princess Sophia's house, a convenient and inconspicuous rendezvous—and this 'set the Queen very much against her, and she resented it so much that she never took any notice of her aunt except making her a formal visit once a year'.

Mr Greville was mistaken. It may be that the Queen cared more for Princess Augusta, and her favourite aunt seems to have been the Duchess of Gloucester, but there is no reason to believe that she slighted or neglected Princess Sophia. 'I grieve', she wrote on one occasion to the Duchess, 'to hear that Aunt Sophia is still so suffering'; and in acknowledging gifts from both aunts to her children at Christmas 1847 she alludes affectionately to 'Dear Aunt Sophia', whom she visited at Kensington more than once in the early months of 1848. She was too essentially compassionate to be 'set very much against' so patient and so pathetic a figure.

The Duke and Duchess of Cambridge came often to the small brick house beyond Palace Green, sometimes bringing their charming young daughters with them. Princess Sophia joined with the Princesses Augusta and Mary in presenting Prince George of Cambridge with a complete set of Wellington's dispatches as a birthday gift. The Duke of Sussex and his morganatic wife, the Duchess of Inverness, would come across the Green from their home in Kensington Palace; and now the 'vile whiskers' of the Duke were no longer visible to his sister. But the most faithful of the Family was 'dearest Miny', who sometimes tempted the recluse out to 'take the air' in a drive round the Parks. The Duchess of Gloucester wrote to Miss Louisa Adams in a letter which must belong to the last stage of Princess Sophia's life:

> You will be rejoiced to hear dear Sophy went out in the carriage yesterday, for the first time since Xmas, and I had the happiness and comfort of going out with her in my carriage in the old, usual way. We went round Hyde Park, and she was not as much fatigued as I expected, and assured me it brought on no more pain in her limbs or side, but she is sadly sunk in her chair, and appears much more infirm to-day.
>
> We went out again round Hyde Park and lengthened the drive by going round St James's Park, and she appeared quite to enjoy it.

To Amelia Murray, Princess Sophia confided her reason for refusing to have a resident lady-in-waiting: 'Not being able to see, she would always fancy the lady sitting opposite her, looking weary'. Four readers came every day, one English, one French, one German, and one Italian, to keep the Princess *au courant du jour*, but she would allow each to read to her only for an hour, so that 'the fatigue would not be too great for them'; and all the while her hands were busy tearing paper or winding silk.

With the aid of Sir William Ross's sketch, made in 1845, it is not difficult to imagine Princess Sophia in these last years, a little, stooping figure with braided hair, a crisply goffered muslin cap tied under the chin, and still an elfin quality in her face. On the third finger of her left hand she wears two rings, of which one at least seems to be a plain gold band.

'The last time I saw this amiable Princess,' writes Amelia Murray, 'in addition to her blindness she was in some degree deaf, and could not move from her seat without being carried; yet still she was as patient and uncomplaining as ever.' Some trace of Queen Charlotte's early religious training appears sometimes in Princess Sophia's resignation, as when she wrote to the Duke of Cambridge apropos of her failing sight,' Let happen what will, I trust I may submit with humility to it—but it is a severe trial, and as such is assuredly for my good'.(w)

Queen Victoria wrote to King Leopold on 11 January 1848, 'Louise will have told you that poor Aunt Sophia is decidedly sinking', but it was not until the morning of 27 May that her condition caused alarm. The Birthday Drawing Room arranged for that day was duly held, as the Queen had not been told the real gravity of the Princess's condition.(w) Four days later Princess Mary of Cambridge wrote to her friend Miss Draper:

. . . thank God my poor dear Aunt Sophia did not suffer much in her last moments, and died without a sigh, with Mama's hand in her own. She had been insensible for two hours before death released her from a life of suffering.

'The Princess', writes Greville, 'left a letter for the Queen which was delivered to her in the garden of Buckingham Palace by Andrew Drummond on Monday morning'—apparently a memorandum concerning her personalty, and her desire for a private funeral. Andrew Drummond was the head of the famous Bank at Charing Cross.

After William IV's funeral at Windsor, with its confusions and delays, and clashes over precedence, the Duke of Sussex had made up his mind firmly that when his turn came he would be interred in an unobtrusive manner in the cemetery 'laid out' in 1832 at Kensal Rise—a spot then two miles distant from London. 'No sooner was the cemetery opened', says a mid-Victorian writer, 'than the boon was eagerly embraced by the public.' If its seclusion and comparative remoteness appealed to the Duke of Sussex, how much more strongly would they appeal to Princess Sophia. Her recollection of his words may have influenced her, and her wishes were respected; but Henry Greville wrote in his diary on 5 June 1848: 'Princess Sophia's funeral, which she had desired should be conducted with privacy, cost £1,500—a monstrous example of the cheating carried on by the tradesmen employed by the Government'.

The hearse, drawn by six horses, and preceded by a mourning coach conveying the dead Princess's coronet 'in the charge of the Vice Chamberlain of Her Majesty's household', left Vicarage Gate at 5.15 and did not reach Kensal Green till 7. At the entrance to the Chapel waited the Prince Consort, the Duke of Cambridge and his son Prince George, the Bishop of Norwich and the Bishop of Hereford. The Duchess of Kent was represented by Lady Augusta Bruce, later the wife of Dean Stanley.

It has been stated more than once that Princess Sophia's grave at Kensal Green is marked by an austere stone bearing the one word *Sophia* and a text from St Matthew xi. 28. But she rests beneath a lofty and dignified monument, of which the sarcophagus, carved with a design of masks and scrolls, is so high that it is difficult to see the coronet which surmounts it. The Commissioners of Woods and Forests purchased a plot, one hundred feet square, south of the chapel, 'intended to serve also for such other members of the royal family as may desire to be interred there', but only the Duke of Sussex and his wife share it with Princess Sophia. His monument, facing his sister's across the gravel path, is clumsy and squat by contrast. Not only her name, as sentimental rumour declared, but her full titles as 'fifth daughter of his Majesty King George III', are set forth upon one end of the stone oblong supporting the sarcophagus; but it is true that on the side are carved the words, 'Come unto Me all ye that are weary and heavy-laden, and I will give you rest'.

6
Princess Amelia,
1783–1810

I

On 6 August 1783, George III wrote to Lord North from Windsor, 'The Queen, finding Herself not quite Well has desired Me to stay with Her, and Dr Ford having told Me it will probably prove a Labour You will give notice to the other Ministers that I shall not come to town till Friday. As soon as the Queen is delivered, You shall certainly receive an account from Me, who till then cannot but be in a state of great anxiety.' The next day the Queen gave birth to a daughter.

It was the fifteenth occasion upon which his Majesty had awaited the imminent arrival of yet another scion of his House, and it was to be the last. Two little Princes, Octavius and Alfred, had died in the year immediately preceding the birth of this sixth Princess, and it is possible to trace a progressive decline in the vitality of the royal children after Princess Mary's birth in 1776.

The new baby was christened Amelia, after her great-aunt, the ruddy-faced, rather masculine 'Princess Emily', whom in looks and character she resembled so little. Among the royal chaplains who assisted at the ceremony was the Rev. Dr Butt, father of the future authoress of *The Fairchild Family*. Her godfather was her eldest brother, the Prince of Wales.

Princess Amelia's cradle-curtains and coverlet are in the London Museum, lovely things of ivory satin embroidered with roses, fringed pinks and streaked tulips, worthy to shelter the sleep of as pretty an infant as ever laughed at its coral and bells. Mrs Delany gives this picture of her at two years old:

> I have been several evenings at the Queen's Lodge with no other company than their own most lovely family. They sit round a large table, on which are books, work, pencils and paper. The Queen has the goodness to make me sit down next to her and delights me with her conversation, whilst the younger part of the family are drawing and working, the beautiful babe Princess Amelia bearing her part in the entertainment, sometimes in one of her sisters' laps, sometimes playing with the King on the carpet.

With the possible exception of the long-lamented Octavius, Amelia was the King's favourite child; she was certainly his favourite daughter, as the rest were quick to recognize. Fanny Burney was characteristically lyrical about her, and few things in her journals are more delightful than the description of the baby Princess walking on the Terrace on her third birthday, 'in a robe-coat covered with fine muslin, a dressed close cap, white gloves and a fan'. After greeting Mrs Delany 'like a little angel', the Princess caught sight of the modest Fanny and then, 'with a look of inquiry and recollection', slowly toddled behind the elder lady to examine the younger more closely. 'I am afraid', whispered Fanny, stooping down, 'your Royal Highness does not remember me?' Princess Amelia's answer was 'an arch little smile and a nearer approach, with her lips pouted out', proffering a kiss. 'She then', records the delighted diarist, 'took my fan, and having looked at it on both sides, gravely returned it to me, saying, "O! a brown fan!"'

On 20 November 1810, about three weeks after the death of Princess Amelia, her executors, the Prince of Wales and the Duke of Cambridge, delivered into the hands of Queen Charlotte a number of letters written by George III. One of these was preserved by her Majesty's secretary, Sir Herbert Taylor, and is here quoted from the unpublished Taylor MSS. It is addressed 'To my Dearly Beloved Daughter, the Princess Amelia'. The oval seal, on scarlet wax, bears the royal arms; on the outer wrapping the Prince and the Duke have splashed black wax over red before applying the seal.

The King wrote from Cheltenham on 4 August 1788:

My Dearest Amelia,
As I shall not see you on the dear 7th of this Month I have sent to Gooly a writing-box and a wooden shoe which is a nutmeg grater, as signs of my not having forgot you. Were I to express all the wishes I make for your prosperity in this world and Eternal Happiness in the next in a letter Vollumes would not contain them. I shall on Sunday the 7th be at Kew before you are out of your bed, to bring you to Windsor and to see your two sisters.—Believe me, ever, my dearest Amelia, Your most affectionate father,

GEORGE R.

Princess Mary was able to assure the King on the birthday that 'Dear little Amelia was vastly pleased with all her presents and laughed exceedingly at the shoe'.[w]

Between that birthday and the next occurred the King's first attack of insanity. When he recovered, and rejoicings were loud and general, one of the most remarkable manifestations of pleasure was the huge 'transparency' painted by Biachio Rebecca and erected at Kew at the Queen's expense. It represented a life-sized Aesculapius holding a medallion of the King upon which Providence, descending at the request of Britannia, was shown in the act of dropping a large laurel wreath. Neither the King nor anyone else seems to have been in the least embarrassed by these symbolic reminders of his recent affliction.

To emphasize the beauty and significance of Rebecca's work, Fanny Burney's services were enlisted, and that flattered little person produced a 'set of verses' which the Princess Amelia kneeling presented to the King, before leading him to the window to see the newly illuminated 'transparency'. The two first stanzas may be quoted here:

> Amid a rapturous nation's praise
>   That sees Thee to their prayers restor'd,
> Turn gently from the general blaze—
>   Thy Charlotte woos her bosom's lord.

> Turn and behold where, bright and clear,
>   Depictur'd with transparent art,
> The emblems of her thoughts appear,
>   The tribute of a grateful heart.

The Princess, not then quite six years old, did what was required of her with engaging grace, and it is easy to imagine with what alacrity the King acted upon the hint contained in the postscript:

> The little bearer begs a kiss
> From dear Papa for bringing this.

With her nurses, Mrs Williams and Mrs Cheveley, Princess Amelia remained on affectionate terms. 'Chi-Chi', whom Fanny Burney describes as 'rather handsome, and of a showy appearance', receives praise for her 'admirable management of the young Princess', whom she always 'treated with respect, even when reproving her', yet without giving way to any of her humours where it was 'better they should be conquered'. 'Our valuable, kind friend, dear Chi-Chi', Princess Sophia called her when she died in 1807—after 'one of her spasms'. Mrs Williams survived her nursling, by whom she was urgently summoned to Windsor in the last months of that sorrowful young life. Princess Mary wrote once to the Prince of Wales concerning their youngest sister that she had never seen 'so grateful a Soul as she is for any kindness shown to her by anyone'—a quality all the more charming because she had been in childhood, as Miss Burney bears witness, 'universally indulged'.

When due allowance has been made for that lady's ecstatic bent, it must be admitted that the 'lovely little Princess' of her *Diary* is lovable as well as lovely. Even the solemn Mr Smelt, of whom Mrs Delany remarked that 'his character is that of the most noble and delicate kind, and deserves the pen of a Clarendon to do justice to it', cast aside his dignity and joined with Fanny one day in pretending to put the Princess in a phaeton and drive about to make visits with her to Mrs Delany and Mrs Smelt. The King's entry interrupted them at a moment when Mr Smelt was 'choosing to represent a restive horse', and Amelia resented the interruption so much that she begged her father to withdraw. 'Go, Papa, you must go!' she reiterated, while he held her in his arms and kissed her—nor would she be content until Papa had gone, and the game was resumed.

Though Lady Charlotte Finch was nominally in charge of Princess Amelia's education, regular lessons were made impossible after 1798 by increasing ill-health. At the New Year 1791 her ladyship gave an evening entertainment to the younger Princesses and their schoolroom attendants, which was graced by the presence of the King and Queen and the elder members of the Sisterhood. 'The supper', remarks Mrs Papendiek, 'was excellent and elegant. A trifle was considered a New Year's dish . . . this depicted the principal events that had taken place during the previous year of pleasurable recollection: the Mornington election, Rebecca with his palette, a rowing match at Eastbourne.'

Up to 1798, when the tuberculous trouble in her knee manifested itself, Princess Amelia had no outward signs of delicacy, being then 'full as tall as the Princess Royal and as much formed'. She was, according to Marianne Moula, '*d'une taille prodigieuse*', and had '*un air de force et de vigueur*'. Her fourth sister wrote of her, even after she had become more or less of an invalid, 'she promised when I last saw her to be very large indeed *in time*'.[w] Madame d'Arblay, more poetical than either Mademoiselle Moula or the Princess Mary, exclaimed that Princess Amelia had 'an innocence, an Hebe blush, an air of modest candour, and a gentleness so caressingly inviting of voice and eye, that I have seldom seen a more captivating young creature'.

The good-natured Marianne was full of pity for the poor Princess, packed off to Worthing with General Goldsworthy and his sister, and Mrs Cheveley, to take sea-baths and be treated by the well-known surgeon, Mr Keate. '*Si*', she wrote, '*c'eut été une dame ordinaire une de ses sœurs l'auraient accompagnée; c'est ce que je ne pouvais m'empêcher de remarquer à la P.M., qui me dit, "Vous avez bien raison. Si nous étions les Miss Guelph surément quelques unes de nous auraient été du voyage."*'

Worthing was evidently regarded as more suitable than Weymouth for Princess Amelia's complaint. It was quieter than the Dorset resort, which royal favour had made a centre of much obsequious activity; it was also within easier reach of Brighton, where the Heir Apparent was spending much of his time.

Already Princess Amelia was corresponding affectionately, though unobtrusively, with her 'Godpapa', the Prince of Wales. 'Pray, my sweet love,' she wrote to him, 'don't answer this, and when you come here take no notice to *high* or low of having heard from me.'[w] From Weymouth, in September 1797, she sent him a purse netted by herself, 'small and not half so pretty as it ought to be', and a batch of lively letters, one of them poking fun at Lady Pitt, otherwise 'Pitty Witty':

The dear soul was very amiable and merry. *She whined more than ever.* Yesterday morning she gave the colours to the Dorchester Volunteers and made them a speech. I would have given the World to have seen her do it.[w]

Then comes a hint of that sensitiveness to noise which was later a feature of her illness: 'I wish the wind would go down. *It hurts the Drumsticks of my Ears.*'[w]

Princess Mary, knowing how kindly an interest the Prince took in his godchild, went out of her way to praise her to him. 'I do believe', she wrote in 1798, 'that was it not for her own very *heavenly disposition* nothing can be *more dull than Worthing*, or the life she must lead wherever she is, from being quite confined to the couch and suffering so much pain.'[w] Far away in Würtemberg the eldest Princess was 'very uneasy' about her, and wrote to the King:

I am sure she is much mortified at being prevented accompanying your Majesty. However, from the moment she cannot enter into the life lead [*sic*] at Weymouth, or at Windsor during the camp, she appears to me happier at a distance, as she is not then daily tantalized with hearing of parties which she cannot partake off [*sic*].[w]

Princess Amelia seems to have been quite free from that vague distrust of the Princess Royal manifested about this time by her sisters Mary and Sophia. She wrote to Lady Charlotte Bruce, otherwise 'Chassy', who was in waiting on the eldest Princess for part of the way to her new home in Germany:

I cannot let you leave this dear Island to accompany my beloved sister without troubling you with a line to say how sincerely I regret my dear Chassy's Departure, though only for three Weeks, and how I shall rejoice when I shall see you again. . . . Oh, my dear Angel, my Heart is so full with parting with my dear Sister that I can scarce write.
  Pray say everything that is kind to dear Royal—tell her how sincerely I love her.[w]

The Princess Royal was at the same time conscious of a particularly tender interest in her stepdaughter, the Princess Catherine, because she was 'the same age as dear Amelia'.

In August 1798 the Prince of Wales drove over from Brighton to visit his ailing godchild, with whom he spent what she called 'a charming hour', and to whom he sent a gift of 'pretty hats'. He evidently charged her with some persiflage for Miss Goldsworthy, as the Princess tells him, 'Goully says you are much too bad, and don't pay *proper respect to her Age*'.[w]

A letter from Queen Charlotte to the Prince of Wales dated 19 September 1798, shows that he was not satisfied with the accommodation provided for his

sister at Worthing. 'I am truely grateful', writes her Majesty, 'for your offer of
the Pavillion, and should, were I to act for myself, not hesitate to accept of Your
goodness at once. But as others must be spoke to, I must seize *un beau moment*
to settle it.'[w] Either the others were opposed to the idea, or the *beau moment*
did not come, for Amelia never enjoyed a visit to 'that fine building', as Mr
Turveydrop called it.

On her way home from Worthing in December the Princess broke her journey
at Juniper Hill, the Surrey house of Sir Lucas Pepys, and by special permission
of the Queen, subject to the approval of Sir Lucas and Mr Keate, Madame
d'Arblay went to visit her there, accompanied by Alexander, who 'seemed
enchanted to see her again', and was so demonstrative in his pleasure that his
mother was 'alarmed lest he should skip upon her poor knee with his caressing
agility'. Madame d'Arblay's well-known description of Amelia on this occasion
will bear repetition:

> The Princess was seated on a sofa, in a French grey riding-dress with pink
> lapels,—her beautiful and richly flowing and shining fair locks unornamented.
> Her breakfast was still before her, and Mrs Cheveley in waiting . . . she received
> me with the brightest smile, calling me up to her, and stopping my profound
> reverence by pouting out her sweet ruby lips for me to kiss.

Sir Lucas had given the visitor 'the most cheering accounts of the recovery of
the Princess', but when the interview ended she had to be 'painfully lifted from
her seat' between him and Mr Keate.

In the spring of 1799 Princess Amelia was at Queen's Lodge, delighting in the
society of her 'perfect Miny'; and by the summer of that year she was bathing in
the sea at Weymouth, and writing to the Prince of Wales to beg a chaplaincy for
Sir Harry Neale's brother, and a new gown for herself, which she is 'in great want
of'. She had sent him a pattern belonging to 'dear Miny' who was anxious to have
it returned.[w] The chaplaincy materialized, and we may hope the gown also.

Christmas was then the accepted time for Confirmations and First
Communions, and at Christmas 1799 the sixteen-year-old Princess was
confirmed by the Archbishop of Canterbury, to whom she showed the 'dear,
dear letter' written to her on that occasion by her godfather, the Prince of Wales.

'Dear Amelia', wrote Queen Charlotte to the Prince on 26 December,

> went through the Confirmation on Tuesday and yesterday extreamly well.
> She declares herself happy and uncommonly easy in Her Mind, which is most
> Natural, as at all times the Preparation for such a sacred Scene is awfull, and
> her very delicate state of Nerves must, of course, have increased it considerably.
>
> She is, however, thank God! in a very good state of Health and in good
> spirits, and the Noise in the throat at times much lessened.[w]

It was in 1801, when she was close upon eighteen, still graced by the 'Hebe blush' and the caressing charm which had delighted Madame d'Arblay, that Princess Amelia was left alone at Weymouth so that, after the rest of the Family had returned to Windsor, she might enjoy the benefit of regular exercise on horseback and the much-prized sea air a little longer. With her were Miss Jane Gomm, the colleague and crony of the faithful Miss Goldsworthy, and the King's aide-de-camp, Colonel (afterwards General) the Honble. Sir Charles FitzRoy,[14] second son of the first Lord Southampton, and nephew of the third Duke of Grafton.

If General Garth was an unlikely hero for a royal romance by reason of his advanced age and his honourable reputation, still more unlikely was the sedate, self-contained, and rather frigid Charles FitzRoy for such a dashing role. Born in 1762—the same year as the Prince of Wales—he had taken his soldiering seriously, even extending his studies to Prussian Army methods, thereby attracting the favourable attention of Frederick the Great. During his Continental travels he had visited Brunswick, and had won the goodwill of the Duchess—never long withheld from any personable young man of good family hailing from her native England.

For FitzRoy was decidedly personable in his wooden way. Neither the ugliness nor the genial temper of his royal ancestor Charles II had descended to him. George III, who would not have been amused by a Restoration turn of wit, regarded the promising soldier with benevolence. Imaginative biographers and novelists have even suggested that FitzRoy's royal blood may have been drawn from a source less remote than the veins of Charles II, and that he was actually King George's son; but this theory collapses upon inspection.

No breath of gossip linked his Majesty's name with that of Lady Southampton; Hannah Lightfoot was already a legend; Lady Sarah Lennox had been an innocent interlude. A God-fearing young Prince preparing himself for marriage with a Princess of unblemished virtue would hardly have indulged simultaneously in an intrigue with the wife of a peer of the realm. But there is a type of mind to which facts do not present any obstacle. The circumstance that George, Prince of Wales, and Charles FitzRoy were born in the same year has not deterred some writers from seeking to add horror to pathos in Princess Amelia's story by suggesting that the man she loved was not even her half-brother—which would have been bad enough—but her nephew.

The behaviour of FitzRoy when he realized—as he must have done on the return to Windsor if not before that she was falling in love with him is hardly excusable. Even if he had fallen in love with her, it would have been wiser as well as more merciful on his part to throw up his post at Court and seek military employment abroad. Sir Brent Spencer, though his feelings towards Princess Augusta were evidently warmer than FitzRoy's for Amelia, had acted with greater credit to himself and with greater consideration towards the royal lady in question. But FitzRoy remained cool and quiescent, even when Miss Gomm perceived how things were, even when Amelia openly dropped behind the rest of the royal riders at Windsor in order to be near him, or sent fond glances towards him in church, thus making the situation perilously clear.

Miss Gomm, grown suddenly either more scrupulous or more apprehensive, now resolved to break silence, and spoke her mind to Princess Amelia herself, to Princess Mary, and to Miss Goldsworthy. From this it was but one stage to informing the Queen, and in May 1803 the distressed Amelia wrote to her mother complaining that she had been badly treated by the two old ladies, as well as by her sister.

The Queen's reply is a marvel of evasion. Not once does she refer frankly to the real cause of all the trouble. She pleads for Miss Gomm that she was bound in honour to put the Princess on her guard if she knew of anything that would be likely to injure her:

> and as she has seen much of the World knows by experience that the Higher the Rank in Life, the more the World will expose them, because the World expects more Circumspection in their Conduct.

Her Majesty also pleads for Princess Mary that she had shown 'a very amiable delicacy' in determining not to mention the subject to her sister, and in offering to remain with her at Windsor when she was 'confined with those Boils', so that the invalid should not be 'left alone with those Ladies'. 'Circumspection' was the text of the royal discourse. The Princess had been 'struck' by a warning from the Queen that she should ride near the King 'and not keep behind':

> This, my dear Amelia, might with reason strike you, having this affair in your Head, but you are wrong in your supposition—I had myself made this observation several times last year, when I went out with You and the King, and named it to those ladies who were in the carriage with me with disapprobation—You see by that how dangerous it is to suspect.

The Queen rejected her agitated daughter's plea that she should not be compelled to have anything more to do with the Misses Gomm and Goldsworthy. This was reasonable, for both were old and attached servants and friends, and a rupture would have been painful as well as conspicuous. But the equally firm rejection of the Princess's plea that her rides should be discontinued is curious. Surely her Majesty must have realized that she was throwing her daughter and FitzRoy together when her chief aim should have been to keep them apart? The obvious thing to do would have been to take steps to eliminate the equerry, but this could not be done without 'this affair' coming to the knowledge of the King, from whom it was of the highest importance to conceal it.

So circumspection, reticence, the suppression of 'all anger and suspicion' were to be the order of the day. The Princess is asked to promise 'neither directly or indirectly to name a word of this unpleasant business' to her brothers. Her mother is sorry that she should have spoken about it to her sisters, 'but what is done is done, and it is better to forget it'. It is with surprise that we find Amelia writing to 'dear Miny' that 'Mama's conduct has been such as to endear her more to me than ever'; but she may have been grateful to the Queen for keeping her secret from the King. 'I glory in our attachment,' she wrote to FitzRoy in 1807, 'only I think the Dear too Royal and Kingly, if he knew it, to pity.'

FitzRoy's letters to the Princess have not been preserved, but it is not difficult to divine that he was the less ardent correspondent. 'My own dear love,' she writes, 'I am sure you love me as well as ever.' She begs for 'a kind look or a word', for a lock of his 'dear hair'; she is anxious that he should sit where she can see him in chapel. No longer chained to her 'sopha', she slips little notes into his hand walking in the garden at Frogmore.

Queen Charlotte's insistence that her youngest daughter should not give up riding might have cost the Princess her life when her mount came down with her near Cuffnells in the summer of 1804. Mr George Rose, at whose Hampshire house the King and part of his family were staying, describes how her horse 'on cantering down an inconsiderable hill came on his head and threw her Royal Highness flat on her face'. The King insisted that if she was 'at all hurt' she should get into one of the carriages and return to Cuffnells; otherwise, she must mount another horse and continue the ride. Not without an effort, as Mr Rose perceived, she chose the second course; and when he, alone of all the gentlemen in attendance, ventured to urge that it would be better for her to drive home, the suggestion was 'certainly not well received' by his Majesty, who observed sharply that he 'could not bear that any of his family should lack courage'.

It may be to this episode that the Princess refers in an undated letter to the Prince of Wales about the 'beautiful horse', his own gift to her, which had fallen down and 'hurt his knees very much'; but her assurance that she kept her seat does not tally with Mr Rose's account, unless she fell 'flat on her face' without being actually thrown. She adds:

> I believe, and so does all the gentlemen, that the fault was owing to the carelessness of the servants than [*sic*] to the poor dear Annimal, as the Grooms do not pay that attention they ought to Ladies' Horses. . . . As being my dear G.P.'s gift it was a very precious horse to me.
>
> Edward was with me at the time, so he will be able to explain.[w]

The Duke of Kent was not left long in ignorance of his youngest sister's infatuation with their father's equerry; the Dukes of York and Sussex soon knew, and, each after his fashion, sympathized. Like the Queen, they prescribed circumspection, but, unlike her, they infused a vague note of hope into their counsels of patience.

In June 1804, when the Family were at Kew, Princess Amelia made the acquaintance of two people destined to play a role which remains a little obscure to this day. They were the Honble. George Villiers, third son of the first Earl of Clarendon, and his wife, a sister of Lord Boringdon, afterwards first Earl of Morley. This lady would appear to have enjoyed the role of confidante to the secretly unhappy, for another of her closest friends was Byron's half-sister, Augusta Leigh. We have Mrs Villiers' word for it that it was not until 1807–8 that Amelia first alluded to FitzRoy in conversation with her, but during the preceding years she was establishing herself firmly in the confidence of the Princess, and in time she acquired such an ascendancy over her that the other Princesses asked her to urge their sister to be more prudent. This she declined to do until she herself broached the subject.

In view of the part played by the Prince of Wales in the FitzRoy affair, both before and after Princess Amelia's death, it is interesting to notice how early she begins to reiterate her faith in her brother's affection for her. 'I hope', she wrote in 1797, 'you will ever continue the kindness to me that I have ever experienced from you', and four years later she exclaims, 'If you ever changed towards me it would break my heart, but I assure you I have no fear of that'.

The Prince evidently encouraged her to call herself his 'Child'. On 11 August 180, she wrote to him from Weymouth:

> I cannot tell you how deeply I feel your invariable kindness to your *own Child* as You call me, and how delighted I was with Your Message, which our dear Miny gave me. She is as amiable as ever, and I hope, *like you* that dear Charlotte will turn out like her, for I never saw such a dear as *she is*. I have dressed *her*, dear little love, from Top to toe for tomorrow, and dear Miny has dressed *me* for the day.(w)

Princess Mary had written *à propos* of the same birthday:

> Amelia, your *old* Child, has dressed little Charlotte new upon the occasion, and I can assure you she will be very smart, and I flatter myself Amelia will look in great *beauty*, as I have given her a dress in my own stile to *make her look* less like an old woman than usual.(w)

It is difficult to imagine Princess Amelia in any circumstances looking 'like an old woman', though she did affect close-fitting lawn caps and Tudor ruffs. Ill-health and tribulation gave an ethereal grace to her beauty as years passed, but when she was in her middle 'teens it would have needed an intuitive eye to discern the delicacy behind her bright colour and her full curves. The resemblance which Princess Mary noticed in after years between Princess Charlotte and her youngest aunt is visible in the miniature of herself given by Princess Amelia to Admiral Sir Harry (Burrard) and Lady Neale. Sir Harry was Captain of the royal yacht, and it was his brother for whom the young Princess obtained a chaplaincy from the Prince of Wales in 1799. The miniature and other relics of her friendship with the Neales are preserved in the family of the late Colonel Jacques Reboul, C.B., grandson of their adopted daughter.

The Princess was very fond both of Sir Harry and his wife, and she poured forth her misgivings about the King's health to Lady Neale in a letter which suggests other sources of distress besides the one defined:

> I am often obliged to put on a happy and merry face when my feelings are quite different, for though I am assured there is no reason for alarm as long as that dear Angel has any *Malady* I must feel very anxious. If anything happened to him or Mama, what would become of *us*!
>
> My dear Lady Neale, all this is quite private, and therefore I must intreate of you to name it to no one but Sir Harry. . . . I pray of you once more not to betray me to a soul—write to me soon, and enclose to Mrs Cheveley, Kew House.

Queen Charlotte cannot have objected to the friendship between her daughter and Lady Neale, with whom her Majesty also was on terms of affectionate intimacy, but she had probably impressed upon all the Princesses the importance of keeping strictly to themselves the fact that the Family were once more anxious about the King. In the same letter Princess Amelia reveals that her own health had been 'indifferent', owing to 'Bile and a caught attack of St Anthony's fire' in her face, and interjects the warning, 'but this is private'.

As erysipelas was one of the contributory causes of her death nine years later it is significant to see the tendency manifesting itself so early. This attack cannot have been grave, for she remarks, 'we are here entitled to take a little exercise, which during our stay in London was impossible'.

During the summer of 1804 anxiety about the King's mental condition steadily rose. 'God knows', wrote Princess Amelia to the Prince of Wales, 'we want some little comfort—I neither dare think or look forward. Things indeed wear but a sad appearance. I think *You* might be of great *use* with the Queen, who indeed wants a *real friend* to help her.' 'You say', she wrote a month later, 'the present undecided state of things *vous navre le cœur*. God knows I feel it the same. The longer it lasts, the more I feel it.'[w]

At the time of the King's previous breakdown in 1788–1789 Princess Amelia had been too young to understand the rumours of an impending Regency which filled the air; but she must now have realized that if the 'state of things' should become admittedly hopeless the headship of the Family would pass from a father 'too Royal and Kingly' to pity her and FitzRoy to a brother whose views might be more liberal. It is perhaps this thought which underlies the letter she wrote to the Prince on 19 August 1804. 'Our situation' apparently means hers and FitzRoy's, and the 'us' then clearly refers to them both.

> . . . God knows I am more wretched than I can express, and could an Extinguisher fall upon the whole family I think as things are it would be a mercy. . . . I trust we shall meet *soon* the moment will be a most trying one— *none will feel it more than myself* but I hope that my dearest dear Brother *Nothing* will prevent it. You know our situation, and I know you love us, especially *your own Child*, and God knows how much ours [*sic*] particularly My own happiness and comfort depends on this meeting.
>
> . . . I love you more and more dearly—could you see my heart you would see *how* I love you—how I *feel* and *suffer* for You. What would I not sacrifice to promote what would make You happy.[w]

The last paragraph presumably refers to the Prince's estrangement from his father over the custody of Princess Charlotte and other matters.

On 12 November 1804, when Princess Amelia had seen her brother and talked with him, she wrote, 'I go to bed to-night with a happier heart than I have had God knows when'. It was shortly after this confidential conversation that she took to signing herself A. F. R.—*i.e.* Amelia FitzRoy. Two plain silver cups still in the possession of his brother's descendants bear Charles FitzRoy's monogram surmounted by the royal crown and cypher, and various pieces of plate found among the Princess's possessions after her death were engraved with cyphers and monograms which her executors caused hastily to be erased.

This raises the still-unsolved problem as to whether any ceremony was performed to satisfy at once the scruples and the sentiments of the Princess. The lady whom FitzRoy married six years after Amelia's death is said 'at one time' to have believed that some such ceremony took place, and there is a persistent tradition to the same effect in the FitzRoy family. The Princess of Wales declared in 1810 that 'everyone believed it'; and Lady Louisa Connolly wrote in 1811, on the authority of Lady Clancarty, that the King had been 'so much affected with the discovery of Princess Amelia's marriage that his illness came on in consequence of it'—an assertion frequently found both in contemporary and later memoirs. It was certainly the Princess's own wish, and she is quite frank about it to her 'own dear Angel', to whom she wrote:

> I really must marry you—though inwardly united, and in reality that is much more than the ceremony, yet that ceremony would be a protection. O my precious darling, how often do I say—would to God my own husband and best friend and guardian was here to protect me!

She told Frederick, Duke of York, that she 'considered herself married' to FitzRoy, and she went so far as to write to FitzRoy himself, 'We are married. Every thought and every sorrow we must impart to each other.' It is quite possible that this should be read figuratively, as Mr Childe-Pemberton suggests, and that the ceremony, if any took place, was regarded by Amelia merely as binding them 'tighter and more sacredly together in spirit'. This view is supported by her own words, 'I own I can never help praying and hoping a time yet may come when the Almighty may bless and join us in person as we are in hearts, ever inseparable'; and elsewhere, after apostrophizing him as 'My husband!' she adds, 'though alas! the rights, from situation, I have not enjoyed!'

On the other hand, she does not describe him as her husband in any of the various wills and testamentary memoranda which she drew up at intervals between 1803 and 1810, leaving everything she possessed to her 'beloved Charles FitzRoy'; and Mrs George Villiers, writing in 1847 to her daughter Theresa (Lady Lewis), says, 'My firm conviction is, amounting as near to certainty as any one person can feel about another, that she never was married, or ever had a child'. This last clause is interesting, as rumour, which ascribed several children to the Princess, had included Theresa Villiers in their number.

Glenbervie also denies that there was any private marriage, but says that the Prince of Wales had promised to permit his sister to marry FitzRoy 'if he came to be King'. His lordship does not mention any child, and adds that her 'amours with FitzRoy have long been notorious to the courtiers. Whether carried to extreme lengths seems uncertain.' It speaks well both for the Princess's reputation and the General's that the old gossip should have felt any uncertainty upon the question.

None the less, rumour, reinforced by the traditions of more than one family, associates the death of Princess Amelia with the birth of a child, or even of children, for the FitzRoys have preserved a legend of twins! The medical bulletins of the Princess's last year are so full of sickroom details as to leave little doubt that she died of tuberculosis complicated by erysipelas—but uncomplicated by pregnancy. FitzRoy does not seem to have visited her at Weymouth, and after her return in a dying condition to Windsor he saw her only once, with the connivance of Princess Augusta. But there is an intriguing passage in a letter written to the Prince Regent by Princess Mary shortly after Princess Amelia's death. 'The King', she says,

> has enquired of Sir Henry [Halford] when poor Amelia saw FitzRoy, but *of course* Sir Henry answered '*Never* to *his* knowledge in the illness', which I trust you will not disapprove of, and this I believe we *must be steady to*, and as the King may ask you the same question it is very necessary You should be informed of the *decided* answer Sir Henry has given.[w]

This looks as if rumour had already begun to busy itself with the matter, and suggests an effort not to suppress a scandalous truth but to forestall a dangerous fable. The affectionate interest shown by the Princess in various girls, ranging from her niece, the Duke of Sussex's daughter, down to the orphans of low degree to whom she played the part of fairy godmother, may have been responsible for the persistent reports that she had a daughter, or daughters, of her own.

A parallel to the story connecting Isaac Corry with Princess Sophia is to be found in the equally insubstantial story of a secret marriage between Princess Amelia and the Prince of Wales's friend, Edward Phelps.

Phelps, who assumed the surname of McDonnell in 1817 when he married Anne Catherine, Countess (in her own right) of Antrim, is alleged to have been the father of a child, Selena Eliza Phelps, in giving birth to whom Princess Amelia died. Selena Eliza Phelps certainly existed, and it is at least curious that she should have received the present of a book in 1823 from 'her very affectionate friend and governess, Miss Burney'. Her descendants treasure Princess Amelia's gold watch and a tea-set of Sevres china with her cypher.

Humbler protégées of the Princess, on whose behalf no such claims could be made, sometimes proved disappointing. Mr Hone, in his *Every Day Book*, discourses at large upon the misfortunes of one of these, an orphan called Mary, whom Princess Amelia apprenticed to her own dressmaker, Mrs Bingley, in Piccadilly. 'The seduction of this young female', he says, 'deeply afflicted the Princess', and he quotes in full the compassionate though platitudinous letter which her Royal Highness wrote on that occasion. This epistle contains two reproachful allusions to the kindness of Mrs Bingley, whom the unfortunate Mary had 'accused of harshness'.

Light is thrown upon the Princess's own views for her 'young females' in this unpublished and undated letter to Lady Harcourt:

> Miny tells me, and ashamed am I that it should have escaped my Memory, that I have a bill to settle with you about the little girl you so kindly placed at Nuneham—and may I hope you will continue to place her where you think best and have her brought up well, and fit for her own situation, and not above it, for doing that I think the most *criminal* thing instead of friendly that can be done.

Indiscriminate charity, and a certain degree of personal extravagance in the matter of jewels, plumes, and shawls, involved Princess Amelia in debt, and on more than one occasion she was fain to borrow not only from her sisters Mary and Sophia, but even from FitzRoy. In a letter to her 'beloved Angel' she mentions money anxieties in connection with some orphans at Kew, 'one of a labourer, another a poor soldier's child, and a little girl of an old nursery maid we had'. Carking cares were thus added to the more romantic sorrows of her last years.

Towards 1807 anonymous letters began to circulate, and one of these accused Miss Goldsworthy and Miss Gomm of having winked at the FitzRoy affair because they knew that the Queen herself had agreed that the lovers should be married 'the moment the King was dead'. Not unnaturally the Queen was 'outrageous', and a complicated, far-reaching quarrel ensued, involving her Majesty, the Duke of York, Princess Elizabeth, Miss Goldsworthy, and Miss Gomm. It was indeed, as the Duke called it, 'a sad row', but the trouble was not all caused, as he seemed to think, by 'that'd——d Miss Gomm'. He had reason to revise his opinion of that conscientious if officious gentlewoman, and before long the indignation of Princess Amelia's sympathizers was focused upon Lady Georgiana Bulkeley, daughter of John, second Earl de la Warr, and a goddaughter of the King's. The Princess herself never overcame her resentment against the two ex-governesses, felt aggrieved when Princess Mary continued to kiss them both, and upon the report of Gooly's impending retirement wrote to her in terms so frigid that it would have been kinder not to write at all.

Though Queen Charlotte ended by dismissing Lady Georgiana, she would not throw Miss Goldsworthy or Miss Gomm overboard, and an admission that the conduct of the latter lady had been 'ill-judged' was as far as she would go. Mr Childe-Pemberton quotes from the Lowther Papers a curious letter written in April 1807 by the Queen, when these tumults were nearing their height:

> In you, my dear Amelia, I have allowed much for your youth, ignorance of the world, and a consideration of the indulgence you have met with, during a long series of ill health, which both affection and humanity led myself and those about you to yield to at that time, and which none of your sisters were ever allowed to enjoy. You are now beginning to enter into years of discretion, and will I do not doubt see how necessary it is to *subdue* at once every Passion in the beginning, and to consider the impropriety of indulging any impression which must make you miserable, and be a disgrace to yourself and a misery to all who love you. Add to this the melancholy situation of the King at this present moment, who could he be acquainted of what has passed would be rendered miserable for all his life, and I fear it would create a breach in the whole Family.

There follows a passage which leaves us wondering which of the two, the Queen or the Princess, was indulging at that time in a little diplomatic duplicity:

> You seem by your letter so much inclined to get the better of this unfortunate indulgence, that I am truly inclined to believe you sincere, and shall not cease to offer my sincere prayers to the Almighty of giving you strength of mind to overcome it.

Was Princess Amelia at any time 'inclined to get the better' of her love for FitzRoy? The evidence of her own words, reiterated and reinforced up to the time of her death, forbids us to believe it. And according to Mrs George Villiers only the haunting dread that the ensuing scandal would scatter the King's wits for ever deterred her from eloping with FitzRoy on more occasions than one when things were intolerably difficult at home.

It seems doubtful whether FitzRoy would have lent himself to any such perilous projects, though if confronted by a fugitive Princess he might have found it hard to persuade her to leave him. After her death he alluded to her as 'the adored Amelia', but while she lived his affection seems to have demanded stimulation from her side. When she wanted a letter from him to herself that she might show to the Duke of York, she found it necessary to draft it with her own hand. In it she makes FitzRoy say, 'Judge then how anything injurious to you, and above all to your *blessed virtue* and *character*, must be galling to me'—surely a clause which would not have been possible if their love had been illicit as well as illegal.

The Duke of York, though it is not clear whether any such 'inspired' document was ever laid before him, proved sympathetic, as was his wont. The Duke of Cumberland proved unsympathetic, as was *his*. The former deprecated 'the violence of Ernest's conduct, highly unfair and improper', adding, in a kind letter to Princess Amelia, that if she should have further trouble, he could have no objection to her telling Ernest fairly that she would tell it to *him*, 'as you are sure that I will not let you be worried or ill-treated'. He recommends her, however, to 'cut him [Ernest] very short' if he begins to speak upon any subject 'belonging to this'.

The letter from Princess Amelia to the Prince of Wales, to which allusion has been made in Princess Sophia's chapter, does not appear to be concerned with the FitzRoy affair, but it affords an illustration of the relations between the Duke of Cumberland and his youngest sister towards the end of the year 1806:

> There are many things I highly disaprove in him, and as to his being *in my confidence* or *me in his* it is not so, it is perfect mistake [*sic*]. . . . I am grieved to think that there should be a necessity for avoiding being alone with him, but I fully understand, and you may depend upon me remembering your kind injunctions on the subject. I don't know how it has occurred that lately I have heard the offnest from him. . . . He has desired me to let him know from time to time how we all are, but the letters might be read at Charing Cross.
>
> Unless I *quarrell* with Ernest I fear I cannot keep him out of my room, but I always can avoid being alone.[w]

Of all the Family the Duke of Cumberland would have been the last to inspire confidence in a sensitive girl, beset by hostile observers, and conscious of the increasing difficulty of her position.

In the letter quoted earlier the Duke of York alludes to the 'violent and vindictive' character of Lady Georgiana Bulkeley, who probably played the part of *âme damnée* to Miss Gomm and was later suspected of having written the anonymous letters which did so much damage. 'I am convinced', wrote the Duke, 'that she will not stay long in the family.' But efforts to dislodge Lady Georgiana were at first unavailing. She threatened to appeal to the King. This threat was too much for the Queen, who grasped the nettle by commanding Lady Bath to write in the name of the King and herself to Mr Bulkeley in the following unequivocal terms:

> Ly Bath is desired by their Majesties to acquaint Mr Bulkeley that they having been informed some time ago that Ly Georgiana Bulkeley had spoken very disrespectfully of the royal family were disinclined to give any credit to such report, but that lately the same being again repeated by persons whose veracity they cannot doubt their Majesties are under the necessity of stating that under such circumstances it cannot be pleasant to either party to have any further communication with one another, but that out of regard to the memory of the late Lord de la Warr the Queen is inclined to receive her resignation through Lady Bath.
>
> The reason why Mr Bulkeley is charged with this message is to render this intelligence less painful to Lady Georgiana Bulkeley.[w]

Confused though the composition may be, the meaning is clear, and it is impossible not to pity Mr Bulkeley, charged with the task of breaking the news of her dismissal to his 'violent and vindictive' lady. She consoled herself in her enforced retirement by declaring that she had incurred the Queen's wrath by conniving at a secret marriage between the Princess Amelia and General FitzRoy.

Mrs George Villiers was now high in the favour and confidence of the young Princess, whose financial tangles she and her husband set themselves good-naturedly to straighten out. Opinions may differ—they differed sharply in the Family—as to the part played by this couple, but Mrs Villiers showed wisdom in at least one regard when she urged Princess Amelia to pay back the loan of £5,000 made to her by FitzRoy. One-fifth of that sum had been repaid at the time of Amelia's death. The aid of the Prince of Wales was enlisted in the complicated task of getting her affairs into order, and the Princess wrote to him from Weymouth in September 1809, 'I long for your seeing Mr Villiers— he will I think tell you many things that I did not from being so interrupted by people coming in. I wish you particularly to know from him about my debts.'[w]

Up to the year before Princess Amelia's death the Prince was quite ready to collogue with 'our excellent friend G. V.', whom he later repudiated when he found that Villiers upheld FitzRoy's claim to the Princess's legacies.

One sad result of the Gomm-Goldsworthy affair was a temporary estrangement between Princess Amelia and the sister whom she had so often called her 'dear, perfect Miny'. Christmas was the season when the Family took stock of their spiritual condition, and then it was that they used all to receive the Sacrament. At the end of 1807 Princess Mary, desiring to be 'in love and charity with all men', wrote an anxious letter to Amelia about the 'awfull ceremony', saying that it was out of her power to approach the Communion Table till she had represented 'how deeply, how keenly' she had felt the 'very great alteration' in her sister's manner towards her. What answer she received is not known, but only after two years was their reconciliation perfected, when Princess Mary, at Princess Amelia's own desire, went with her to Weymouth on that last quest for restored health.

In 1808, the same year in which the negotiations took place for a marriage between Louis Philippe and Princess Elizabeth, Mrs Villiers obtained for her royal friend a copy of the full text of the Royal Marriage Act. From this Princess Amelia perceived that upon attaining the age of twenty-five she would be entitled to notify the Privy Council, through the Lord Chancellor, of her desire and intention to marry General FitzRoy. Even her realization of the effect that such a proceeding would have upon the King's mind did not deter her from drafting the necessary letter, and another for the Prince of Wales. In these drafts she refers to George III as her 'late father', and it has been argued from this that they were not intended to be used during the lifetime of the old King.

The wording of the documents is so naïve, so artlessly sentimental, as to be obviously her own:

> My being the youngest of so large a family takes off many objections. . . .
> In the state the Continent is in, no settlement could happen there; besides, I
> never would marry where I could not give my affections, and General FitzRoy
> possesses all my affection, and nothing can ever alter that; and for years I have
> considered myself his lawful wife, though suffering all the trials of that without
> ever enjoying my rights.

The last clause does not remove the uncertainty as to whether any religious ceremony had taken place, but there is a passage in a note among the Lowther Papers which diminishes without positively removing that uncertainty.

> May my blessed Charles and I never forget it was to Thee, O God, and
> through Thee we first promised to be kind, constant and true; that these
> blessed vows and feelings are not to be sported with, nor their obligations
> profanely cast away. May we, C.F.R. and A.F.R. never forget to pray for Thy
> blessing on our mutual connection![15]

Up to this time it had appeared as if the ministrations of Sir Lucas Pepys and Mr Keate had been more or less effectual. Nothing more is heard of the 'poor knee' which had given her so much agony ten years before. She was able to ride, to walk, and even to dance; and Miss Burney's prophecy that in looks she would be 'another Princess Augusta' had been fulfilled. But already in 1806 the doctors had found it necessary to insert a 'seton'[16] in her chest, and in March 1808 she was ill with some complaint which caused the apprehensive Princess Elizabeth to take a great deal of snuff and hang herself about with camphor bags in order to escape infection. Princess Amelia notes with apparent irony in a letter to the Prince of Wales that the Queen had sent her 'a few figs and grapes', and it looks as if we might date from this period that suspicion of the Princess's— unfortunately shared by Mrs Villiers—that the Queen was not anxious for her recovery.

It was—according to the lady herself—at the instigation of Mrs Villiers that Princess Amelia asked leave to put herself in the hands of Dr Pope, a Quaker physician of Staines, and of Sir Henry Halford, a step which the Queen opposed, ostensibly from reluctance to dismiss Sir Francis Milman, who had been attending the invalid.

Pope, who misread the symptoms as stubbornly as the rest and diagnosed 'inflammation of the membrane of the liver', ordered 'the warm bath every other night, 5 drops of antimonial wine twice a day, some elm-bark tea, to sweeten the blood', and a little sudorific powder at night.

Later he prescribed calomel in large doses, and the inevitable sea air.

'Dr Pope', wrote Princess Amelia to the Prince of Wales, 'is very sanguine in his opinion that the result will be a perfect *cure*—I have often felt tired of myself, and felt I only was a plague, but I thought it wrong not to do whatever was ordered for my good.'

The same note of weariness is audible in an unpublished letter to Lady Harcourt (Harcourt MSS.) in which she says:

> I know you will be angry if I don't mention that tiresome subject *self* I don't loose [*sic*] ground, and the physicians think me going on well, tho' I don't feel much different. . . .
>
> Don't mention having heard from me, for people are very kind but I feel unequal to writing to many, and therefore if it is known I may offend some even of my own family.
>
> Will you enclose your letter to Miss Gaskoin, King's House, St Albans Street, Windsor.

'Miss Gaskoin' was the aunt of the faithful and devoted Mary Anne Gaskoin, who used to act as the Princess's confidential secretary and wrote a better hand than her royal mistress.

It was no doubt for the sake of her beloved Charles FitzRoy that Princess Amelia was loth to leave Windsor and go to Weymouth in the summer of 1809. When Milman was still in charge, Princess Mary had written to the Prince of Wales:

> ... he says everything depends on her being kept as quiet as possible, and she ought to be *considered* in everything to make her as comfortable and happy as possible—must be *worried* about nothing, which, Entre Nous, in our House is very difficult, and with such a fine creature as she is, who possesses such very strong feelings, it requires great care to manage her well.[w]

Pope was of the same mind as his more eminent predecessor, and it may have been as much the insalubrity of Windsor as the salubrity of Weymouth which led him to urge the change. When the Princess went, Princess Mary went with her, 'trying to make up to her for all the misery she had endured from want of health' during the last six months.

There had been some opposition on the part of the Queen, 'but the King', wrote Princess Amelia to the Prince of Wales, '*not only* consented to my request to have Miny, but said he was *determined she should go*'. 'I am full of hope', wrote Princess Mary to the King, 'I may have the happiness to bring her home much restored to health if not quite so, and that alone will reward us for all we have suffered.'

This letter was written from Hartford Bridge, where the two Princesses had halted on their way to the sea. Amelia had been 'much relieved by tears', and was then perfectly composed, laying down on the couch'.

By way of Woodgatestone and Blandford they continued their journey to General Garth's house at Ilsington—fully described in Princess Mary's letter quoted above. The Princess, seeing the General 'much overcome' at the change in the invalid, 'begged he would recover himself before he went upstairs to her, during which time Amelia revived, and we got all very cheerful at breakfast, so much so that Amelia was quite comfortable before we set off on our journey again'.

The King, almost blind and already half demented, had planned everything for the comfort of his darling. A little couch had been sent on ahead for her, and placed in a room 'near her bedroom', formerly the King's sitting-room and now to be hers. Orders had been given, and were faithfully obeyed, that the carriage should drive right into the courtyard of Gloucester Lodge, and the Princess be installed at once upon the couch. The Navy, in the person of Admiral Sir Harry Neale, took charge of these things, and the Army, in the person of General Garth, attended to the commissariat. Of the General, Princess Mary wrote to the King:

> ... he has made every arrangement you desired and thought of *everything* for our comfort, not even forgetting to have asses' milk ready if Dr Pope

found it necessary. He has secured good milk and butter for our breakfast, and fruit of all sorts, particularly grapes, for Amelia—he has forgot nothing and remembered everything. He intends to be with us tomorrow by dinner.[w]

A bathing-machine formerly used by the King was turned by Garth and Neale into a sort of parlour on wheels, with a couch from the royal yacht inside, and a green canvas curtain over the door to keep off the glare of the sea. 'This machine', wrote Princess Mary, 'puts me in mind of our dear old Baby House at Kew.' Into it Princess Amelia was carried straight from her own room, and it was then drawn into the sea 'as if she was going to bathe'. On the first occasion she remained for a quarter of an hour, after which 'the motion of the sea made her feel faint'.[w]

Anxious that his beloved child should miss no opportunity of inhaling the ozone, his Majesty gave orders that General Garth was to rig up a tent in the field next the Lodge, but Mr Beavor, the local apothecary, suggested that it would be better to wait, 'on account of the rainy weather'. Princess Mary wrote to the King:

> It appears to me as if Beavor perfectly understood her complaint. He is very attentive, and when once we got over his dreadful manners he certainly talks most reasonably and [I] may add comfortably as to her recovery with care, but calls her a 'Hot House Plant'.[w]

Three days later the Princess is happy to tell her father that for the first time since they came to Weymouth 'Amelia has passed a night without moaning in her sleep'. Bad nights were a constantly recurring symptom, and she was always 'dreaming that she was in prison'.[w]

A small red notebook exists in which Princess Amelia kept notes of her medical expenses between April 1809 and March 1810, and the items and charges are interesting. In April 1809 she paid Dr Pope £42; in May £60 18s; in July £58 16s; in August £52 10s; in September, at Hartford Bridge, £2; in the same month, at Weymouth, two sums of £105 each. In November the doctor received £150 for accompanying the Princess back to Windsor. Mr Beavor, of the dreadful manners, received only £22 17s. Other items include 'making seatons', one at £5 5s and one at £10, two 'Cuppings' at £5 5s each, and 'the Warm Bath', £8 8s. Total, £928 17s—no inconsiderable sum for an impecunious Princess to disburse.

These 'seatons' which loom so large in the treatment adopted by Princess Amelia's advisers were the early nineteenth-century equivalent of the surgical drainage tube. A sinus was artificially produced, and kept open with a skein of silk or a quill until the surgeon was satisfied with the amount of the discharge. Their insertion and renewal was an agonizing business, and if the surrounding surfaces became inflamed they were treated with caustic. Princess Mary's reports to the King and to the Prince of Wales contain a distressing number of allusions to these measures, which were designed to relieve the pain in the patient's side but had no effect other than to aggravate it.

At the King's earnest wish the Princess was taken out on calm days in his own 'most beautiful boat', where the resourceful Sir Harry Neale hauled her up in a slung chair, as she was apt to faint or fall into fits of coughing upon any exertion, such as climbing the seven steps of the pier.

General Garth was constant in his attentions, leaving the Princesses only for a day or two 'to receive Dolly', who had gone to shoot at Ilsington. On his return he thought he could discern some improvement in Princess Amelia, and he and Neale were both struck by the more active way she got into the yacht. Pope too was pleased with the results of the 'seatons', though Mr Beavor did not attach so much importance to their action as did his senior. The improvement was short-lived.

The Princess is now described as alternately languid and cheerful. She could not cross the room without coughing, but found 'great comfort in resting quiet all day and not speaking'.(w)

Her kind sister wrote to their father every day, enlivening her letters whenever possible by some little touch of humour. One day she tells the King that Sir Harry Neale had charged his horse up the hill to measure the height of the hat upon the colossal equestrian statue of his Majesty, and found that it was fourteen yards high. General Garth said 'nothing but a sailor or a madman could ever have charged a horse up that hill'.(w)

There was perhaps a reason for Princess Amelia's desire to rest quiet 'without speaking' all day. Upon the subject nearest her heart her lips were sealed. Princess Mary wrote to the Prince of Wales a few weeks after the death of their youngest sister, *à propos* of 'that most unfortunate and fatal attachment which destroyed her health by degrees':

> As far as I am concerned on the subject that I look upon as having *killed her* I have nothing to reproach *myself* as I never encouraged what could not be for her happiness, and during the number of years the attachment lasted was never in her confidence, and though I attended her all the time of her long illness (I may not be believed, but it is a fact, though) I don't believe I ever named the subject *three times*, and then I was so situated that I could *not help it*.
>
> I must do her the justice to say her great object was never to distress my feelings, and her wish was never to drive me into an awkward situation, as she called it.(w)

But though Princess Amelia could not open her heart to her 'dearest Miny', there were others with whom she was less reticent, the Prince of Wales, and Mr and Mrs Villiers, among them. On 29 September 1809, after a visit from her eldest brother, she wrote to him:

> I feel most grateful to the Villiers's, who, I am sure, take much interest about me, and have proved their friendship so strongly for me, for amidst all my enemies nothing shook them. . . .
>
> Dear Miny is very well. I have not named to her Mrs Villiers' letter of *course*, as I wish that to remain entirely between us and I know you will not betray me, and I have never said *more* of my conversations to her except the delight your visit had been to me, how I liked to think of it, and was sorry those days were gone by.
>
> I always loved you better than any of my brothers, I knew, and *now* very much more. I shan't mind the Queen's *ill* and *cross* looks now, or Fatima's.[w]

'Fatima' was obviously Princess Elizabeth.

It was during this visit of the Prince to Weymouth that Princess Amelia put her affairs in his hands and gave him power of attorney, at the same time authorizing him to employ a solicitor to investigate the conduct of Mr Bolton, her man of affairs.

In a letter written on 5 October the Princess wrote to the Prince evidently referring to that part of their talk which touched upon FitzRoy:

> . . . tho' I don't doubt dear Miny's kindness and affection for me, yet as the subject on which I have opened myself so *thoroughly* to *you* is one on which I never speak to my family, I think it better to *tell* you when that is alluded to I shall not shew Miny your letters.[w]

Meanwhile Princess Sophia, in what she called the 'Nunnery' at Windsor, was pouring forth her apprehensions to him:

> Anxious as you and I are about this dear Child how can we be easy under the present circumstances?
>
> All her letters as well as those from dear Miny are full of your affectionate kindness to *them* and of the happiness they experienced during your visit.
>
> As to dear Amelia your kind heart will rejoice to hear that thanks to the conversation with you her poor harrassed mind has found relief, and I can trace by her letter how much more composed she is.[w]

This looks as if Princess Sophia were deeper in Princess Amelia's confidence than was their elder sister. Perhaps 'this dear Child' felt instinctively that of the two sisters the younger was better fitted both by character and by experience to understand the secret of her heart.

The Prince of Wales evidently feared, not without reason, that the King did not realize the seriousness of his beloved child's illness. 'I assure you', wrote Princess Sophia, 'the dear King does not deceive himself about Amelia.' But she was wrong; and the reaction when no hope remained was terrible to behold.

Meanwhile Sir Herbert Taylor had been writing affectionate though ponderous letters to Weymouth at his Majesty's dictation, some to Princess Mary, full of fatherly approval, some to Princess Amelia instinct with anxiety and love. Once at least, in October, the blind King made a pitiful effort to dispense with a secretary's aid, and to write with his own hand. 'My dearest Amelia,' begins the heavily blotted scrawl, 'I attempt to write a few lines to accompany the Book.' Then the 'few lines' merge into an almost indecipherable confusion from which, with unconscious irony, one incomplete sentence alone stands out: 'I am most happy——'

II

The immediate sequel to the Prince of Wales's appearance at Weymouth in September 1809 was the arrival of five pelisses, each of a different colour. 'A *new dictionary*', wrote his delighted sister, 'must be invented for saying "I love you".' She asked him to send her a yard of each colour for Gaskoin to 'make up for her head', and added, 'Oh, *naughty me*, but I should have enjoyed seeing the Queen's seeing your bounty laid out on all the *Chairs*! How she would have envied, and So'd——I will write her word of it, I am determined, or rather communicate it through Eliza, that *two* may enjoy it together.'(w)

The Prince's reply (quoted by Mr Childe-Pemberton in *The Romance of Princess Amelia*) contains no comment upon these uncharitable interjections; but he assures his sister that her orders are 'obey'd by this day's coach, as a small Parcel will go down by it, containing a yard of silk of each of the Pelisses'.

The weather at Weymouth, which had at first been calm enough to permit the invalid to spend some time on the royal yacht, broke in the first week of October, when a young naval officer, John Burrard, Sir Harry Neale's nephew, was drowned in an effort to 'bring in the King's barge'. He had volunteered to replace a 'little Mid' who was seasick.(w) The Neales were naturally distressed when it became known that the boat carrying their nephew to the barge had capsized, and that, though the two sailors with him had been saved, he himself was missing. To conceal their anxiety from Princess Amelia, Lady Neale made an excuse for not coming to 'spend the evening as arranged', but the Princess, conscious of the atmosphere of suspense, wrote next day begging 'for God's sake to know what had happened', which 'obliged Lady Neale to tell her the truth'. The storm continued to rage, and sailors were posted at various points along the beach to keep a look-out for John Burrard's body, which 'was expected to be washed ashore at any minute'; and Princess Mary arranged that the invalid should remain in her bedroom at the back of the house, where she received Sir Harry and his wife, and was 'much relieved by tears'.(w)

As the autumn wore on, and it became increasingly evident that Princess Amelia was losing rather than gaining ground, the question of an early return to Windsor arose. She herself was pining, if not for home—since the Castle held many painful memories—at least for her father, and doubtless for FitzRoy. Moreover there was no fire in the room where she 'took the warm bath', and she was 'chilled both in the bath and coming out'.[w] Still her fortitude would not yield, and she reiterated her willingness 'to do anything, or submit to any pain or inconvenience for the sake of promoting the recovery of her health'. So wrote Princess Mary to the King on 21 October, after a visit from the Duke of York, which had 'roused Amelia much', and given both Princesses pleasure.

The Duke of Kent also went to Weymouth about this time, and Princess Sophia, in an anxious letter to the Prince of Wales, remarks that 'Edward will tell him how he found Amelia'. She adds:

> Alas! I am quite out of *heart*, for this obstinate pain in the side yields to nothing, and what she has to go through nearly breaks my heart. I trust in God everything will be considered for her comfort if she returns here, and as far as the dear King I am certain he will do what he can to make her situation as easy and tolerable as possible. I long to see her yet am aware our House and its *appendages* will not suit her.[w]

Princess Amelia's conviction that the Queen and Princess Elizabeth were her enemies now amounted almost to an obsession, but it must be acknowledged that her Majesty's behaviour was a little lacking in tenderness. 'I must tell you', wrote the young Princess to the Prince of Wales in October 1809,

> of the Queen's last letters to Miny. She don't name me, but in a postscript says 'I am glad Amelia is better, and hope very soon to hear she is perfectly well'.
>
> This has provoked Miny, [who] owned then, tho' she has always tried to make me think the Queen's letters not unkind, that hers to her were all kindness and affection but to me certainly the very reverse.[w]

Who had told Queen Charlotte that Amelia was better? Not Princess Mary, whose letters were full of anxiety. Not Dr Pope, who now wished to have her under supervision nearer home than Weymouth, and 'hinted at Frogmore or Kew'. 'Amelia', Princess Mary told the King, 'has no wish for any particular place', apart from her desire to be nearer her father, but would like to be 'under Pope's own eye', so that he may be able 'to pursue the calomel in larger doses, which he would not venture to do if he was not near enough to watch the progress of the Calomel'.[w]

Sir Francis Milman, be it recorded to the credit of the medical profession of the time, did not agree with Pope in the 'pursuit of calomel in ever larger doses'. But the old Quaker had won his patient's confidence. 'I am always sorry', she wrote to the Prince of Wales, 'when he is obliged to go, for he attends me both with *skill* and *feeling*, and not from interested motives, which never was the case before.'[w] Another point in his favour was that he was *persona non grata* with Queen Charlotte.

It now became necessary for Princess Mary to write to the King with a candour which must have been painful to both of them upon the subject of the Queen's treatment of Amelia. In the letter of 21 October, already quoted, the Princess, after touching upon the calomel treatment, says:

> I cannot disown to you, painful as it is to me to be obliged to say so, that innervated as Amelia is from the length of the illness any *harshness* in a sharp *word* goes very deep with her, and if she is so situated as to be liable to have those coming in and out she cannot with any propriety refuse to see, I cannot answer for the *consequences* at present, having seen what the effect was before she came *here* and even how some letters since we are at Weymouth have vexed her.
>
> I am the last person that have any right to complain myself, as nothing can be kinder or more Affe than all the letters wrote to me but upon one subject, which is my *being absent* from home and making myself so necessary to Amelia, which is not thought right, and considered as *selfish* of Amelia. If that is ever said to Amelia you must perfectly understand it will *half kill her*, who really, poor soul, never thinks of herself, and only wishes to give us all as little trouble as possible.[w]

'I have taken care', wrote the King in reply, 'to have it understood that you are not to be separated from her.'[w]

Princess Amelia herself now desired to go to Kew on her return from Weymouth, but to this the Queen would not agree, and finally Augusta Lodge, Windsor, a house formerly occupied by one of the King's physicians, Dr Heberden, was agreed upon. Princess Mary welcomed the idea. 'It would be', she wrote to her father, 'the greatest relief and comfort' to be near him, and to be able to apply to him for advice 'upon every trifling circumstance that may arise in the course of the day'. She adds that the King's letters to Amelia 'act like magic upon her, and calm and revive her for hours after'.[w]

On 26 October Princess Mary was full of plans for the return journey, which was to be broken, as the outward journey had been, at Ilsington. The Dukes of Cambridge and Clarence were to form part of the escort, and the Princess wrote to the King, 'General Garth says he can lodge us all very well and appears quite delighted at the idea of his house being made use of by Amelia'.[w] On 26 October the Duke of Cambridge arrived, and the invalid was 'much agitated' at seeing him. A day later the Duke of Clarence joined them 'in high spirits', and both royal Dukes attended a ball the same evening; Princess Mary records that 'it was very full', and 'Dolly got home about half past two o'clock'.[w]

Princess Amelia's brothers were much in evidence at this anxious time, and the Prince of Wales sent down to Weymouth for her use on the return journey a special carriage of his own, easily hung and comfortably built. A short drive in it convinced the Princess that it was 'easier than any carriage she had been in since her illness', and at Princess Mary's request Dr Pope drove round and round the courtyard with Amelia 'to determine the best method of arranging the cushions etc. for the journey'.[w] Finally Sir Harry Neale was called into consultation to see if he could contrive to sling one of the cots (hammocks) from the royal yacht inside the vehicle, 'to swing backwards and forwards' with its motion. 'Sir H. I trust has succeeded', wrote Princess Mary hopefully on 2 November.[w]

The next day they set off in bright sunshine. On arriving at Weymouth two months earlier Princess Amelia had been 'very much overcome indeed', and then 'greatly relieved by tears',[w] but she seems to have quitted that place of many memories without sign of regret. While she was there, and during the long hours when she lay quietly 'without speaking', thoughts of her father and of FitzRoy must have filled her mind—the two people whom she loved best in the world—and such thoughts cannot have been happy ones.

'Dolly', wrote Princess Mary, 'is kind enough to go all the way with us, and William will go as far as General Garth's drive with us, and then set off for Windsor'; but this arrangement seems to have been altered, for Miss Knight records on 7 November that the Duke of Clarence, Princess Mary, and Lady George Murray were with Princess Amelia when she reached home, and 'the Duke of Cambridge rode in before them'.

On the first day of the journey the carriage was brought frequently to a halt, as the cot was not as easy as they hoped it would be. The next day they were at Ilsington. 'Nothing', wrote the elder Princess, 'can be more comfortable than we have found this House. The General gave us a *famous dinner* and very good Beds, and is all attention.'[w] Sir Harry Neale joined the party at Ilsington, and readjusted the cot, which then 'did better'. The two Princesses were full of concern for his anxiety about Lady Neale, left at Weymouth in precarious health.

Next day the travellers reached Salisbury, where the invalid was 'very faint, and in great pain with her side', and on the 7th Princess Mary wrote to the King from Hartford Bridge that Amelia was 'all anxiety to get to Windsor' as soon as she could. At last they were safe in Augusta Lodge, where Princess Sophia shortly afterwards joined them.

In spite of the recurring note of discouragement in Princess Amelia's letters, she had not given up hope of recovery. Life was still sweet; she was not aweary of the sun. Firm though her faith in Dr Pope might be, she began to feel as the year waned that it would be well to seek other opinions. So on Christmas Eve 1809 she wrote to the Prince of Wales:

> . . . the dear King has fully *entered* into my wishes for further advice in the most kind way you can conceive, and has chosen Sir Henry Halford and Dr Bailey [sic]. I found Sir Walter Farquhar *would not do*.[w]

After some remarks upon the contrast between the Queen's manner and the King's when they had visited her the previous day, she adds a pathetic postscript, 'I certainly am no better, and going on so was absurd'.

In addition to Halford and Baillie, Saunders and Heberden were called in, and Mr Battiscombe was also in constant attendance. The results of the consultation between Saunders and Heberden are thus summarized by the Princess herself in a letter to the Prince of Wales:

> ... they are both of opinion that the principal disease was an Inflammation which had taken place in the back part of the right side, and had caused considerable swelling in that part. From its origin being in the neighbourhood of the Liver they think it probable it may have been disordered in its functions and perhaps suffered a degree of superficial inflammation. .... *Dr Pope* had not perceived the *swelling*, nor did he see my side with the two Drs, but this evening on examining it he thinks if anything there may be a little fulness. the Kg is much pleased with Pope's honesty, for he told him he had not perceived the swelling.
>
> I am to be kept a good deal in bed. I am quite resigned, for they say it will be a long *case*.⁽ʷ⁾

On 15 January Princess Mary reported that Amelia had a cold and slight erysipelas about the head and eyes, but was 'insisting on a cold meat dinner' against Pope's wishes. Next day Halford, supporting Pope, said 'no more solid food was to be thought of', so the menu was altered to beef-tea, arrowroot, and panada of chicken. If the doctors had realized that the malady was tuberculosis they might have restricted her, as Sir James Clark did John Keats, to one sardine a day, but, before the calomel was begun, the regime at Weymouth might almost have been prescribed by a modern physician—fresh air, milk, fruit, soup, and sleep. Sir Henry Halford now introduced another element, Madeira wine, and among George IV's papers is this neatly written note dictated to Mary Anne Gaskoin:

> Sir Henry Halford wishes me to try Madeira Wine and I am sure you are so good you will not object to send me some, for I know yours is much better than any we have here.⁽ʷ⁾

There was an illusory improvement in March, but in April a set-back followed the news of the attempt of Sellis upon the Duke of Cumberland's life, 'Amelia's nerves being so completely shook with the length of her illness'. This intelligence apparently caused the Prince of Wales to hurry down to Augusta Lodge, and on the morrow of his visit Princess Amelia wrote to him in a feeble hand:

Having been to [*sic*] ill my beloved and most kind brother, to speak to you when you were here, I cannot help, now I can hold a pen, attempting to express my gratitude for your kindness, for I plainly saw your affection and feeling brought you to me, and it has made a deep impression on my mind, and endeared you, if possible, more to my heart than ever.

In the midst of the severest sufferings your affection ever was a cordial, and most tenderly do I love you, and how much I wish the *rest* of the family had hearts and feelings like yours. To you, my beloved Brother, I will confess as my best friend, anxiety and ill-usage I am sure having preyed on my mind and brought me to the state I now am.[w]

She adds kindly, 'How grieved I am about poor Ernest, and how like you to be the friend and brother always in distress'. This evidently refers to the Prince of Wales's action in placing the Pavilion at the Duke of Cumberland's disposal during his convalescence.

In another undated letter, which must belong to the first half of 1810, the Princess wrote to the Prince of Wales:

I hear General FitzRoy is returned, and the Queen was particularly *cross to him*. She always tells me how very agreeable Sir Brent Spencer is, and Col. Disbrowe, but regularly names no one else except Munster. She has never invited the Villiers's once since I returned except the birthday of Augusta.[w]

She adds that 'the Princess'—*i.e.* of Wales—had sent 'to offer and beg' to come and see her, but that Miny had sent word she was too ill to see anybody.

The Sisterhood seem to have been unfortunate in their man of business, Mr Bolton, roundly described by the youngest as 'that old rogue'. Misgivings as to his handling of her affairs had preyed upon Princess Amelia at Weymouth, and had formed one of the chief topics of her conversation with the Prince of Wales. Some undated letters evidently written not long after her return to Windsor suggest that Bolton was not the sort of person to be entrusted with the financial resources of royal ladies. He had apparently sent her some drafts to sign long before 'the quarter was due'. These, as she reminds the Prince, she had shown to him, whereupon he had told her not to sign them, as it was a trick, the man thinking she would die. Two years earlier the Duke of York had given Bolton a bond for £5,000 for her use, but this she never knew of, and 'certainly did not understand'. In August, apparently just before leaving Windsor, she signed a bond for £9,000 which Bolton had raised for her, but did not know 'if Frederick's £5,000 were included'.[w] It was clearly her anxiety upon this point which led her to give her eldest brother power of attorney to employ a solicitor to investigate.

The Princess goes on to say that the Duke of York had told her he had detected Bolton 'acting very improperly with regard to some money matters of Sophia's', and in consequence he was 'authorized by Miny and Sophia to act for them'.[w] The Duke was proposing to raise a sum for Amelia at Drummond's Bank, but she had begged him to consult the Prince first.

In the next letter the Princess declares that she has been 'cheated and robbed beyond all belief', but she will not take one step, or listen to any advice, without the Prince's concurrence, even though 'other parts of the Family have offered and even *pressed* their interference'.[w] 'I have been', she says,

> beset and hurried to such a degree since you left me that all my complaints are increased. . . . That vile Bolton seems to have blended all our money matters together, and I dread being made the sacrifice, so pray dont name it.[w]

Mr Bucknill is mentioned as the solicitor who is to act for her. He also played an important part in the subsequent transactions over her will.

One of the motives for the Princess's anxiety was her debt to FitzRoy, of which £4,000 still remained unpaid. In conversation with the Duke of York she represented that this sum had been lent to her by the Prince of Wales. 'He asked', she says, 'when you lent it to me, and I said I really knew so little about my affairs that I couldn't answer. 'But speaking confidently for FitzRoy, she adds,' I feel sure the *person* who assisted me with that £4000 will feel as much obliged as myself for your kindness on this subject'.[w]

The Princess was harassed, too, about the £5,000 of Princess Sophia's which Bolton declared she had used. 'I own I doubt it', she wrote, 'and therefore I wish you very much to do it all for me, and not let F———ck, for you know his partiality for Sophy, and I do dread being sacrificed.' However partial the Duke of York may have been to Sophia, he was not the sort of man unscrupulously to sacrifice one sister to another, and it is possible that Princess Amelia's long illness had induced in her a slight touch of persecution mania.

Beyond all these preoccupations with her financial position lies the Princess's increasing anxiety that FitzRoy shall be her heir. Her hopes of recovery must have been flickering out when she wrote to the Prince of Wales, probably in July, but certainly in the summer, of 1810:

> My Dearest Brother,
> It is impossible to describe to you the good your visit has done me. I am so little accustomed to kindness from my own family that I always feel as if in a dream when you have been with me. . . .
> I send you as you desired my Will, sealed up, which you will be kind enough to deliver to Mr Bucknill. I am most grateful to you for so kindly allowing me to name you as my Executor, for I cannot disguise from You that on no one else could I have depended for the faithful execution of my wishes. *In your hands I know I am safe.*[w]

She mentions that at the Prince's request she has 'named Adolphus joint Executor', but asks the Prince to tell him this, as it 'rather agitates' her to talk of it. It had at one time been her intention to make 'dear Mr George Villiers' her executor, but she thought it 'more delicate not to do it'. (Mr Villiers was himself chronically impecunious, in spite of the valiant efforts of his wife to 'place' him.) A duplicate of this will, witnessed by Mr Battiscombe, would be put in a red box belonging to her, and she would tell Princess Mary that it was there. She continues:

> ... With respect to Sir Henry Halford, who you are so kind as to intend seeing, I really should be very gratefull to You if you would impress upon him how greatly You know the unhappiness of my mind encreases my bodily sufferings, for I think he is now become so good a courtier that he does not venture to oppose anything that the King or Queen like, tho' it may be very contrary to my wishes. For instance, they want me to see all the Ladies and others who are in the Castle, whether I like them or not.[(w)]

This letter was to be delivered to the Prince by Mr Villiers, whose fidelity she commends. 'Frederick's inveteracy against him', she says, 'proceeds entirely from his thinking him so attached to you, and so anxious that you and the King should be well together.'[(w)]

Princess Amelia's misgivings about her own condition must have been accentuated by the second set-back which she suffered in May 1810, when the Prince of Wales had offered to come and see her. Princess Sophia wrote to him that 'dear Amelia shed tears' when she heard how much the Prince felt for her, but that as she was allowed to see nobody but the King and Queen, and then only for five minutes at a time, no plans could yet be made for his proposed visit.[(w)] Next day she reported that the patient had had three hours' sleep, and that when she told her of the Prince's 'offer of coming to her at any moment she expressed a wish for it, she was much affected, and answered *He has judged right*'.[(w)] The letter is sealed on scarlet wax with the device of a cornucopia, and the legend *Le Bon Temps Viendra*.

This relapse in May may possibly have been aggravated by Princess Amelia's distress at parting from her old nurse, Mrs Williams, who had been staying with her. She had written to her before the visit, 'I wish you to come as soon as you can, and bring the Girls, pray'.[(w)] The Princess engaged a lodging for them in Windsor, and hoped Mrs Williams would not be in a hurry to leave her. 'Gaskoin', she says, 'is really very unwell, and more ill than she owns to me.'[(w)] Indeed, poor Gaskoin seems to have paid the price for her constancy to the Princess which Queen Charlotte had feared that Princess Mary might be called upon to pay.

Mrs Williams duly came, accompanied by her two cheerful daughters, and their presence seems to have had a tonic effect upon the invalid. Sensitive to sound though the Princess was, the fresh young voices of 'the Girls' gave her pleasure, and she liked to watch them playing card games in which she herself had not sufficient strength to join. Her faculties were, however, sufficiently alive for her to be struck by the alteration produced in the appearance of the Duke of Clarence by the absence of his wig, and she managed to reach the fourth volume of *Clarissa Harlowe*. 'It grows', she remarks, 'very interesting. Much to like and much to abhor in the work.'[(w)] There was certainly nothing in the character of Lovelace to remind her of FitzRoy, who had more affinity with Sir Charles Grandison; in the luckless Clarissa there was more than a touch of Amelia herself.

In June the intractable cough, which might have warned the physicians of the real nature of her illness, became more marked, and it was now complicated by pains in the head. Dundas, who had been added to the medical constellation, joined with Pope in declaring that she was no worse, and that 'they were not losing ground'.[(w)] Her appetite was capricious, and nothing seemed to 'go down tolerably well'[(w)] except green peas served with vinegar. 'Her spirits', reports Princess Mary, 'are flagging more than at any time during her long illness.'[(w)] On 4 and 5 June she lay on a couch in the adjoining room for twenty minutes while fresh linen was put on her bed. 'Pope will not call her worse, only less well than yesterday'—a nice distinction.[(w)]

Among the old friends with whom Princess Amelia continued to correspond during that weary last summer was Miss Finch, Lady Cha's daughter, concerning whom she had written to Lady Harcourt in February 1808, 'I love her for her dear Mother's sake, and tho' she is odd she possesses many charming good qualities'. Lady Charlotte's own health was fast failing, though she lingered three years longer. Early in May 1810 Princess Amelia wrote:

My Dear Miss Finch,
Very many thanks for your most kind letter I got last night. I feel all the kind things you say most deeply, and upon the whole thank god you give a tolerable account of our dear Ly Cha——

I have no hope to see you as I have no chance of going to town, for I am [a] poor Creature yet, tho' I trust in god mending by degrees. Dearest Miny stays with me till the 3rd of June in the evening, and I move to Frogmore the day after they all go to town, as it will enable me to be moved out without fatigue, for I am forced to be carried to the carriage.

In regard to your question about dear Lady Cha's present I think like you anything from her will be acceptable and valuable but I really think a *snuff-box* would delight her, if it is what she can wear in her pocket.

I am so glad your opera went off so well. I quite enter into all you feel—even living retired, without illness or anxiety of mind, makes going into public a great exertion and flurry still more under such circumstances. . . . My dear

Nurse, Mrs Williams, is with me, which is a great comfort to me.—Ever yours
most affectionately,

AMELIA

Queen Charlotte was obviously the person to whom Lady Cha's snuffbox
was to be offered. Like others of the Family and the household, her Majesty
got her supplies from Messrs Fribourg and Treyer in the Haymarket, where
the formulae are preserved of the blends preferred by the Queen—'the Duke of
Cambridge's Special' and 'Sir Herbert Taylor's Special' figuring frequently in her
accounts.

On the morrow of Mrs Williams's departure her other foster-child, Princess
Sophia, wrote to her:

How much we all owe you, my beloved Mrs Williams, for giving up so much
of your time here—you must derive comfort in feeling of what spiritual use you
have been to your darling Child, and I speak not only for her but for *myself* to
whom you have been so *very, very* kind. Yesterday we dined at Frogmore, and
to my sorrow left that dear Child all alone till eight o'clock. As soon as we went
home we went to her and you can have no idea how dull the apartment looked
without the three merry companions who cause life wherever they are. . . .

I have only to lament not having seen more of you, but you know full well
I could not take you away from your dear Child. . . . As to your dear Girls I
think them the most delightful children that exist.[w]

On 28 July 1810, Princess Amelia drew up and sent to General FitzRoy a
memorandum regarding her two wills. In this document she describes him as her
'ever most beloved, chosen, and valued Charles', and assigns everything to him
except a few personal mementoes to relatives and friends. Gaskoin and Mary
Anne are to have her clothes, and 'some mark of favour either by annuity or
remembrance'. And she inserts such reminders as, 'Remember Theresa [Villiers]
is my adopted child' and 'Pray remember my dear Mrs Williams'.

While Mary Anne Gaskoin was still at her post she wrote at the Princess's
dictation a letter to FitzRoy, thanking him for the visit he had paid her that same
evening, and asking him 'whilst riding tomorrow' to express in the strongest
terms to Princess Augusta 'how much both the Princess Amelia and yourself *felt*
the very great kindness HRH had shown concerning this visit'—but Princess
Augusta was not to be told that Gaskoin was in the secret. This visit must have
taken place rather near the end of Amelia's life, for the letter contains a statement
that 'Sir Henry Halford is come, and finds the pulse considerably reduced since
he was here'.

The Princess's beauty was unaffected by her illness, as Miss Knight bears
witness, who saw her a few days before her death. She then took off her glove,

and revealed a hand 'perfectly transparent'. That hypersensitiveness to noise which had been a symptom of her early illness at Worthing had returned, and 'she could not bear the sound of a pianoforte even in another room'. Princess Augusta therefore gave her a bird which sang 'with a very soft note', and to which she could listen with pleasure. Two days after its owner's death, when Miss Knight was sitting with Princess Augusta, one of the dressers

> entered the room with a birdcage in her hand and her fingers at her eyes. 'Princess Amelia', she said, 'gave orders before her death that this bird should be returned to your Royal Highness; but not on the day she died, nor the day after, that it might not afflict you too much in the first hours of your grief. But she wished you to know how much she was obliged to you for giving it to her, and what a comfort its sweet voice had been.'

On 16 September Princess Mary wrote, at Princess Amelia's request, to let the Prince of Wales know 'that the Eruption he saw the beginning of in her face had increased every day since and had run nearly all over the body'.[w] Pope and Halford were now in agreement that 'it had an alarming appearance'.

The King, though he exacted bulletins from the doctors six times a day, still refused to be dismayed. On the anniversary of his accession, 25 October, the whole Family was present except the eldest and the youngest daughters. Guided by the Queen's hand, he went round the circle, peering in an agitated way at the people whom he could hardly see. 'It was the custom', says Miss Knight, to speak to him as he approached, that he might recognize by the voice whom he was about to address. I forget what it was I said to him, but shall ever remember what he said to me: 'You are not uneasy, I am sure, about Amelia. You are not to be deceived, but you know that she is in no danger.' At the same time he squeezed my hand with such force that I could scarcely help crying out. The Queen, however, dragged him away.

Two six-lined stanzas, beginning

> Unthinking, idle, wild, and young,
> I laughed, and danced, and talked, and sung,

were attributed to Princess Amelia only a decade after her death, on no stronger evidence than the existence of a copy in her writing. The gods, as Lady Louisa Stuart observed, had made none of the children of George III poetical, and it is hardly likely that this rather touching product of the late-Georgian Muse was the Princess's own composition. It must have been during the closing months of her life that she felt the force of some of the phrases she had copied out, though there were others that could never have been applied to her:

Unthinking, idle, wild, and young,
I laughed, and danced, and talked, and sung,
And proud of health, of freedom vain,
Dreamed not of sorrow, care and pain,
Concluding in those hours of glee
That all the world was made for me.

But when the hour of trial came,
When sickness shook the trembling fame,
When folly's gay pursuits were o'er,
And I could dance and sing no more,
It then occurred how sad 'twould be
Were *this* world only made for me.

As October waned she lost ground, and the King's visits to her became more agitating to them both. He would hold her hand and bend over her to scan the face in which he was too blind to discern the onset of death. Sometimes he would speak with simple fervour of the consolation of religion, 'the means of grace and the hope of glory'. It must have been on such an occasion, near the end, that she whispered, 'Remember me, but do not grieve for me', and gave him the ring that she had had made, set with her own hair. The story has often been re-told, usually with the comment that at the very moment that the ring was pressed upon the King's hand 'his reason fled for ever'. This was not so. Anxiety and sorrow had already almost broken the frail thread of his sanity, and it was her death rather than her dying gift that finally snapped it. 'No entreaty was spared', says Miss Albinia Cumberland, 'to induce Princess Amelia not to give the ring to the King, but nothing could prevent her.'

He was distressed because she had given no keepsake to the Queen, and as greatly pleased when she relented and gave her a locket with her hair.

The King was thus conscious sometimes of the Princess's danger. Outside the Castle it was common knowledge, and in August Lady Ailesbury wrote from Bath to Lady Louisa Stuart that everyone there had bought their mourning. At the end of October her heart was giving way, and she lay by turns semi-conscious and delirious, but suffering no more pain. When Mr Digby, one of the royal chaplains, read the service for the Visitation of the Sick to her, she became aware that he was omitting to rehearse the Articles of the Faith. 'She reminded him of it', writes Miss Albinia Cumberland, 'and answered every question perfectly clear.' The time had come when she had to declare herself to be 'in charity with all the world', and to make a special confession if her conscience was 'troubled with any weighty matter'. She had wished to live, but was composing herself quietly to die.

Towards noon on 2 November Sir Henry Halford, with his hand upon Amelia's pulse, said to Princess Mary, 'Your Royal Highness had better retire'.

Princess Mary answered that she was determined to stay till the last. 'Then Sir Henry asked for a candle', and, putting it to Princess Amelia's lips, looked at the unflickering flame, and said 'It is over'. While Princess Mary, after kissing her sister, went upstairs, Halford sat down and wrote to the Prince of Wales:

SIR,

It gives me pain to inform your Royal Highness that the Princess Amelia is no more. I have just witnessed her last expiration.—I am ever, Sir, Your Royal Highness's faithful

HENRY HALFORD [w]

12 o'clock.

It was Princess Amelia's own women, directed by Mrs Adams, who measured her for her coffin, put on 'the nightclothes she always wore', and wrapped her in her white satin shroud. She had left instructions that some lockets given to her by her father, and also a picture of him, should be buried with her.

Disregarding the express wishes of the King and the protests of Mrs Adams that he 'knew her orders', the Prince of Wales insisted upon seeing his sister in her coffin. 'My brothers', he said, 'are all coming to see poor Amelia'; and they all came.

On 7 November, when the leaden coffin had been closed, Lady Albinia Cumberland and Mademoiselle Julie Montmollin sat up in the next room and kept watch by the light of two candles. Two sofas 'made up as beds' were provided for them, but no refreshments. Another night Lady George Murray and Miss Cornelia Knight sat there, and noticed on the table Tillikeper's *Thoughts on Religious Subjects* marked in pencil by Princess Amelia's hand. 'The passages thus distinguished', says Miss Knight, 'testified to the feelings and judgement of the Princess.' In the room with the coffin two women of the Augusta Lodge household were on duty all the time between the day of the Princess's death and the day of her funeral—2 November to 14 November.

Meanwhile Sir Henry Halford had broken the news to the King,[17] 'who went off in a low, rambling way, which lasted some time, when he became more composed and mentioned her again, saying, "Poor girl"'. During a short interval of lucidity his Majesty gave directions about the funeral ceremonies, and himself chose the anthem, from the sixteenth Psalm: 'Thou shalt show me the path of life. In Thy presence is fulness of joy and at Thy right hand is pleasure for ever more.'

Seven royal Dukes followed the hearse, which was drawn by eight black horses on its short journey to St George's Chapel. Trumpeters of the Royal Horse Guards preceded the coffin, and the black velvet pall with its eight escutcheons was borne by Yeomen of the Guard. Miss Goldsworthy, Mrs Williams, Mrs Adams, Mademoiselle Montmollin, Miss Planta, and Mary Anne Gaskoin, all heavily veiled, were among the feminine part of the procession. Among the men were Mr Battiscombe the apothecary, and Mr Charles Bucknill, the solicitor in whose hands the will of Princess Amelia had been lodged.

The grief of the Family for the Princess was complicated by the terms of that will, which at first nobody dared communicate to the King. Princess Mary wrote to the Prince of Wales on 18 November 1810, that Augusta Lodge would not be shut up until the Prince had 'personally settled and arranged poor dear Amelia's affairs'. 'The King', she says,

> gave orders to Brawn some days before his illness that as soon as the event took place the House was to be shut up. I have begged Brawn untill you have been again at Windsor to leave things as they are, which of course he sees the necessity of, and is of opinion it would be improper to leave her things in an empty house.[w]

The shock of Princess Amelia's death had overwhelmed her father, and not until three months later was he in a state to see his family. On 5 February 1811, Queen Charlotte wrote to the Prince of Wales, newly created Prince Regent:

> The King being now Informed of everything relatif to Public Business there still remains one Point to be broke to Him Namely, poor Amelia's Will, the Ignorance of which may lead to very Unpleasant Conversations should He see His Family before that is done. But as the Ld Chancellor's coming down to Windsor solely for that purpose might distress the Kg if his Mind was not prepared for it, would You and Your Brother Adolphus have any objection to Sir Henry Halford preparing Him for it, as a Man in whom the Kg knew she put great Confidence and who would be able to answer more satisfactorily any Questions which most naturally arise upon the subject. . . .
>
> The sooner this Unpleasant Business is over the better, as it is likely to forward a meeting between the Kg and his Family and prevent many distressing altercations.[w]

The Regent was aware that Princess Amelia had not put 'great Confidence' in Halford at the end, but he and the Duke of Cambridge made no objection to the proposed arrangement. According to the 'Lady of Quality', Halford, in his account of what followed, said that Mr Perceval and the Lord Chancellor had shrunk from the duty, and had imposed it upon him. Even if Sir Henry exaggerated the importance of his own role, his description of the scene is worth reading. He stood with his Majesty by a window, with the light falling full on his face so that 'even the poor nearly blind King could see it', and asked whether it would be agreeable to him to hear how the Princess Amelia had 'disposed of her little property'.

'Certainly, certainly, I want to know'—with great eagerness. Sir Henry reminded him at the beginning of his illness he had appointed FitzRoy to ride with her; how he had left him with her at Weymouth; how it was natural and proper that she should leave him some token for these services; that excepting jewels she had nothing to leave, and had bequeathed them all to him; that the Prince of Wales, thinking jewels a very inappropriate bequest for a man, had given FitzRoy a pecuniary compensation for them . . . and had distributed slight tokens to all the attendants and friends of the Princess, giving the bulk of the jewels to Princess Mary, her most constant and kindest of nurses. Upon this the poor King exclaimed, 'Quite right, just like the Prince of Wales'.

Princess Mary then wrote to the Prince of Wales:

I take up my pen to say that now that the King is informed of poor Amelia's will I hope you will have the kindness the next time you see the Queen to make her sensible, as well as every one of the Family the necessity and propriety of dropping the subject for ever, and make them all *feel* it is what we owe to poor Amelia's memory. Nothing [*sic*], thank God, can have taken it more properly than the King, and he feels as he ought your *conduct* on the *occasion*; & I trust & hope *no questions will be asked*, but if any conversation should take place I am sure you will *strongly* recommend nothing more being said but that we were not ignorant that poor Amelia preferred *him* to all *others*. The laying any blame upon any soul (which after all can only be conjecture) is the most horrid of all things, and can in my opinion only make mischief and yet not be proved.

The object of this letter, my dearest Brother, is to implore that you will use *this language* the very first opportunity you come to Windsor, as you must be aware an unguarded word dropped by the Queen may bring on a thousand unpleasant things, and I am sure we ought to let *her rest in peace now* and for her sake be silent on FitzRoy.[w]

At the time of Princess Amelia's death FitzRoy was suffering from 'a bilious fever', but at the earliest opportunity her two executors appealed to his honour and discretion not to stand upon his rights as residuary legatee, but to authorize them in writing to act in his stead. An interview took place at which, according to the Villiers Papers, the Prince of Wales and the Duke of Cambridge embraced the General with a 'fraternal hug'—upon which Mr Villiers remarked drily that he was sure the General had been cheated in some way.

No doubts seem to have troubled FitzRoy at first. He wrote to the Prince, 'to ease a grateful though distracted mind in thus pouring forth its inward vows of the most unfeigned veneration'. But Mr Villiers continued to be sceptical as to the Prince's intentions, and took courage at a subsequent interview to remind HRH of 'the actual debt in money due to General FitzRoy from Princess Amelia'.

The reminder was not well received. The Prince 'expressed great displeasure, and was very intemperate in his manner', though he expressed willingness himself to settle his sister's debts 'up to the amount realized by the sale of her jewels'. These had been valued in 1808 at between £2,500 and £3,000, and the diamonds alone were now valued at £1,800. But they were not sold. Upon one point at least Halford had not misled the King: the jewels were given to Princess Mary.

It has been stated that the Princess refused this gift, but a letter in the Windsor Archives shows that she accepted it, though not without demur. Thanking the Prince for his 'very *practical* kindness to me during all my life—but more particularly during all my misery and anxiety concerning my blessed and ever-to-be-lamented Amelia', she adds:

> Your kindness in giving me *her jewels* (though I feel it is more than I ought to have had) is deeply felt by me, and of course *valuable* as all that comes from you will ever be in my eyes.[w]

One reason for the Family's anxiety that in his calmer moments the King should ask no questions may have been the failure of the executors to pay to FitzRoy the 'pecuniary compensation' of which Sir Henry had spoken. The attitude of the Prince and the Duke of Cambridge has been severely criticized, and it has always been assumed that they treated badly a man who had been the faithful and devoted friend of their sister. The story has been told only from FitzRoy's point of view, and mainly in the words of his partisans, Mr and Mrs Villiers.

But there is another side to the picture. Princess Amelia's brothers believed that her infatuation for FitzRoy had been the cause of her death, and that belief was incompatible with full approval of his conduct. 'Monk' Lewis wrote in his diary at the time of the Princess's death that 'he treated her very cavalierly'; and adds, 'the more the shame, for she was a sweet creature, so amiable, and really pretty at one time'. All her letters to her 'beloved Charles' suggest that most of the ardour was on her part. *Il y a toujours un qui aime, et un qui se laisse aimer.*

FitzRoy was the one who 'allowed himself to be loved'. Perhaps he was flattered rather than pleased. He wrote to the Prince after her death, 'to the memory and transcendent purity of affection of the adored and departed angel I owe every self-value I can ever possess'. His self-esteem no less than his regard for her memory was wounded when the executors sent him several waggon-loads of badly packed odds and ends, including empty bookshelves, a few books, a few pieces of plate from which the Princess's cypher and coronet had been partly erased, a mahogany box, open and empty, without a key, and a red box, probably the red box of her memorandum, locked, but also without a key.

Instigated no doubt by Mr and Mrs Villiers, the affronted General made some attempts to enforce the fulfilment of Princess Amelia's wishes; but he succeeded only in ruffling the feathers of the Prince Regent, who turned his back on him when he came to pay homage to him at a levée, 'as representing the crown'.

In the meantime George Villiers had written to Sir Henry Halford a letter which he showed to the Queen; and Princess Mary wrote breathlessly to the Regent on 25 January 1811:

> To describe the feelings of my *heart* upon the Queen's informing me yesterday of a letter Mr Villiers had wrote to Sir Henry Halford no more can I find words to say the *horror* it has left in my mind and the *shock* it gave me to find that a Man who my *adored* Amelia had really *heaped* with kindness, and gave such proofs of Affection to Mrs George Villiers and all the children to her *very last hours*, that he can do so atrocious an act as to rake up a *subject* which he knows was the *real cause* of her death (for she died of a broken heart) as that most unfortunate and most fatal attachment destroyed her health by degrees. . . .
>
> She died, poor Angle [*sic*], in perfect Peace with all the world, and it is hard not to leave her departed Spirit *in Peace*—and that Mr Villiers, who she looked upon as her Friend, can use her Memory so cruelly *half kills me*, and I am certain, my dearest Brother, your feelings must be as deeply affected as mine are upon *this* occasion, for your affcn for poor Amelia was full as strong as mine.
>
> God knows she suffered enough in mind and body in this world.[w]

The Princess adds that she cannot recollect naming FitzRoy in any letter to Mrs Villiers, 'but in the number of years Mrs G. Villiers was *intimate* in our House I cannot pretend to say I may not have wrote many things I should be sorry appeared before the Public'. She had not written to the lady at all during the last two years of Amelia's life, firstly because she had not the time, and secondly because she looked upon her as 'a very *bad friend* for Amelia'.[w] Fearing lest she might be accused of keeping Mrs Villiers away from the dying Princess, she reminds the Prince that not only had she herself suggested a meeting between them, but got the Prince and the Duke of Cumberland to do the same. Amelia declined, saying, 'It will be my death if I see my adored friend'.[w]

It seems that Mr Villiers had been threatening to put pressure upon the Prince in the matter of the will, for Princess Mary concludes:

> The *conduct* Mr Villiers proposes is a very strong proof of his *great affec* for her. I don't care what he says and does to the Liveing, however disagreeable, but to disturb her *poor Ashes* is more than I can stand.[w]

Two years later, when Miss Knight mentioned the name of Princess Amelia, the Regent burst into tears, 'regretted he could not more fully comply with her last wishes', and 'seemed embarrassed and exceedingly overcome'. His conscience was evidently not quite at ease; but his conduct would have been more reprehensible if FitzRoy had been a more chivalrous and self-forgetting man.

The executors lost no time in distributing mementoes of their sister among her friends and servants. Notable omissions from the list were Princess Elizabeth and Miss Goldsworthy. To Mademoiselle Montmollin they gave a small coral necklace; to Miss Planta, a gold brooch; to Mrs Adams, an enamelled box;[18] to Mrs Williams, a topaz cross; to Miss Finch, a fan. The ring inscribed 'When this you see, remember me', which was given to Lady Neale, is believed by the descendants of her adopted daughter to be a facsimile of the ring given by Princess Amelia to her father.

In conjunction with Princess Mary, the Prince promptly began to arrange the future of Mary Anne Gaskoin, whom they proposed to place in Princess Charlotte's household, where her father already held a post. Princess Mary had several conversations with Gaskoin, who looked forward to his daughter 'being one of Charlotte's attendants, as it brings her more immediately under his own eye' and would be a proof that the Prince was satisfied with Mary Anne's conduct 'in her trying situation about poor Amelia'. But, said Gaskoin, 'the King had promised to make Mary Anne one of his pensioners, and it might be more respectfull to him not to let her move to Carlton House or Warwick House till the King is in a position to be informed of his [Gaskoin's] future plans for his daughter', and of the Prince's kind intentions towards her. In the same letter Princess Mary tells her brother that 'things go on much as before' in the King's apartments, 'quiet, but under great delusion at times'.

The least painful of George III's delusions, to himself if not to others, was the idea that the beloved child was not dead, but living in Hanover, 'where she would never grow older, and always be well'. Hanover seems to have been for him synonymous with Heaven, for he believed that Prince Octavius was there too, and when one of his physicians lamented the loss of his wife, the King assured him that she was not dead, 'but living in Hanover with Amelia'. Another time he thought that Octavius had told him that 'Amelia was at Weymouth in perfect health'. This did not prevent him from remarking, in a gleam of sanity, that 'both Halford and Baillie had misunderstood poor Amelia's case'.

Mary Anne Gaskoin did not live to enjoy the rewards of her fidelity at the hands either of George III or George IV. After a short holiday at Bristol, designed to 'set her up', she died in February 1811 at the age of thirty-one. The date of her death must have coincided with one of the King's clearer intervals, for he gave orders that she was to be buried in St George's Chapel 'as near as might be to her royal mistress', and himself composed the inscription for the mural tablet at the entrance to the cloisters, placed there 'in Testimony of his grateful sense of the faithful service and attachment of an amiable young woman to his beloved daughter'.

No monument marks the resting-place of Princess Amelia, and yet, by virtue of her youth, her unhappy love, and her untimely death, she is the one daughter of George III who lives in English memory. On 18 January 1818, Princess Mary wrote to the Prince Regent that she was sending him at last the offering she wished to have had placed on his table on New Year's Day:

The only merit is it comes from one who *loves you* most affly and tenderly, and that the two hands of the Eternities contain the hair of both Charlotte and Amelia, and I had them twisted together, trusting they are entwined together in a happy Eternity.

Endnotes

1. His chapel was in Friary Court.
2. *Sire, on ne joue pas ici en conquérant!*— Sire, we do not play here as a conqueror!
3. A letter written by Sir Henry Halford to Mrs Fitzherbert during the last illness of George IV contains allusions to the sufferings of the King and his brothers, the Dukes of Clarence and Sussex, 'under their attacks of spasmodic asthma', and this may indicate the character of the 'spasms' which afflicted the Princesses.
4. He was afterwards Treasurer of the Household to George IV and William IV; knighted, 1827.
5. The first part of this letter has been published in the *Taylor Papers*.
6. *Letters of Princess Elizabeth*, ed. P. Yorke. Cf. p. 120 *supra*.
7. The name is spelled sometimes 'Miny', and sometimes 'Minny'.
8. General Thomas Garth (1744–1829). Garth was an Army officer and chief equerry to King George III. He was the son of John Garth (1701–1764), Recorder and MP for Devizes, and Rebecca, daughter of John Brompton. He entered the Army in 1762 as a cornet in the 1st Dragoons, rising to the rank of General by June 1814. In 1795, he had been appointed an equerry to George III. Garth rented Ilsington House at Puddletown, which was often visited by the royal family *en route* for Weymouth.

    General Garth was the father of Thomas Garth of the 15th Hussars (1800–1873), who it is believed was the illegitimate son of Princess Sophia. In the 1861 census Thomas Garth is living at 30 Hans Place, Chelsea, lists his occupation as a Captain in the 15th Hussars, and gives his place of birth as Weymouth It seems highly likely that the assertion that Sophia was his mother is correct. He lived at Hans Place with his unmarried daughter, Georgina, aged '22'

    'Tommy' Garth was a notoriously intemperate; he so depleted his assets that within a year of General Garth's death he was committed in October 1830 for debt to the King's Bench Prison, Southwark. Even before then, however, he was the subject of widespread gossip and the butt of satirists following his elopement in 1826 with Georgiana Caroline (b. 1796), wife of Sir Jacob Astley (1797–1859). The unhappy lady shared young Garth's disgrace, living with him in debtors' prison until her death there from scarlet fever on 29 June 1835, five days after giving birth. The most serious of 'Tommy' Garth's escapades occurred during 1829, when he attempted to blackmail the royal family over his parentage, hoping for a lump sum and an annual pension of £3,000. His ploy failed and the Press's opinion of him being 'a silly youngster,' 'the reckless one who has violated private friendship' and 'the most contemptible of human beings' seems to have been widely shared.

Georgiana Rosamond Caroline Garth was actually 25 not 22. She was the illegitimate daughter of Thomas Garth by Lady Astley, née Georgiana Dashwood (1796–1835). Born 24 June 1835, she died unmarried at Croydon General Hospital, in April 1912 from pneumonia following an accidental fracture of the thigh. There Sophia's line ended.

9. Charles and Joseph Surface were two fictional brothers whose entanglements provide one of the two plots of *The School for Scandal* by Richard Brinsley Sheridan.

10. On 2 May 1816 the Prince Regent made a presentation to General Thomas Garth of a silver two-handled tray, made by Paul Storr for Rundell, Bridge & Rundell, London, 1815, after designs by Thomas Stothard. It sold by auction on 9 July 2014 for £170,500.

11. The history of this letter is curious. It was sent to Sir Herbert in April 1830 by a wine merchant called Hansley, who was apparently one of the creditors of Captain Garth, and it may have been an example of the 'documents' in the Garth case, discussed shortly.

12. Augustus Snodgrass, a character from Charles Dickens' *The Pickwick Papers*.

13. Charles Boone, Esq., in his 90th year was buried in the family vault at Lee in Kent, attended by his afflicted relatives, General Thomas Garth and Captain Thomas Garth, RN—*The Gentleman's Magazine* March 1819.

14. He was the great-grandson of Henry FitzRoy, 1st Duke of Grafton (1663-1690), an illegitimate son of King Charles II by his mistress Barbara Villiers.

15. Quoted by Childe-Pemberton, *op. cit.*

16. A seton or seton stitch is, in medicine, a procedure used to aid the healing of fistulae, a thread or the like inserted beneath the skin in order to maintain an artificial passage, often used to drain pus or other infectious material in the wound.

17. Mr Rose says that the King 'not only understood but anticipated' the news.

18. Now in possession of her descendants the Fulford family at Great Fulford, near Exeter.

The Children of King George III and Queen Charlotte

George
(12 August 1762–26 June 1830). Prince of Wales from birth, King George IV from 29 January 1820.

George married 8 April 1795, Caroline of Brunswick, (17 May 1768–7 August 1821); one daughter, Charlotte, (7 January 1796–6 November 1817).

Frederick
(16 August 1763–5 January 1827). Duke of York and Albany and Earl of Ulster, 27 November 1784.

Frederick married on 29 September 1791 at Charlottenburg, Berlin, and again on 23 November 1791 at Buckingham Palace, his cousin Princess Frederica Charlotte of Prussia, the daughter of King Frederick William II of Prussia and Elisabeth Christine of Brunswick-Lüneburg. The marriage was not a success and the couple soon separated.

William
(21 August 1765–20 June 1837). Duke of Clarence and St Andrews, 16 May 1789; King 26 June 1830.

From 1791 William lived with an Irish actress, Dorothea Bland, better known by her stage name, Mrs Jordan. The couple had ten illegitimate children—five sons and five daughters, each was given the surname 'FitzClarence'. They separated in 1811 and Mrs Jordan was given an annuity. She died in 1816. William married, 11 July 1818, Adelaide Amelia Louise Theresa Caroline; (13 August 1792–2 December 1849); one daughter, Elizabeth Georgiana Adelaide, (10 December 1820–4 March 1821).

Charlotte
(29 September 1766–6 October 1828). Princess Royal, 22 June 1789; Princess of Würtemberg 18 May 1797; Queen consort of Würtemberg, 1 January 1806.

Charlotte married, 18 May 1797, Frederick, Hereditary Prince of Würtemberg; one stillborn daughter, 27 April 1798.

Edward
(2 November 1767–23 January 1820). Duke of Kent and Strathearn and Earl of Dublin, 23 April 1799.

Edward married, 1818, Princess Victoria of Saxe-Coburg-Saalfeld; one daughter, Victoria (Alexandrina Victoria; 24 May 1819–22 January 1901); Queen of the United Kingdom of Great Britain and Ireland from 20 June 1837 until her death.

Augusta Sophia
(8 November 1768–22 September 1840.

Unmarried

Elizabeth
(22 May 1770–10 January 1840).

Elizabeth married, 1818, Frederick, Landgrave of Hesse-Homburg; no issue.

Ernest Augustus
(5 June 1771–18 November 1851). Duke of Cumberland and Teviotdale and Earl of Armagh, 23 April 1799; King Ernest Augustus I of Hanover from 20 June 1837 until his death.

Ernest married, 1815, Frederica of Mecklenburg-Strelitz; one son, George V (George Frederick Alexander Charles Ernest Augustus, 27 May 1819 – 12 June 1878). George was the last king of Hanover. The kingdom was ended by the Unification of Germany.

Augustus
(27 January 1773–21 April 1843). Duke of Sussex, Earl of Inverness, and Baron Arklow, 27 November 1801.

Augustus married first, 1793 (in contravention of the Royal Marriages Act 1772) Lady Augusta Murray; there were two children: Augustus Frederick d'Este, (1794–1848) and Augusta Emma Wilde, Baroness Truro (née d'Este, 1801–1866). An annulment was forced upon the couple in 1794 and the children took the surname of d'Este in place of Hanover. Both parents were descended from the house of d'Este. Augustus married secondly, 1831, (again in contravention of the Act) Cecilia Underwood, Duchess of Inverness; no children.

Adolphus
(24 February 1774–8 July 1850). Duke of Cambridge from 1801 until his death.

Adolphus married, 1818, Princess Augusta of Hesse-Cassel. There were three children: George William Frederick Charles; 2nd Duke of Cambridge, (26 March 1819–17 March 1904); Augusta (19 July 1822–5 December 1916), married into the Grand Ducal House of Mecklenburg-Strelitz and became the Grand Duchess of Mecklenburg-Strelitz; Mary Adelaide (27 November 1833–27 October 1897), who married, 1866, Francis, Duke of Teck.

Mary
(25 April 1776–30 April 1857).

Mary married, 1815, Prince William, Duke of Gloucester; no children.

Sophia
(3 November 1777–27 May 1848).

Unmarried; one illegitimate son, Thomas Garth, (1800–1873).

Octavius
(23 February 1779–3 May 1783).

Alfred
(22 September 1780–20 August 1782).

Amelia
(7 August 1783–2 November 1810).

Bibliography

Charlotte Augusta Matilda, Princess Royal, Queen of Würtemberg

Windsor Archives. Fanny Burney (Madame d'Arblay), *Diary and Letters*, ed. Austin Dobson. *The Harcourt Papers* (privately printed), ed. E. Harcourt. Mrs Papendiek, *Journals: George III, His Court and Family* (Anonymous). *The Cambridge Modern History. Meyers Lexikon. The Dictionary of National Biography.* Unpublished letters in the possession of Viscount Harcourt.

CHAPTER 1, PART I.—Viscount Esher, *The Girlhood of Queen Victoria.* C. B. Todd, *Life and Letters of Joel Barlow. The Works of Peter Pindar, Esq.* Henry Angelo the Younger, *Reminiscences. Diaries of Robert Fulke Greville*, ed. F. M. Bladon. *Letters of Horace Walpole*, ed. Mrs Paget Toynbee. *Mary Hamilton at Court, Family Letters*, ed. E. G. and F. Anson. Mrs Papendiek, *op. cit.* Information kindly given by the late Mr Hubert Carr-Gomm. Lady Mary Coke, *Journals* (privately printed). Mrs John Buchan (Lady Tweedsmuir), *Life of Lady Louisa Stuart.* Miss Frances Williams Wynn, *Diaries of a Lady of Quality. Selection from the Letters and Correspondence of Sir James Bland Burges, Bart.*, ed. Hutton. Lady Charlotte Bury, *Diary of a Lady in Waiting*, ed. A. F. Steuart. *The Lady's Magazine*, Vol. I, 1797. British Museum, Additional MSS, 38364, ff. 280-88, Miss C. A. A. Disbrowe, *Old Days in Diplomacy.* Joseph Grego, *Works of James Gillray. Briefwechsel der Königin Katharina und des Königs Jerome von Westphalen, sowie des Kaisers Napoleon I mit Friedrich von Württemberg*, ed. A. von Schlossberger. Edward Barry O'Meara, *Napoleon at St Helena, The Connoisseur*, November, 1910. Emma Sophia, Countess Brownlow, *Reminiscences of a Septuagenarian.*

PART II.—*Cambridge Modern History. Meyers Lexikon. Politische und Militärische Correspondenz König Friedrichs von Württemberg mit Kaiser Napoleon I*, ed. A. von Schlossberger. Dr J. Holland Rose, *Napoleon.* E. B. O'Meara, *op. cit. Correspondence of Harriet, Countess Granville*, ed. Leveson-Gower. Miss F. Williams Wynn, *op. cit.* C. de Bourgoing, *Le Cœur de Marie Louise.* Princess

Lieven, *Letters to Prince Metternich*, ed. P. Quennell and Dilys Powell. Frédéric Masson, *Napoleon et sa famille. Briefwechsel*, etc. *Letters and Despatches of Lord Castlereagh*, 3rd Series, Vol. IX. W. A. Shaw, *The Knights of England. The Letters of King George the Fourth*, ed. Dr A. Aspinall. Baron Stockmar, *Memoirs. The Creevey Papers*, ed. Sir Herbert Maxwell. *The Annual Register. The Gentleman's Magazine.* Sir Walter Scott, *Song for the Anniversary Meeting of the Pitt Club of Scotland.* Mrs John Buchan (Lady Tweedsmuir) *op. cit.*

Princess Augusta Sophia

Windsor Archives. Unpublished letters in the possession of Viscount Harcourt, Mr Heneage E. B. Harrison, Mr Herbert Adams, and Mrs Keele Home. Fanny Burney, *op. cit.* Mrs Papendiek, *op. cit. The Annual Register. The Gentleman's Magazine. The Army List.* British Museum, *Additional MSS.*

CHAPTER 2, PART I.—Lady Mary Coke, *Letters and Journals* (privately printed). The Rev. G. Cecil White, *Glimpses of William IV and Queen Adelaide.* Charles Abbott, 1st Baron Colchester, *Diaries and Correspondence. Letters of Lady Louisa Stuart*, ed. R. Brimley Johnson. *The Annual Register*, 1789. Colonel George Landmann, *Adventures and Recollections.* James Harris, Earl of Malmesbury, *Diaries and Correspondence.* British Museum, Additional MSS., 30128, f. 18, and 30007, ff. 55-62. *Lift and Letters of Frances, Baroness Bunsen*, ed. Augustus Hare.

PART II.—Miss Cornelia Knight, *Autobiography. Finance Accounts of Great Britain.* Lady Charlotte Bury, *The Diary of a Lady-in-Waiting*, ed. A. F. Steuart. Charles Greville, *Memoirs*, ed. Lytton Strachey and Roger Fulford. *The Taylor Papers*, ed. Ernest Taylor. Thomas Ashe, *The Spirit of 'The Book'. The Dictionary of National Biography*, article, 'Brent Spencer'. Unpublished MSS. in the possession of Viscount Harcourt. Raymond Smythies, *Historical Records of the 40th (2nd Somersetshire) Regiment. Burke's Peerage. United Services Journal*, II, 1829. Stepney, *Leaves from the Diary of an Officer in the Guards.* Sir Charles Oman, *The Peninsular War.* John Wilson Croker, *Correspondence and Diaries*, ed. L. J. Jennings. Sir Harris Nicholas, *History of the Orders of Knighthood of the British Empire.* Rev. G. Cecil White, *op. cit. Letters of a Young Diplomatist and Soldier* (Ralph Heathcote), ed. Countess Gunther-Groben. Roger Fulford, *George IV.* Baroness Bunsen, *op. cit.* Lloyd Sanders, *Old Kew, Chiswick and Kensington.* W. H. Pyne, *Royal Residences.* British Museum, Additional MSS., 38261, f. 186. Tom Moore, *Memoirs, Journal and Correspondence*, ed. Lord John Russell. Frances, Lady Shelley, *Diary* ed. R. Edgcumbe. Princess Lieven, *Correspondence with Earl Grey*, ed. J. Le Strange. *Letters during her Residence in London*, ed. L. G. Robinson. *Letters of Princess Lieven to Prince Metternich,* ed. Peter Quennell and Dilys Powell. *Diary*, ed. Harold Temperley. Lytton Strachey, *Queen Victoria*. British Museum, Additional MSS., 38368, ff. 282-83, *Letters of Queen Victoria*, ed. Viscount Esher.

Princess Elizabeth

Windsor Archives. Fanny Burney, *op. cit*. Mrs Papendiek, *op. cit*. *Letters of Princess Elizabeth*, ed. Philip Yorke. Unpublished letters from Princess Elizabeth to Mrs Dering in the possession of Mr Heneage E. B. Harrison, and to Mrs Adams in the possession of Mr Herbert Adams and Mrs Keele Horne.

CHAPTER 3, PART I.—Mary Hamilton, *op. cit*. *Letters of Horace Walpole*, ed. Paget Toynbee. Henry Angelo, *Reminiscences*. Mrs Delany, *Autobiography and Correspondence*, ed. Lady Llanover. W. S. Childe Pemberton, *The Romance of Princess Amelia*. F. A. Crisp, *Visitation of England*. *The Court and City Register*. *The Royal Kalendar or Complete and Correct Annual Register*. *The Works of Peter Pindar, Esq*. *Notes and Queries*, 3rd Series, Vol. VIII. Thomas Ashe, *op. cit*. Bland Burges, *op. cit*. *The Dictionary of National Biography*. British Museum, Additional MSS. (Holderness Letters), 33132. *The Diary of Sylvester Douglas, Lord Glenbervie*, ed. Francis Bickley.

PART II.—Roger Fulford, *Royal Dukes*. Cochin, *Louis-Philippe*. Lady Charlotte Bury, *op. cit*. Information kindly given by Miss Myra Battiscombe. The Taylor MSS. John Wilson Croker, *Correspondence and Diaries*. *The Harcourt Papers*. *Letters and Despatches of Lord Castlereagh*. Richard, Duke of Buckingham and Chandos, Memoirs of the Court of the Regency, Memoirs of the Court of England. E. B. O'Meara, *op. cit*. Introduction to the *Letters of Princess Elizabeth*, ed. P. Yorke. *Remains of the late Mrs Richard Trench*, ed. by her son. R. Rush, *Recollections of the English and French Courts*. *The Lady's Magazine*, 1818. Letter in the possession of Mrs Leggett. Letters from Princess Elizabeth to Lady Banks, by courtesy of Messrs Myers & Co., New Bond Street. Miss Cornelia Knight, *Autobiography*. *Memoirs of Sir William Knighton*, by his widow. Roger Fulford, *George IV*. Thackeray, *The Four Georges*. *Letters of Princess Elizabeth*, ed. P. Yorke. Letters to Mrs Dering, in the possession of Mr Heneage E. B. Harrison. Information kindly given by Lord Hylton.

Princess Mary

Windsor Archives. Unpublished letters in the possession of Mrs Keele Home and Mr Herbert Adams. Fanny Burney, *op. cit*. Mrs Papendiek, *op. cit*. Charles

Greville, *op. cit.* John Wilson Croker, *op. cit.* Thomas Creevey, *The Creevey Papers*, ed. Sir H. Maxwell. *The Harcourt Papers.*

CHAPTER 4, PART I.—Letters of Princes and Princes of the House of Orange to Madame de la Fite, British Museum, Additional MSS., 19589. *Mary Hamilton at Court*, ed. E. G. and F. Anson. *George III, his Court and Family.* Harriet Martineau, *Biographical Sketches. Autobiography and Correspondence of Mrs Delany*, ed. Lady Llanover. Captain Landmann, *Adventures and Recollections.* Frances, Lady Shelley, *Diary*, ed. R. Edgcumbe. James Harris, 1st Earl of Malmesbury, *Diaries and Correspondence.* Unpublished letters in the possession of Mrs Keele Home and Mr Herbert Adams. P. Trehearne, *Spencer Perceval.* J. Grego, *Works of James Gillray.* Roger Fulford, *George IV.* Information kindly given by Miss Lucy Webb-Hawkins. H. Twiss, *Public and Private Life of Lord Eldon.*

PART II.—V. Biddulph, *The Three Ladies Waldegrave and their Mother.* Miss Cornelia Knight, *Autobiography.* Frances, Lady Shelley, *Diary.* G. W. E. Russell, *Collections and Recollections.* Unpublished letters (as above). Twiss, *op. cit.* Lord Albemarle, *Fifty Years of My Life.* Dormer Creston, *The Regent and his Daughter.* C. E. Vulliamy, *Farmer George. Letters of King George the Fourth*, ed. Dr A. Aspinall. Byron, *English Bards and Scotch Reviewers.* W. Thornbury, *Old and New London.* Viscount Esher, *Girlhood of Queen Victoria.* The Duke of Argyll, *Passages from the Past.* Sarah, Lady Lyttelton, *Correspondence*, ed. the Hon. Mrs H. Wyndham. Information kindly given by the late Miss Adams. *Letters of Queen Victoria*, Vol. I. Sir Clement Kinloch-Cook, *Life of Princess Mary Adelaide, Duchess of Teck.*

Princess Sophia

Windsor Archives. Works cited under the Princesses Augusta, Elizabeth and Mary. Information kindly supplied, from family papers and traditions, by Mr Ernest Taylor, Miss Madeleine de Soyres, Miss E. C. Tyler, Mrs Keele Home, and Miss Geraldine Heckrath.

CHAPTER 5, PART I.—*George III, his Court and Family. Mary Hamilton at Court.* Fanny Burney, *op. cit. The Illustrated London News*, May–June, 1848. Family papers of Miss Madeleine de Soyres. Letters in the Neuchâtel Public Library, kindly communicated by Miss E. C. Tyler. *The Marlay Papers.* John Wesley's *Journal*, October, 1784. Viscount Esher, *Girlhood of Queen Victoria.* Information kindly given by Lord Hylton. *The Annual Register.* Information kindly given by Mr Evans Lewin. *The Harcourt Papers.* Roger Fulford, *Royal*

Dukes. Charles Greville, *op. cit. The Gentleman's Magazine. The Army List*. Captain Gronow, *Reminiscences*. J. Watkins, *A Biographical Memoir of Frederick, Duke of York*. Information kindly given by Mrs Harold W. M. Tollemache. Gronow, *op. cit*. Information kindly given by Mrs Hurford. W. Munk, *Life of Sir Henry Halford*.

PART II.—Lady Charlotte Bury, *op. cit*. Taylor MSS. *The Army List*. Information kindly given by Miss Madeleine de Soyres. Article by Mr Osbert Lancaster in *The Cornhill Magazine*, Vol. 155. J. Watkins, *op. cit*. Sir Herbert Taylor, *Memoirs of Illness and Decease of the Duke of York*. Greville Memoirs, British Museum, Additional MSS, No. 41095. *The Taylor MSS*. Information kindly given by Miss Geraldine Heckrath. *Girlhood of Queen Victoria*. Miss Cornelia Knight, *op. cit*. The Hon. Amelia Murray, *Recollections. Letters of Queen Victoria*. Sir C. Kinloch-Cook, *Life of Princess Mary Adelaide, Duchess of Teck*. W. Thornbury, *London Old and New. Leaves from the Diary of Henry Greville*, ed. Viscountess Enfield. *The Annual Register*, 1848.

Princess Amelia

Windsor Archives. Fanny Burney, *op. cit*. W. S. Childe-Pemberton, *The Romance of Princess Amelia*. Article by Jennet Humphreys in the *Dictionary of National Biography. Autobiography* of Miss Cornelia Knight.

CHAPTER 6, PART I.—*Letters of George III*, ed. Sir John Fortescue. Mrs Sherwood, *Autobiography*. The Taylor MSS. Letters in the possession of Mr Herbert Adams. Mrs Papendiek, *op. cit*. Manuscript letters at Neuchâtel, kindly communicated by Miss E. C. Tyler. Fanny Burney, *op. cit*. Childe-Pemberton, *op. cit*. George Rose, *Diaries and Correspondence*. Ethel Colburn Mayne, *Lady Byron*. George Villiers, *A Vanished Victorian*. Information kindly given by the late Colonel Jacques Frédéric Reboul, C.B., Paris. Letter to Lady Neale in the possession of Madame Reboul. Information kindly given by Mrs Harold W. M. Tollemache. *The Marlay Papers*. Information kindly given by Mr A. King-Smith. W. Home, *Everyday Book*. Harcourt MSS. Notes of medical expenses from small red book in the possession of Mr J. C. Farrar. Taylor MSS.

PART II.—Miss Cornelia Knight, *Autobiography*. Harcourt MSS.
    Letter in the possession of Mrs Wood. Information kindly given by Messrs Fribourg and Treyer. George Rose, *op. cit*. Miss F. Williams-Wynn, *op. cit*.